Mr. Peale's Museum

MR. PEALE'S MUSEUM

Charles Willson Peale
and the First Popular Museum
of Natural Science and Art

CHARLES COLEMAN SELLERS

A BARRA FOUNDATION BOOK

W. W. NORTON & COMPANY, INC.

NEW YORK • 1980

THIS BOOK WAS EDITED AND PRODUCED BY
REGINA RYAN PUBLISHING ENTERPRISES, INC.

Designer: Ulrich Ruchti

FRONTISPIECE: THE FOUNDER
Charles Willson Peale's self-portrait of 1822 was painted at the request of the trustees of the newly incorporated Museum, as a monument to the major accomplishment of the artist's long life. The composition is innovative, with the light source behind rather than in front of the subject. Symbolic palette and brushes have been laid aside in preference for natural history, as represented by taxidermist's tools, mastodon bones, and a wild turkey from the recent expedition to the Rocky Mountains. In the left background a father is instructing his son, while a Quaker lady raises her hands in wonder before the great mastodon skeleton. (Pennsylvania Academy of the Fine Arts.)

1 2 3 4 5 6 7 8 9 0

CONTENTS

TO HORACE
AND THE PEALE TRADITION

FOREWORD

As early as the summer of 1970, Edgar P. Richardson had been urging the writing of a history of Peale's Museum, as a work that would be "fascinating and important. It would offer, as nothing else could, a view of the American Enlightenment. . . . I see this as a landmark contribution to American intellectual history."

This was a challenge indeed to an author well versed in Peale biography but new to the history of science. It was hesitantly accepted, and I am still aware others will have much to add. But in 1973, with the friendly interest of Robert L. McNeil, Jr., behind it, and a liberal supporting grant from the Barra Foundation, the work was begun. It had by that time another advantage. The Peale Papers were being assembled for publication under the editorship of Lillian B. Miller, with whom a happy cooperative relationship has contributed much throughout. Once under way, institutions and individuals everywhere responded with information and guidance.

As with earlier projects, the Peale Papers at the American Philosophical Society were the home-base resource, and Whitfield J. Bell, Jr., Librarian, was constantly helpful. Other Philadelphia institutions contributing were the Academy of Natural Sciences, the College of Physicians, the Historical Society of Pennsylvania, the Library Company of Philadelphia, the Pennsylvania Academy of the Fine Arts, the University Museum, and the Wagner Free Institute of Science. Harvard University's Peabody Museum of Archaeology and Ethnology and Museum of Comparative Zoology, together holding most of what survives of the Peale collections, have assisted generously, particularly, at the first, Marie Jeanne Adams, Elinor Reichlin, and Edwin L. Wade, and, at the second, Clifford Frondel, Barbara Lawrence, and Raymond A. Paynter.

Cordial assistance came also from staff members or associates of the American Antiquarian Society, the American Museum of Natural History, George Arents Research Library at Syracuse University, the Australian Museum in Sydney, the Bishop Museum in Honolulu, the Boston Athenaeum, the British Museum (Natural History), the Center for Bibliographical Studies at Uppsala, the University of Michigan's William L. Clements Library, the Eleutherian Mills Historical Library, the Jefferson County Historical Society, Jefferson Papers at Princeton University, the Jones Memorial Library at Lynchburg, the Library of Congress, the Maryland Historical Society, Mount Vernon Ladies' Association of the Union, Muséum National d'Histoire Naturelle, the Museum of Southern Decorative Arts, The National Archives, the New Hampshire Historical Society, the New-York Historical Society, New York Institution for the Blind, New York Public Library, the New York State Museum, the Oneida Historical Society, the Peabody Museum of Salem, the Peale Museum in Baltimore, the Pennsylvania Historical and Museum Commission, the Polynesian Society, the Swedish Royal Academy of Sciences, the Smithsonian Institution Archives and Joseph Henry Papers, the United Church Board for World Ministries, and the Washington State Museum.

Among the many who have volunteered help or responded to appeals for it are Mrs. Mark Aldrich, Edward P. Alexander, Toby A. Appel, Donald Baird, Mrs. Eric Wollencott Barnes, Frederick E. Bauer, Jr., Roland M. Baumann, Sally Bond, Julian P. Boyd, Richard J. Boyle, Linda Burcher, Alford Carleton, Raymond J. Cunningham, Francis James Dallett, John C. Dann, Michelle De Garme, Davida Deutsch, John d'Entremont, Roger A. Derby, Jr., Ernest S. Dodge, Mrs. Catherine Gordon Dosker, Rolf E. DuRietz, Edward H. Dwight, Joseph Ewan, John C. Ewers, Norman Feder, Peter Fetchko, Eric Frank, Mrs. Ellen Gartrell, Charles E. Gilette, Roy E. Goodman, John C. Greene, Charles H. Haines, Max Hall, Robert M. Hazen, Brooke Hindle, Bill Holm, Wilbur H. Hunter, William A. Hunter, Mrs. Edward C. Hutter, Helen C. Isherwood, Daniel W. Jones, Jr., Adrienne L. Kaeppler, Lisa Kamisher, Donald Castell Kelley, David J. Lakari, Mrs. David H. Low, Mrs. Robert L. McNeil, Jr., Basil Marlow, Kenneth R. Martin, Nancy L. Mautner, A. Hyatt Mayor, Christine Meadows, Hannah Miller, Mrs. Elizabeth M. Moyer, William D. Myers, G. O'Donnell, Douglas M. Preston, Peter Ranby, Nina J. Root, Nina Dodds Schlick, Mortimer Newlin Sellers, Nicholas Sellers, Susan Pendleton Sellers, Wendy J. Shadwell, Margaret W. M. Schaeffer, Martha

Calvert Slotten, Murphy D. Smith, William Stanton, James A. Steed, Barbara B. Stevens, Iris J. Swab, Nicholas B. Wainwright, Kathleen Waldenfels, Carolyn J. Weekley, the late Walter Muir Whitehill, K. Beverley Whiting, Richmond D. Williams, Mrs. Jacob Wirth, Mrs. Barbara Wiseman, Edwin Wolf, II, Harrison Morris Wright, and Henry J. Young.

The author's warm gratitude goes also to Mrs. Nell K. Barr who, with a constant watchful eye upon the project as a whole, transcribed the almost indecipherable minutes of the Philadelphia Museum Company (a benefit shared with owners of the original manuscripts), and to Keir Brooks Sterling, whose critical oversight from the viewpoint of an historian of science was most valuable. Finally, appreciation and apologies are due to those who advised so laboriously as to a style appropriate to the subject.

C. C. S.

LIST OF ILLUSTRATIONS

LIST OF ILLUSTRATIONS

CREDITS

Photographs from the collections of the American Philosophical Society are by Bertram V. Dodelin, Jr. The Cree Indian dresses were photographed by F.P. Orchard, and photographs of all other objects from the Harvard University museums by Hillel Burger.

CHAPTER ONE

A NEW SCIENCE
FOR
A NEW ERA

Peale's Museum and the Peales— it is a story of vision and adventure in science and art, of labor and love, of struggle and study and delight within one family. There had been nothing like it in the world before. Other existing museums were for the cognoscenti or the rich amateur's pleasure, but this one was to be for all. It was to attract, to teach, to offer to everyone a knowledge of their world and themselves.

Begun in the aftermath of the American Revolution, it was marked by the eager, innovative spirit of those times, by the idea of a liberated people extending the frontiers of civilization and knowledge into a new world era of human happiness. Far ahead of its time, it had the triple function of a modern museum of science: actual specimens were systematically arranged and documented, research was fostered, and, above all, the "diffusion of knowledge" was promoted by a happy process formerly known as "rational amusement"—enjoyment while learning.

The educational theory it implemented came straight from Jean Jacques Rousseau. Teaching is a sublime ministry inseparable from human happiness, and the learner must be led always from familiar objects toward the unfamiliar—guided along a chain of flowers, as it were, into the mysteries of life. "Rational amusement" was this museum's instrument but also, by a curious irony, its eventual undoing. Imitators sprang up almost at once. A collection of oddities, unencumbered by scientific purpose or accuracy, was

I

found to be good business. Tawdry and specious museums soon appeared in almost every American city and town. Here was cheap popular entertainment to attract what would someday become the cinema audience. It reached its peak with Barnum, who in the end obtained and scattered the Peale collections.

Yet throughout its years, from 1784 to the final dispersal of 1845–1854, Peale's Museum played a strong supportive role in the development of the sciences in this country, preeminent in its primary goal of exposition in accordance with the latest canons of scientific order. It inspired amateur collectors and intelligent collecting; it stirred the enthusiasm of young professionals-to-be like Joseph Henry of the Smithsonian Institution, and because of it all professionals worked with the stimulus of greater popular understanding. The scientific specialists who emerged during the Museum's midcourse each tended to isolate his specialty in his own collection. Peale's Museum stayed with the total concept: each natural form should be shown in all variations, in its natural environment, and with related species in a comparable view.

The Museum's influence, though often acknowledged, eludes precise assessment. We shall never know whether the museum of the East India Marine Society at Salem, Massachusetts, copied Peale's in its wax figures of mankind—only that Salem captains had seen the Philadelphia collection, and Salem merchants had contributed to it. Both exhibits have their place in the prehistory of anthropology, a science unknown to any but the last of the Peale naturalists. We do know that the great Peale collection of birds inspired the first definitive work on American ornithology, Alexander Wilson's, and also influenced those of Charles Lucien Bonaparte and John James Audubon. But its full influence can only be inferred. There was the Museum, and others drew from it what they could. And there were the Peales—father, sons, and daughters—riding this new wave of their own with memorable zest, prime examples of collecting, arranging, exploring. Their joy in the hunt, in discovery, in confounding error with truth, had a part in sending others like them across rivers and seas in search of the unknown.

Such was the creation of the portrait painter Charles Willson Peale, soldier in the War for Independence, radical politician, and irrepressible optimist. John Adams, who could only deplore Peale's politics, found him at their first meeting "a tender, soft, affectionate creature," and so he was and had been from childhood.

Peale had grown up in Annapolis, eldest son of a widowed

mother and heir presumptive to a manorial estate in England which, if he could ever claim it, would put an end to his poverty and struggle. With that inheritance he could make his two brothers gentlemen, his two sisters ladies, of the proud little Maryland town. Meanwhile, throughout his formative years, he was bound apprentice to a saddler.

Hope, pride, and poverty can make an explosive combination. Those ten long years under a master brought an enduring horror of enforced servitude in any form and an utter delight in freedom, fancy-free. But they also brought the habit of hard work, a self-drive so compulsive that inactivity would always be painful—"the pains of ennui" was his phrase. He acquired manual skills, learned delicate metalwork, and delighted in mechanical problems. With the roving interests came a passion for neatness and order, as if to see the whole world a smoothly running machine.

When free at last, a saddler on his own, Charles Peale married his boyhood sweetheart, dark-haired Rachel Brewer, and then recklessly expanded his business while breaking away from it when he could into music, poetry, and finally the more earnest pursuit of painting. This free-running hedonistic drive echoed the lives and thought of the easygoing Maryland aristocracy around him. By and large, these gentlemen belonged with the Enlightenment; they read Locke and Pope and Hume, Montesquieu and Voltaire, smiled on the new doctrines of Reason and Nature, natural religion, natural rights. Young Peale, rather quaintly regarding his Huguenot grandmother as of one heart with the *philosophes,* felt he had his own kinship with France, with Rousseau and Montesquieu. Voltaire was too sharply witty for his taste. God was the "Great First Cause," but not an ever-active presence. Men must work out their own destinies together or alone. Among the older men he knew, John Beale Bordley, lawyer and planter, was a profound influence. Bordley was gentler, more seriously idealistic than the others, such as Charles Carroll, the barrister, always jovial and friendly, or scowling Samuel Chase, who had the young Peale whole-souled behind him in the rough-and-tumble "Chase and Liberty" election of 1764.

These and other gentlemen, bethinking them that Maryland needed a painter of her own, raised a purse that sent Peale to London to study art. There Benjamin West became his mentor and friend. After discovering, as he promptly did, that his right to the fortune of Dr. Charles Wilson had been lost by his father's sentence to transportation as a forger, he gained from West a new and compensating self-image—the artist as superior to all common

3

RAPHAELLE AND TITIAN RAMSAY PEALE I

In The Staircase, *C. W. Peale's famous eye-fooler portrait of 1795, his eldest son, Raphaelle, is shown stepping upward with maul stick and palette in hand, while Titian peers down. Raphaelle had been his father's first museum assistant, but with only sporadic interest in the work. Titian was already the dedicated naturalist whose career would be cut short by his death in 1798. This is the painting which President Washington, visiting the Museum to see its new wax figures of the races of mankind, mistook for reality, doffing his hat with a bow.* (Philadelphia Museum of Art.)

REMBRANDT PEALE

Rembrandt, younger than Raphaelle, older than Titian I, dedicated himself wholly to art while still a child. He saw museums, only however, as an additional support for an artist's career. He joined Raphaelle in a short-lived museum venture of 1797, and in 1814 established the present Peale Museum in Baltimore. After his father's death, as a stockholder and director of the Philadelphia Museum he urged exhibitions for profit, and used his profits to visit the galleries abroad. This miniature by Lemarchand was painted in Paris, about 1834. (Author's collection; Frick Art Reference Library photograph.)

RUBENS PEALE
Rubens, younger than Raphaelle, Rembrandt, and Titian I, dedicated himself early to museum management, since his weak eyes unfitted him for painting or other fine work. He directed the Philadelphia Museum from 1810 to 1821, then took on a dual operation in Baltimore and New York. Rubens, breaking with his father's broad educational purpose, conceived his museums as scientific entertainment and ran them as a business. He scorned the humbug of Barnum, but was unable to compete with it. This portrait was painted by Rembrandt Peale in 1801, before the two left home to exhibit a mastodon skeleton in England. Rubens had become an enthusiastic botanist, and the geranium was then a rarity that Thomas Jefferson had found difficult to cultivate. (Mrs. Norman B. Woolworth.)

TITIAN RAMSAY PEALE II
Titian II, named for his naturalist brother who had died in 1798 at age eighteen,
became the only naturalist in the family with recognized professional standing. His
father's portrait of 1819 shows him at the beginning of his career, aged nineteen,
wearing the uniform of the civilian scientific corps that participated in Major Stephen
Harriman Long's exploring expedition to the Rocky Mountains. (Private collection.)

notions of gentility. The true nobility was that of virtue and talent, open to all. And to be an American was to hold a firm foothold on the future. Lonely, intense, and fiercely contemptuous of British complacency, Peale made himself a painter in those two and a half years in London and gained skills in engraving and sculpture as well. When he returned to Maryland, he brought with him as masterwork a huge and turgid portrait of William Pitt in Roman costume, standing at the Altar of Liberty. Copious symbolism reinforced its title, *Worthy of Liberty, MR. PITT Scorns to Invade the Liberties of Other People.*

The London training brought success. Old debts of saddlery days were paid off in the first few years. He ranged from Virginia to Philadelphia, painting many of the best portraits of his career. By 1774–1775 he was adding battle flags, replete with rebel device and sentiment, to his repertoire. In 1776, just as the city became a chief British military objective, he brought his family from Maryland to make Philadelphia their permanent home. He captained a company of city militia, joined Washington before Trenton, fought at Princeton, and was on active service through the next year's campaign. With the end of military operations in Pennsylvania, he returned from Valley Forge to enter politics, defending the radical state constitution against attacks by the wealthy merchant class.

He was in the legislature for one term (1779–1780), the session which enacted America's first law for the abolition of slavery. His ability to present an extremist view in gentle and reasonable terms—in a scene teeming with violence and unreason—brought him to the head of the "Furious Whig" party, where Thomas Paine was his closest ally and friend. But Peale's more interesting, and probably more effective, contribution to the revolutionary cause came with his "transparencies," those jubilant propaganda pictures painted on thin fabric and placed in windows, where they were lighted from behind to create a brilliant and novel nighttime spectacle. The success of American arms was vaunted, the vileness of the enemy exposed, and, always, France glorified in a blaze of poetic allegory. Each was larger than the one before, up to the last enormous Arch of Triumph lit by a thousand lamps, celebrating peace and independence.

But peace brought problems. Peale had a growing family to support. Patrons of art were few, and the best of them were cool to a Furious Whig who had publicly investigated Robert Morris as a profiteer. Yet praise and applause for the transparencies still resounded, encouraging the idea of an art for the general populace, one that would be freer and more interesting than any sort of portraiture.

Like other painters in England and America, Peale had always had a small gallery show, mostly of his own work, attracting visitors and enhancing his reputation. In 1782, with victory in sight and friends urging it as the duty of an artist to record all for posterity, he had built a large addition to his studio modeled roughly on that of Benjamin West in London, and was filling it with portraits of the heroes of the Revolution and toying with the idea of becoming, like West, a painter of history. It was here, in the first skylighted gallery in America, that the museum idea emerged—not full-fledged, but simply as a possible new way to mend a bleak financial outlook.

Sometime in 1784, Peale's brother-in-law Colonel Nathaniel Ramsay stopped in from Maryland to see how the family fared, his great bulk towering over them all, the face florid from good living, the alert and easy eyes and mouth of the lawyer and businessman. The Peales adored him, gathering around, the growing children Raphaelle, Angelica, and smart little Rembrandt all vying for attention, and, at his mother's side, toddling little Titian Ramsay, whose christening honored both the famous Venetian painter and the beloved American soldier. Colonel Ramsay had been sabered down when his regiment checked the British advance at Monmouth, but as a prisoner on parole had used his leisure well. He must now advise upon the new gallery and the future.

They all stepped out into the long high-ceilinged chamber, bathed in light. Facing them at its farther end was Washington's portrait, full-length, one hand resting on a cannon, and behind him the Princeton battlefield just as Peale himself had seen it on that frosty morning, with the college buildings on their hill beyond and redcoat prisoners being marched away by men in blue. Along the wall the Colonel saw an array of familiar faces looking back at him: Smallwood of the Maryland Line, his old commander; Howard and Moultrie; "Light Horse" Harry Lee and William Washington, both in the distinctive fighting dress of Virginia dragoons; the foreign allies Steuben, Kalb, Laurens, Lafayette, Luzerne, Rochambeau, and Gérard, full-length with an allegory of the French alliance (perhaps too many Frenchmen to suit Ramsay's taste). Charles had known them all, had gabbled with them in their own language.

Then Ramsay's eye fell on the gigantic bones, piled on and around a table. Charles explained, excitement in his voice. This was the great scientific mystery of their time. For a hundred years

9

CAPTAIN PEALE
Self-portrait of Charles Willson Peale (1777), in the brown uniform of
the Philadelphia regiments. (American Philosophical Society.)

explorers and learned men had tried to determine from such
scattered, tremendous relics as these what races of enormous beasts
or people had once roamed the forests of America, or might still be
prowling through the shadows of its farthest wilderness. Dr. John
Morgan owned this collection of nearly fifty pieces, brought to him
in 1766 from Big Bone Lick in the Ohio country. Now Dr.
Christian Friedrich Michaelis, a Hessian army surgeon, wanted
drawings to take back for study by the savants of Göttingen.[1] While
stationed with the British in New York, he had heard of bones
discovered in Orange County within the American lines. Peace
brought an opportunity to dig for a skeleton, and General
Washington had offered men, tools, and wagons. Heavy rains had

COLONEL NATHANIEL RAMSAY
The redoubtable hero of Monmouth saw the museum idea as a sure
solution for an artist's financial worries—a more popular public
attraction "than any paintings whatever." Portrait by Rembrandt
Peale. (Independence National Historical Park Collection,
Philadelphia.)

defeated the effort. Then Michaelis heard of Dr. Morgan's collection. Morgan had refused to sell, and drawings were the eventual answer. Brought to this public place for the purpose, they had been attracting much attention.

They attracted the Colonel's, no less. He lifted, hefted and handled, speculating in wonder. Then he gave blunt advice. Paintings were not the answer. There were any number like himself, he said, who would go twenty miles to see bones like these and would get more satisfaction from "such articles of curiosity than any paintings whatever."[2]

After all the labor and expense Peale had given to his gallery of paintings, such frankness from a trusted friend might have been jarring. But the idea held attractions even beyond the artist's need for a better livelihood. Soon the painter took it to other friends and put the question broadly: Should he attempt to found a museum of natural history?

David Rittenhouse, astronomer and mathematician, old friend and fellow politician of the left, liked the idea yet advised against it. "While collecting and preserving subjects," he said, "you will neglect your pencil, and consequently it will be a great injury to your interest in a pecuniary point of view."

But Dr. Robert Patterson, professor of mathematics at the University of Pennsylvania, was encouraging. The contrast between the two advisers is interesting. Mild-mannered Rittenhouse, with that thin, sensitive face so much like Peale's, gave first thought to his friend's career in art, and may have seen the proposal in terms of what the Swiss artist and connoisseur Pierre Eugène Du Simitière had built up into his "American Museum" on nearby Arch Street. This collection was a magpie's nest of historical and scientific rarities to which small parties were admitted on certain days at a charge of fifty cents per person.[3] This was not impressive "in a pecuniary point of view." Peale could earn from two good portraits as much as Du Simitière took in in a year.

Patterson, an old soldier with a rugged face, large mouth and steady eyes, was a man intent upon combining the philosophy of a thing with its practical application. He not only endorsed the plan but gave king's shilling to it, a gift Peale would cherish as a cornerstone, the first small step toward what should in time become a great national institution. It was a paddlefish, a cigar-shaped freshwater monster about four feet long, dried and preserved.[4] The creature may be glimpsed in Peale's full-length self-portrait of nearly forty years later, *The Artist in His Museum,* shown upright against the cases at the left of the picture and inscribed: "With this article the Museum commenced, June, 1784. Presented by Mr. R. Patterson."

Yet Peale's Museum did not truly commence that June, and, when Du Simitière died in October, Peale made no attempt to set up a successor to the American Museum or to take over its collections. He had been swept off his feet in a new direction. Word had come from London of an astonishing breakthrough in art—pictures in motion. The actual techniques were still unknown to him, but if such a thing had been done, he could do it too. Pursuit of this aim would absorb all that bounding, boundless energy for the next two years.

He built a small skylighted moving picture addition at the end of the new gallery. The gallery became, in effect, a theater where the audience faced a small proscenium, like a picture frame. By unseen cords, curtains could be drawn over the long skylight to darken the hall. Wonder of wonders! There, in the summer of 1785, overhead fans mysteriously stirred the air above each expectant audience as the pall of darkness closed over it. Then, faintly at first, the picture could be seen—a landscape nocturne into which, slowly, came the light of dawn. As birds began to sing, hills, trees, and a mansion appeared, carrying the picture toward a climax of light and sound. Next came a city street scene, and then a mill with splashing water and turning wheel. The repertoire of six scenes moved up to a dramatic pinnacle from *Paradise Lost*—since boyhood Peale's favorite book—smoldering mountain, fiery palace, Lucifer and his hosts. Later, Peale added a dramatization of the great sea battle between the *Serapis* and *Bonhomme Richard*. Peale would have had the story from John Paul Jones himself, whose portrait hung there on the wall.[5]

Philippe de Loutherbourg, Garrick's scene painter at Drury Lane, had first produced such little scenes in 1781 under the name "Eidophusikon." Peale's initial cumbersome title, "Perspective Views with Changeable Effects; or, Nature Delineated and in Motion," was soon shortened familiarly to "moving pictures." It was all part of a continuing search for greater realism and a more popular impact in art, to be climaxed in Robert Barker's invention of the cyclorama (1789), a panoramic picture that surrounded its viewers in a closed circle and where, to complete the illusion, actual objects at the spectators' feet blended cleverly into the huge painted scene beyond. The trend is worth noting, apropos of the form which the Peale museum exhibits would later take, in their similarly realistic presentation.

Philadelphia's "moving pictures" caused a great stir and were profitable for a while. "The meed of praise," always brighter to this painter than pounds and guineas, he had. Financial returns, however, soon diminished. The labor of creating each scene with its movable panels and intricate lighting was enormous, and people would not return repeatedly to see the same repertoire. Then, too, competition had come promptly as Charles Bousselot, a dashing young Frenchman who had married a sister of the lively American actor Charles Durang, produced his own transparent moving pictures and a puppet show as well, on Second Street near Pine, not far from the Peale home at Third and Lombard.[6] Peale added his sea fight sequence in February, 1786, apparently as an improvement

DR. ROBERT PATTERSON
Brigade major of the Revolution, professor of mathematics and
vice-provost at the University of Pennsylvania, and president of the
American Philosophical Society—Patterson was the Peale friend who
encouraged the museum idea as a scientific necessity of national
importance. Portrait by Rembrandt Peale. (American Philosophical
Society.)

over one by Bousselot. But active competition was not at all to Peale's taste, and as the promise of the picture shows faded, his thoughts had been returning to the paddlefish and bones, to natural history and the prospect of a museum like the great museums of Europe, national yet universal, an American revelation of herself and of the world.

Natural history was a new science, freshly conceived, rising and popular—a new science for a new era. Linnaeus, the great Swedish botanist and physician, had founded it upon a systematic base that gave all life new meaning. His binomial nomenclature of genus and species set fixed or implied relationships and brought unity and coherence where before there had been only a perpetuating confusion. His books and lectures, terse, direct, and factual, brought him an influence greater than that of any of the abstract philosophers of the Enlightenment. Here, truly, was an exultant break from the past, which seemed to bring the whole world into view, and with it the divine creator—the "Frame of Nature," the "Great Chain of Being," infinite variety within an irrefragable whole. "Order is Heav'n's first law," Alexander Pope had written, and

All are but parts of one stupendous whole,
Whose body Nature is, and God the soul.

Peale, deist and devotee of the poet, would in time dare to speak openly of his Museum as a temple, more truly a revelation of God than could be found in any church. Over its door and repeatedly in its publications he would cite these lines from Fettiplace Bellers' *Injur'd Innocence,* a poetic drama of 1732:

The Book of Nature open,
. . . Explore the wondrous work,
. . . an Institute
Of Laws eternal, whose unaltered page
No time can change, no copier corrupt.

Clergy, however, were inclined to look askance at natural history, though there was a notable exception in Nicholas Collin, pastor of the Swedish churches on the Delaware and a member of the American Philosophical Society. He had been a friend and student of Linnaeus, and he gave Peale his warm and steady support Doctors, instead, saw natural history as a branch of their own science. Peale had many friends in the profession, and there was a

15

strong element of medical theory in the undertaking he now had in mind. Natural history would teach natural living, right food and drink, healthy exercise, and reverse that tide of corruption to which Rousseau had pointed in the opening sentence of *Emilius:* "All things are good as they came out of the hands of their Creator, but everything degenerates in the hands of men."[7] Natural history had persuaded him that, in proportion to the immature period, human beings should live as long an adult life span as other animals. Through right living a man could put two active centuries behind him before feeling his age. He laughed, but he believed and preached it. His naive and charming little *Epistle to a Friend, on the Means of Preserving Health, Promoting Happiness, and Prolonging the Life of Man to its Natural Period* was addressed to Thomas Jefferson in 1803, for Peale was fearful that under the pressures of the presidency so valuable a life and so dear a friend might be in danger.

Patriotism, too, touched natural history, with Jefferson in the picture here as well. In his *Notes on the State of Virgina,* begun in 1781 and published in 1787, Jefferson was at pains to refute the doctrine of Western Hemisphere degeneracy that was widely held in Europe but profoundly irritating to Americans. The great Comte de Buffon had endorsed it in his authoritative multivolume *Histoire Naturelle,* stating that all natural life of the Americas, even the Indians, was smaller and weaker than commensurate species in other parts of the world, and that even species brought into the American climate from Europe tended to degenerate. To Americans

FIRST GIFT TO THE MUSEUM
"A curious Non-descript Fish . . . termed by those who caught it a paddlefish." A freshwater monster, 4 or 5 feet in length, now classified as Polyodon spathula, *Dr. Patterson's gift served as an example of the innumerable strange discoveries awaiting American naturalists. (From the* Columbian Magazine, *November 1786.)*

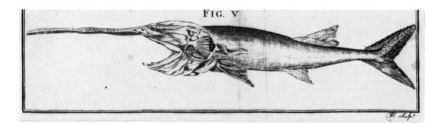

the fallacy was obvious, but it persisted. Jefferson, going to France in 1784 to succeed Franklin as minister, brought abundant evidence directly to Buffon and others, topping it off with the impressive hide and skeleton of a moose, imported at great expense. Peale, never one for heated controversy, answered the Europeans only with mild ridicule, particularly for their equating of animals known to them with vaguely similar but quite different species in the west. Their errors gave him self-confidence. He must rely much on Buffon's work, but had no fear of challenging it.

One other, and important, impulse behind his museum idea came with Benjamin Franklin's return from France in 1785. Welcomed with all the joy and gratitude his long service abroad had earned, Franklin once more presided over the learned society he had founded so many years before. The American Philosophical Society Held at Philadelphia for Promoting Useful Knowledge responded to his presence with renewed activity and new plans for the future. Franklin was friendly to Peale's museum project as soon as he heard of it. The Society encouraged Peale's decision, took him into membership when it was made, and would serve him as a formative influence and a collaborator through the ensuing years.

His friends in the society could give him some general idea of what models there were to follow. This would be sketchy, leaving much to the fertile Peale imagination. He learned that the great museums of Europe were state-supported, but that they had started as private collections. Inevitably, from the first, he expected his own to follow that pattern. The venerable Ashmolean at Oxford had been assembled by John Tradescant, King's Gardener to Charles I. The inscription over its door, "MUSEUM ASHMOLEANUM, SCHOLA NATURALIS HISTORIAE, OFFICINA CHYMICA," may have inspired the plain English he would place over the door of his own ("SCHOOL OF NATURE"), and the added "OFFICINA CHYMICA" (Chemical Laboratory) perhaps gave a blessing to the chemical experiments that would eventually become a feature of Peale's museum.

In London the British Museum had been founded in 1753, when the collections of Sir Hans Sloane were purchased by the nation. Visitors could gain admission but only recognized scholars had free use. Londoners could get more satisfaction from Sir Ashton Lever's private museum covering a vast range of natural history. It was open to the public for half a crown, and it is unlikely, at that price, that Peale had seen it in his student days. What Philadelphians could tell him of the Leverian was not too encouraging. Sir

Ashton had begun it as a man of wealth but had exhausted his fortune in building and maintaining it through the years. Now he was finding Parliament cool to the idea of placing it on a national foundation.

Nicholas Collin could give Peale a similar account of the Swedish collections. Later, primarily from Jefferson, he would hear of the museum at Paris, the one which became his chosen model. There was very little in the way of American precedent. Besides Du Simitière, various gentlemen had become collectors. Philadelphia's Library Company cherished a cabinet of curious objects. More significantly, the Charleston Library Society in South Carolina had laid a foundation for a full-scale museum of natural history on January 12, 1773.[8] This modest beginning had been interrupted by the war, but Peale must have heard of its revival in 1785, since one of its promoters was Dr. David Ramsay, brother of the Colonel.

But for the idea of popular education in natural history there was no precedent at home or abroad. That was Peale's alone, and with it, at first, a total innocence of the vastness of his undertaking. As the magnitude of his task appeared, so also his sense of its importance grew. He must specialize, yes, but the framework must nonetheless embrace all nature—the inanimate, the living from simplest forms up to the races of mankind in every character and occupation. It must attract, delight and inform all comers. It must

> . . . diffuse a knowledge of the wonderful works of creation, not only of this country but of the whole world. Also to show the progress of arts and science, from the savage state to the civilized man; displaying the habits and customs of all nations; to show the progress of arts and manufactures from the raw materials to their finished fabrics.
>
> To form a school of useful knowledge, to diffuse its usefulness to every class in our country, to amuse and in the same moment to instruct the adult of each sex and age—with a zeal far surpassing the bounds of fatigue, did I exert every nerve by increasing labours, for fifteen years: by day and by night, as long as I could keep my eyes open, did I labour to preserve animals, common as well as those more rarely met with . . . .[9]

European museums of this time had no such concern for "usefulness" to "every class" and "each sex or age." Peale declared freely that "the Fair Sex" and children possessed equal rights to every advantage. Beautiful rarities of a museum, too, should be seen against a background of the commonplace—barnyard poultry along with peacock and lyrebird:

> We might suppose it unnecessary to display animals so universally known, yet when we consider that a Museum should possess specimens of every genus; that there should be no c[h]asms, if possible to be avoided: and as the diffusing of knowledge is the great object of such an institution, it ought to display the common as well as the uncommon.[10]

Specimens should also be seen in natural attitudes and groups and with the natural environment of each represented by appropriate objects and a painted landscape background. Here was the origin of the habitat groups which would be brought to full perfection a century later (and with the eclat of a new discovery) at the American Museum of Natural History in New York. With Peale it had come naturally from his artist's eye. He created his museum as he would a picture, and for years he had been painting men and women against a background of household settings. Another of his innovations can be traced to his apprentice days and the woodwork supporting the saddle leather: he mounted the skins of larger animals on sculptured forms showing the muscle action appropriate to each.

He pioneered also in conducted "walks," public lectures, and, long before the advent of photography, lectures illustrated by actual specimens or lantern slides. He published a visitors' *Guide,* a *Scientific and Descriptive Catalogue,* along with other occasional productions of "The Museum Press," and even attempted a popular journal. Gifts were encouraged and scrupulously recorded, and a system of exchanges was set up, bringing him into touch with the museums of London, Stockholm, and Paris, as well as institutions and collectors throughout Europe and the Americas. His activities also stimulated a correspondence with naturalists eager to exchange information. Field trips ranged west to the Susquehanna, east to the Jersey shore, south into Maryland and Virginia, and, most important of all, north into New York State in 1801, where America's first organized scientific expedition (the Museum supported by American Philosophical Society and federal government) solved, where Michaelis had failed, the mystery of the gigantic bones. In time, collecting for the Museum was to reach into South America and across the Pacific to Australia and China.

"Moving pictures" in the Peale gallery had brought, for the first time, an admission charge. There was a trend in this direction; Du Simitière had followed it, as had old Dr. Chovet at his anatomical waxworks, long one of the town's more titillating educational experiences. In London, artists such as Copley were now showing their paintings for a price. So Peale's Museum began with the 25-cent admission fee that would continue throughout its history. At first it provided a helpful supplement to his income from painting, and after ten years a more and more comfortable living; yet it was never adequate for expansion, renewal of exhibits, and all the other envisioned programs. The modest admission charge would become, actually, one of the many obstacles to the national or state endowment so ardently hoped for. Congressmen or legislators could appreciate the Museum's public service, but not its need for public aid. Peale must contrive what he could on his own. Musical evenings and an emphasis on popular and entertaining aspects of science were devices that came easily, as they have to our present-day museums when financially hard-pressed.

Where all this could lead was obvious enough to Peale from the many other proprietary museums that were oriented entirely in this direction. Other scientific endeavors of his time were one-man affairs: James Woodhouse's Chemical Society of Philadelphia, or the learned journals put out by Benjamin Smith Barton, Archibald Bruce, Thomas Cooper, John Redman Coxe, and that ponderous man of universal learning, Dr. Samuel Latham Mitchill of New York. Yet the story of Peale's Museum centers upon his vision of a great national institute, a continuing, elusive hope, pursued with all the fateful ardor of tragic drama.

He had reached the age of forty-five when it all began, young at heart, with a boyish zest for collecting and for adventure, freed from the drudgery of "face-painting" and happy to be constantly before the public in this protean, momentous fulfillment. There were no "pains of ennui" here, and no room for them. Give him a hundred years if need be, and he would prove his point beyond all cavil. The fascination of it all amazed him as it did others. Sometimes it seemed like happenstance, like taking the grand prize in a lottery. It might never have come about if as an artist he had not been reduced to making portraits of Dr. Morgan's old bones . . . if Ramsay had not stopped in that day . . . if Patterson and the others had not responded with their warm approval . . . if the work itself had not been such a joy, from the start and on through the years. "I have always made myself happy by a constant employment in one way or another," he confessed to one of his sons three decades later, "and that habit accidentally led me to the formation of a Museum which in some future day will be the admiration of the world."[11]

CHAPTER TWO

"WITH HARMONY SMALL BEGINNINGS EFFECT GREAT THINGS": 1784-1790

Politician Peale, appointed a commissioner for confiscated estates, had bought one of them for himself in 1780, at the end of his term in office. A mass exodus of Tories with the retreating British army had glutted the market with properties, and the house at Third and Lombard Streets had been a bargain. It was of brick, two and a half storeys high, with tall lombardy poplars along its Lombard Street front and an ample backyard shaded by a large willow. He soon saw the need to add a small studio room at the side, since the house itself was filled to overflowing with family.

Besides his own Raphaelle, Angelica, Rembrandt, and Titian, he had adopted two war orphans, the awkward teenager Charles Peale Polk and bouncing, laughing little Betsy, the children of his sister Elizabeth. Elizabeth had succumbed to tuberculosis, and her husband, the belligerent Captain Bobby Polk, had died amid cannonfire on the quarterdeck of his little privateer *Black Joke,* disputing the British invasion of Delaware Bay. Here, in the new house, during the founding years of the Musuem, Rachel's last three children would be born: Rubens, Sophonisba, and Rosalba. Add to these one young art student—the deaf mute son of General Hugh Mercer, killed at Princeton—and you have a handful. Charles's mother and his childhood nurse, old Peggy Durgan, had remained with his family, helping Rachel with the household tasks. Two former slaves also helped out; both had been acquired in Maryland, apparently as payment for portraits of masters eager to be rid of them. One, a mulatto named Moses Williams, a youth and, later, a man of both humor and resource, was destined to figure prominently in the Museum years.

Over a fireplace in the heart of this ménage there hung a Swiss engraving, an allegory honoring Jean Jacques Rousseau as the liberator of childhood. The author of *Emilius* had been the first to speak out against rule by the rod, and in favor of education by example and happy experience. Peale heartily approved. There would be no "reign of terror" in his home. Here the young would be led "to the paths of virtue by a chain of flowers."[1] This was the view of the master, and no other would dispute it. Gentle and beautiful Rachel was slowly fading in health; Margaret Peale and Peggy Durgan were far advanced in garrulous, cheerful old age, and the servants were irresponsible and content. Thus, the Peale swarm of infants and young people grew up without discipline, but always with new interests, new excitements, a free share in whatever the paterfamilias had in hand. They all learned to paint, learned French, read prolifically, wrote verses, sang and played. They were sent to school but never required to follow through in any regular fashion. It was a chain of flowers.

In the summer of 1782, Peale added his skylighted gallery to the painting room and, in November 1784, added on to that the moving picture room, bringing the total length to 77 feet. He was able to buy an adjoining lot on Third Street, with a small stable, in the next year. He would need this for what would soon become the Museum's lively and diverse menagerie. A large proportion of its animals would be received alive and, generally, young. They must be kept to maturity (and sometimes longer), as Peale studied their habits or became fond of them. And what joy for the young Peales! Winged and four-footed pets, including serpents, overflowed from stable into the house. The old Peale homestead of family-plus-painting-room would never be the same again. By June 1786, the change was well under way, and an announcement in the

MR. *PEALE*, ever defirous to pleafe and entertain the Public, will make a part of his Houfe a Repofitory for Natural Curiofities—The Public he hopes will thereby be gratified in the fight of many of the Wonderful Works of Nature which are now clofeted and but feldom feen. The feveral Articles will be claffed and arranged according to their feveral fpecies; and for the greater eafe to the Curious, on each piece will be infcribed the place from whence it came. and the name of the Donor, unlefs forbid, with fuch other information as may be neceffary.

Mr. PEALE will moft thankfully receive the Communications of Friends who will favour him with their Affiftance in this Undertaking.

Corner of Lombard and Third ftreets, Philadelphia.

N. B. All the Portraits are now removed into the former Exhibition Room; and Exhibitions of the *Moving Pictures with Changeable Effects*, will only be made for private companies, confifting of twenty or more perfons; on previous notice being given.   r

FIRST APPEAL TO THE PUBLIC
Published in the Pennsylvania Packet, *July 7–November 12, 1786,*
with insertions in other newspapers north and south.

Pennsylvania Packet of July 7 invited the nation at large to participate:

> MR. PEALE, ever desirous to please and entertain the Public, will make a part of his House a Repository for Natural Curiosities—The Public he hopes will thereby be gratified in the sight of many of the Wonderful Works of Nature which are now closeted but seldom seen. The several articles will be classed and arranged according to their several species; and for greater ease to the Curious, on each piece will be inscribed the place from whence it came, and the name of the Donor, unless forbid, with such other information as may be necessary.
>
> Mr. PEALE will most thankfully receive the Communications of Friends who will favour him with their Assistance in this Undertaking.
>
> *Corner of Lombard and Third Streets, Philadelphia.*
>
> N.B. All the Portraits are now removed into the former Exhibition Room; and Exhibitions of the *Moving Pictures with*

Changeable Effects, will only be made for private companies, consisting of twenty or more persons, on previous notice being given.

Two weeks later, Peale was elected to membership in the American Philosophical Society, where a transformation was also in progress. The Society, with a world-famous figure at its head, must now have a more active program than before, publications, closer ties with savants overseas, and, as a final element of institutional stability, a building of its own, right beside the State House on Independence Square. Thirty-four new members came in at this meeting. As befitted Franklin's position as chief executive of the Commonwealth, a fine political impartiality was shown—bringing in both George Bryan, leader of the political radicals of wartime, and Robert Morris, their stoutest opponent; both radical Peale and Robert Edge Pine, the English artist to whom many of the conservative camp had transferred their patronage. Foreign notables Franklin had known as minister to France sparkled on the list: Marquis de Condorcet, Duc de la Rochefoucauld, and Jacques Charles, the aeronaut. Peale had already painted from life a new portrait of Franklin for his gallery, and he presented an earlier one from Colonial days to the Society, to hang in their new building when that should be completed.

He continued to run the newspaper notice until November 12, and it was reprinted in other papers over a wide area. Dr. Franklin himself was one of the first to respond, contributing the body of an angora cat. A parting gift from a delightful and flirtatious neighbor of his Paris days, Madame Helvétius, the animal had survived only briefly after the voyage from France. Franklin also lent Peale a treatise on the preservation of birds and other natural history subjects that had been given him by Louis Marie Jean Daubenton, one of Buffon's collaborators on the great *Histoire Naturelle.*[2] Its information was little help with preserving the cat, which had to be discarded as a failure. Peale saw that, as with the moving pictures, he must work out these new techniques for himself. Some of his procedures may be traced to a little manual by another of Franklin's friends, the London physician John Coakley Lettsom, but eventually Peale developed his own system and took pride in it as better than anything being done in Europe.[3] He drew first on his own painter's materials for preservatives, then changed from turpentine to arsenic solutions, variously brewed, with bichloride of mercury (corrosive sublimate) for larger specimens. Glass eyes were difficult to find and import, and for small birds or quadrupeds a bead of black sealing wax would do. For the larger specimens he used his skill in molding concave glass for miniature settings, making a hollow crystal on the inside of which he painted the precise markings of the original eye.[4]

Franklin's cat had been a failure, but, improving rapidly with experience, Washington's pheasants were successfully preserved. They are extant today to prove it, pecking and strutting contentedly, the earliest of Peale's mountings. He had heard of the gift of Lafayette, the farmer of La Grange, to the farmer of Mount Vernon—Chinese golden pheasants from the Royal Aviary in Paris. Peale had written at once: When they died, might he preserve them for posterity? The birds did die soon, and the General was happy to oblige. The remains of the first, delayed on the road, arrived in poor condition; "yet," as the response came back from the Museum, "I was richly repaid in being able to preserve so much beauty. Before this time I had thought those Birds which I had seen in the Chinease paintings were only works of fancy, but now I find them to be only aukerd Portraits. I am sorry that their lives cannot be preserved. I did not find this body very lean. The musls of the Thighs were strong which with the smallness of the wings makes me think that they run fast & fly but little. When you have the misfortune of loosing the others, if the weather should be warm be pleased to order the Bowels to be taken out and some pepper put into the Body. But no salt which would injure the feathers."[5]

Judge Beale Bordley, his oldest and dearest friend, sent a gift from his Maryland plantation, and, although Peale left plant life largely to the Bartrams of the famous botanical garden on the Schuylkill, he responded warmly. "Your favour of the Silk Grass, Cabbage seed and Nut I have recd. and placed among my other articles of Curious Nature. I have just returned from the warf where I have been assisting to get out of a ship's bottom a piece of a Sword of a Sword Fish. It is supposed that the fish had taken the ship for a whale and made the dreadful attack, which broke off the end of his sword, & which we immagine is about 5 or 6 Inches sunk into the Ships Timber." He and Bordley, an amateur, had painted together, and Peale added a note on the "Marble Chalk" someone had given to his growing mineral collection. He had sensed a useful new pigment, and was trying it out on his palette.[6]

Friends were sending in donations to the collection, and Peale was reaching out to them. A letter was dashed off to Dr. David Ramsay in Charleston: "I suppose you have seen my advertizement respecting my Intention of appropriating a part of my House for a repository of natural curiosities. My colection already is become interesting. My Labours to increase the stocks and get a knowledge of the Business is great." He had gotten into something, he now confessed, much vaster than he had at first realized. No matter. Could the doctor find him a stuffed alligator? Ramsay's marriage to Martha Laurens, daughter of the former president of the Continental Congress, was then impending, and it was not a time for alligators. Peale brushed that thought aside as the correspondence continued, asking for birds of Carolina also and other specimens, "either in spirits or dry."[7] He knew a fellow enthusiast when he had one, and the South Carolina doctor would respond in time.

The collection had indeed "become interesting." It was found so by the editor of the *Packet,* whose column of city items for October 31, 1786, reports: "We hear that Mr. C. W. Peale has acquired the means of preserving birds and animals in their natural form, and that he intends to place in his collection of curiosities every species of birds and animals that he is able to obtain, belonging to North and South-America." ("Curious," it should be noted, signified an object of intellectual interest, and is not to be taken in its present, often pejorative sense.) Recognition also came in the new *Columbian Magazine,* an illustrated journal of science, politics, history, and literature. A gigantic tooth, another relic of the mysterious "American *Incognitum,*" had been found on the upper Susquehanna by David Rittenhouse and Andrew Ellicott. The Philosophical Society had asked Peale for a drawing, and this now appeared in the magazine's first volume, together with "A Description of the Soldier, or Hermit Crab, from one in Mr. Peale's Museum."[8]

Peale had set out, as he put it, "to bring into one view a world in miniature," and that, after a fashion, was what visitors to the corner of Third and Lombard beheld.[9] Spreading out under the lofty skylight they found an artificial landscape, a low bank of hills around a glass-covered pond, trees and bushes with birds, beasts, and fish seen everywhere. It was an artful beginning which disguised the actual smallness of the collection—an attractive nucleus to be continually expanded until individual exhibits first supplemented and then replaced it. It was growing, as he wrote to Bordley on December 5, 1786, "most by my labours in disecting and preserving Birds and Beasts. I have, I believe, nearly compleated the class of wild Ducks belonging to this river, ducks & Drakes which I have disposed in various attitudes on artifical ponds, some Birds & Beasts on trees and some Birds suspended as flying. I have not yet been able to get [any] of the large wild Beasts and it is necessary it should be so, as I have been practicing on the smaller to gain knowledge of the business. . . . And if my life is preserved for any length of time, it is most likely that my labours will make a museum that will be considered of more consequence than anything of this sort in America. It is to be lamented that too many rare & valuable things have already been sent & [are] still sending to the other side of the Atlantic."[10]

Or, see the Museum in this early stage through the eyes of a visitor from Massachusetts, as he stepped from the painting room into the exhibition hall:

At the opposite end, under a small gallery, his natural curiosities were arranged in a most romantic and amusing manner. There was a mound of earth, considerably raised and covered with green turf, from which a number of trees ascended and branched out in different directions. On the declivity of this mound was a small thicket, and just below it an artificial pond; on the other side a number of large and small rocks of different kinds, collected from different parts of the world and represented in the rude state in which they are generally found. At the foot of the mound were holes dug and earth thrown up, to show the different kinds of clay, ochre, coal, marl, etc. which he had collected from different parts; also, various ores and minerals. Around the pond was a beach, on which was exhibited an assortment of shells of different kinds, turtles, frogs, toads, lizards, water snakes, etc. In the pond was a collection of fish with their skins stuffed, water fowls, such as the different species of geese, ducks, cranes, herons, etc.; all having the appearance of life, for their skins were admirably preserved. On the mound were those birds which commonly walk the ground, as the partridge, quail, heath-hen, etc.; also, different kinds of wild animals,—bear, deer, leopard, tiger, wild-cat, fox, raccoon, rabbit, squirrel, etc. In the thicket and among the rocks, land-snakes, rattle snakes of an enormous size, black, glass, striped, and a number of other snakes. The boughs of the trees were loaded with birds, some of almost every species in America, and many exotics. In short, it is not in my power to give a particular account of the numerous species of fossils and animals, but only their general arrangement. What heightened the view of this singular collection was that they were all real, either their

27

substance or their skins finely preserved. . . . Mr. Peale was very complaisant, and gave us every information we desired. He requested me to favor him with any of the animals and fossils of this part of America, not already in his museum, which it might be in my power to collect.[11]

Already, this early in the day, the difficulties of museum management were appearing. The historian Ebenezer Hazard, who was then Postmaster General of the United States, contributed a number of articles. These probably had come from Du Simitière's estate, of which he was one of the executors. Small objects, Peale reported back, "especially those that are delicate must be kept under Glass to prevent the abuse of fingering, and I am getting made some Glass cases with sloping shelves for that purpose, which will be opened for the Curious when desired."[12] But he could not prevent handling among the objects comprising the large exhibit of pond and hill. Signs were put up conspicuously:

DO NOT TOUCH THE BIRDS.
THEY ARE COVERED WITH ARSNIC POISON.

No use. People would finger the feathers even while reading the warning.[13]

The next step would be the glass-fronted cases, each backed with its view of native habitat, rendered in watercolor on paper. Alas, that these little paintings by Peale, many of them actual views, have all disappeared. At the breakup of the Museum, they were thrown out and the birds were rudely torn from their mountings. Universally accepted as the habitat arrangement is in natural history museums today, yet late in life Peale must needs defend his controversial innovation:

It is not customary in Europe, it is said, to paint skys and landscapes in their cases of birds and other animals, and it may have a neat and clean appearance to line them only with white paper, but on the other hand it is not only pleasing to see a sketch of a landscape, but by showing the nest, hollow, cave or a particular view of the country from which they came, some instances of the habits may be given.[14]

The gallery became filled, then crowded. The former painting room at the front part of the museum, and then the old moving picture addition, eleven feet deep and with a skylight of its own, was transformed into the semblance of a seaside cavern, as appropriate background for marine life and reptiles. Floor and walls were plastered and painted in imitation of rough stone, and the skylight was "disguised like a hole in a rocksome height."[15] It must have been very much like the stage cavern he had created for little Nancy Hallam's appearance as Fidele, the forlorn maiden of *Cymbeline,* back at the Annapolis Theatre in 1771. A wooded hill! A lake and shore! A grotto by the sea! Thus Peale's Museum at its inception was presenting nature in the poetic and romantic terms of the garden art so popular in eighteenth century. One wonders whether he had visited Twickenham in his London days, as did other admirers of Pope, to walk down its paths, encounter surprises and delights at every turn, and peer into the shadowy grotto there.

For all that, a sense of duty to truth and science underlay the emphasis on beauty. In January 1788, the Philosophical Society elected Peale one of the curators of its own scientific collections, a responsibility he would hold for twenty-one years. At its meetings the importance of discovery, standards of proof, and ideals of order and exactitude prevailed. Undescribed species must be brought into the mainstream; anything, however slight, was to be added to the riches of knowledge. Peale even preserved an unusual fish without a head, deeming it worthwhile to preserve that much until more could be learned.[16]

All nature must be the scope of this museum, but birds were its favored department from the first—their beauty and enchanting variety—the great ranges open to new discovery beyond Mark Catesby's pioneering works of many years before, those of George Edwards, and the few others who had thus far attempted to describe American species. American ornithology was still a chaos crying out for order and correction and, above all, for an assembling of type specimens. The allure of collecting and of the hunt were there. In April and May, year after year, Peale would be out with his gun in neighboring woods and river marshes. He and his sons became famous hunters. His very first bird taken in this way, a grebe or "water witch," was an experience never to be forgotten. Out on the water, the bird would dive at the flash of his gun, seeming to elude the shot. Peale outwitted it at last by running nearer to the shore each time it dived and standing still when it came up, thus getting within easy range and "pulling the Trigger before the water had run out of its Eyes."[17]

He inserted a four-line notice in the papers inviting "gentlemen sportsmen" of the city to join him in enriching the Museum.[18] But word came constantly of natural prizes at distances beyond his reach. "My finances are such that I cannot leave my family to go after any article of Curiosity however valuable and easily obtained," he complained to Hazard in July of 1787. "The fine arts have no encouragement here. I hope to see better times. Much worse will not do."

This was the summer of the Constitutional Convention. Important men and their families had come to Philadelphia from north and south, yet portrait commissions lagged. Not many faces were added even to the Museum gallery, which now represented *Homo sapiens* in the "Chain of Nature." General Washington came to see his pheasants in their new setting and posed for a half-length portrait in uniform, from which Peale made and published a mezzotint print. The delegates, so many of whom Peale knew personally, dropped in and he had an opportunity to plant the ideas of a national museum among them, of natural history as a source of public health and happiness, of natural law as a guide to peace among nations. James Madison was there with a more intelligent, encouraging interest than others, citing Buffon's monumental work with familiarity.

Times were hard, but lively too, and with a sense of better things impending. One of the few businessmen of the town who shared Peale's political views, John Swanwick, merchant and poet, had imported a collection of Italian paintings for sale, which were hung in the Peale gallery for a while. This was a cultural novelty for Philadelphia and a wonderland that awakened nine-year-old Rembrandt, an intense and impressionable child, to visions of undying fame in this magic realm.[19]

There were lighter diversions as well, more suited to the temperament of Rembrandt's elder brother Raphaelle, now thirteen. As the Italian paintings were echoed in the career of the one, so the fun and fascination of the wax figure would be reflected in the other. Their father had mastered the technique of wax sculpture, perhaps from young Joseph Wright, painter-sculptor son of Patience Wright, the waxwork portraitist and wartime spy in London, or perhaps from Rachel Wells, Patience's sister, whose waxwork show had long been one of the sights of Philadelphia. Later, Peale would use this skill in creating costumed figures of the races of mankind. Now, as a first trial, he had made a figure of himself. The story comes to us from the Rev. Manasseh Cutler, a New England clergyman and naturalist who, in July 1787, had been brought around to Third and Lombard by Peale's neighbor Dr. Gerardus Clarkson.

A boy, surely Raphaelle, met them at the door, led them in, and, surely with twitching lip and dancing eye, pointed to a narrow corridor and asked them to walk through to where the "curiosities" could be seen.

> I observed, through a glass at my right hand, a gentleman close to me, standing with a pencil in one hand and a small sheet of ivory in the other, and his eyes directed to the opposite side of the room as though he was taking some object on his ivory sheet. Dr. Clarkson did not see this man until he stepped into the room, but instantly turned about and came back to say, "Mr. Peale is very busy taking something with his pencil. We will step back into the other room and wait till he is at leisure." We returned through the entry, but as we entered the room we came from, we met Mr. Peale coming to us. The Doctor started back in astonishment and cried out, "Mr. Peale, how is it possible you should get out of the other room to meet us here?" Mr. Peale smiled. "I have not been in the other room," says he, "for some time." "No!" says Clarkson, "Did I not see you there this moment, with your pencil and ivory?" "Why, do you think you did?" says Peale. "Do I think I did? Yes," says the Doctor. "I saw you there if I ever saw you in my life." "Well," says Peale, "let us go and see." When we returned, we found the man standing as before. My astonishment was now nearly equal to that of Dr. Clarkson; for, although I knew what I saw, yet I beheld two men so perfectly alike that I could not discern the minutest difference. One of them, indeed, had no motion; but he appeared to me to be absolutely alive as the other, and I could hardly help wondering that he did not smile or take part in the conversation. This was a piece of waxwork which Mr. Peale had just finished, in which he had taken himself. To what perfection is this art capable of being carried![20]

The diversions of that summer were followed by the 1788 campaign for adoption of the Constitution. Though many of Peale's old political allies were hostile to ratification, he was heartily for it and supported the movement with a huge, exuberant transparency entitled *Horrors of Anarchy and Confusion and Blessings of Order,* similar to his propaganda paintings of the war. It was shown with great éclat in his native Maryland, where, as he now discovered, he was even more welcome than of old. The people of the towns and plantations there received him as an honored guest, were eager to have their portraits made, and were complaisantly ready to contribute whatever of interest they might have to the new museum. There followed a series of trips to the south for Peale, traveling in a light carriage and bringing not only paints but his gun and a supply of wire, oakum, cotton, and preservatives used in stuffing birds, so that each journey became a museum expedition as well as a campaign for support. Each brought him a replenished purse and busy days of rearrangement and expansion at Third and Lombard.

Peale's diaries flash glimpses, here and there, of the scene. On Saturday, June 6, 1788, he is a guest of the gentlemen of the Fish Club at Annapolis. He dines with them under a marquee by the creek and, while they are amusing themselves afterward with skittles and quoits, wanders off with his gun. When he returns to them, it is with birds he would preserve the next day, among them a bluebird and a "nondescript but commonly called the Peewe." We see him on the boat from Annapolis to Baltimore occupied, as usual, every moment. "I employ myself in preserving one hen Red-Bird and a Cock, & hen of a species of Wood red-Bird."[21] That was on the homeward trail, followed up by the arrival of packing cases filled with much else—a pelican, a swan, a mink, a variety of ducks, and more.

At home he had a helper in the younger brother to whom he had always been close. James Peale had been with him at the moving pictures, and was still by his side whenever needed. They had shared home and studio until James's marriage in November 1782. James's health had suffered from his service in the war as a lieutenant, and then captain, in the Maryland Line of the regular army—a quiet, steady soldier, no dynamo of energy like Charles, but a gentle, ready brother and friend. In painting, Charles now turned all the miniature work over to James, whose art was slowly maturing into a style of his own. Charles's diaries show them together at the Museum, making over a bookcase into a display of small birds, placing others on the "artificial Bank," grinding watercolors and painting landscape backgrounds for the cases.

RED-LEGGED PARTRIDGE
Peale's original habitat groups have been dispersed, and his painted landscape backgrounds are lost, but his mountings can still be identified by their animated natural attitudes. (Museum of Comparative Zoology, Harvard University.)

Charles brewed the arsenic preservative and applied it till his fingertips broke out in sores and by night a fever came on:

> Before breakfast make in part the trees for fixing my Birds in the Case. Afterwards I worked the whole day in washing my Birds & Beasts in Arsenic water. I put 2 lb. of arsenic into a large kettle, the[n] pour Water 3 parts full, & stir it well & lett it settle & put such Birds &c as are small into it, but the larger kind I am obliged to laidle it up in a porrenger and pour it upon them. Bought 1 lb. more of arsenic & put the most of it into the Kettle & add more water in order to have it impregnated for tomorrows use.[22]

On Sunday, after a week of this, there was an outing to Gray's Ferry with James's family and Betsy Polk, friends and laughter in a hired carriage, a picnic by the Schuylkill, where the brothers gathered moss and evergreens "to decorate the Museum."

John Cram, who had devised the cooling system of fans for the moving pictures, came in to build special cases in which to show the East India insects, the gift of Mrs. John O'Donnell of Baltimore.[23] Captain O'Donnell's return from the Far East had made him at one stroke a man of fame and fortune. Peale painted the O'Donnells' portraits and contributed one of their tiny daughter in acknowledgment of their gifts to the Museum: the brilliant insects, a collection of beautiful shells, a cockatoo and a bird of paradise from the Spice Islands of Molucca, a "hanging bird's nest," East Indian bow and arrows and match gun, and Mogul slippers and saber.[24]

What O'Donnell's vessel *Pallas* had brought to Baltimore, Robert Morris's *Alliance* echoed in Philadelphia; and like Mrs. O'Donnell, Mrs. Morris joined her husband in enriching Peale's Museum. Again, at this early date, all is not recorded, but there were among the rest a mandarin cap, boots and shoes, a mandarin spear and pipe, a paddle from "Morris Island," a Chinese lady's shoe, and a Chinese "silver pheasant which I dressed & put into a attitude."[25]

From New England, Salem's great merchant prince Elias Hasket Derby sent the skin of an antelope of Senegal. Derby often instructed his captains to bring back living animals that might be of interest or value on the American scene; later, perhaps after hearing of Peale's proposals for domestication of the bison, he sent the Museum a live sheep from Russia.[26] By that time, live animals were filling the Peale stable and yard and fluttering, stomping, or creeping through the house. One may well wonder how far Rachel, fading, sweet and pale, could share the communal delight of the children, her husband, and the cheerful servants in it all—the surprises, mysteries, revelations, the occasional wild fights of specimen against specimen, and then the days of death, dissection, arsenic solution, and mounting required for an artistic return to the semblance of natural life. In a day when every child had his toy Ark, here for the Peale offspring was the thing come to life, better even than Noah. In 1788 Captain Thomas Bell came up the river with a cargo from Sumatra and the Coromandel Coast of India, bringing Peale a jackal and an "animal I believe of the monkey tribe. It is called *Mongoose*. . . . I find from reading that this is a very rare animal—much esteemed for their destroying the Eggs of the Crocodile

MODEL OF CHINESE LADY'S FOOT AND SHOE
Richard Dale, John Paul Jones's second-in-command at the famous battle off
Flamborough Head, sailed the merchant ship Ganges *to Canton after the Revolution.*
In 1797 he presented this "Model of Chinese ladies foot with dress and shoe" to Peale's
Museum. (Peabody Museum, Harvard University.)

in Egipt."[27] In from Fort McIntosh on the frontier came Captain William Ferguson of the Artillery, with a pair of snarling, snapping cougars and a sleepy porcupine for good measure. Peale mentioned the cougars in writing to Washington: "Male & Female of full groath, most terrifick animals." These, nor a porcupine either, were no family pets, and they appeared indoors in short order, "neatly preserved."[28]

Snakes, too, were dangerous, but the Peale boys were taught to handle a rattler without fear. The rattlesnake, so deadly at one end and so ready with a warning at the other, was a creature of great interest in Europe as well as America, and Peale set up a special exhibit that has been cited as a noteworthy early example of museum exposition:

> [July] 19th [1788] . . . after breakfast fixed the Teeth of a Rattle Snake in the bird case with a Lens to show the passage and the manner that the Snake communicates it[s] poison. Waited on Doctr. Ewing to endeavor to get him to sett for the finishing his picture which he could not do untill after next week. I then called on Mr. Patterson who went with me to the Library of the University and looked over Buffons works &c. . . .
>
> 20th (Sunday), put arsenic water with Spir[i]ts [of] Turpentine on most parts of the skin by lifting up the feathers of the large Birds presented by Capt. Bell called Albatross and put one of them into the Exhibition Room. Struck off 29 Tickets (Admission). . . .
>
> 21st, got a Blank book from Mr. Siddons cost 5 to class and number the articles of the Museum, & spend this Day in writing the several Classes & Order[s] in the same. . . . [29]

Here, with the rattlesnake, is our first word of two essential developments. The charming little ticket he had etched himself, admitting the bearer to "the Wonderful works of NATURE! and Curious works of Art," with a design of playful animals and a smiling admonishment: "The Birds & Beasts will teach thee." "Equal to 25 Cents," it could also pass as currency. More important was the beginning of a catalogue for the collection. In these books, now unhappily lost, the classes and orders of the Linnaean system were each given ample space for specific entries. Each had its number, to be keyed to a Museum label. The numbering would be revised several times, as Peale was forced to recognize the real extent of his undertaking.

FIRST TICKET TO THE MUSEUM
Etching by C. W. Peale, 1788. (Elise Peale Patterson de Gelpi-Toro.)

Compiling the catalogue required much close study, with many returns to Buffon at the University and to the resources of the Library Company of Philadelphia. Quaker botanist and philanthropist Zaccheus Collins—shy, inconspicuous, yet a figure of influence in the natural sciences through many years—lent Thomas Pennant's *British Zoology* and Richard Pultney's recent *General View of the Writings of Linnaeus.*

Reading and fine workmanship are a strain on the eyes as one nears fifty; while researching and writing labels and catalogue entries, Charles was also helping James to make his start as a miniature painter. On Sunday, August 24, 1788, for instance, we find them at it together—James grinding colors while his brother reads aloud, then lends a guiding hand to the painting, and next day sets himself up with a pair of bifocals: "bought 2 pr. Spectacles, one of 9 Inch focus & the other of 18. I cut the glasses of both pr. and put the longest focus above and the shorter below in each frame, so that I have 2 pr. of Spectacles which will serve for a near or greater distance."[30]

Regular newspaper advertising had begun, and the papers were awakening to the well-known fact that animals are news. We read of a strange "aquatic bird" driven into the city by a storm and of a five-foot rattlesnake lugged in from Maryland, alive, both to be seen at the Museum. Elsewhere in the sheet the following modest announcement was having a month-long run:

Mr. *Peale's* Museum,
Containing the Portraits of Illustrious Personages, distinguished in the late Revolution of America, and other Paintings—Also, a Collection of preserved Beasts, Birds, Fish, Reptiles, Insects, Fossils, Minerals, Petrifactions, and other curious objects, natural and artificial.

Intended to be an easy and pleasing Instruction in Natural History.

As this *Museum* is in its Infancy, Mr. *Peale* will thankfully receive the Assistance of the Curious.[31]

"The Curious" were responding well. A collection in appreciative hands tends to snowball, and so it was with Peale's. Constant expansion kept public interest alive and alerted that of donors. The best form of advertising stimulus, regular publication of the Museum accession lists, began in August 1788. Here the chronicler is tempted to open full throttle, hold onto his hat, and race through the whole panoply of the all-and-sundry that poured into the Peale home in these formative years. A sampling, however, must do. There were the sixty-three young vipers, gift of the Chevalier D'Anmour, the French consul at Baltimore with whom Peale had spent an afternoon discussing Buffon's classification of minerals. There were the hornsnake's horn and tail bestowed by Miss Araminta Alexander, the pelican shot by Colonel Tench Tilghman, a coral tree from Benjamin Laming, lava of Vesuvius from Londoner James Worrel, and—on December 11—the Museum's first material from "the Islands of the South Seas," clothing made of bark, fishhooks, and a spear "of fine workmanship," all the gifts of George Harrison. Harrison was a sophisticated young man in his twenties, a bird fancier like Peale, who had been with Franklin in France during the war and supercargo on the *Alliance* to China, and was

OPOSSUM FAMILY
This engraving from J. D. Godman's American Natural History *of 1826 may show the "opossum with nine young ones" presented to Peale's Museum in 1790 by Dr. John Foulke.*

Drawn by C.Burton

Engraved by W.E.Tucker

Opossum Male & Female

with their Young.

now in public service as Navy Agent at Philadelphia, in an excellent position to be helpful. So he would be, his gifts continuing for twenty years.[32]

As the lists roll on, we read of "A Piece of the Bastille" from Peter Du Ponceau, a philologist who had come to America as aide-de-camp to Baron Steuben; a large iguana, alive, from Captain Stephen Decatur; a hyena of Bengal, alive (presently, we are assured, "confined in an Iron Cage") from Captain Willet; "Likenesses of the King and Queen of France, executed on white sattin, and each produced by a single spark of electricity— Presented by Wm. Temple Franklin, Esquire"; the Koran in Arabic, from William Thompson of Virginia, and more live creatures galore: an opossum with nine young from John Foulke, physician and amateur painter; an East Indian goose from Mrs. Robert Morris; "A Cock with a curious Crest, from Holland— Presented by His Excellency Thomas Mifflin, Esquire, President of Pennsylvania." Michael Hillegas, first Treasurer of the United States sent "Racou Seeds in the Pods; used as a dye for silks and stuffs, and for colouring cheese in Gloucestershire, Great Britain"; William Turnbull, a petrified snake from Fort Pitt; and William Barton, elder brother of the naturalist Benjamin Smith Barton, "A chip cut from the Coronation Chair in Westminster Abbey."[33] Samuel Latham Mitchill appears in 1789 with an important gift of ores, minerals, and fossils. Another naturalist of high repute, Dr. Samuel Brown of Kentucky, sent Indian relics to join the Museum's growing store of pottery, weapons, clothing, scalps, and skeletons.

The Peale sense of order was being challenged by a streaming mélange of treasures among trivialities. Captain Daniel Howland's strange fish of the South Sea—"4 feet long, and not more than 4 inches in the girth, the head and eyes disproportionately large and the jaws set with a single row of very sharp teeth"—was followed by John Galt's clothing and canoe models from the Northwest Coast of America and across the Pacific to Sunda Strait in the Java Sea, as well as a "War Cap and Cloak" of feathers from some island in between. Another feather cape and cap from "Owhyee" followed in 1791, and, in March 1792, the Museum's first government deposit gave evidence of President Washington's continuing friendly interest:

> An Otahitian dress, consisting of a long cloak and a cap, made of feathers, and very elegant. Being a present to the President of the United States, by some gentlemen of Boston,

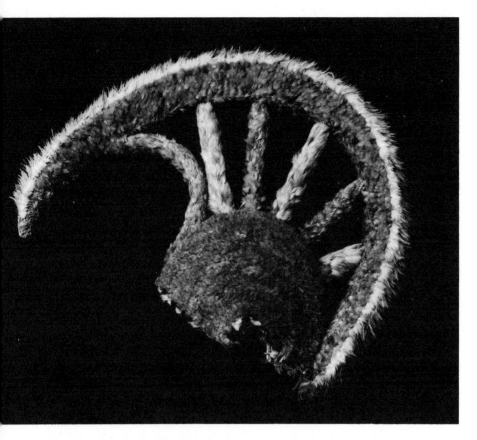

FEATHER HELMET OF HAWAII

*This brilliant yellow, red, and black feather headdress on a
wicker frame may be the helmet in "Roman Style" which
crowned the "Crown Prince of Owyhee" as he landed at
Boston in 1790 and marched up State Street to greet the
Governor, with Captain Gray at his side and the ship's
company of the* Columbia *following. The long feather cape
he wore, with its yellow sunbursts on a scarlet background,
has vanished. Two years later, this costume was presented to
President Washington by the "gentleman adventurers" of the
voyage and then given to Peale for safekeeping, the first
government deposit in the Museum.* (Peabody Museum,
Harvard University.)

adventurers in the first voyage made from thence to Nootka Sound, and the Otahitian Islands, now deposited in this Museum for preservation and safe-keeping for the President.

The gentlemen "adventurers" of Boston—their gift to the nation reechoed the triumphant return of Captain Robert Gray in the *Columbia,* after three years of voyaging around the world. Cannon had thundered the city's welcome on that brilliant summer afternoon in 1790, and the bold seafarers had paraded up State Street through the crowds, preceded by "the Crown Prince of Owhyee" in flowing feather cape and tall feather helmet, a vision of scarlet and gold.[34]

Peale's diary jottings give us a better, but still fragmentary, view of purposeful collecting. His pages swarm with winged, finned, and hooved creatures; fliers, creepers, leapers, and swimmers; a mud iguana with external gills, colorful insects, a "tyger-cat"; and on into the somber silence of minerals, fossils, petrifactions, sponge and coral and shell, and grasses from Madagascar or the coast of India. We glimpse a shark from the "western ocean, 17 feet long," a copy of Hultman's *Instructio Musei* of 1753, and then a collection of South American birds new in beauty and color. But the gifts, year after year, reflect only too well the American public's persistent concept of a museum as a wonderworld of the offbeat and weird, the two-headed pigs, the root resembling a human face, the knot tied by the wind in a storm at sea. People presented what they themselves delighted to see. Such trivia were merely interruptions of Peale's plan. *Lusus naturae,* he explained over and over, were exceptions to the rule, objects for a museum to keep but only to show upon reasonable request.[35] One such that could not be hidden in a drawer, however, was the five-legged cow with six feet and two tails, the gift of a Maryland planter. She lived in the Peale stable and yard for a number of years, faithfully giving milk. Her fame brought her at last, perserved, into the Museum. Public pressure swept aside Peale's attempt to cover the least attractive deformities with a curtain, and she remained fully exposed, an appalling error of Nature and a popular delight. In later years, when Raphaelle had a hand in the mountings, she won further éclat by suckling a two headed calf.

An even more worthless and morbid item was exhibited for a while, by virtue of the moral it was supposed to convey: the trigger finger of the murderer Broliman, presented to the Museum by Philadelphia merchant George Plumsted in July 1790. Surprising as it may seem, its display was expected to draw attention to the value of courteous behavior. Broliman, an officer in the French and Indian War who was despondent after being cashiered, had determined upon suicide by committing a murder. Gun in hand, seeking a victim, he had passed a girl, too pretty to be killed. Then Dr. Thomas Cadwalader appeared, doffing his hat with a cordial, "Good morning, sir! What sport?" Broliman walked by. Had it not been for that genial politeness, the doctor would have been destroyed. Instead, it was in a billiard room that a young man, intent only upon striking the ball, was struck down by Broliman's gun.[36]

"The African Bow," on the other hand, remained on display throughout the Museum's history and was prized as both an ethnological rarity and a profound moral lesson. It was also a genuine relic of one of those swift, fierce little battles of the Southern campaigns, and therein lay the moral. This weapon with which an African warrior had defended his freedom in vain had been used with success in the cause of American independence. Liberty for man or nation is equally dear. The slave is the hero of this parable, his mistress its heroine, and "a British Merchant" its villain, as Peale tells it.

> An African Prince, subdued in Battle, capitulated for his bow and quiver. A bauble bought his life. A British Merchant sent him to South Carolina, where he was sold as a slave.
>
> A placid countenance, and submissive manners, marked his resignation, and preserved him, in all situations, the possession of his arms; the only companions he had left—the sole objects of his affections.
>
> His stateliness and strength recommended him to Colonel Motte, a humane Master in whose service he died, in stedfast faith of a certain resurection in his native state.
>
> The Bow and quiver were preserved as relicks of a faithful slave in the Colonels family, who gratefully remember the services, the fortitude and the fidelity of the trusty, and gentle Jambo.
>
> In the Campaign of 1781, the widow of Colonel Motte (who died a patriot) was banished from her House on the river Congaree, then fortified by a British Garrison; the Garrison was besieged by a small detachment from the American Army, whose approaches were soon within bow shot.

The widow, who lived in a Cottage in sight of the *Fort,* was informed of the expedients proposed. Here, said she (presenting the African bow & quiver) are the Materials— Jambo never used these arrows, and I fear they are poisoned. Use them not, therefore, even against your Enemies. But take the bow. Any arrow will waft a Match. Spare not the House so you expel the foe.

The blazing roof produced submission. The Britains drop'd their arms. The Americans entered the House, and both joined to extinguish the Flames.

The Misfortunes of a Prince, and the Heroism of a Lady, are not uncommon. The Novelty is the Bow—a stem of genuine Bamboa—which, destined for the defence of Liberty in Africa, served the same cause in America, was preserved by an Officer of the Patriotic Army—presented to Mr. Peale, and deposited in his Museum.[37]

The anonymous donor of the ornate bow, quiver, and arrows was Otho Holland Williams, who had been Nathanael Green's adjutant-general in the South and commanded a regiment of the Maryland Line in successive battles. "Fort Motte" had been the South Carolina plantation house of Colonel Isaac Motte, a prisoner of war at the time of the action—May 12, 1781.

In September 1789, Peale came back from Maryland laden with specimens of natural history and with $360 in gold, good earnings for a single painting tour. Fall and winter were before him; it was a high point, and yet a low. A strange, dark climax was near. He was now entering his fourth year of intense preoccupation with the Museum, and through all that time Rachel had been growing more and more frail. The home life so dear to him was receding in a fateful slow ebb tide, raising the more sharply all his memories: their young days at Annapolis, proud hopes alternating with despair, his flight from angry creditors north to New England, leaving her behind . . . his return and first successes as a painter . . . the years away from her in England, the eventual return to acclaim and prosperity, she in silk and ribbons and he with gold lace on his coat and a sword at his side . . . and then the war with all its sorrows and alarms, he in the field, she and the children refugees in hiding . . . and now the Museum, holding a prospect brighter than everything before. He had worked so hard for that! Afterward he himself would look back on the Museum years with amazement that he could have labored as he did, daylong and far into the night, "to accomplish," as he put it, "an end of so much importance as the giving a school of wisdom, and at a time when nothing had been done even to make known what our country alone possessed." He would tell of that night in the winter of 1786–1787 when he had gone to bed exhausted by long hours of work by candlelight, unaware as he slept that robbers had broken into the house, "opened every door on the ground floor & took the little silver plate he had possessed, and also feasted on the contents of the Pantry, drank the liquors of the sideboard, opened the draws in the adjoining Painting-room and must have spent some time to examine what was worth carrying away."[38]

During his last few painting trips, Peale had had a nurse come in to care for Rachel until he returned. Returning, the feverish labor went on, driving away the thought of separation and bringing forward the hope of some high achievement which she could share. Surely, all that he had done at such personal pain and cost now deserved recognition by the nation. He had assembled more than a thousand objects he would call "The American Museum." On February 1, 1790, in the newspapers and in a small broadside he sent to members of the newly established government, to friends and men of influence everywhere, he issued his first call for a national museum.

To the CITIZENS
of the
United States of America

Mr. PEALE respectfully informs the Public, That having formed a design to establish a MUSEUM, for a collection, arrangement and preservation of the objects of natural history and things useful and curious, in June 1785 [i.e., 1784], he began to collect subjects, and to preserve and arrange them in the Linnaean method. His labours herein have been great, and disappointments many—especially respecting proper methods of preserving dead animals from the ravage of moths and worms. In vain he hath sought, from men, information of the effectual methods used in foreign countries; and after experiencing the most promising ways recommended in such books as he has read, they proved ineffectual to prevent depradations by the vermin of America. But, in making various other experiments, he at length discovered a method of preservation, which he is persuaded will prove effectual: it has a very favourable appearance in practice, and far surpasses all others that have come to his knowledge. Nevertheless, it will be obliging in gentlemen to inform him of the best practices in Europe, or elsewhere.

The difficulties in preserving subjects being thus overcome and the Museum having advanced to be an object of attention to some individuals—who, it is hoped, may gain from it information, which, with pleasing and elevated ruminations, will bring them nearer to the Great-First-Cause—he is therefore the more earnestly bent on enlarging the collection with a greater variety of birds, beasts, fishes, insects, reptiles, vegetables, minerals, shells, fossils, medals, old coins, and of utensils, cloathing, arms, dyes and colours, or materials for colouring or for physic, from among the Indian, African or other savage people; and all particulars, although but in model or delineation, promising to be useful in advancing knowledge and the arts; in a word, all that is likely to be beneficial, curious or entertaining to the citizens of the world. But, alas! in compleating the design, a collection of all animated Nature, alone (in the infinite variety of which she wonderfully delights—so great—so vast) requiring an age to enlarge it to the full consideration of a national magnitude; and yet these and other subjects are to be unremittingly pursued, and far as possible obtained, by an individual of but slender circumstances.

All the national museums in the world (as far as he is informed) were from beginnings of individuals: The Public are therefore the more chearfully solicited to help forward this tender plant, while it is yet under the nurturing care and anxious attention of its present possessor, and until it shall have grown into maturity, and become a favorite establishment in the hands of the great Public of the American States. He hopes this may be the case: For—"with harmony small beginnings effect great things."

Much might be said of the importance that such a collection and arrangement would be of to society: but the present address means only to give a concise report of the rise and progress of this infant design, and excite exertion in the friends of science favorable to it: A design that, whilst countenanced by the Public, may grow into a great national museum, or repository of valuable rarities, for more generally diffusing an increase of knowledge in the works of the

Creator—God, alone wise!—At all events, Mr. PEALE intends to prosecute the design with such means as are in his power. Should it happily receive the smiles of the Public, the progress will be proportionately great; whereas, if it is to depend only upon his solitary efforts, the progress must be so slow, that the whole may fall through, not for want of men of superior abilities, but for a successor equally zealous in building up and enlarging the noble fabric, for the emolument of mankind—a fabric which, with due attention, must be continually improving to the end of time.

With sentiments of gratitude, Mr. PEALE thanks the friends to the Museum, who have beneficially added to his collection a number of precious curiosities, from many parts of the world;—from Africa, from India, from China, from the Islands of the great Pacific Ocean, and from different parts of America; some whereof are the more curious, as they have been but very recently discovered, even by the great voyagers of Europe.

He respectfully asks a continuance of their favors; and the assistance of all persons who may be possessed of things curious that they can spare; whether they be of America, or any other part of the world: all will command his grateful acknowledgment; and such deposits will surely be pleasing to men of genius, lovers of science, as well as obliging to their

Thankful and humble servant,
CHARLES WILLSON PEALE.

Note. Mr. PEALE keeps a register of the subjects of his Museum, arranged systematically; together with the names of the promoters of this important institution. *Philadelphia, Feb. 1, 1790.*

Years later, sending a copy of this to Thomas Jefferson, he wrote beneath it: *"Experience thus far has justifyed the above statement, and posterity will do justice to the labours of CW Peale."*[39]

With this arrow in the air, he turned his attention to two large rattlesnakes, sluggish enough from the cold to be measured and studied in detail. The *Address* was bringing a response in gifts and annual tickets, and in one opinion which may be taken as representative of many, for much of the public that was enough. In the *Pennsylvania Packet* of March 27, 1790, "A Lover of Nature" mingled personal encouragement with a clear rebuff to the idea of public support: "A fellow citizen so truly meritorious cannot fail of

47

encouragement from a people who pride themselves on republican virtue and patriotic honor . . . , but—

> In European countries princes can, by a portion of the public treasure, promote science and the useful arts: our jealousy of liberty will not permit such liberality; and indeed in our present exigencies it is not very practicable—But to make up for this, the generosity of individuals is amply sufficient. Thanks to Heaven, we are not poor; many of us can, without the least disadvantage, spare a dollar per annum; this contribution would arise from saving *one farthing every day.*

Peale may have seethed at this invocation of liberty. Liberty and light were the stars he followed! And *a farthing a day!* If he could have realized then that this was exactly where the American public stood and would continue to stand throughout his lifetime, we would have had a different story. The "Lover of Nature" concludes with praises Peale must have thought weak indeed, though they also reflect precisely the value that most people placed on natural history in his day:

> Parents may regard Mr. PEALE's Museum as a school of education for their children: a young gentleman who does not know the natural riches of his country is indeed very deficient; a young lady, with all her taste in finery, is wanting in *fine taste,* if she has no desire to be acquainted with the sweet little humming bird, the gay paradise-bird, the golden pheasant, the beauteous ring-dove, and many other lovely fellow beings.

Two weeks later Rachel, thin and wan against her pillows, asked that the children be brought to her for a last farewell. Their father, fearful that the sight of all seven by her bed might be too much for her to bear, brought them in one by one, the elder first—Raphaelle, listening wide-eyed to his mother's faint voice and nodding his promise to be an obedient good boy. Then came a tearful Angelica Kauffman, followed by Rembrandt, Titian, little Rubens blinking his weak eyes, Sophonisba Angusciola too small to understand, and tiny, sweet but fragile Rosalba Carriera, carried in her father's arms.

Rachel died on April 12, 1790. But when the women came to make her ready for burial, the widower sent them away. Nature is full of instances of false death, suspended animation, astounding revivals. He remained with her, hour after hour, oblivious to the whispering at the door, a man slow to believe that half his life had ended, and forever.

CHAPTER THREE

FOUNDATIONS FOR A NATIONAL MUSEUM: THE ELITE (1790–1795)

"God alone wise!" It was not a mere pious ejaculation intended to add persuasive force to that address "To the Citizens of the United States of America." It came, rather, from tense emotions of hope and tragedy. In pointing to the mysterious First Cause behind all the truths of Nature, it waves aside the priests and prophets of traditional faith. It echoes Peale's contempt for "enthusiasts" in religion. No child of his bore a scriptural name. He had chosen their names from Matthew Pilkington's *Dictionary of Painters,* and, as preferable to the usual large family Bible, their births were recorded on a flyleaf of Pilkington. Now the Museum was making him a religious enthusiast himself, though of necessity a cautious one. His reverence for the Creator grew and his deist dismissal of the idea of ever-watchful divine interventions was confirmed. Brought up an Anglican, and now occasionally attending St. Peter's Church, he gave Christianity no more than a pat on the head as an "excellent code," which could be much improved as to "charity, love and forbearance" by the study of nature.[1] Yet he was also aware of the danger of arousing what his dumpy, truculent friend Dr. Thomas Cooper, chemist and veteran of many battles for freedom of thought, called "the inveteracy of the *Odium Theologicum*." Peale had felt obliged to announce that his moving pictures could not "offend the most rigid Religionist," and years later he would warn his son "to keep clear of every offense to religious societies; you must know that if they take it into their heads that such exhibitions are improper, their inviteracy knows no bounds."[2]

The Museum was this man's temple, his offering, his service to mankind, his link to a future beyond himself. It was also, in the 1790's, just beginning to become a livelihood—although, as he would pause to reflect from time to time, the same amount of labor at painting alone should have brought him a far more substantial return. The Museum was for the future, his and his sons. His family would grow up with it into greater things in a greater America.

He was alone, and yet surrounded and sustained by the young Raphaelle, Angelica, Rembrandt, Titian, Rubens, and Sophonisba. Little Rosalba died in the fall of 1790. Grandmother Peale and old Peggy Durgan were both gone by the following spring. Charles Peale Polk now had a family of his own and was painting portraits remarkably hard in line and harsh in color—a style that somehow,

ELIZABETH DE PEYSTER PEALE
Museum silhouette,
c. 1802.

touchingly, recalls his father's bold clear orders from the quarter-deck and the red flash of cannonfire. Betsy Polk, who had married a relative of James Peale's wife and was plumper and bouncier than ever, popped in from time to time to share jokes and laughter with the children. One wonders what induced Peale, just two weeks after Rachel's death, to announce that children under ten would have free admission to the Museum if accompanied by their parents. This dispensation must have proved a burden, for some months later it was changed to half price (12½¢) for youngsters under twelve. [3]

But man, in Peale's frankly declared view of nature, is an animal that needs a mate, and children need a mother. He turned first to his Maryland homeland to find one, but Molly Tilghman's hesitation and her brother's outright contemptuous opposition to the match left Peale stricken in a way that only Beale Bordley's understanding kindness could assuage. Appropriately and auspiciously, it was in the Museum that he found a mate and a mother for his brood.

President and Congress had moved in from New York, and in the spring of 1792 Philadelphia's ten years as national capital were just beginning. A group of young New Yorkers, government workers and friends, had come to see the Museum, chattering and laughing, and then, as its proprietor watched with pleasure, sat down on one of the benches and broke into song, one after the other. The voice of Miss Elizabeth DePeyster, in her turn, floated over the wonders of Nature, charming him, stirring his heart—

CHARLES WILLSON PEALE
Museum silhouette,
c. 1802. (Author's collection.)

Hush ev'ry breeze, let nothing move,
My Delia sings, and sings of love . . .

Betsy was Dutch to the core, round and rosy. At twenty-five, she was half his age but, as in a few days he learned with pleasure, not at all abashed by the thought of marriage to a widower with a family. It was a whirlwind courtship, but with parental consent and all the formalities properly observed. They were married in New York on May 30, 1791.

In New York the couple visited a new museum, just established in imitation of Peale's own, but with one significant difference. It was supported not by an individual but by an association, the Tammany Society. Tamanend was the legendary Indian chief who had welcomed William Penn and endeared himself to the gentlemen of Penn's town by permitting them to fish in the Schuylkill River. A fishing club of the seventeenth century had in 1772 become the "Sons of King Tammany," at whose social, jovial, and patriotic gatherings the old chief was further exalted into "St. Tammany." Charles and James Peale appeared at some of these outpourings of spirit at the close of the war. Then John Pintard, a scholarly merchant-philanthropist of New York, had imported the convivial idea from Philadelphia, and in 1789, after three years' preparation, a constitution had been adopted, a Grand Sachem elected (with Pintard as Sagamore, or master of ceremonies), and a museum adopted as their first project in civic improvement. It was called, like Peale's, "The American Museum," and a broadside declared its "purpose of collecting and preserving every thing relating to the history of America, likewise every production of nature or art." When the Society petitioned the Common Council for exhibition space in City Hall, September 1, 1790, it was granted on the very next day.[4]

Peale found the New York collection small but, he thought, of good promise. Six substantial citizens served as its trustees, and a salaried keeper was in charge. The keeper was a friendly fellow—no naturalist, no idealist, but an anti-Federalist and admirer of Revolutionary France like Peale. Gardiner Baker would be remembered in New York as a "snub-nosed, pock-pitted, bandy-legged, fussy, good-natured little body, full of zeal in his vocation." A zeal for collecting was another trait they had in common, and gifts and exchanges would later attest their congenial relationship. As Tammany turned more and more to politics of the left, Pintard and others withdrew, so that by 1795 Baker would be sole proprietor of the collection in new quarters, with Tammany's blessing but on his own.

Peale, however, returned from New York with new thoughts in mind: prestigious trustee support and a salaried staff. In addition New York's American Museum had been opened under the eye of the new Federal government. Now, and for nine years more, his own would have that same advantage.

The newlyweds turned south for a wedding trip in Maryland, the groom eager for his Betsy to see and share the pleasures of the land and people he knew so well. To her, city-bred, it was an alien world, and soon she was happy to be back in Philadelphia, mother to the motherless children. They returned laden, as usual, with gifts for the Museum and with one portentous—so it seemed—scientific discovery. The skin of a mulatto slave of Somerset County, dark brown in color, had changed, first in spots and then completely, to a paper-white. Vitiligo, a harmless disease causing depigmentation of the skin, was then unidentified. Peale's neighbor, the great Dr. Benjamin Rush, bold in medical theory and practice, would later associate such cases with leprosy. Peale did not attempt to explain the phenomenon and gave only the man's genealogy and a history of his gradual alteration, but its social implications fascinated him. He had satisfied himself that the Negro lacked only an equal advantage of education; only ignorance and skin color set the race apart. If, as Buffon had theorized, subtle influences in the American climate were causing changes, might not some benign influence be at work here? Whatever it be, this was something that more than matched the lesson of the African bow. He had painted a portrait of James, "the White Negro," and hung it in the Museum gallery—a revolutionary figure indeed. The facts of the case he brought to the American Philosophical Society and published for the general public as well.[5]

The Society's Philosophical Hall had at long last become a reality, standing close beside the old State House, where once more state and national governments were seated. The sense of a new era, too, was sweeping in from overseas as the tides of revolution rose in France. The American Museum must be in the mainstream of it all; it must exchange knowledge and specimens with museums abroad, just as the Society was doing with its publications. The foremost influence here was Peale's lifelong friend and partisan—that lean, sharp-nosed, kindly man of God and science, the Rev. Dr. Nicholas Collin.

Collin, almost the same age as Peale, had come from Sweden

in 1771 to minister to his countrymen on the Delaware. He became a member of both the Society for Political Inquiries, of which Benjamin Franklin was president, and Franklin's American Philosophical Society. To the first Collin lectured on the advantages of "a cheerful temper" in politics, and to the second he read, on April 3, 1789, "An Essay on those Inquiries in Natural Philosophy which at present are most beneficial to the United States of North America." Collin's priorities for study would be reflected in the Peale's Museum collections. He urged the society to establish a botanical garden, to fill a scientific need that Peale had been reluctant to enter. Collin's treatise on American trees was published by the Royal Academy in Stockholm, and he had begun to assemble a description of the natural life of all America—too large a project ever to complete.[6]

Collin was a direct link to the fountainhead of natural history. Now he offered to bring Peale's Museum into rapport with Stockholm through an exchange program with the Swedish Royal Academy, of which Linnaeus had been founder and first president. Letters went forth, and Peale entered copies of them in a new book reserved for foreign correspondence. On the advice of other friends, he also approached the British Museum, through Sir Joseph Banks.[7]

Surely these new lines of scientific endeavor could not be pursued without a broader base of support. The summer before, Peale had found selling annual tickets from door to door "rather irksome" and had made his plea in print instead, publicizing a showing of three of his moving picture scenes as a bonus attraction.[8] That sort of thing would never place his Museum on par with the staid activities in Stockholm, London, or Paris. He would now bring together a group of distinguished citizens to serve first in an advisory capacity and then, should they succeed in obtaining a public endowment, as trustees. Though Tammany's was the first museum with such an organizational basis, it was accepted practice in establishing other educational institutions. "I am putting my museum under the patronage of a number of Gentlemen of Science," he wrote to a friend in Baltimore, "the first step toward

REV. DR. NICHOLAS COLLIN
While he and Collin were cataloguing the Library of the American Philosophical Society, in 1798 Peale made these quick caricature sketches of his, and the Museum's, warm friend. (American Philosophical Society.)

54

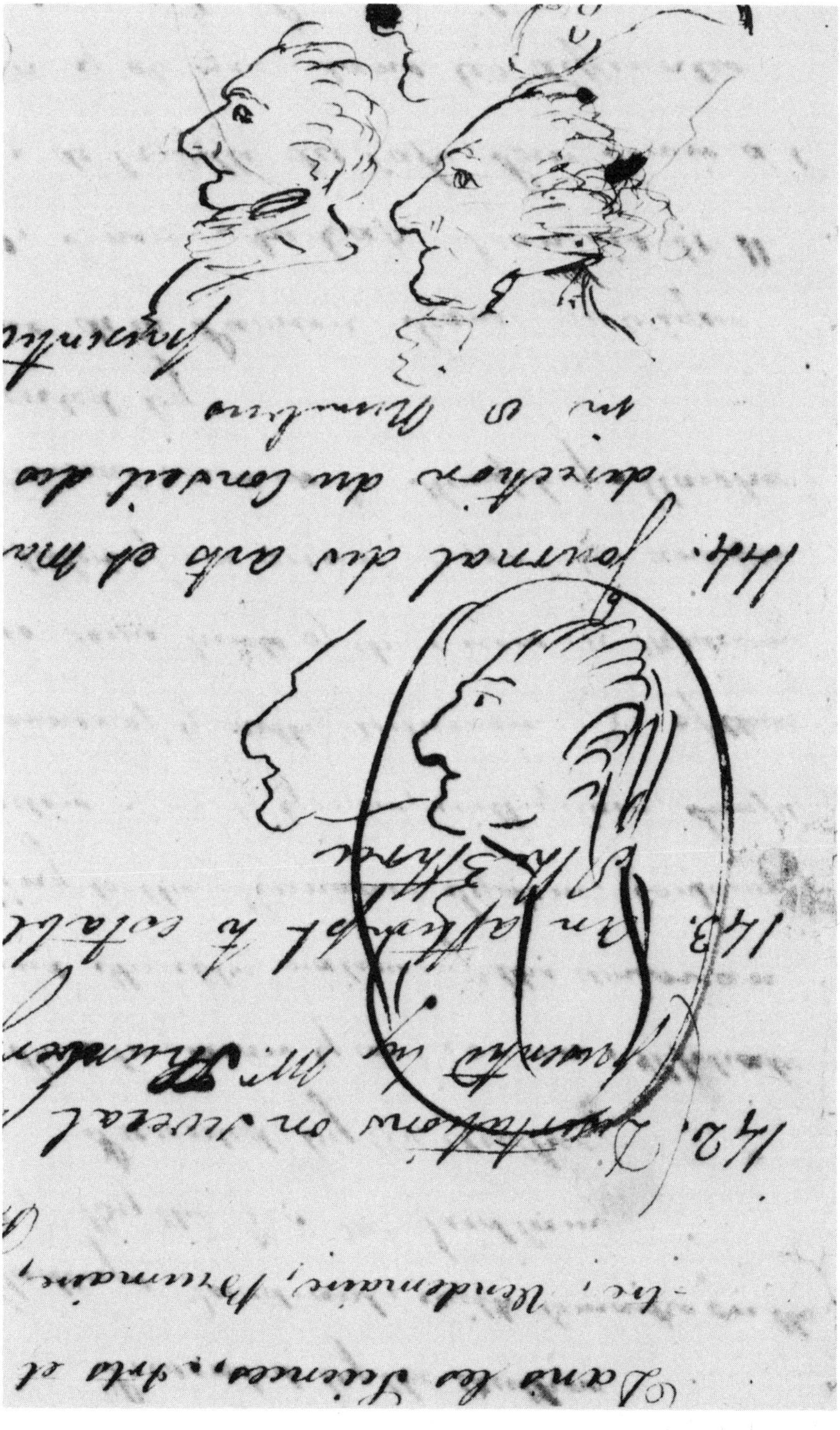

making it a Public Establishment, of which the particulars will shortly appear in the papers."[9]

He had already made his first move in the papers, on January 19, 1792. It was another address to the citizens, asserting again the value of a museum of natural history classified and arranged in the Linnaean system. In it Peale again asked their aid in raising "this tender plant, until it shall grow into full maturity and become a *National Museum.*" As his first step:

> Mr. Peale means personally to solicit the assistance of gentlemen whose regard for science is well known; if there are those who would become *Inspectors* or *Visitors* of the Museum, their united aid and influence, he is confident, would greatly promote a design that is truly worthy of American patriots and citizens of the world.[10]

The term "Inspectors or Visitors" might imply little or much. "Visitor" and "trustee" were interchangeable. Philadelphia's academy, college, and university had trustees. At the College of William and Mary, as later at Jefferson's University of Virginia, visitors were in charge. Yet there was a shade of difference. A visitor might also be an official supervisor under some higher authority such as a sponsoring church. The appointment of visitors, in this sense, at times preceded formal trusteeship under an independent charter—and such as Peale's present hope.

Twenty-seven responded to his personal invitation. He wanted an elite group, and he had it: three members of the President's cabinet were there, along with the nation's two richest men, and the whole an impressive roster of influence and reputation. "Public Establishment" might still be in doubt, but no other institution in the country had a better committee of endorsement.

All but three were members of the American Philosophical Society, and one of these, Peale's lawyer, John Francis Mifflin, would be elected to membership later. The other two nonmembers were his old friend John Page of Virginia, congressman and governor, and Miers Fisher, a prosperous Quaker lawyer influential in state and city politics who was later an associate of the ornithologists Wilson and Audubon. The two friends from whom Peale had first sought advice on founding a museum were present—Robert Patterson and David Rittenhouse—as were Rittenhouse's nephews, William and Benjamin Smith Barton. Also included were Beale Bordley, of course, and Nicholas Collin, who was probably chief architect of the visitor plan. Ebenezer Hazard was another and genial, learned John Vaughan, who was to be prominent through many later years as librarian of the Philosophical Society.

Henry Hill, another, had marched out with Peale in the city militia in 1776, and was now a prosperous businessman, as was Michael Hillegas, Continental Treasurer from 1776 to 1789. Hillegas may have been included because of a passion for music he shared with Peale, or because of his new financial interest in anthracite coal, consonant with Peale's declared purpose of bringing American natural resources and their usefulness to the public in his Museum.

There were three physicians on the Museum board. Dr. James Hutchinson, the Peale family doctor, was professor of chemistry at the University and secretary of the Philosophical Society. After carrying out a dangerous mission to France during the war and then returning through the enemy lines to Valley Forge, he had joined Peale and Paine in the city as a "Furious Whig." Now, fat and jocose, he was regrouping old political allies in opposition to Washington, Hamilton, and Morris. Caspar Wistar, an authority on vertebrate paleontology, would add the Peale family to his practice after Hutchinson's death a year later. The third physician was Samuel Powell Griffitts, founder of the Philadelphia Dispensary and professor of materia medica at the University.

Religious influence, not to be underrated or ignored, was present in the Rev. Dr. Ashbel Green, who was young and smoothly aggressive, a power in Presbyterian affairs, professor of mathematics and natural philosophy at Princeton, and now in town as chaplain to Congress, and by the scholarly Episcopal bishop of Pennsylvania, William White.

Thomas Jefferson was not only Washington's Secretary of State but also Franklin's successor in scientific reputation and influence. Alexander Hamilton, Secretary of the Treasury, was present too, and Peale might well have felt pride that two such opposite leaders could find common ground in natural history. Edmund Randolph, Attorney General of the United States, was also on the board, as were Congressman and future President James Madison, Senator Robert Morris (now as friendly to Peale the naturalist as he had been wary of Peale the politician), and the enormously wealthy William Bingham, who would soon succeed the enormously wealthy Morris in the Senate.

State-level political influence was present in the person of Governor Thomas Mifflin, genial and heavy-drinking, an occasional donor to the Museum; of Alexander James Dallas, Secretary of the Commonwealth and the most powerful figure in Mifflin's administration; and of Jonathan Bayard Smith, a Philadelphia alderman and Auditor General of Pennsylvania.

Conspicuously absent from the list was Dr. Benjamin Rush, who should have been an obvious choice. Rush, who had declared with such vehemence that the treaty of peace marked the beginning, not the end, of the American Revolution, had included instruction in natural history supported by a museum in his "Plan for a Foederal University" of 1788.[11] He was promoting new educational projects with single-minded, battling zeal, intent upon safeguarding revealed religion and conservative policy in the new republic. He had founded Dickinson College in Carlisle—then regarded as the far west of the new nation—with a board of trustees almost twice the size of Peale's but similarly selected for political influence and in hope of public endowment. Of the two, the Museum group was the more prestigious by far, and while only fifteen of Peale's twenty-seven "visitors" attended meetings, that, again, was much better than the general average of such groups.

On Sunday, February 5, 1792, eleven Visitors met at the Museum—the two Bartons, Bordley, Collin, Hazard, Hutchinson, Madison, Page, Patterson, White, and Wistar—and adopted the constitution which Collin had drafted.[12] It limited the board's number to thirty-six. Any seven could transact ordinary business, but only a majority of the entire board could elect new members, petition for public aid, approve the sale of any part of the Museum, or enact regulations for its management.

Thomas Jefferson, present at the next meeting, on February 14, was elected president of the body. Peale had ready a printed statement as a basis for discussion. It detailed his purposes and present situation.[13] He had set out to create a great national resource covering every aspect of natural history, with only the vegetable kingdom excepted. "Yet it has so increased as to have become too weighty for me alone to arrange and govern it; and my circumstances are too confined to admit of the requisite advances towards enlarging it. If it has produced to me some income, yet this is but partial, and has become disproportioned to the encrease of labour and the calls for rooms requisite for the further extension of the design. These difficulties, together with the desire to have your countenance and assistance as Visitors and Directors, with the hope that it may induce a more public and general notice of it, are the motive for requesting your friendly services."

THOMAS JEFFERSON
The future U.S. President was the Museum's constant friend and president of its
Board of Visitors. Painting from Museum portrait gallery by C. W. Peale, c. 1791.
(Independence National Historical Park Collection, Philadelphia.)

Peale next reviewed for the board the Linnaean system, from the primates on down, noting that men, like it or not, must recognize that they themselves are animals and be content with their place at the head of the list. In the Museum they were represented by portraits of outstanding human beings, but—and here some of his listeners surely smiled—he hoped someday to have actual specimens of *homo sapiens* preserved like the rest. Dr. Franklin would have agreed, Peale was sure, and would very likely have given his own body for the purpose. The races of mankind must be represented with "the arms, dresses, tools and utensils of the aborigenes of divers countries." The mystery of the huge *Incognitum* must be solved by the discovery of a complete skeleton. He touched upon his own favorite study of birds, their physical characteristics, habits, and migrations, then upon his research on serpents, and so on down to the lowest classes, the insects and worms.

Specimen mountings must be in proper form and attitude. "Mere stuffed skins are but a poor resemblance." Deviations from the normal must be "received with caution" and stored separately. (Teratology, the study of malformations and monstrosities—or *Lusus naturae,* "jest of nature" in Peale's day—had a long way to go till Barnum.)

Peale's lengthy statement ended with a plea for public support, but under some arrangement by which "my family may not lose the benefits of my assiduous labours of years past." He was teaching his sons all that he had learned and soon meant to send one of them "to collect articles for the Museum from that wonderful store, South America."

Public financing was his collection's greatest need; but, failing that, he told them, he would nonetheless continue work as before. Always naive in financial matters, he may have been unaware of the near-panic conditions of the moneyed world around him at this time. Not so his hearers, who understood only too well the political hazards of any new burden upon taxpayers, and the taxpayers' unwillingness to encourage the collecting mania of a family who seemed to be managing well enough on the 'leven-penny bits taken in at the door.

Other meetings followed, but without the quorum needed to apply for public funds. Peale, having felt "the pulse of our great officers of Congress," saw the hopelessness of any immediate Federal grant. The state government of Pennsylvania, where the Museum was a presence as a major Philadelphia attraction, offered the better hope. "The American Museum" now yields to "The Philadelphia Museum" as official title—though "Peale's Museum" was already so firmly fixed in common parlance that it would never be wholly dislodged. When a quorum of sixteen visitors at last met on March 8, a petition to the General Assembly was approved, but asking only that a legislative committee inspect the Museum and recommend measures that would "raise the superstructure and render the Institution a lasting honor and benefit to America and a successful rival to the boasted Museums of Europe."[14] Interestingly, in Mr. Jefferson's absence, Mr. Hamilton was presiding. The others present were William Barton, Bingham, Bordley, Collin, Dallas, Griffitts, Hill, Hutchinson, John Mifflin, Morris, Page, Patterson, Vaughan, White, and Wistar.

The petition to the Assembly went out, but too late in the session for action. Well—Peale accepted the blow cheerfully. He would see that it came to the floor at the opening of the next session, and, with the backing he now had, action could be expected. In the meantime the board settled into its advisory capacity under an "Acting Committee" of three, changed each month: first Collin, Randolph, and B. S. Barton, then Hutchinson, Dallas, and William Barton, then Bordley, Wistar, and Vaughan, after which the practice was continued with three-month terms.[15]

The board members' advice was sound, and Peale enjoyed the institutional prestige their presence brought. Bordley, Wistar, and Vaughan, who made up the most active group, exhorted Peale to emphasize clays, minerals, and fossils and "Resolved, that it be recommended to Mr. Peale to form a Cataloge of his Museum in which all the articles belonging to the great kingdoms of Nature shall be arranged according to the most approved methods." These were men of affairs, with an eye both to scientific interest and to practical applications.

Peale responded. In minerals he had Franklin's gift from the unusual Derbyshire deposits to build on, as well as collections from Congressman Vance Murray and others. Samuel Latham Mitchill had sent in the first mineral ore, and that department would be enriched through the years by promoters eager to publicize their mines: the nearby lead mine of Francis Da Costa, better known to fame as the guardian of young John James Audubon; the lead mines of Stephen and Moses Austin, uncle and father of the founder of Texas; and the ironworks and kindred interests of Mahlon Dickerson, a senator and Governor of New Jersey. By the end of

1793, Peale had a display ready in glass-covered drawers, each specimen labeled with "references to a book of description" and a note on the usefulness of each.[16] The "book of description" was probably Richard Kirwan's *Elements of Mineralogy* (London, 1784), the text used in this way from 1806 until the appearance of an American authority in Parker Cleaveland's *Elementary Treatise on Mineralogy and Geology* (Boston, 1816). American mineralogists would still prefer to work with their own collections, but the Peale Museum's, as Clifford Frondel of Harvard's Geological Museum has pointed out, was our "first organized and effective public display of minerals and geological materials."[17]

Inevitably, the visitors had foreign models in mind. Only Collin could describe what was at Stockholm. Jefferson knew the resources of Paris, but now France was in turmoil and the survival of royal institutions in doubt. All, however, had seen or read of Sir Ashton Lever's world-famous museum in London, and saw its parallel to what they had in Philadelphia. It also was a one-man affair, begun in 1760 in Manchester, then moved to London in 1774, as wide-ranging but a far richer collection than Peale's, and with a more generous admixture of useless oddities. Sir Ashton had called it "Holophusikon," not quite the Greek equivalent but similar in sense to Peale's "World in Miniature." Sir Joseph Banks had replied to Peale's proposal of exchanges with the British Museum by advising him to turn instead to James Parkinson, the new and somewhat bewildered owner of the Leverian's vast store.[18]

The Leverian stood as prime example of a proprietary musem; but everyone knew of Parliament's refusal to purchase it. Peale wanted a museum so well adapted to the life of a free people that they themselves would recognize their need for it. For him the national museum of liberated France would become the true model, and news of it was soon coming through. On June 10, 1793, the Revolutionary government had reorganized the old Jardin du Roi as its new Muséum d'Histoire Naturelle, "for the teaching of natural history in all its branches." Broadly conceived, amply endowed, its faculty of professors would give lecture courses in mineralogy, geology, chemistry, botany, agriculture, zoology, anatomy, and— recognizing the need for pictorial supplement of the collections— iconography. In addition, a library was instituted to sustain the whole.[19] Here was a flat and forceful answer to that querulous "Lover of Nature" of 1790 and his claim that princes might spend their treasure on museums but a free people dare not.

The foreign exchanges initiated by Collin were expanding, though they would never bring Philadelphia into a close cooperative relationship with any foreign museum. The first shipment from Sweden failed to arrive, and the aggressive young Dr. Barton was eventually suspected of having appropriated the birds. In London, Peale ignored Parkinson and began a fruitful correspondence with Thomas Hall of Moorfields, a taxidermist and dealer.[20] With Hall, he refused either to buy or sell, but insisted on exchange of equivalents only, and this decision became fixed Museum policy through the years. He had devised airtight cases to be used for both storage and shipment of duplicates, and these moved back and forth between Philadelphia and London to bring Peale some prized rarities, among them the Australian lyrebird (*Menura superba*) and duck-billed platypus.[21] He was flattered, too, to find that his preservation and mounting were better than the Englishman's.

Other significant relationships are glimpsed—Abraham Gevers, naturalist of Rotterdam, with whom Peale exchanged birds, insects, and minerals, and Gustaf von Paykull, Swedish statesman and naturalist, poet, and playwright who was building the collection that would become the National Museum at Stockholm after his death. Gifts and encouragement came from Adriaan Valck, the convivial Dutch consul living on a large estate near Baltimore. Peale brought all their letters and his replies before the Visitors, who advised publishing extracts in the papers to lend force to the appeal for gifts. Reaching farther, as he had told them he would, Peale sent museum assistant Raphaelle Peale, his nineteen-year-old son, on a collecting tour of the Southern states and later, in December 1793, armed with passports and recommendations from the French and Spanish embassies, to Cayenne and Mexico. Raphaelle would return with exciting treasures, some of them alive—toucans and the spotted mangay cat, *Felis tigrina*.[22]

Fish, like minerals, were of economic importance. Many specimens were added to the Museum from New York's famous fish market during visits to Betsy's family, and one notable accession of this time was the hammerhead shark brought in by a mariner. Fossils depended more upon chance finds than purposeful collecting. Bones of the *Incognitum* turned up in New Jersey. Peale explored a site near Bladensburg, Maryland, with high hopes of finding a complete skeleton. Disappointed in that, but astonished to come upon a wealth of sharks' teeth, shells, and other marine objects sixty feet above sea level; these added to the mystery by suggesting an aquatic environment for the vanished monster.[23]

Peale continued to encourage donors by citing his board of visitors as a step toward institutional permanence—"a society for better securing the property of the museum to the public after my decease." That was an eventuality of small concern to a man who insisted that idleness and unnatural diet were all that stood in the way of anyone's living to be two hundred years old.[24] Driving home that point, he added to the Museum gallery a portrait of John Strangeways Hutton, then in the one-hundred-and-eighth summer of his career as sea fighter, Indian fighter, and master silversmith, and at the same time published an account of Hutton's life.[25] This would be the first of half a dozen long-lived primates to be seen on the Museum walls.

Peale had promised his visitors to have a descriptive catalogue ready soon, and in print. The project would be on his mind over the next several years, but held back by the flow of other work. He had declared his intention of giving names to the undescribed species of American birds in his collection, and that alone posed a formidable task. Rapid growth of the Museum's inventory impeded study, and also made an exhibition of specimens in the Linnaean sequence more and more difficult. It should be possible to examine the collection with catalogue in hand, but for that more space would be needed. As it was, he could only arrange the various-sized cases to please the eye.[26]

By 1793, effort and accumulation were sharpening the sense of an approaching crisis. But the crisis of that year, when it came, was of a totally unexpected sort, devastating for the city as a whole. First, there were the events in France, echoed across the sea—a king and queen wiped out at the guillotine, followed by the arrival of the sister republic's first official representative, brash Edmond Charles Genet, who boldly summoned America to rise again in defense of liberty. Among the attentions lavished on Genet was a ticket to the Philadelphia Museum, sent "with the most cordial wishes for the success of the Republic of France." It was a compliment Peale would repeat some months later for another champion of freedom, the great chemist Joseph Priestley, a refugee from persecution in England. Some of the Museum's board of visitors—Dallas, Rittenhouse, Hutchinson, and William Barton—joined in welcoming Genet at a great mass meeting in State House Yard. Others were cold. The town seethed with partisanship, Federalists for England and the rising Democratic-Republicans for France.

Then came the sultry heat of July, and with it the first refugees from the bloody slave revolt in Santo Domingo, anguished, destitute crowds of them with every ship from the island. Over a thousand came to Philadelphia alone in July and August. Peale, speaking French, was in the forefront of those helping them, and lifelong friendships began here, among them, with Dr. René La Roche, a physician with a taste for music who would remain in America, and Dr. Louis Valentin, author of numerous medical works and of a description of the United States, mentioning Peale's Museum, in *Nouvelle Geographie Universelle.*[27]

Quiet had returned late in August, when Peale left for a stay at Cape Henlopen. It would be a vacation for Betsy, whose first child, then eleven months old, was in delicate health. Her lively businessman brothers had been clamoring from the first for "a Dutch painter," and now they had one, Vandyke Peale. Titian, aged thirteen, also went along. He and his father would be gunning and gathering specimens along shores teeming with wildlife—tall cranes, high-swinging gulls, curlews, snipe, and blackbirds in a dark cloud over the sea of marsh grass—a scene that would return to Peale's memory years later, a vision of its myriad "inoffensive animals that almost darken the shores by their numbers; either busied in picking up their proper food, thrown up from the abundant bosom of the Ocean, or regaling themselves with the refreshing waves! Where a sweet harmony reigns as far as the Eye can reach, and the prattling notes of 10,000 tongues mingle with the murmurs of distant waters and the surges of succeeding billows which forcibly strike the Ear with pleasing yet awful Solemnity."[28]

Father and son made a team, as they shot, dissected, preserved, and mounted new specimens. Peale scribbled in his diary their day-to-day discoveries and excitements:

[August] 25th. Sunday. A fine morning but after breakfast it rained and the wind blew hard at N.E. which makes a damp cold air from the Sea. I get the remaining undressed birds, and Titian and myself dress 2 more of them. These birds ["Mother Carey's Chickens"] are curious, having only one Nostril, which is a round pipe placed on the top of its [sic] beak. I find that they have no gizzard but a stomack like the Hawks & other carniverous birds, the feet webbed. It is curious to see them, as it were, resting with their feet on the water, as they pick up the fat which we threw overboard for them. Being a light bird, a small motion of their wings suspends them, while their feet touch the Top of the waves. They must I suppose come to the shore to lay their Eggs, however the[y] are seldom seen there. We find them at great distance from the land and generally in bad weather. I do not find any difference in the appearance between the Cocks & hens. Some I found had very small Eggs in them, but I could not be certain whether the others were Cocks or not . . . .

Or, again,

[August] 29. Before breakfast finishing the puting the Eyes and dressing the feathers of the birds mounted the day before. After breakfast borrowed Mr. West['s] Bateau and went down the Creek after Game, having got two boys to row for us. We shot will willets, mud hens, Curlews, Gull, & did not return untill near dinner time. The going by water after Game I found to be much less fateaguing, having assistance to row the boat. We found it rather hard labour to mount each of us 2 Birds. Not being in good feathers made the task still harder. The days becoming shorter deceives me in my expected quantity of Labour which contrarywise in the increasing length of days I have found that I can do no more than I have generally promised myself . . . .

When the time came for return from Cape Henlopen, Peale bought thirty-eight chickens and a duck to bring back alive, an act of thrift for which he was to be profoundly grateful. New arrivals from Philadelphia had brought frightening news of disease and death; the great yellow fever epidemic of 1793 had begun. The Peales hurried their departure, fearful for the children left behind at home. The one friend they met at the wharves was amazed they should have come deliberately into such danger. He advised them as to what streets they should follow to avoid those where the contagion was rampant.

Up to the door they rattled, followed by a cartload of gear, trunks and boxes, mounted birds, live birds, snakes and shells, the skeleton of a whale, and other trophies from the shore.[29] Moses was there to greet them, with Angelica, Rembrandt, Rubens, and Sophy. The Peale house and Museum became, forthwith, a fortress besieged by the surrounding terror. The crates of poultry gave them a supply of food. Peale sprinkled vinegar and fired a gun from room

SHOREBIRDS

Curlew, snipe, and godwit, painted by Alexander Wilson—probably from Museum specimens—for his American Ornithology. *Peale's "Will Willet" is third from the left. Wilson classifies it as "Semi-palmated Snipe.* Scolopax Semi-palmata. *Peale's Museum No. 3942," with the following description: "The Willet is peculiar to America . . . its loud and shrill reiteration of* Pill-will-willet, Pill-will-willet, *resounds, almost incessantly, along the marshes."*

to room—measures supposed to purify the air. He alone went out, to seek advice from a Santo Domingo family to whom he had lent furniture. They had lived with this contagion before and had no fear of it. They went about the town freely, though always, they told him, "with a clove of garlic" in the mouth.[30]

Within walls, the Peales were, as ever, busy. Of the fifty shorebirds brought back, thirty-three specimens new to the collection were boxed behind glass with painted backgrounds. Identification of the minerals was completed with whatever help could be gleaned from Linnaeus's *System of Nature* and a recent gift from Beale Bordley, Abraham Rees' *Supplement and Modern Improvements* (to Ephraim Chambers' *Cyclopaedia; or, Universal Dictionary of*

AMERICAN BUFFALO
The bison was the earliest large animal to be mounted in the Museum. Peale expanded the exhibit into a proposal that the bison be bred for domestic use, to provide meat, milk, and wool from an animal hardier than imported cattle. This drawing, made by Charles A. Lesueur for J. D. Godman's American Natural History *of 1826, may give two views of the Museum specimen.*

Arts and Sciences). Then, somehow, the fever crept through the walls. First Betsy was stricken—effluvia, they imagined, from a passing corpse—and then Moses. Day after day, Peale nursed them both, with a gentle regimen of his own that seemed to check the swift progress of the sickness until, feeling himself suddenly overpowered by weakness, he called to Angelica to make a bed for him on the floor. He felt no loss of appetite but expected it soon. Prudently, he would fortify himself for the coming ordeal with a hearty meal, and so made his way to table, for bread and molasses, gin, and water. That did it. He was himself again.[31]

Not until late October were citizens who had fled from the pestilence returning. Because they still shunned gatherings, there was poor attendance at the Museum. Peale himself was confident that, with a few mild preventive measures encouraging the body's natural resistance, one had little to fear. The yellow fever would return in later summers, but never with the same virulence, and for now he would simply take advantage of the enforced quiet to refurbish the Museum for an autumn reopening. With improving techniques of light and heating, winter was becoming its most successful season.

But he must have more ample space. Accessions, mounting, arrangement—each was treading on the heels of the other, so that now the whole length of the place, from former painting room to "rocksome height," was completely filled. He had acquired an adjoining lot, one hundred feet by twenty. Given funds, and funds were now at a very low ebb, he could put up a new building that would double his floorspace.

Some firsthand descriptions of the congestion and the wonders at Third and Lombard have come down to us. On entering, one was confronted first of all by a huge American buffalo and could read a long explanatory label on its potential value if domesticated—"a substitute for the Cow," more hardy in winter, a source not only of milk and meat but of wool. Yarn spun from its fur was exhibited, and could not be distinguished from sheep's wool.[32] Beyond this imposing guardian of the gate, one moved on among all the other creatures of land, sea, and air, cases of birds and small animals with charming painted backgrounds, and the huge leg bones and dreadful teeth of the *Incognitum,* now given a name borrowed from Russia, the mammoth. Savage weapons and utensils of distant lands and the American wilderness were there—and always the more enlightened primates gazing benignly from above. Then on to brilliant shells, corals, insects, minerals, fish great and small, and the live serpents that, for a favored visitor, Peale would draw out of their cages and handle fearlessly. "Lang Syne," an anonymous old-timer writing in 1828, recalled the scene as memorable not only for its wealth and variety but also for the compact and orderly arrangement. "He had so contrived everything in his Museum with an eye to economy in *space,* that there appeared to be a place for everything and everything in its place, decorated and enlivened by miniature scenery of wood and wild, blended and intermingled with insect, bird and beast, all seemingly alive, but preserving, at the same time, the stillness and silence of death."[33]

In 1794, the English traveler Henry Wansey was

entertained for two or three hours in viewing his collection of artificial and natural curiosities, some of which I shall proceed to enumerate. It is not yet so extensive as the Leverian

Museum in London, but is every day encreasing. Mammoth's teeth, found on the banks of the Ohio; several of them that I measured were sixteen and seventeen inches round; one that was broken in two, appeared of the same horney substance within, so as to confirm me in the opinion of its being the real cheek tooth of some animal now utterly unknown. Dr. Caspar Wistar, professor of anatomy in this city, I am told, has collected a vast variety of huge bones of this animal, which he is endeavoring to systematise. There were several of these delicate birds' nests of which soups are made. A pair of Chinese shoes, worn by the lady of a merchant at Canton, with whom the donor transacted business, only four inches long; Chinese fans, six feet high; Asbestos, found a few miles from the city; curious and rare birds preserved in their plumage; the red and blue Manakins; Birds of Paradise, and Humming Birds, in great variety; Toucans, with their remarkable bills; Spoon-bills, natives of Georgia; Batts of Pennsylvania, carrying their young; Scarlet Curlews of Cayenne, etc. Medals, fossils, insects, rare and uncommon. Very curious Petrifactions, from their cataracts and grottos. Scalps, tomohawks, belts of wampum, of curious variety; Indian and Otaheite dresses, and feathers from the Friendly Isles.[34]

An American in the same year pictures it all as "a beautiful garden" where smiling Nature welcomed him. Yet he found its most fascinating single object the "live female Opossum with its young in Embryo visible, through the aperture of the bag, to the eye of an observer. An European naturalist would not have thought a voyage across the Atlantic too great a price for this sight."[35] Indeed, the live exhibits inevitably held an advantage over every other—back beyond the grottos and the den of snakes, where the rattler rattled at one's approach, and then out to the yard and barn, where eagles, owls, wildcats, apes, and heaven-knows-what-other-surprises lived in noisy discord. Amid that scene "Lang Syne" could still hear the roar of laughter when Moses Williams tossed the baboon a quid of tobacco instead of its expected apple.[36]

James Hardie's *Philadelphia Directory and Register* (1794) gave the Museum top place among the city's scientific institutions, extolling it for beauty and taste and also praising Peale's discretion in keeping disquieting *lusus naturae* out of sight, as well as his patriotic zeal in having placed the whole under "a board of Visitors and Inspectors." Hardie's account conveys much of the printed address to the visitors' board but adds one perceptive comment on the character of the proprietor—"remarkable for his ingenuity and perseverence rather than for pecuniary abilities."[37]

Senator William Bingham had promised to present the board of visitors' petition to the Pennsylvania Assembly, but Peale in the meantime had opened the year 1794 with a drive for annual subscriptions. This time it was a special effort, and subscribers' names were entered in a new record book handsomely bound in red morocco.[38] President Washington headed the roster with four tickets, followed by Vice-President Adams, eighteen senators, nine representatives, the board of visitors, and other friends. By the end of January 1794, 159 subscribers had signed, at one dollar apiece. French names abound, among them the botanists André Michaux and Candide Frédéric Antoine de Grassi and the young Parisian Alexandre Lerebours, whom Peale brought to a meeting of the Philosophical Society to present a paper on the progress of science in France since the Revolution.

Then, on February 24, Bingham brought the board's message before the state legislature. It was "read and laid on the table."[39] Would the appeal for public aid end there? Not if the Museum's busy proprietor could prevent it. He reran old newspaper announcements and alternated them with a call for needed objects emphasizing both the broad scope of the collection and its practical applications:

> He especially wishes to collect into one view, specimens of the various kinds of wood growing in America; they may be in cubes of two or three inches; all sorts of fossils,—minerals, spares, stone, sand, clay, marle, and earthly substances; from a better knowledge whereof the arts will derive improvement, especially in the manufacturing of porcelaine, earthen and stone wares, and in the various useful metals.
>
> It will always be acceptable to have some account (if known) where they grow, or where found, and whether alone, or with but a few, or with the appearance of their being in large quantities, and with any particular circumstances that may attend them.
>
> Besides the above particular subjects, curiosities or rare things of every other kind are desireable; birds, beasts, reptiles, insects alive or dead, tools, dresses, utensils, or other articles heretofore or at present in use among the Indians of America. One or more of their clay or stone pots are particularly desired.

MUSEUM ANNUAL MEMBERSHIPS

The Museum's subscription list opened in January 1794, its title and preamble engrossed in Peale's hand, with Washington, Adams, and members of the Senate leading the signatories. (The Historical Society of Pennsylvania.)

Philadelphia, Jan.¹ 10.ᵗʰ 1794.

As the MUSEUM is now in a fair way of becoming a permanent and important Institution of rational and instructive Entertainment, The Records of its rise and progress will be valuable Monuments. On these the Names of its generous Promoters claim a place, that the Friends of Science may be known to each other and to future Admirers of the Creator's Works; Charles Willson Peale, the present Proprietor, therefore respectfully desires the favor of Subscribers to enter their Names by their respective Signatures, and receive Tickets of Admission for a Year from the day of Subscribing.

If numbers of the articles are collected in the museum, a part of them will be exchanged with the proprietors of other collections for other foreign subjects, for our information.

It will be obliging in the Printers, friends of science, of the other states as well as this, if they will give the above a place in their newspapers. Mr. Peale respectfully invites them to view his museum; and will be happy to see them when they visit Philadelphia.[40]

Faithful to his trust, Mr. Bingham persisted, and the Legislature, as the board had requested, appointed a committee to visit the Museum and return with its recommendation for assistance.[41] Peale got word of this brightening prospect on the morning of March 20, 1794, just after Betsy had brought her second son into the world. Their first, little Vandyke, had died in infancy. This latest gift to the future would bear not the name of a painter, but that of a naturalist. A jubilant, slightly incoherent father dashed off the news to Dr. Collin: "The first Linneus perhaps so named in America was born this morning—may he be a light to this New World, like him of Sweden whose percevering labours in Natural History hath eluminated the Old World."

Charles Linnaeus! A doubly inspired thought, for it also satisfied Betsy's strong feeling about family names. But the boy, from babyhood on into his rough-and-tumble career, would answer only to "Lin." There was a postscript to Collin:

Dr Sir, the Committees of the Legislature have promised me to "*make a point of attending at the Museum* at 7 o'clock this evening," And I have sent notice to the other gentlemen of the Acting Visitors.[42]

Peale had made clear what he would ask of the legislators. It was little: Let them grant him a sufficient loan on easy terms, and with the new building there would be no problem in repayment. He had a threat, too, with which to urge compliance, one that would have weight with the Philadelphia business community: He might move everything away to some more appreciative city. This was the first time he had posed such a possibility. He saw its effect and would use it again. The Museum was famous. Editors throughout the nation had learned that the Peale accession lists made good reading. Right at this time, for instance, there was the story of the bright little Brazilian moor hen (*Porphyrio Americanus*) that had fluttered down to a ship in the Gulf Stream and was now

74

winning friends at the Museum. Tame but timid, it was being fed on bread crumbs and, on finding any piece too large to swallow, would carefully dip it into its water until soft. Soon after, Dr. Samuel Brown sent him storied skeletons of a man and a woman of the Wabash nation, and later in the year Musuem news was enlivened by a medical phenomenon—James Gallaway, "the horn-breasted man."[43] A large horn had been growing from the scar of a wound he had suffered in a sea battle. Peale himself sawed it off and recorded the case in a portrait. Gallaway then capitalized on his fame by exhibiting himself at the Black Horse Tavern.

The Museum could not be ignored and must not be slighted. In *Claypoole's American Daily Advertiser* of March 27, 1794, "A Lover of Nature," perhaps the same churl who had expressed doubts in 1790, now took up his quill in full approval:

> The Legislature will do a very popular act by granting to Mr. Peale the moderate loan he requests.
>
> The general interest of science demands in all civilized countries aid and patronage, because it exalts mankind to the dignity and felicity of her destination.
>
> The cultivation of natural history is in this country very important in many respects. It brings to light our many treasures in animals, plants and minerals, suggesting thereby new branches of manufactures and commerce, which otherwise might lie dormant for a long time. Mr. Peale's collection of ores and fossils does already merit attention. What sums may we not save in articles of copper and tin, queensware, &c. &c. by exploring and improving the treasure we often tread upon! The hair of wild animals, the feathers of birds, the skins, bones and oil of fishes, are in several countries employed by divers manufactories, for example: the strongest glue is made from the skin of a species of Perch, by Laplanders. The offals of herring are by a late improvement converted into valuable oil, by the Swedes. In England and Germany a great variety of elegant feather muffs are made. The skins of Elk are in the north of Europe made into Buff so firm as to be a defensive armor.
>
> The Moral effect of a Museum is very considerable. I appeal to all who have seen this sublime inscription in that of Mr. Peale:
>
> "Ask the beasts, and they shall teach thee; and the fowls of the air and they shall tell thee; and the fishes of the sea

declare unto thee. Who knoweth not that in all these, that the hand of the LORD hath wrought this? In whose hand is the soul of every living thing, and the breath of all mankind." [Job, xii, 7. 8, 9. 10 verses.]

How many thousand pounds do we throw away upon foreign gew gaws; Let ladies and gentlemen who admire true elegance, view the Summer Duck, the Humming Bird, the Scarlet Sparrow, the Brazilian Creeper, the Gold Finch, the Poweese, the Ruby Crested Ren, &c. they will be charmed at very small expense.

Numbers wish with myself that Mr. Peale may have sufficient encouragement to remain among us. The removal of the Museum would not only be severely felt by the votaries of science, but also diminish that circulation of wealth which arises from the commerce of liberal arts.

The legislative delegation was received by the Museum's proprietor and its Acting Committee, and was shown the collection, the adjoining lot, and the plans for a building. Costs and prospective income were discussed. Yet money is money, precedents are dangerous, and Mr. Peale's "ingenuity and perseverence" must be balanced against his "pecuniary abilities." The Assembly would be grateful for some avenue of escape, and it came. It came just in time, in a proposal that the American Philosophical Society lease to Peale, for both Museum and living quarters, almost the whole Philosophical Hall. After all, the building stood on land which the state, responding to Franklin's great prestige, had granted to the society. One condition of the grant had been that the society might rent parts "for such purposes as have affinity with the design of their Institution and for no other." That Peale's Museum met this condition could not be disputed. One room of Philosophical Hall had been leased to the College of Physicians since 1791, but that lease would expire on June 10, 1794.

The matter was discussed by the society at a well-attended special meeting, on May 30. The prevailing affirmative view is reflected in the offer of David de Isaac Cohen Nassy to help bear the expense of the removal *"du Museum de le Monsr. Piltz dans la Salle de la Societé."*[44] Dr. Nassy, physician, historian, and botanist lately arrived from Surinam, was only slightly acquainted with the Peales but had no doubts as to the value of their Museum. The lease arrangement was worked out and approved. At an annual rental of £130, Peale was to have all but the two rooms reserved for society use, for a term of ten years. He was to act as the society's librarian, its first. He was to be responsible for care of the society's own collections and for heating and cleaning throughout. Some areas still unfinished could be partitioned at his convenience and their cost deducted from the rental.[45]

Peale hesitated, but not for long. He needed space, yet here there would be less than with the addition he had planned. Against this, his close ties to the society, and the respect in which it was held, augured well. His view of the future was always a bright one. Might not the state someday do for the Museum what it had already done for the society—permit erection of a museum building on State House Yard? On that site it could be a full block in length, right in the heart of the city.

He had never considered the monetary advantage of one location over another, but now his friends presented a convincing case in favor of Philosophical Hall as against the Third and Lombard site. At the Hall the Museum would become virtually a part of the city's most attractive park (today's Independence Square), with its winding walks, small trees, and shrubbery, and would stand right alongside the seat of national, state, and city government. Then, too, the old Third and Lombard property could be sold or rented, to bring a clear financial advantage. Although Peale's dream of public support remained remote, the means for creating a museum of unquestionable public value, a public necessity, had come closer with this offer.

Friends' persuasion and congratulations swept him along to an agreement; carpenters and plasterers went to work on both a new home and a new museum. Museum arrangement again became a central problem: strict Linnaean order weighed against "handsome appearance" in the sequence of many-sized cases. And the live specimens! Peale applied to the legislature for permission to fence off part of State House Yard for hutches and cages, and this was speedily granted after an assist from convivial Governor Mifflin, in effect, adding a small zoo to enhance the attractions of the yard—"State House Garden," as it was called.[46]

With the whole spacious square at their door, its walks and shrubbery where children could play, the caged animals, the passing people, sometimes a band of Indians even, the Peales had all the excitements of the day before them. War overseas, Whiskey Rebels in the west—Raphaelle joined the crack "Macpherson's Blues," taking along ten-year-old Rubens as regimental mascot, uniform and all. Rubens raised his own regiment of children, armed

them with wooden swords made from lath discarded by the carpenters at the Hall, and drilled them handsomely in State House Yard. On that bright July day when all friends of France were celebrating the fall of the Bastille five years before, the children's troop, carrying a French flag with the British banner ignobly set beneath it, paraded to the home of Monsieur Fauchet, the French minister. His house at Twelfth and Market was swarming with patriotic Gauls. Vastly pleased and flattered, they brought in the little soldier and put a glass in his hand to drink with them to liberty and victory. Rubens later remembered standing by an obelisk on which the red cap of liberty was raised, while all the others marched round and round him, stamping in rhythm to the tune as they sang the "Marseillaise." After that the drunken little boy barely made his way back—along the twists and turns, and past the leaping monkeys, staring bears, and startled deer—to the wide and welcoming door of Philosophical Hall.[47]

Autumn came—and with it, moving day. To transfer the whole collection from Third and Lombard to Fifth and Chestnut required two weeks, and the effort was climaxed by a parade of another sort. Peale, as a third-person narrator, describes the scene in his *Autobiography:*

> Almost the whole of the articles belonging to the Museum must either be carried in hands or in hand barrows. However, to make [it] easy and at the same time expeditious, he hired men to go with the hand barrows. But to take advantage of public curiosity, he contrived to make a very considerable parade of the articles, especially of those which was large. And as Boys generally are fond of parade, he collected all the boys of the neighbourhood, & he began a range of them at the head of which was carried on men's shoulders the American Buffalo—then followed the Panthers, Tyger Catts and a long string of Animals of smaller size carried by the boys. The parade from Lumbard to the Hall brought all the inhabitants to their doors and windows to see the

RUBENS PEALE, BOY MASCOT OF "MACPHERSON'S BLUES"
Painted by Raphaelle Peale in 1794, the year of the "Whiskey Rebellion," this youthful portrait also probably celebrated Rubens's salute to the flag of France and his march to the Marseillaise. (Private collection.)

79

cavalcade. It was fine fun for the Boys. They were willing to work in such a novel remooval, and Peale saved some of the expence of the remooval of delicate articles. Yet he was obliged to use every means to prevent injury & loss with so numerous a meddley, and yet with his care he lost only one article, a young alligator, and had only one glass broke among the many boxes of that kind.[48]

Indeed, "It was fine fun for the Boys," one of whom, as always, was the Museum's proprietor.

CHAPTER FOUR

FOUNDATIONS: THE PUBLIC (1795–1801)

This to an old friend in London:

> My Museum is creeping up—yet it is like roling a heavy stone up a steep sandy hill, having no funds to support it but of my own earning. The Government has not yet done anything for me, but my having placed it in the Philosophical Hall, this situation being the best in the City, the products have increased.[1]

The Board of Visitors, formed to obtain and control funds, would do no more in that direction, and the whole effort was soured by a suspicion that one member had taken possession of the first exchange shipment from Sweden—birds from the collection of Gustavus von Carlson, sent on behalf of the Swedish Royal Academy of Sciences. Benjamin Smith Barton had been under similar suspicion as a medical student abroad.[2] That had been hushed up, and Peale said nothing of what he knew until long after the doctor's death. It had required an effort to bring the board or Acting Committee together, and when Peale ceased to summon, they ceased to come.[3]

But with increased income, the move to Philosophical Hall also brought a more continuous association with the learned world, new prestige, and a quickened sense of new directions in science. Peale, in turn, enlivened the Philosophical Society, not only with

PHILOSOPHICAL HALL FROM STATE HOUSE YARD
Philosophical Hall housed the Museum from 1794 until 1810. In 1802 the collection
expanded to the upper floors of the State House, and from 1810 to 1827 the entire
collection was concentrated there. One of a group of visiting Indians gestures toward the
Hall, seen in the center background with a small sign reading "MUSEUM" over its
door. Drawn and engraved by William Birch, 1799. (Philadelphia Museum of
Art.)

his zest for constant improvement but by fanning the fresh winds
that blew from France. Fauchet's successor as Minister Plenipotenti-
ary, Pierre Auguste Adet, was an admirer of the Museum, a
naturalist of ability, and in chemistry a defender of Lavoisier against
Joseph Priestley's controversial phlogiston theory. The Duc de la
Rochefoucauld-Liancourt praised the Museum's collection of minerals, thought its collection of animals of the New World must surely
be complete, and noted its proprietor's "intelligence, et son
Industrie indefatigable," which might have earned him a fortune

and must indeed be rewarded eventually with public support.[4] The tall, amusing lawyer and author Moreau de Saint-Méry, whose bookshop and printing house was a meeting place of francophiles, wrote in the same terms: "His interesting children help him in this estimable work and will share in the recognition which will come to it in time."[5]

Closest of all to Peale in friendship and temperament, beloved by the "interesting children" too, was the serene and gently humorous botanist Ambroise Marie François Joseph Palisot de Beauvois—or, as he stood in those days, plain A. M. F. J. Beauvois. While studying the flora of Africa, Beauvois had been driven from there by illness and suffered the loss of all his collections. The revolt in Santo Domingo had later brought him a similar loss and an even narrower escape. He arrived in Philadelphia destitute, only to learn he had been proscribed in France as an emigré nobleman and an enemy of the state. He lived by playing the French horn in theater and circus orchestras until Peale, with his increased income at the Hall, came to his aid.[6] Here was someone admirably qualified to carry out that recommendation of the Board of Visitors, to compile a catalogue of the collection. Peale and Beauvois worked together, planning an ambitious publication and bringing the crowded collections, as best they could, into Linnaean order.

Their *Scientific and Descriptive Catalogue* was to be published in parts, by subscription, with the whole eventually becoming an octavo volume of from 300 to 500 pages, with the subscribers' names listed as Patrons of Science. These patrons of science were slow to respond, however, but Peale went ahead anyway with the first number. Beauvois wrote in French. A refugee schoolmaster, Jean Thomas Carré, supervised the translation into English. Both versions were printed. By December 1795, aid from Congress was being sought, the members cool, however, to Peale's plea on the Museum's "beneficial tendency . . . in a Republic, to instruct the mind and sow the seeds of Virtue." Looking to other sources, Peale tried to raise funds by portrait painting, but with little success. No other number of the catalogue was published.[7]

Yet the work of compilation went on, with Peale continuing it alone after 1798 when Beauvois, no longer threatened by the guillotine, returned to France. Back in Paris he became Peale's best contact at the Muséum d'Histoire Naturelle—yet also a lingering presence in the Philadelphia home, dear to the children, loved by all. Beauvois had been especially close to Titian, his companion on many hunts, and at their parting made the boy a present of a fine new gun. Peale, at times of difficulty, would always console himself with Beauvois' favorite saying, "Never mind."

The Museum was now a way of life for the family like no other, excitingly modern, always adventurous, and the children were growing up with and into it. Mother Betsy had to adjust, and she did so with good humor while bringing her own solid Dutch sense of propriety to bear. Angelica had married in the summer of 1794 and was living in Baltimore. Raphaelle, at twenty-one much out and about the town, would rather dabble in paint than arsenic solution, and declared, as he would throughout his short life, that artistic talent lay only in those who could whistle, sing, or play some musical instrument. Only Rembrandt, a mature seventeen, had dedicated himself wholeheartedly to art. It was primarily for Rembrandt's sake that Peale brought some sixty artists and amateurs together in America's first art academy, the Columbianum of 1794–1795. During its brief and stormy existence, it gave the art profession in America its first experience with life classes and the exhibition of contemporary work. It has a lasting memorial, too, from that exhibition, in Peale's celebrated full-length trompe-l'oeil portrait of sons Raphaelle and Titian, *The Staircase*. *The Staircase* remained with the Museum, a permanent and popular feature.

Titian also was carefully preparing himself in art, but as a recorder of natural history. He looked after Rubens, *enfant de la patrie,* with a view to making a naturalist of him. Rubens had a garden at Third and Lombard where he planted seeds sent to the Museum and raised the first tomatoes seen in Philadelphia. He was provided with pets to his heart's content, including big birds, waddling furry beasts, and one great blacksnake that reputedly would follow him protectively about the house or yard and attack any threatening presence at his command, even a dog. When Rubens was very small, Dr. Franklin had come upon him struggling with little success to make a picture and had patted and encouraged him by writing a one-word maxim on a card, "Perseverantia." Rubens, the delicate child sent to school riding on Moses' shoulder, had never, even with perseverance, done well

"NEVER MIND"
Baron Palisot de Beauvois after his return to France. Lithograph probably from Rembrandt Peale's portrait of circa 1808. (Jane Loring Gray Collection of Portraits of Botanists, Gray Herbarium, Harvard University.)

Institut Royal
de
France.

Acad.º des sciences. (Botanique)

LE BARON PALISOT DE BEAUVOIS,

(Ambroise-Marie-François-Joseph.)

Membre de la Légion d'honneur.

Né à Arras le 27.º Juillet 1752, Elu en 1806, mort le 21 Janvier 1820.

TITLE PAGE
Hand-printed title page of the first Titian Peale's
work on American insects, 1796. (United States
Agricultural Library.)

there. Now, at the Hall, he made a scientific discovery on his own, and it changed his life. He found a magnifying glass and, looking through it, saw things that had always been blurred before standing sharp and clear. Wild with excitement, calling the news, he rushed for the stairs. Still holding the lens before his face, he misjudged the steps and went hurtling down into his father's arms. He was fitted with spectacles at once. A boy of eleven with glasses on his nose—Peale warned him anxiously that he must be ready to face the laughter of other children.

"Since I find them useful," his son replied, "I do not regard anything they may say about my use of spectacles."

Sophy, now nine, was the only one left to help her new mother with the new baby. Peale painted her portrait holding fat little Lin in her arms as a record of family continuity, the old brood and the new. Sophy had always been fleetfooted as a deer, sudden as a fairy. Peter Du Ponceau, eminent in the law and of rising eminence in philology and history, would always greet her on entering the Hall, bowing over the small hand with a courtly, "How does my little Miss Quicksilver do?"

Betsy was expecting another child in the autumn of 1795, and in that summer Angelica's first was due. A visit to Baltimore was planned. Betsy and Sophy would cheer and encourage Angelica, and Peale would paint a preaccouchement portrait of her—with her husband, if he would consent to pose. The rub here was that Alexander Robinson, her Irish-born businessman husband of aristocratic tastes, nursed a strong contempt for museums and museum people—"showmen," in short. This was a painful aspersion, and it much enhanced Peale's dislike for the sordid ignorance of those who live only to "buy cheap and sell dear."

The visit did nothing to appease their mutual disregard. Peale found a congenial friend nearby in John Daniel Kurtz, a young Lutheran clergyman who collected insects, and the two were out together in the fields, netting butterflies, scraping the bark of trees, and turning over stones, carrion, or clods of dung to gather what they could find. Peale's diary alternated between reflections upon those "who have no pleasure but in their prospects of gaining wealth" and those whose passion it is to pursue the arts and sciences. We read:

> Some collectors like myself have only looked for subjects large and striking to the sight—but now I declare I find an equal pleasure in seeking for an acquaintance with these little

animals who[se] life is spent perhaps on a single leaf or at most on a single *bush*.

It is diverting to watch a flower as you approach a bush and see the little being watch your approach, turning round a *twigg*, or part of a flower to avoid your sight, and in an Instant draw in its leggs and roll off, sometimes falling from leaf to leaf to get a passage to the ground—some others as quickly take to their flight—some other depending on the thicking [thickness] of their shelly coats, remain where you first see them regardless of danger. Others depending on the velosity of their flight stay until you give them the alarm, after which it becomes almost impossible to come near them.

Mr. Kirtz had taken a Fly with transparent wings, a slender Insect with a tuft of feathers on its Tail. It appeared to us a rare species. We could not find any more of them at this time, however I frequently went to the same meadow, and there only I could find them, but altho' I ardently wished to possess them, altho' I have seen at different times about 5 or 6 of them, yet I could not take one of them. Sometimes I have had my forcepts within a few Inches of them, but their quick motion aided by quick sight, they always avoided my trap.

The pleasure of this pursuit is great, for altho' we do not always find the Insect we go in search of, yet our labours are often overpaid by the obtaining new subjects, these perhaps before quite unknown or described.[8]

Treasures of the field brought back to his house, though praised for beauty and rarity, did nothing to soothe Mr. Robinson's feelings, which rose to fever heat when he learned that Raphaelle and Rembrandt planned to set up a small museum of science and art in Baltimore—bringing disgrace, as it were, to his own doorstep.

Back once more in the rarefied atmosphere of the Hall, on October 15, 1795, another child joined the rising generation— Aldrovand—but with a qualifying note added to the record of the birth in Pilkington, "if he likes that name when he comes of age." Plainly, Ulisse Aldrovandi, museum man of the distant past, was not being honored by unanimous consent. Among the Dutch families of New York, family names were the custom. And Aldrovand! Four months later, Peale brought the issue across the corridor to a meeting of the society, where it was voted unanimously that "the first child born in the Philosophical Hall . . . should be called *Franklin*."[9]

Linnaeus and Franklin—fresh hopes for a future day, but

THE NATIONAL BIRD
Peale objected to "bald eagle" as a misnomer, and Alexander Wilson
followed his lead in calling it the "white-headed eagle." A drawing
by Wilson now at the Museum of Comparative Zoology, which
identifies this as one of the few surviving specimens from Peale's
Museum, shows that the bird was originally mounted on a rock with
a large fish under its claws. (Museum of Comparative Zoology,
Harvard University.)

meanwhile help was hard to come by. Raphaelle would pitch in
occasionally, but had no heart for the routine. Only Titian was
dedicated like his father and gave his days and nights to the work
while dreaming of exploration and discovery in far places. Rain or
shine, there were the animals to be cared for, monkeys and baboons,
llama and elk and antelope, bears, panthers, wildcats, and the rest,
and above them all the famous bald eagle in his high cage with the
sign below proclaiming his expected longevity, "FEED ME DAILY
100 YEARS."[10] Though faithfully tended, the bird would not live
out that span. At the sight of Peale on the walk below, he would

scream his recognition. All, sooner or later, would become exhibits indoors, such as the five-legged cow and the elk in the first winter at the Hall—the one's peculiar feature concealed by a curtain, and the other's displayed to show what dissection had revealed. In the latter case, it had long been accepted as fact that the American elk had a unique reserve breathing system through "tear holes" near the eyes. Peale had found no passage from these to the lungs and made it clear by his exhibit that the supposed orifice was of superficial character only.[11]

Beauvois had commended Peale to the National Museum of France as a source of correct information on American zoology and of well-preserved specimens for exchange. In due course a letter dated June 30, 1796, arrived from Paris. Under a letterhead emblazoned "LIBERTÉ, EGALITÉ, FRATERNITÉ," two of the French institution's professors jointly initiated the cooperative relationship Peale so much desired. Jean Baptiste Antoine Pierre Monet de Lamarck and his young colleague Étienne Geoffroy Saint-Hilaire were seeking "a solid opinion" on generative functions and changes in species. Buffon's theory of degeneration did not enter into it. "We are about to proove," they explained, "that no species of the ancient continent exists in the new, et vice versa, and that great proof founded in the contrary opinion by wich both continents were formerly united towards the north would fall as groundless."[12]

They had a long list of needs, beginning with "those enormous bones wich are found in great quantity on the borders of the Ohio, the exact knowledge of those objects is more important towards the theory of the earth than is generally thought of." One or more pairs of live opossums were needed for dissection. A list of skins and skeletons followed: bison, bear and deer, and on down to beavers, moles, and bats. "It is incredible what variety these animals offer to the attentive eye. How many analogous forms are taken for Species. It would be interesting to know what degeneration had produced on their economy, They would lead us to a more exact knowledge on the nature of the Species and even of the Species in general."

The letter confirmed Peale's opinion that Buffon had been misled primarily by believing American species analogous to those of the Old World. Today its significance lies in placing Lamarck's interest in transformism, forerunner of the doctrine of evolution, at least five years earlier than had long been supposed. The prevalent firm belief that every species remained precisely as it had come from the hand of the Creator was falling before these revolutionaries. Lamarck was the theorist; Geoffroy, the zoologist studiously building a collection. It was to Geoffroy that Peale addressed his enthusiastic response. His supply of duplicates had been depleted by Raphaelle and Rembrandt with their Baltimore venture. He had appealed to the merchants of the city for gifts, and now issued a longer, more urgent appeal to the public at large.[13] Beauvois, financed by Adet and now collecting in the South, would contribute. Adet, a failure as a flag-waving diplomat, would be returning to France and the first great shipment could cross the ocean under his protection.

It had been hoped that Adet could join in a great rattlesnake hunt, but the tightening international situation prevented that. The creatures must be found while cold weather still kept them torpid, and the snake hunters waited into February 1797, longer than was safe. With them was Beauvois, making a new study of the "rattle viper," as Peale insisted it should be called. The backwoods of New Jersey was the scene, and Dr. Jonathan Elmer of Bridgeton was their guide. Peale astonished the others by the nonchalance with which he dragged out the serpents, writhing and squirting their venom.[14] Nine were deemed a sufficient catch, and the prize among them was a monstrous female with nine rattles. She would be the one to send to France, as Beauvois' personal gift. Back at the Hall, all the Peales, young and old, gathered to watch Beauvois study and select. Young Dr. Barton was there, readying for publication his paper "On the Fascinating Faculty of the Rattle-snake," and seemed to fear the fascinating faculty himself, for he made his observations seated on a table at a safe distance. Into this scene, unexpectedly, came a party of Indians, alert spectators. Too quick to be stopped, one warrior reached in, whipped out the largest, slashed out her still-beating heart with his knife, and munched it down. "They have an idea," Rubens noted in his serious way, "that if a living heart of a rattlesnake is swallowed, that no harm will attend them thereafter."[15]

So much for the Muséum National. Three smaller rattlers were substituted, along with a large blacksnake. The first consignment was generous, and subsequent ones were actively in preparation. As for the Indians, they were already involved, even more memorably, in doings at the Hall.

The Indian nations of the Northwest Territory and their British allies had been defeated by "Mad Anthony" Wayne at Fallen Timbers on February 12, 1795. Blue Jacket, war chief at the battle, sued for peace, and the Treaty of Greenville that August was followed in the next year by ceremonial visits to the Great Father at

Philadelphia. The campaign had brought gifts to the Museum. Wayne sent pipes smoked at the treaty fire—a Chippewa pipe, a pipe of the Kickapoos, Piankashaws, and Kaskaskias, and a pipe of the Sauk nation on "the Tyger and Missouri Rivers," claiming a muster of 10,000 warriors—as well as a buffalo skin mantle colorfully decorated with dyed porcupine quills.[16] General William Irvine added Indian leggings, garters, and moccasins.[17]

Meanwhile the tribes of the South, too, had been mending fences and hearkening to the Great Father. Thus it happened that on December 1, 1796, by chance (or, as it seemed for some long moments, *mis*chance), tribesmen of the Northwest Territory and the South, some of them traditional enemies, met unexpectedly at Philosophical Hall. While the rival tribesmen eyed one another, silent, hand on knife, the government interpreters hastily explained to each that each had come only for the pleasure of seeing a musuem. The result was an agreement to meet again at the Museum, next day. Having made their peace with the United States, the Indians would come to terms among themselves. And so they did, with Blue Jacket himself a principal orator.[18]

Peale would ever after cherish the lesson he saw in this happy event: the harmony of Nature leads to harmony among men. He commemorated it in wax portraits, figures in full costume of Blue Jacket and his friend Red Pole of the Shawnees, and when the one-time terror of the frontier, Thayendanegea of the Iroquois came to town not long after, Peale painted his portrait for the Museum gallery—a gentle characterization of a man, as the artist saw it, now won over to love for his fellow men. Here was Nature's own "Equality and Fraternity."

Eight other wax figures were added to make a group of contrasting races of mankind, completed in August 1797: a "Carib, or Native Indian of Gu[i]ana—South America," a native of the "Oonalaska Islands on the north west coast of America," natives of Kamchatka, of the Sandwich Islands, "Otaheite," of the Gold Coast of Africa, a Chinese laborer, and a Chinese mandarin. Their faces were casts from types brought in by ships' crews perhaps, but the Chinese likenesses were probably taken from servants who had arrived from Canton in the retinue of Andreas Everardus Van Braam Houckgeest in 1796. This Dutch traveler, who had been promptly elected to the Philosophical Society, made loans and gifts from his large collection to the Museum, Chinese clothing and utensils for the figures and artifacts from the islands of the South Seas, including a "throne of the King of the Pelew Islands."[19] President

CAPTAIN JOSEPH BRANT (THAYENDANEGEA)
Museum portrait by C. W. Peale, 1797. The war chief of
the Iroquois, long an enemy of the United States in battle
and massacre, was added to the Museum portrait gallery
both as a racial type and in hope of promoting peace among
men. (Independence National Historical Park
Collection, Philadelphia.)

Washington was invited to inspect the ten wax figures and, to the delight of all the Peales, bowed politely to the painted Raphaelle and Titian as he passed the *Staircase* portrait. The Indian peace conference, the wax figures—these were real steps forward toward Peale's goal, and he gave the waxworks a public announcement in his most effusive style, quoting a poet, "Whom Nature's works can charm, with God himself hold converse." This promptly drew the fire of the Federalist *Porcupine's Gazette,* whose irrepressible William Cobbett declared Peale's show not worth the price of admission unless some "stuffed Democrats" could be included—"Never mind their being of *your own tribe.*"[20] That last sally satirizes Peale's and other naturalists' talk of "the feathered tribe," "the finny tribe," or "the vegetable tribe" and takes a side cut, too, at Thomas Jefferson, the emerging head of the Federalist opposition and now president of the Philosophical Society.

To Federalists the Peale involvement with France was little better than treason—and ergo natural history, a tainted and frivolous subject. President Adams' undeclared war was looming, and Frenchmen were returning home. Lerebours departed for his homeland and took another shipment to Paris in his care, and Dr. John Rouelle, a friend of Beauvois who had been studying the mineral springs of Virginia, soon followed with a third consignment. Beauvois himself returned. But the ties with Paris, begun so auspiciously, would not flourish. The sea-lanes were now closed by war. Geoffroy left for Egypt with Bonaparte's scientific corps. Beauvois, too, left Paris but managed to get a letter through from time to time with some friendly suggestion or new contact, such as introducing Peale to a Dr. Perrein, "Officier de Santé," of rue J'adore L'egalité, Bordeaux, who would later turn up in New York with specimens to exchange.

Though cut off from France, the Museum must still show itself in the forefront of scientific progress. New inventions served that purpose. In 1794, Peale had invited all inventors to record their ideas in a book at the Museum. This project languished, as it should have, for to have pursued it correctly would have taken much time and only duplicated one of the Philosophical Society's functions. But models of various devices were exhibited and received more attention at the Museum than in the government's small and neglected collection of patents.[21]

Inventiveness was running high among the Peales themselves. In 1797 Dr. Elmer's suggestion that a bridge might link State House Yard to the adjoining open square set Peale's mind to work

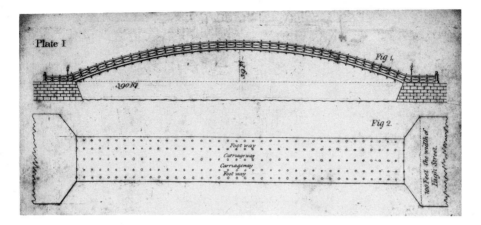

Plate I   Fig 1.   390 ft   Fig 2.   Foot way   Carriageway   Carriageway   Foot way   100 Feet the width of High-Street.

THE PATENT WOODEN BRIDGE

Engraving from C. W. Peale's Essay on Building Wooden Bridges, *1797. A large structural model was long a popular feature of the Museum. Visitors could walk across it and test its strength. Cheapness of building materials and simplicity of construction were expected to speed the country's westward advance—a hope not realized.*

on the idea of a wonderful single wooden arch, cheap and easily put together, something to carry roads and trails over watercourses everywhere, thus speeding the whole westward advance. He took out a patent on this idea, printed a pamphlet of directions, and built a model of it for the Museum, so strong "that 12 Indians and all stout men stood on it together and did it no injury."[22] At the same time he expanded on an idea of Raphaelle's for improved heating, and the pair won a Philosophical Society prize with it.[23] For the Museum itself, better heat and light would mean better income. The argand lamp, brought from France by Benjamin Franklin, had been a great blessing, and now there was a new brick stove, also a French invention, which like the argand lamp consumed its own smoke. Lamp and stove put the Museum in the front line of modern progress, and the news reechoed in the press to north and south. Regular evening hours began at the Museum in January 1797, on Tuesdays and Saturdays. Philosophical Hall now shone by day and night, with its new glass and the new wonders of Creation behind it, generating a new excitement. Happy that day in 1797 when the Comte de Volney stepped in from Fifth Street, exclaiming, "This is the Temple of God! Here is nothing but Truth and Reason!"[24]

95

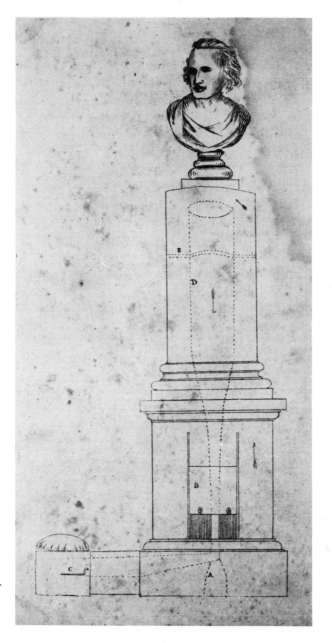

SMOKE-EATER

Heat and light were essential amenities to promote Museum income, and each new practical improvement attracted interest in itself. In this device smoke, forced back through the firebox, was cleansed of soot. From a drawing by C. W. Peale, engraved for the Weekly Magazine *(vol. 2, 1798, p. 353). The portrait bust, probably also by Peale, may represent Linnaeus.*

Everyone had been discussing Volney's *Ruins, or Meditations on the Revolutions of Empires,* a new philosophy of history with a vision of all religions united in the recognition of one basic truth. At the Hall, the importance of ideas over objects stood out; objects were only a means from which to derive facts—and from facts, discoveries. Day-to-day entries in the Museum catalogue, Peale's first draft of a catalogue of the Society's library, and his constant emphasis on the idea of a "school of wisdom" were all reminders that the Museum must not be voiceless. Scientific lectures were popular in Philadelphia. Even the English actor James Fennell, lacking a part on the boards, had lectured successfully on "natural philosophy" with help from Rittenhouse and Dr. Barton: scientific experiments dramatically presented, some with Franklin's own electrical apparatus. With study, Peale felt sure he could do better. In the spring of 1796, he announced his intention in the papers, soliciting books and information. When ready, he would have a novelty—lectures on natural history illustrated with actual specimens.[25]

Alexander Robinson, Angelica Peale's husband, had done all in his power to discourage the Baltimore museum of his brothers-in-law, and its brief life-span ended in 1798. But both young men were married and must have livelihoods. Calling it "The American Pantheon," Rembrandt took the portrait gallery of the Baltimore collection on tour to New York and other towns. Raphaelle sold his share and went back to chores in Philadelphia—skinning, mounting, dousing with arsenic. This gave Titian more time for his work on entomology, accumulating in beautifully precise watercolors of American insects. He was dreaming of exploration. Raphaelle had gone at it slapdash; Titian would proceed as a naturalist should, missing nothing. His father had written to his friend Pierre Adet for a passport to Cayenne for Titian. General Wilkinson had promised full cooperation from the army anywhere in the western territories.

Titian's precise little watercolors were building up toward an exciting and definitive work just at the time when a name had to be found for a newly-arrived half-sister, born October 27, 1797. Once more, Pilkington's *Dictionary of Painters* provided an answer in Sibylla Meriam, the German artist-naturalist, famous for her drawings of insect life. One volume of them was in the museum library. We can only guess as to whether it was Mother Betsy, or the child herself, who later transformed this name into the more fanciful, Sybilla Miriam.[25A]

The elder Peale took his Betsy for a visit to the DePeysters in June and, unexpectedly, found them all eager to have their portraits done. Happily he wrote to Beauvois that there would be money now for another number of the *Scientific and Descriptive Catalogue.* There was shooting in the neighboring woods and a search of the wonderful New York fish market. With complacent good nature, the DePeysters accepted what would have brought Alexander Robinson to a boil—the skinning, the mounting, and even the polecat that brought crowds to the street outside when Peale, experimenting with ways to rid it of odor, stationed it on the eaves of the house. Fumigation at the back of the kitchen chimney eventually did the trick.

Peale found Gardiner Baker's museum much changed. John DePeyster, Betsy's twin brother, had written him in 1794 of the Tammany Society's rebuke to Baker for advertising as an "elegant addition" a guillotine complete with the wax figure of a body and severed head. In 1795 the New York group had thrown up its hands and, in settlement of unpaid wages, let Baker have the whole exhibition. Here, then, was the pattern of the Barnum years—a manager intent only on showmanship, but with a naturalist as well as a billposter in his employ. Baker's naturalist was Jotham Fenton, a knowledgeable collector of insects with a mechanical bent that would lead him eventually into the manufacture of scientific instruments.[26]

Then, in the late summer heat, word came that yellow fever had returned to Philadelphia. Titian was ill, and Rubens too. Their father hurried back, confidently, to care for them: No bleeding. No calomel. Warm baths. Cool drinks. Both recovered. Returning to New York, Peale brought Titian with him because he was still very weak, and must be watched. But then the New York relatives were stricken, too. They had the good sense to follow the Peale regimen, and all of his patients recovered—all but one. Titian suffered a relapse and died, on September 19, 1798, aged eighteen. This was sudden cold tragedy in a form the Peales had never known before. For them Titian had been the future's brightest promise, forever mourned in the words and music of his brother Rembrandt's memorial ode:

> His early loss let Science mourn
> Responsive to our frequent sighs—
> Sweet flower of Genius that had borne
> The fairest fruit beneath the skies.

Young though he was, he had a soul
>   That urged to schemes the greatest scarce had thought,
Yet could his energy control
>   The harshest obstacles that danger brought.[27]

When the Peales returned to Philadelphia, Jotham Fenton came with them. He was taught their method of taxidermy and became useful at once in the display of insects and in other ways. Raphaelle, Rubens, Moses—even Sophonisba, at twelve a neat hand with brush or any fine work—all pitched in as the head of the house labored with them. They had, rising beyond the shadow of their sorrow, a new, great opportunity for the Museum.

Once more that vision of a national institution was in sight and in a new way practical, exciting—carrying them forward at no cost into a time when even the most pinchpenny taxpayer would be willing to help with the Museum overhead, staff, and faculty. Pennsylvania had long been debating the selection of a more centrally located capital, and in April 1799 the Assembly voted to seat itself at Lancaster pending a final decision. With this transfer and the impending move of the national capital to Washington, the old State House would be empty. Let the Assembly dedicate that to natural history, and the space problem of the Museum would be solved, for a few years at least. Thus spread out, the Linnaean system would appear in its full clarity, natural law revealed and transcendent. In time, the whole of State House Yard might be granted for additions. There was even a precedent, for in 1797 another artist, Joseph Steward, had been given use of the Old State House in Hartford, Connecticut, for his museum.

Washington's final message to Congress two years before, his Farewell Address, and even his will each embodied his strong desire for the founding of a national university. That idea would stay alive, and with solid Federalist as well as Democratic backing. A national university must have a museum, just as even small colleges would have until photography came in as a teaching tool. To Peale, the museum could well come first, and the time had arrived to bring out his own museum's teaching function. Professors he would someday have, but meanwhile there was only himself. As in painting he had turned from individual patronage to the public at large, so now he was turning from Board of Visitors to the visitors coming in from the street. As far as Assembly support was concerned, he must win not only the politicians but the citizens they represented. Philadelphia must stand with him. In contributing one day's receipts (amounting to $144) to sufferers from a great fire at Savannah, Georgia, he had included a reminder to his own city of its duty to "enrich and improve" its Museum.[28]

By February 1799, as he was opening his heart to—of all people—His Most Serene Highness, Louis, Prince of Parma in the royal house of Spain, the ultimate goal still seemed far away: "In the close of my life I have the hope to see this Museum rich in the three departments of Nature and become an object of National Patronage." Jefferson had advised Prince Louis to turn to Peale for American subjects. A consignment had gone off at once to the young aristocrat, Peale explaining his preference for person-to-person relationships and exchange rather than sale. "When I want funds for the increasing or improving [of] my Museum, I can earn it by my Pensil with less labour." This brought long, meticulous "want" lists of fishes, birds, and more, for which European specimens would be returned. More, indeed, were requested than the one-man operation at Philadelphia could possibly supply.[29]

Four months later Peale was writing to Beauvois of his determination to begin lectures that fall. "I am induced to undertake this ardious task, under a belief that it will be an important means to appreciate my Museum with the Public." The novelty of a course of lectures illustrated by its own subject matter would be attractive, he thought, "opening the eyes of an Ignorant people." It would require study beyond all the work given to the catalogue, but he would find an escape from the "canker-worm" of grief for Titian—"my loss, & I may justly say, a *public loss*."[30]

New York expenses had wiped out all of Peale's gain from portraiture. To Beauvois he could confess that he had relieved the financial stringency by "the triffling circumstance of adding a young oran-outang to my collection, and giving a number of handsome experiments with an excellent Electrical Machine." He may have taken his cue from the showmanship of Baker. One sees a gradual shift in Museum policy, more marked as the younger Peales took over, moving from an emphasis on overall growth toward special and temporary attractions.

The projected lecture course was to be a special attraction, but not of a trifling sort. It must, however, in keeping with Peale's total concept, seek to "amuse as well as to instruct." Dr. Benjamin Rush had promised his help with style. Peale could well feel happy for having brought the doctor into the circle of Museum friends. Famous as lecturer-teacher, Rush was an active champion of the national university idea. He, his wife, and daughter would all be subscribers to the course, and certain passages on the force of revealed religion in the first introductory lecture savor strongly of Rush. Peale had jotted down an outline for that introductory piece during a bird-hunting trip to the Jersey shore in May, stressing the importance of his subject to all classes of society, "the honor and importance of being teachers," and the "mode of instruction."[31] In a copy of Rousseau's *Emilius* owned by one of his heirs, it may have been he himself who has marked the passage urging teachers never to substitute representation for reality, shadow for substance—to teach, in short, from actual objects as he now meant to do.

Peale's forty lectures of 1799–1802, with their verbal description of each specimen as it was presented, bring us the substance of the *Scientific and Descriptive Catalogue,* the published first number and all that had been added in the three ensuing years. They were the most comprehensive effort by an American up to that time to summarize all that was known on mammals and birds.[33] A general summary of Museum holdings, as of April 1799, somewhat underestimates the number in those two categories as they appear in the lectures: over 100 quadrupeds, "near 700" birds, 150 amphibious animals, "many thousands" of insects, "a number" of fishes, minerals and fossils given a guestimate of 1,000, and one new wax figure of the racial type, bringing that group to eleven.[34]

The course was to occupy four months, November to February, with lectures twice a week, and was planned to coincide with the medical lectures at the University of Pennsylvania. "For want of time," Peale ended the first course after twenty-seven lectures. The 1800-1801 series was completed in thirty-nine sessions. The introductory lecture (different for each and, as was customary, published afterward in pamphlet form) was given in the Hall of the University, and the others at the Museum. "Much cannot be expected with the opportunities I have had for improvement," Peale confessed in approaching the trustees of the University, "yet I am pleased in a hope that some person better qualified will follow the path that I shall open."[35]

On Saturday, November 16, 1799, he rose to face his first audience, opening with a prayer—"Grant to ONE of thy works, strength to declare the praise of ALL!"—and then moving on to the more familiar ground of poets, quoting Pope and Thomson at length and from these launching into his argument:

> Natural history is not only interesting to the individual, it ought to become a NATIONAL CONCERN, since it is a NATIONAL GOOD,—of this, agriculture, as it is the most important occupation, affords the most striking proof.[36]

He cited the concern of other governments for the natural sciences, their research, their museums, and then the history of his own. With Paris and the teaching faculty there in mind, he "publicly and with earnestness" solicited the "aid of the several professors belonging to this honourable institution, the University of Pennsylvania."

As groundwork, Peale's first lecture introduced the four "grand sections" of nature: 1, the terraqueous globe; 2, fossils as distinguished from minerals; 3, vegetation; and 4, animals. He then divided animal life into six classes, each subdivided into orders, and the orders into genera:

1. Viviparous
2. Oviparous
3. Amphibians (One ventricle and auricle)
4. Fishes (Breathing by gills)
5. Insects (One ventricle, no auricle)
6. Worms (No feelers or wings)

The primates, of course, led off with a discussion of "the animal man," and then the genus *Simia*, with the orangutan (or "Wild Man of the Woods") leading the parade. It would be pleasant to think that the young specimen just acquired, alive, had a chance to win further applause here before being followed by the silent company of the preserved and mounted. Nearly 200 quadrupeds were described, though only 122 were actually shown, some represented only by an essential part—zebra skin, rhinoceros horn, a tiger's skull. Quadrupeds filled the first twelve lectures; the rest dealt with Peale's great and growing collection of birds, of which he was able to show 765 examples.

One can assume that the younger Peales were present and perhaps brought each specimen in its turn to the demonstration table before the audience. The monotony of the descriptive entry that came with each was relieved by accounts of how traditional lore had been tested by reason or experiment, or by random anecdotes and occasional reflections upon the usefulness, beauty, morality, and harmony of nature as a whole. Peale championed his science with arguments very close to those with which he had always defended the fine arts. He quoted poets and philosophers alike, citing both Alexander Pope and William Smellie (author of the recent *Philosophy of Natural History*) in support of the concept of "the great chain of nature," and was fully convinced of "a ballance of life that fills space."[37] Orthodox religion saw an immutable, divinely fostered creation. Peale's view admitted change but warned against disruptions of the interdependence of all forms of life. As Nicholas Collin had put it, "Each crawling insect holds a rank which lost would break the chain, and leve behind a gap which nature's self would rue."[38] Changes in species had occurred, but Peale, like Jefferson, hesitated to believe that any had actually become extinct. Surely the mammoth, the *Incognitum* of the mysterious gigantic bones, was still the terror of some distant wilderness.

All this the younger scientists were sweeping aside. Dr. Barton had no doubts: "There is no such thing as a chain of nature," no absolute dependence of one species on another, and some animals were indeed extinct.[39] Eventually it was young Rembrandt Peale who would convince his father, soon after, of the truth that some species had vanished from the chain.

Buffon had seen a deterioration of animal life in the western continent—the tapir a poor thing beside the elephant, or the cougar beside a lion or tiger. Thanks to Jefferson, that theory was now discredited, but the possibility of significant changes remained. As to Lamarck's plea for evidence on the transformation of species, Peale could only suppose that he and Geoffroy were making a further test of Buffon. "In the course of my correspondence with some naturalists in Europe," he told his audience, "a question has been put to me whether the animals *imported* into this country have degenerated or not." Only so, he had decided after investigation, in instances where climate and food were adverse. Buffon's idea of all American life being smaller and weaker was "a ridiculous idea." Peale cited comparisons seeming to bear the idea out, then demonstrated that these were actually quite different species and so dismissed the whole matter. "It is wonderful how far local prejudice will carry even scientific minds."[40]

Peale gave his sources, and the lectures show a familiarity with all the available literature of natural history, as well as a critical discrimination that compares well with the work of other and more scholarly writers of his time. To this he added much from personal observation, particularly on his favorite subject, the birds. He noted many examples of territoriality, a factor given far more attention by the writers of our own day than of his. He was always ready to put

Drawn by C.A. Le Sueur

THE AMERICAN ELK
Peale both studied the living animal for possible
domestication and, in order to correct popular
errors, dissected specimens before mounting. At his
farm an elk did a daily work stint on a
treadmill, pumping water. Drawn by Charles A.
Lesueur, probably from the Museum mounting,
and engraved for J. D. Godman's American
Natural History *of 1826.*

ADVENTURE WITH AN ELK
Right: In his lectures of 1799, Peale describes the
elk in detail. The female was "good humoured"
and affectionate, "yet so sensible of the enjoyment
of liberty that we generally found it a
(Academy of Natural Sciences of
Philadelphia.)

difficult task to get her ~~haltered~~ again.
altho she would come at my Call and suffer
me to handle her, yet the sight of a bridle
would make her spring away in an Instant.
          I can never forget the narrow escape
I once had by endeavouring to ~~halter~~ catch ~~her. the Elk.~~
          I quoiled a long rope and put it in my pocket
and left out only a piece of the end with a loop, which
I carefully kept out of her sight. calling her to me I
stroked her gently, making much of her, until I
made sure of puting the rope over her head. No sooner
~~this was~~ done, but she darted off like an arrow ~~shot~~
~~from~~ a bow, and the rope not delivering sufficiently
quick from my pocket, the Elk jerked me round,
~~& threw me off my feet~~ in an instant, thus thrown
I was draged on my back, about 20 yards, in expectation every moment of having my brains beat
out. but most luckily, the Skirt of my coat gave
way, and was torn off, and thus my life most provi-
dencially saved.   This instance may serve to
shew how ~~a~~ dangerous an animal the Elk would
be to domesticate for the draft; ~~through~~ as well as their agility
and strength. I have heard that the American Elk
~~has~~ been used in a carriage, but ~~however~~
~~I know~~ from my observations on this Animal
when alive, I should never advise any person to
                                                              make

what he had read to the test of experimentation and to look for new evidence in the specimens themselves. His dissection of birds had taught him much about their feeding habits and was helpful in identifying species—aware that male and female were often mistaken for separate species and that crossbreeding could add further confusion.

He delighted in putting popular beliefs to the test and in refuting that "Pillar of Error," the mere antiquity of an idea. He had experimented with the breathing of frogs to refute a notion that "swallows, those daughters of the air, which seem destined to circle in that subtle fluid, live six months without breathing."[41] This he treated with special care, for the delusion that swallows wintered under water had been accepted even by Linnaeus. So also with the "tear holes" of the elk mentioned earlier.[42] Would niter turn mice white? He proved that it would not.[43] Was it true that porcupines were the mortal enemies of snakes, that the porcupine rolled itself upon the serpent to destroy and devour it? He had longed to "make a tryal" of this, but "compassion for the poor Reptiles always prevented me from putting any of them into the porcupine's cage."[44] Buffon had described the flight of flying squirrels as a mere downward floating through the air, but Peale and Beauvois had both seen the animals actually gain height by a vibrating motion.[45] And, for a laugh, he noted that his exchanges from London had brought a "Domesticated Duck of the Mallard kind—it was sent to me . . . as a very great curiosity, having no webs between the toes. It is a variety that may very easily be made with a pair of scissors."[46]

Buffon was quoted frequently; Peale delighted in the lofty eloquence of his style, though deploring his occasional supercilious derision of some poor creature's appearance or faculties. "We should not adopt too hastily the opinions of any great Man," the Philadelphia audience was warned, "but to judge for ourselves whether they deserve credit at all times, and always to distrust that author who shall presume to treat lightly of the works of Creation."[47] It is an engaging trait of naturalists to become advocates for the creatures they describe, and Peale took both Buffon and the Englishman John Latham to task for characterizing the spotted-belly barbet of Cayenne as "clumsy, ill-made," and the Toucan likewise. The First Great Cause knew what He was about, and Peale defended both birds as well adapted each to "its particular mode of living."[48] Only man had marred the symmetry of a perfect whole with aberrations of his own. One glimpses Rousseau again. Worst of all man's follies was the irrational, unnatural fury of war.

He alone had learned to prey upon his own kind. "Nature, who designed him for love, denied him arms, and he had forged them for himself to combat his fellow. Oh! What a pity it is that the great nations of the world will not learn wisdom."[49]

Peale was diffident about naming newly discovered species, yet had strong opinions on nomenclature. Names should be descriptive, and accurately so. Latham's "Louisiana Lark" is too local, so Peale renames it "Small Lark of America."[50] And,

> There is another unmeaning custom which is still more essential for us to get rid of. I mean that of naming subjects of Nature after Persons, who have plumed themselves with those childish Ideas of their being the first discoverers of such or such things. How much better it is to give a name which is descriptive of the subject, and if possible in our common language, not in Greek or even Latten, which very few persons understand, even among the many pretenders to classical learning. Hard names almost totally destroy the good effects which the study of Botany might be to mankind. They deter many from attempting a knowledge of the classification of Plants—and with many of those persons who pretend to make a study of this pleasing science, their heads get so filled with those abominable long and difficult names, that there is no room left to contain any thing about the qualities. There skull like a cup is cram[m]ed full of names and will hold nothing about the uses which various plants of this vast continent must contain, for food and Physick. For instance, the Science of Botany is one of the most simple, according to the Linnean method. Linnaeus wrote in Latin for the use of all nations; but is it not Folly in each nation still to retain the Latin terms, so difficult to remember? *These* translated shew the Science is divided into *Classes* & *Orders*—the Classes *chiefly* distinguished by the number of the *Stamina's;* the orders by that of the Pistils: for instance, first class 1 *stamina,* of which the 1st *order* has 1 Pistil; 2d order 2 pistils & so on. 2d Class 2 Staminas, 1st order 1 Pistil & so on. Instead of terms so easy, students are frightened with the classical names of Monandria, Diandria, Triandria, Tetandria & so on—and those of their respective orders, Monogynia, Digynia, Trigynia, Tetragynia & so on.

For an animal, the descriptive name should not only give its appearance but also "its manners, disposition and general character."[51] Thus, Peale's "Gentle Falcon" had earned its name by its acceptance of the caresses of the Peale children.[52]

Through all nature, as the lecturer saw it, beauties and virtues abound, "charming models of every social duty." Much was to be learned of the love of mate for mate among the birds living at the Hall, and for usefulness the owl in the cellar had proved itself a better and bolder rat-catcher than any cat. Always there was that personal rapport between the naturalist and Nature. Peale disagreed with Daubenton's assertion that all animals, even the apes, are "totally devoid of thought." On the contrary, "It is my opinion that every Animal has a Reason, sufficiently adapted to their respective situations," a conclusion he reinforced with some lines from Pope.[53] We see him charmed by all the traits which he had loved to portray in portraiture—serenity, intelligence, parental love, and love for the home scene. His lectures are a parade of animal character, reflecting the lecturer just as a portrait does the painter:

The Cat:
The next Animal following in the arrangement is the Cat, and although an animal of prey, is a useful domestic. It is neither wanting in sagacity nor sentiment; but its attachments are stronger to *places* than to *persons.* The Cat is handsome, light, adroit, cleanly and voluptuous.

The Swallow:
Like all sentient beings, they cherish a partial tenderness to the place that gave them birth; there they felt their faculties first expand; there they tasted the fresh pleasures of the morning of life: necessity compelled them to leave with regret the delicious spot; but its image still dwells in their bosom and incessantly awakens the ardent craving to return and renew the felicity of infant days.

The Elephant:
However rough the form, when blest with *gentle manners,* whether in *man* or *beast,* is *far more pleasing* than the *most splendid beauty.*

The Redheaded Guinea Parakeet:
The male is ever obliging and affectionate to his consort; will hull the seeds for her with his bill, and present them to

her in this state; it seems unhappy at a moment's separation, which is reciprocal on her side: a state which will make even captivity tolerable.

The American Cuckoo, in contrast to that of Europe, prototype of cuckoldry:

Here I feel gratification, nay, pleasure, that I am able to show *this nest & Eggs* belonging to *these American Cuckoos.* They build their *own nest; they* foster *their* young; they diligently chaunt their soft notes to sweeten the Care of Incubation—and I am proud to believe that they are faithful and constant to each other.[54]

Dr. Lillian B. Miller, editor of the Charles Willson Peale papers, has suggested that the defense of the American cuckoo may well have been spoken with a smile. Perhaps. Peale certainly understood that humor has its place in "rational amusement." Just as surely, for a self-proclaimed citizen of the world, he was remarkably sensitive on points of national pride. A gentle note of comedy comes in with the racoon as he describes it: "very good-natured and sportive, but sometimes plays a little too rough. It is almost always in mottion; very inquisitive, examining everything with its paws. It makes use of them as hands, sits up to eat, is extremely fond of sweet things and will get excessively drunk."[55] And then he had the story of a Dr. Foulke and the Museum's red curapow, a huge crested bird with a voracious appetite for anything large and shiny. The doctor would earnestly assure credulous persons who happened by that the creature understood the value of United States currency and would urge them to test its sagacity with their small change. Sure enough, the bird would ignore coppers but instantly seize and swallow the silver, preferring a quarter dollar to eleven pence or a fipenny bit—all of which was largesse later for the Peale youngster, Rubens presumably, who cleaned out the cage.[56]

In lecturing on the whale, Peale had a story obviously enjoyed in private but presented in public with caution. Some visitors to the Museum, on examining the skull of a whale, had speculated on the small size of its throat and inferred that the Bible story must be one of "the fables of Antiquity." But, "at last one of the Gentlemen said he could do it—the others eagerly demanded how. By making a miracle of it." Then, for the benefit of the faithful, the lecturer quickly avers that one species of whale exists that could "easily swallow an ox."[57]

Rarely was any creature censured in the Peale lectures, and then but gently. The titmouse, a little bird, is "tainted with ferocity." Peale's illustration of the terrible voracity of the fox was deleted as too indelicate. On discovering that ladies would form a majority in his audiences, he went through his manuscript to circle every word or passage of doubtful propriety. But the ladies were most welcome and were very much a part of his vision of the future: "If Education is essential for obtaining happiness—have not our Daughters an equal right with our Sons to our instruction?"[58]

During the first course Peale became aware that his "minute descriptions of those small animals may not be so interesting to some of my hearers as I could wish."[59] In the second course the descriptions remained, but with a more generous seasoning of natural history lore to relieve any monotony. But if his first lecture series had ended with doubts about its success, the larger trend of events seemed to be in his direction, and Peale moved swiftly to meet them.

Now the rising tide of Democratic-Republican power was being felt, a wave that at year's end would sweep the Federalists out of office. Thomas Jefferson, president of the Philosophical Society as well as friend of the Museum and president of its Board of Visitors, would become President of the United States. Businessmen were sick of the quasi-war with France and ready for a settlement with the new French leader, Bonaparte. Peace would return, and with it the Museum's exchange program should flourish as never before. It was time for another pronunciamento to the nation, and it came on January 23, 1800. This, the third such, was addressed jointly to the "PEOPLE OF AMERICA and CITIZENS OF PHILADELPHIA."[60] Peale pointed with pride to all he had done—yet how far from his goal, and how inadequate "the income arising from mere visitors." From the nation he needed "the pecuniary aid of government." Philadelphians should at least "take the benefit of an annual ticket." An aggrieved tone is evident, and with it Peale's threat that "some other city in the Union will rejoice in receiving my labours." It is touched throughout by the emotional pique of an artist whose masterwork is not receiving the acclaim he feels sure it deserves.

The flow of events around him, passing him by, sharpened that emotion. Acting in haste, for the legislative session might adjourn soon, he petitioned the Pennsylvania Assembly to grant him use of the State House and reinforced his plea by sending urgent letters and the printed appeal to Governor McKean, Tench Coxe, and everyone else with influence. To his old comrade in the

Revolutionary War and politics, Colonel Timothy Matlack, now Clerk of the State Senate, he put his case in terms that he scrupulously avoided publicly, those of political impact: "I shall open a road that will be followed by men of greater talents, who will keep the way strait and in such manner influence public opinion that republicanism will be highly promoted."[61]

To William Findley, anti-Federalist frontiersman, consummate politician, and now a pillar of the State Senate, he explained that the broadside address was intended "to prove my urgency to bring my Museum into public patronage" and prepare the public for further more explicit proposals. He outlined in a general way what should follow:

> In the first place I declare that it is only the arrangement and management of a Repository of Subjects of Natural History, &c., that can constitute its utility. For if it should be immensely rich in the numbers and value of articles, unless they are systematically arranged, and the proper modes of seeing and using them attended to, the advantage of such a store will be of little account to the public . . . .
>
> A house sufficiently large to contain all subjects proper for a museum would be a very extensive building. Such is not easily obtained, although it need not be ornamented in the least, or have lofty ceilings. Yet a great deal may be done on a smaller scale. Rooms that will hold of large and small quadrupeds rather more than 200, of birds 2000, besides amphibious animals, fishes, insects, minerals and other fossils, shells and other marine productions—these, if possible, should be arranged in one suite, to shew a gradual link in the natural connecting chain. And the light ought to be from the north, as best to preserve their colors. Rooms for utensils, models, arms and clothing of various nations, a picture gallery to exhibit many things that would communicate knowledge, which words would feebly express. A large room to deliver lectures in, and a library to contain at least a complete collection on natural history, none of which should be taken from the Museum but resorted to by all that wanted information on such subjects. Also, an allotment for botany, and some conveniences for keeping a few living animals.
>
> I will now suppose such a museum realized. Persons should be appointed to deliver courses of lectures on the several branches of natural history, having the real subjects before

them. Such professors in a large city ought to get a sufficient number of pupils to reward them for their trouble, especially with the addition of persons who would come from other states to get the advantage of delightful and powerful instruction.

And besides these schools, a museum in perfect arrangement, with a good catalogue to give information on each subject, always open to visitors, would diffuse a beneficial taste and knowledge to those who might not be able to attend the courses of lectures. The price of admission to such visitors should be proportioned to the price of provisions or labor: about as much as I have always heretofore received. And the moneys arising from the visitors should be the support of the proprietors and keepers of the museum—which mode I have ever considered the most beneficial to the public. For if a museum was free to all to view it without cost, it would be over-run and abused. On the other hand, if too difficult of access, it would lose its utility, that of giving information generally . . . .[62]

The Legislature adjourned without action, and the petitioner labored on through the summer revising and completing his lectures. When the second course began, on November 8, 1800, Jefferson's Republicans had been victorious, the dispute with Aaron Burr for the presidency would soon be settled, and peace with France was in sight. Peale's introductory lecture to the second series reflects the speaker's confidence in this new future. He gave it almost the form of a religious service, a sermon with interludes of music. In his first draft he indicated a pause at one point for "One of David's Psalms or an Original," and at another, for "My Soul thy great Creator praise." For these Rembrandt Peale substituted seven stanzas of his own on "The Beauties of Creation," a seven-line "dirge" on the sad fate of Aldrovanus, Renaissance man neglected in his own time (and lately vetoed as a namesake), and his touching "Ode on the Death of Titian Peale." The words were set to music by a new close friend of the family, the English inventor and composer John Isaac Hawkins.[63] The whole savors—distantly—of the attempt of Ethan Allen, Thomas Paine, Elihu Palmer, and other prophets of revolution to formalize Deism into a religious body, a movement furiously resisted by the established churches.

Through December, Nicholas Collin supported his friend in the newspapers with a series of six "Remarks on the Utility of Mr. Peale's Lectures in the Museum," presenting a call to natural history as to worship that pictured the influence of this science for good, its promise for the future, and recalled how the lectures of Linnaeus had moved his own heart.

Both of the introductory lectures were printed, and copies were sent to such friends as Sir Joseph Banks and Parkinson of the Leverian, to the Exeter Exchange Museum in London and the Dublin Museum. Peale told Sir Joseph that he had in mind publishing the whole series of lectures and was already, in this euphoria, composing the prefatory piece for an entirely new course—building it around Raphaelle Peale's highly imaginative "Theory of the Earth"—and topping all that by boldly putting forward his own calculation of 170 to 200 years as the "natural life of man" in a roseate scientific future.[64] He declared once more his determination to press forward, unwavering, "until government may think such work deserving their patronage and support."[65] Hesitating to intrude upon Jefferson's time, he wrote James Madison about the prospect of support from the new administration: If Pennsylvania would grant him the State House, would Congress give him a professional staff?[66]

Most of all, and soon, he needed something that would bring wide recognition to the Museum, something to thrill learned world and world at large in unison. John DePeyster had reported strange petrifactions of the human body in Curaçao. He was following up on that, but an expedition to South America, including himself, Titian, Fenton, and Moses perhaps, promised better.[67] Through these possibilities, another opportunity glimmered, nearer and brighter. Peale spotted it in Samuel Latham Mitchill's *Medical Repository*—in two letters written to Dr. Mitchill in September 1800 by Dr. James G. Graham and Sylvanus Miller, Esq., each reporting discovery of the bones of "an animal of uncommon magnitude" in Orange and Ulster counties, directly north of the city of New York and not far from where a former business partner of Betsy's father had lived. They were found in abundance, though under adverse conditions in the swamps from which farmers were wont to dig white marl for fertilizer. Dr. Wistar had been in touch with Jefferson on the matter, and both had obtained bones from the area.[68] Indeed, all the valuable evidence was being scattered among collectors. No one had sought to find and keep intact a complete skeleton. That must be done, and who to do it but Peale himself? That would give the final answer to this most teasing mystery of the age and win the attention of Europe and America, folk and philosopher alike. No time must be lost.

If this attempt failed, Peale still had the South American expedition nearly ready. He dashed off a note to Victor Hugues, newly appointed French governor at Cayenne. Was it true that the National Museum of Paris had an exploring expedition in Guiana? Would an exchange program with Philadelphia be acceptable?[69] Hugues, in contrast to the Prince of Parma, was a Jacobin in full blood lust, soon to become known as the "Tyrant of Guadaloupe" and "Robespierre of the Islands." To Hugues, all Americans were "double-faced rascals."

That was on June 4, 1801. Next morning at dawn, with hastily packed clothing and equipment, the Museum's proprietor was on the stagecoach for New York.

A COLOR PORTFOLIO

CHINESE PHEASANTS FROM THE
ROYAL AVIARY, 1787
The pheasants were a gift of Lafayette to
Washington; at their death the birds were sent
to Peale. He had not yet fully developed his
system of taxidermy and found these mountings
difficult. "Yet," he wrote back gratefully,
"I was richly repaid in being able to preserve so
much beauty." They are shown here in a restoration
of the original exhibit, with the Peale's
Museum labels at their feet. (Museum of
Comparative Zoology, Harvard
University.)

PAILIONIDAE. PAPILIO. GUNDLACHIANUS.
*Titian R. Peale II continued the study of American insects begun
by his half-brother, Titian I, and painted these butterflies for
a work on Lepidoptera, many years in the making but never
completed.* Above: *Upper and under surfaces of the male.* Below:
Upper and under surfaces of the female. (American Museum of
Natural History.)

"PAPELIO"
*This butterfly drawing by the first Titian Ramsay Peale
is a page from his unpublished work on American insects
(1796).* (United States National Agriculture Library.)

ROCKY MOUNTAIN SQUIRRELS
Watercolor dated about 1821, made for the scientific collections of
Major Long's exploring expedition. Inscribed: "TR Peale delin. Sc
quadravittatus. Natural size. Specimen obtained at the Rocky Mountains
by TRP." (American Philosophical Society.)

Top: STEAMBOAT "WESTERN ENGINEER" AT COUNCIL BLUFFS,
FEBRUARY 1820
Sketch made by Titian R. Peale during Major Long's expedition to the Rocky Mountains. The
little vessel, the first of its kind to ascend the Missouri River, breathed smoke from its figurehead as
well as from its stack, a ruse to intimidate hostile Indians. (American Philosophical Society.)

YOUNG TITIAN AT THE OPENING OF THE WEST
Watercolor sketch in Titian Peale's notebook carried on the Long exploring
expedition to the Rocky Mountains, inscribed "Sundown on the Missouri,
370 miles above its mouth, July 28, 1819." (American Philosophical Society.)

BLACK-TAILED, OR MULE DEER (CERVUS MACROTIS)
This species was first discovered by Lewis and Clark. Drawing by Titian R. Peale
possibly made from the Museum mounting, as it was later published with the
annotation "Philada. Museum N. 1493." (American Philosophical Society.)

KING VULTURE
Inscribed: *"King Vulture* (Vultur papa) *from life. Turbaco, New Grenada. TRP, 1830."* (American Philosophical Society.)

CHOCTAW WARRIOR'S COLLAR
This Indian adornment was presented to the Museum by Miss E. M. Burns, on January 9, 1828. (Peabody Museum, Harvard University.)

THE LONG ROOM, 1822

The heart of the Museum is shown in this painting begun by C. W. Peale as a study for the background of his full-length self-portrait, and then completed in precise detail by Titian Peale. At left are the bird cases, with portraits hung above. In the portrait the "first gift" paddlefish has been substituted for the Indian relics shown here in the doorway. Visible at right is the top of the organ, with busts of scientists by William Rush and of Washington by Houdon above the cases holding the mineral collection. The nearer pedestal holds a "vase of hummingbirds," and the one behind, basalt from Giant's Causeway in Antrim, Ireland. On right wall are four of Peale's recent landscapes. (Detroit Institute of Arts.)

THIRD AND LOMBARD

This painting shows the home of the Museum through its first decade (1784–1794). Extending back from Lombard Street beside the Peale house are the skylighted portrait gallery built in 1782 and the "moving picture" room of 1785, which later became the Museum's Marine Room. Painted by Rubens Peale, 1858–1860. (Author's collection.)

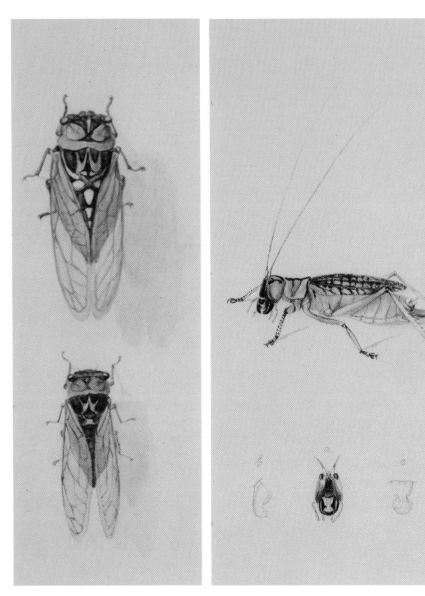

CICADA
Watercolor by Titian R. Peale.
(American Philosophical
Society.)

GRASSHOPPER
Inscribed: "Carthagena, April 4, 1831. Nat. size.
Coloured from the living Specmn. T. R. Peale."
(American Philosophical Society.)

CHAPTER FIVE

THE GREAT AMERICAN *INCOGNITUM* (1801–1804)

$\mathbf{H}$e had booked a seat on the diligence to New York (metroliner of stagecoach days) and climbed aboard in the dawn light of that summer morning, a gray-haired, pink-cheeked man of sixty, adventure-bound, with a small trunk in one hand and a double-barreled shotgun in the other. The trunk contained not only clothing but material for preserving birds and other small animals, gunpowder and shot, paper, ink, and charcoal. Every interval in the search for the *Incognitum* must be used to enrich the Museum, and if he could not bring back a skeleton, at least he must have an authentic record on paper. Here, to all appearances, was a gentleman on vacation, though inwardly alert to the excitement and importance of his quest. The chance of a lifetime lay before him, the hidden monster, the "Behemoth" for those who thought in terms of scriptural majesty. He himself, partial to descriptive names, preferred "Carniverous Elephant of the North."

He had a plan of campaign. He would move step by step rather than in haste. In New York he would get letters of introduction to Dr. Graham of Newburgh, who had reported the largest find. His DePeyster relatives should be ready to lend financial aid. He would go on to Newburgh by way of West Point, where an old friend, Major George Fleming of the Artillery, was in command. The major had visited the Museum in the spring of 1797 with a gift, one of the torpedoes floated down the Delaware in the famous "Battle of the Kegs," on January 5, 1778.[1] Army help might be offered, as it had been to Dr. Michaelis in his earlier attempt, but this time it would be in response to an order from the President of the United States. All through the touch-and-go of Aaron Burr's claim to the presidency, Jefferson had been dividing his attention between the constitutional crisis and the huge fossil bones newly found between Shawangunk Mountain and the Hudson River.

The new President was, and would continue to be, a unique and a controversial figure—a fact that became apparent almost as soon as Peale had settled himself in his seat in the diligence. Stagecoach travel, with passengers close together and jolted about behind the pounding hooves, made for intimacy, likes and dislikes quickly emerging. What Peale experienced as they rattled over the city streets and thudded along the open road is best told by himself:

> June 5th, 1801 began a journey to New York in the Diligence Stage, which was pretty well filled with Company, and we were not a little incommoded with baggage within but to this I contributed my full share, by not suffering my Trunk to be lashed on the outside, for on a former occasion I was a sufferer [by] the carelessness of a Driver in tying on my Trunk, it was dropt by [the] way, hence my dread on the present occasion. Among our Company was a french Gentleman who could not speak English, who afforded me the opportunity of exercising my french. Another passenger was an Englishman who was fond of talking, and I soon found he wished to know my political sentiments by his various questions about our Governor and the President of the United States. Not willing to indulge him, my answers puzzled him, for I told him that I voted my sentiments when called upon to exercise such rights, and whether I gave a successful ticket or not I submited to the power choosen to govern, content to wait and if so pleased to make my objections at the proper time.
>
> However, making some general reflections on the folly [of] Nations making war, hoping I might live long enough to see mankind more wise and not disgrace themselves below the brute Creation, even the more voracious of which did not kill their own species—In such train I leveled at many of our follies & vices—and thus passed the forenoon—but after dinner John

Bull having wetted his whistle, his pipes were louder & more grating to my Ears, and as he throws out some ill natured sarcasms on our public men with much low slander, I then thought his venemous tongue ought not to be allowed to slobber his venum to pison the minds of some of our company, to prevent which I told him, that he should not believe such Idle tales, that as party did not stop to say many things without the least foundation for much slanders both against our President & Govr. McKean. On this he was vociferous & Insolent and he seemed to exult at finding my oppinion. I replied that he had exposed himself sufficiently to my mind, that such sentiments did not accord with my Ideas of what ought to be the state of things, to render a people happy. He called Bonaparte a boy, and wondered france would submit to be governed by a Corsican when they certainly possessed many great men of their own Country— Boy or not, he shewed more good sence than any of the Monarks of Europe, for in his moments of Victory he demanded peace, and many of his actions proved him to be a wonderful man, and it was of little consequence of what country a Governor was, provided he governed with prudence & no man could act with more liberality than actuated Bonapartte. John Bull replied, ah we shall see by & by—Robertspere, once was thought highly of and we shall see whether the President will have resolution to keep to the Sentiments of his Speech. I replied that he had before shewed himself to be a man of firm nerves by his writings. He replied that some of his works had been brought forward to his censure. Yes, but by a party that stoped at nothing to obtain their end, making improper implications & misrepresentations, and more honor than want of just sentiments manifest to every one who will read the whole of his notes on Virginia. We spar(r)ed thus for some time, and I was heartily tired with his gabble. But taking in other passengers in the place of some ladies who gave up their seats at Princeton, these were more rational beings & therefore more agreable.

6th. We sleep at Brunswick, & had an agreable journey to New York where we arrived at noon. Not to leave *John Bull* without further remarks, would be omitting what I thought remarkable, i.e. he has been almust dumb, perfectly chop-fallen, sullen as any hog to this end of our Journey.[2]

He found his New York relatives, some in town, some at their country place in Harlem, everything bright and green. He dined well, suffered a spate of violent indigestion, cured it by his newly invented steam bath and then, having astounded them all with this demonstration, built baths for both households. Brother-in-law Philip was there to tell of his visits to the museums of Paris and Madrid: Paris a dismal building surrounded by a menagerie . . . pictures separate from natural history . . . stuffed birds packed together on shelves . . . in Spain a rare sight of gems, gold, and silver.[3] They all went shooting at Coney Island. Peale preserved birds and fish and looked in again at Gardiner Baker's museum, run by the Baker children now. When he embarked for the upriver voyage on June 19, he had letters of introduction to Dr. Graham from Betsy's cousin, Colonel Henry Rutgers (trustee and namesake of the university), and from Dr. Mitchill. The DePeysters were ready as bankers if needed.

There were two days of waiting for a favorable wind. It was midafternoon when the Little sloop *Priscilla* at last moved out and then sailed on, as darkness fell, to where the towering Palisades threw the whole river into shadow, and then, as darkness fell, into wilder country, the storied highlands of Hudson. Lowland-bred and a romantic at heart, Peale sketched constantly as each new view appeared; the *Priscilla* sometimes speeding around into a new vista, sometimes fluttering her sail below the mountain crags. This was the giant's lair of mountain and marsh. Here was a wildness matching the beast he had heard described at Philosophical Hall—enormous in size but with "the ferocity and agility of the tiger," armed with great tusks and claws, seizing its prey in "one gigantic leap" and then crushing body and bones in the huge teeth.

That had been the paper read to the society by George Turner, Revolutionary veteran, judge of the Northwest Territory, an astute amateur naturalist.[4] Though he endowed the lumbering creature with so much ferocity—"once the terror of the forest and of man!"—Turner's paper still holds a certain respect. He correctly judged the beast to be extinct, though at the same time he conjured a fanciful vision of how it became so: "And may not the human race have made the extirpation of the terrific disturber a common cause?" Drawing his deductions largely from the form of the teeth, he had defined two types of mammoth: one, the American, carnivorous or with a mixed diet; the other, herbivorous. His conclusions were close to those which George Cuvier, friend and colleague of

Geoffroy and Lamarck, published in 1799. Cuvier, however, rightly pronounced both types herbivorous.

Landing at West Point, Peale was entertained overnight by Major Fleming's family, toured and made drawings of the post, and then was driven north to Newburgh, where he found Dr. Graham equally hospitable. On June 25, Peale and the doctor drove out to the nearby farm of John Masten, who three years before had retrieved the greater part of a skeleton from his marl pit and had been exhibiting it for a small sum:

> Bones of a Mammoth found by some rude boor,
> While, heedless of his luck, dug manure . . .

as the incident is cited in a satirical poem of 1802.[5] Here, spread over the old farmer's granary floor, lay the *Incognitum*— incomplete, damaged, yet far more than Peale had ever seen and, a point whose vast importance he fully appreciated, all indisputably from the same animal.

Word of Masten's discovery of the huge dark bones embedded in the white shell marl had been quickly bruited about among his neighbors. A hundred or more had gathered to see and then, encouraged by local savants, mostly medical men, had set to, to heave them out. A gay country frolic had followed, a flow of liquor warming the workers while they dug and dragged, racing against the flow of water into the deepening pit. Now Peale could see ample evidence of their zest and speed in the wreckage around him. There lay some fragments of the head and five feet of one tusk, broken midway. All of the neck, most of the back vertebrae, and some of the tail seemed to be present. Breastbone and ribs were there, but much broken. The pelvis too was damaged. He saw both shoulder blades, both forelegs complete, and one femur, a tibia, and a fibula from the hind legs. Some bones of the feet were missing, but there were enough to reconstruct the form. Missing parts might still be found in the morass; but, lacking that, there was enough to reproduce on one side what had been on the other. The most serious lacks were the upper part of the head and parts of the jaw.

It was known that the old farmer had refused to sell the skeleton, but by now it had ceased to attract much local interest and his income from showing it had dwindled to very little. Peale, all eagerness, was careful not to seem too eager. He asked merely if he might make drawings. Permission was granted, and he set to work. What followed is best told in his letter home to Betsy:

. . . I did not at first give the least hint of my Intention to purchase, & liberty was readily granted me to make my drawings. After examining them I soon determined what part I would take drawings of. Viewing the magnitude of them, a thought instantly struck me, that it would have a better effect to make drawings of the exact size, although they should be ever so slight, and having near a quire of paper in my Trunk, I began to paste a number of sheets together proport[ion]ed to the size wanted, and to sketch with coal an out line, measuring the distances for correctness, and afterwards to line them with India Ink with a long brush & shade them in a rough manner. Having prepaired and just begun the work, I was asked to dinner. While at Table the eldest son demanded of me whether I should not like to buy them. I candidly replyed that I should provided the price was not too high, and in my turn demanded what they would take for them. I could get no answer to my question, but still they insisted to know what I would offer. My mind had been made up on that score purty nearly. Therefore I answered that I would be candid with them, and would at once bid, give as much as I could afford & in a few words, and if the offer that I made was not accepted, I should content myself with only having slight drawings of them. Thus promising it as my ultimatum, I offered 200 Drs. for those now collected and 100 Drs. at some other period when I should be able to bear the expence of getting up the remainder, which should be wholly free of expence to them, and what aid I should want of the family I would pay for, besides the 300 Drs. They answered in a negative. I reasoned a little on the cost of obtaining the residue—and that if any body thought of making money traveling about the country to shew them, the costs of Taverns would often exceed the profits—although money might be made at one place, at others only expence would be incur[r]ed, that in short it was a kind of life very prejudicial to the morals of those who attempted to get a maintinance by such means &c. &c. I could get no answer by which I could then know the issue—and I went again to my drawing. In the evening when I was about to return to the Doctrs. they invited me to stay the night. I excused myself by saying that I had promised to return—that I wished them to consider & consult together, that I would be obliged to them for an answer in the morning, as if they choose to accept my offer, it would superceed my wishes to finish the drawings. The next morning I came to my work & brought with [me] 2 quires of paper in order to have a sufficiency—but I found that the old gentleman had gone into the field to his work, which made me suppose he had determined not to accept my offer, & I set to work again, but I had not been long at it when Mr. Masten came in. When I asked him if I was to continue my drawings, he replyed he believed not—my heart jumpt with joy.[6]

Observing this reaction, boot was demanded, and it was agreed that the bargain should include a double-barreled gun like Peale's for Masten's eldest son and gowns from New York for his daughters. The bones were then packed in hogsheads and crates for shipment to town, where the transaction would be completed.

Back in New York, Peale had his first taste of an excitement that would soon become a national furor. He had wanted to do some business with his patent bath and fireplace, but found that the huge thigh bones he had with him, too large for any container, his drawings, the news of what would soon be revealed in the mounting of the skeleton, had created an excitement that left no room for other topics. He wrote Jefferson an account of it on June 29, but his diary tells more:

> The Vice President of the United States [Aaron Burr], and a considerable number of Ladies and Gentlemen came to see the Bones. The news of them must have blew like wild fire, for upwards [of] 80 persons came to see them that evening. It was a pleasing circumstance to me, that every body seemed rejoiced that the bones had fallen into my hands. It seemed to be a general sentiment that with me they would be preserved, and saved to this Country.
>
> One Person only uttered a contrary sentiment. Doctr. Hosack invited me to dinner with him the next day. I excepted his invitation, and his first salutation was, he was sory that I had got the bones. I asked him wherefore, and he said they ought not to have let them go out of the State. Then I replied, give me sufficient encouragement and I would bring them & the Museum also to New York. I was a citizen of the world and would go to that place which would give most incouragement to my favorite Science.
>
> But Doctr., do you know any man that would put these bones together if they had them, but myself? He replied he did not. Then surely you ought to be glad that I possess them.[7]

The bones were put on a ship bound for Philadelphia, the schooner *David,* under the command of Captain L'Hommedieu. Their owner headed home again by the diligence, an exciting dash through field, forest, and town, down the long highway and into Betsy's arms, greeted with all the eager questions from children, friends, and philosophers at the Hall. The Philosophical Society, fostering the study of this subject over so many years, could muster the most expert knowledge available for a correct assembling and completion of the skeleton. The news was spreading out over the country as all awaited the arrival of the *David* in Philadelphia harbor. "Mammoth" would soon become a household word. As *Kline's Carlisle Weekly Gazette* reported it, on July 22, "Mr. Peale" has now "the bones of the great American animal commonly called the *Mammoth,*" and "within the space of two or three months he expects to have it in his power to put together a complete skeleton for the Museum." On July 24, 1801, a special meeting of the society, with the largest attendance of the year, met to inspect the bones and consider Peale's plea for cooperation in completing the skeleton. The vice-presidents, Robert Patterson, in a sense a founder of the Museum, and Dr. Wistar, had called the meeting. Governor McKean was there, along with Drs. Rush, Barton, Woodhouse, Seybert, and Collin—twenty-six members in all. Peale had asked for a loan of $500 for four months. It was granted, unanimously, without interest.[8]

Preparations for further excavation were already underway. The site to be explored lay under twelve feet of water, but an unusually dry summer, so far, gave promise that it could be drained. Peale had written Jefferson to ask for the loan of Navy pumps and Army tents. He now wrote Dr. Graham and asked him to order lumber delivered to the site. That letter never reached Graham. The President was at Monticello, and his ready agreement, written on July 29, with orders to General Irvine at Philadelphia and to the New York Navy Yard, came too late. The expedition, a party of four, had set forth in the diligence on that day. Rembrandt Peale, aged twenty-three, was joining his father in what would be the only scientific study of his career, but a memorable one. Jotham Fenton was there. Young Dr. James Woodhouse, short, florid, and balding, a professor of chemistry at the University soon to be recognized as America's leading authority in that science, came as the society's representative. A francophile and a friend of all the Peales, like them he loved experiment and relished a joke, but unlike them he gave God the Creator only conditional praise for what He had done.

Peale had succeeded in borrowing an Army tent. In New York he procured pumps and other gear. How to set up and power the pumping operation on which all else depended remained a problem, but in looking over the ground at Masten's a novel idea occurred to him—a huge millwheel, as it were, powered not by water flowing over the outside but by men treading in the inside. Such a power source attached to a chain of buckets would lift the water high enough to be channeled a distance away—a great improvement over separately operated hand pumps.

[August] 3d., [1801] . . . I rode to Doctr. Grayham's where I made some drawings of a wheel & buckets to drain the hole where the bones lay—for last evening viewing the Ground near the Pond I found a considerable hollow over a small hill. This struck me at first sight as a favorable place to carry the water, which I could do with a trough of no great length. . . . By the advice of the Doctr. I went to seek a Mr. Campbell, a very ingenious workman, a wheelwright. Mr. Brown, in whose employ he was, very obligingly consented to let him leave his work to do mine.

[August] 4th. Mr. Campbell began his work. He readily conceived my plan—and after viewing the Grounds round the Pond we determined how to place our wheel and water buckets. [We] went into the woods and fell[ed] some Trees and a number of sapplings, some to make the arms of the great wheel, others to make triangles for fixing the Tackles, &c., and we got the poles hauled to the Pond. A horseman Tent which General Ervin lent me, we set up on a Hill south of the Pond at a good distance to be out of the effluvia of mud. An appearance of Rain toward sun set induced us to make a shed of Boards to work beneath, and also to keep part of the boards dry.

[August] 5. Having slept in the Tent & being so near to the shed altho' it rained, Mr. Campbel & myself set about to compleat the covering of the shed—we had just compleated our work when behold, the whole fell down—having neglected to put braces to support the crotches, & some of the boards being put up in haste had a leaning position. The shaking it got by letting the boards fall against it set it agoing. We had each of us to scamper as fast as we could to escape being

crushed beneath the pile. Each of us rejoiced to see the other safe, and after our surprise was over we set again to work, determined to be more careful in putting the boards perpendicular to brace it. With dilegence we rebuilt [all] of [the] building before breakfast. Mr. Campbel went to get a cross cut Saw, buy nails & engage a Carpenter to assist us. I set about to make a work bench, which I compleated with sundry conveniences for working carpenters work. . . .

The constant attention and labour after we began to emty the Pond of the Morass belonging to Mr. Mastin prevented me from making my daily notes—therfore a sumary from recollection of the events is all I can give at this time, the 31st. of Augt.

When we had raised the wheel & had compleated the Buckets, and made a Tryal of it, I found that when the wheel was not drove fast, that the Buckets delivered most water into the Trough—That thus moving slow & steadily in its best effect emty 20 Buckets in one minute, and altho' these Buckets held 1½ Galln. of water, yet on an average they did not deliver little more than one Galln. I frequently tryed the effect of my Watch, and to proove that my calculation was just, I counted them for 5 minutes together, which make very exactly 120 in that time—12 times which makes 1440 Gallns. pr. hour with the labour of 3 men. Had I known that the Bason into which I carried the water would have absorbed the water so fast as afterwards on experience was the case, I would have used fewer Buckets and not have raised the water so high. The fear of our scaffolding sinking down induced me to raise the water 25 feet. At first I made the Buckets in number to reach the Bottom & supposed they would float on the Surface, but by tryal I found that they intangled together. I then was induced to make a long Barrel about 2 feet in diameter [as base of the bucket chain]. This Bl. floated on the water & answered to my expectation—but too many Buckets I found troublesome, entangled together and encreased the labour of the wheel. At last I took some away. We soon emtyed the hole of water, and began the work of exploring—but the Buckets

BEGINNING TO DRAIN THE MARSH
On-the-spot diary sketch by C. W. Peale. (American Philosophical Society.)

THE EXHUMATION OF THE MASTODON

Painted by C. W. Peale in 1806, to commemorate America's first organized scientific expedition (1801), this lively scene was intended to bring some of the drama of discovery into the Mammoth Room at the Museum. John Masten, owner of the land, is on the foreground ladder, and Peale, with one hand on the large-scale drawing of the bones, gestures toward him. Large crowds gathered every day, and Peale filled up the scene with family and friends, many who were not actually present. Rembrandt, Rubens, and Raphaelle Peale, as well as Coleman and Sophy Sellers (under umbrella), are in the family group behind the drawing. At left, Alexander Wilson watches with folded arms. An exciting moment in the work is shown—the passing nearby of a Catskill Mountain thunderstorm that threatened to deluge and destroy the whole endeavor. (The Peale Museum, Baltimore.)

reaching to the bottom, the gravel soon began to wear the ropes and afterwards was the cause of much labour to repair the damage.

We soon found some of the bone[s] of the feet. At first discovery of them, I forbid the taking them up,* but to my mortification in the next moment the morass began to moove forward with the weight of the mud thrown on it pressing down. The white marle at bottom being soft came upon the bones & we were glad to seize all we could before they should entirely be again Covered. The next advice was to through all the mud further back on the Morass, with the hopes that when thus lightened the bank would stand—but behold we found it began to form cracks of considerable extent back & thus large bodies pressed forward—and . . . on Saturday evening we found the whole of the work like to overset, as the whole bank then began to give way. A Thought suggested as our only resource by Mr. Cambel was to fix a takle from the Top to a small Tree standing near—altho' I thought the assending not a little dangerous, but not a minute was to be lost. I quickly mounted the Scaffolding & brought down the Tackle and thus we saved the works from falling. Numbers of people had collected. All seemed to urge me to work on the day following. The fear of offending made me hesitate, but when even those of various stations, even the clergy, one in particular, said it was a work of necessity—and finding the men willing to labour on Sunday provided I would screen them from harm, I agreed to pay any fine that should be exacted.

[August] 16 (Sunday). We cut down a strong pole of 36 feet length, and raised it by a second takle—placed the foot into the bottom, yet it would not sink sufficiently untill the additional weight of the other Poles & machinery was added, which by a happy thought of Mr. Cambel was effected thus: fixing a takle to its Top, and the other block to the works, they thus threw all the weight on it, & from time to time pressed it down until it had reached the gravelly bottom. We then threw the weight of the mud still father back, cutting bushes and

*"As he wished to see the bones of the whole foot in its proper form." *Autobiography*, p. 292.

small Trees to keep it from sinking. However, the next day we were under the necessity of getting some stought poles, one to extend along the bank and others to brace this back. Then they got a great number of poles and drove them pretty close together, by means of what is called a *Commander,* a very large *Maul.* After we thought we had now made sufficient defense against the bank & began to explore, Mr. Cambel found one of the braces bending. He then got a shorter piece to help it.

We then went to work to emty the space within our bank, and in the course of the week we got part of the Tusk, many bones of the feet—and each day wished to come at the under Jaw, which we hoped to get intire—but among other bones I found other Grinders & some pieces which I knew belonged to the under Jaw. Thus my hopes were dashed on that score. We got a piece of the *Sternum, osnominatum* and one piece of the head & now and then some bones of the feet—but . . . after labouring with our utmost exertions until mid day on friday I was induced to give over further search. Altho' I had 25 men at work for some days, and I paid them for pumping 2 nights, yet the difficulty of obtaining any more bones, would be a waste of money. Thus on friday I paid off my men—and on Saturday I went to Doctr. Grayhams who was so obliging as to accompany me to Doctr. Gallatia, who had advised me to try a morass belonging to Captain Barber from which some few ribs had been found some years back.[9]

There had been one moment of crisis which Peale long remembered, an occurrence told best in his well-known painting of 1806, *The Exhumation of the Mastodon.* With all in order and hopes high, the skies had darkened, and lightning flashed and thunder rolled with all the flamboyant fury of a Catskill Mountain storm. The downpour it threatened would have washed down banks and wheel together, wrecking and flooding all. Boldly, however, his men stayed at their work as the black clouds and downpour passed them by, lightning flash and thunder roll receding into the mountains beyond.

Peale had paid his workmen good wages. He had also, for their own good as much as for thrift, watered the liquor doled out to those who labored in the pit. It had always been accepted that the body should be fortified with alcohol against cold and wet, but two years earlier Peale had defied that dictum, and with success. On an expedition to Cape May with Jotham Fenton, Fenton's weakness for the bottle had become apparent. No strong spirits were forthcoming for either, therefore, in spite of storm and stress, and they came through in fine shape.[10]

The major task of pumping water cost Peale nothing. As in 1794 he had moved the Museum to Philosophical Hall by a parade of boys, at the excavation site he found youths aplenty in the ever-present crowd who were eager for a chance to walk inside the great wheel, laughter and shouts, back and forth, inside and out, 1,440 gallons an hour.

When the expedition, in its search for an underjaw and perfect skull, moved on to Captain Joseph Barber's and other sites, Rembrandt's ingenuity came into play. He had a blacksmith make a number of slender pointed steel rods. These could be thrust easily through the swamp mold, so that one could easily judge the nature of what their point might strike, whether rock, soft root, or a hard substance between rock and root—a bone.

As Peale reported to Jefferson soon after, his work at Masten's had retrieved part of the sternum or breastbone, all the remaining vertebrae and part of the sacrum, a tibia and fibula, as well as those fragments of underjaw and the second tusk. "Some inconsiderable additions of carved pieces," he wrote, "will render this a tolerable compleat skeleton." Still unsatisfied, however, they moved a few miles westward into the township of Montgomery, on lands of Captain Barber and Peter Millspaw, where they expended much labor but with highly satisfactory results.

> . . . I determined to try at some other morasses where some few bones had before been found. I went to a morass 16 miles distant from this where only 3 ribs had been taken up. Here I obtained 43 bones of the feet, 10 tail bones, 2 Tusks, many ribs, some Vertebrae, and a blade bone. I found these bones scattered in every direction, and some of them buried between large stones & even under them, tho' the stones that covered them were not large. After digging about 40 feet square, and spending about 8 or 9 days of several mens labour, I went to another morass 5 miles further, where several bones had been taken up, but as no part of the head had been found, my hopes were particularly to obtain that part. Here I found the bones more scattered than at the last place. This part of the morass was not so deep as those I had explored before. After finding a

number of ribs & some few bones of the feet, and having dug up the manure to a very considerable distance round, in the moment of despairing of getting any more bones and thinking to discharge the labourers—by means of a spear which we used we luckily discovered other bones—which uncovered prooved to be a fore leg beneath which was an intire under Jaw—not a part deficient except one of the lesser grinders, which appears to have been lost while the animal lived. Here we also found part of a foot. From this spot to where we found the heel of the hind foot measured 82 feet. After exploring in every direction [we] at last found the upper head, but in such total decay that no part would hold together except the enamel of the grinders & that part which joins the neck. The place the skull once occupied appeared to be a little blacker than other parts of the mud. The form in part was discoverable, although all was converted into manure, yet it would seperate and shew the rounded parts. All these morasses where these bones have been found have marly bottoms. Bones found in the whitest shell marle are most perfect, those parts found in a bluish coloured marle less so, and bones found in the black marles generally in total decay. The experience I have had enables me to judge with certainty; several bones we have found exhibit these facts in the clearest point of view. The shell marle it is probable possesses much anticeptic qualities. The spring water is also essential to the preservation of the bones. I have brought specimens of the different strata where these bones are found and Doctr. Woodhouse has promised to analyze them for me. When I undertook this journey I was under considerable apprehension of subjecting myself to putrid or bilious fever, by Exposure to a hot sun or great quantity of rotten vegetables &c., also with the addition of much stagnant water. And although the weather was extremely hot and some of the morasses & Ponds were surrounded by woods that prevented the passage of the winds—yet we enjoyed good health. Perhaps the precautions I used in a great measure guarded our health, but I am much inclined to believe that those morasses are not so unhealthy as many people have immagined—For many Gentlemen of that country marveled how I could enjoy health undergoing such fateague. The Bones found in that country are not petrified like many of those found on the Ohio—yet in the vicinity of those morasses we found immence quantities of Petrifactions of shells & even nuts—and what I thought extraordinary near the last place we explored, we found a considerable quantity of petrified Corals, some of which are large. I do not find any saltness in the taste of substances found in those morasses—but on the contrary the water which we took from the springs was the most pure and agreable that I ever meet with. It was so clear as not to impede the sight of the bottom of the deepest vessel that held it.

When we take a view of the mountains through which the North River passes, the Idea naturally occurs that probably once those waters were dam[m]ed up by those mountains and thurce formed a great Lake from thence to the Shawangunk Mountain. Such I find has been the oppinion of many. . . .

But to leave conjectures, and return to the bones. The great quantity we collected at the two last explored morasses with those that had been before taken . . . will enable my son Rembrandt by the aid of his chizel to carve in wood all the deficiencies in order to compleat a second skeleton—with which he hopes to pay his expences of traveling into Europe. He has now long wished to improve his talents in Painting and I am happy to have it in my power to aid him, more especially as by the exhibition of it, there is a chance of his making something handsome and at the same time make an exchange of the duplicate subjects I possess for those of Europe yet wanting in my Musuem, besides settling a good and sure correspondence for a reciprocal exchange of Natural Subjects. It is supposed that a great deal of money may be made in London & Paris with such a Skeleton, but I am taught not to be so sanguine in my expectations. If he can meet all his expences and take the portraits of distinguished characters in the large Cities of Europe, and gain more knowledge with a small addition to his purse it will be well. The first Skeleton might soon be erected in the Museum but the necessity of keeping it apart until my Son had made up the deficiencies of the 2d Skeleton will be a cause of some delay.

Doctr. Wistar has been so obliging as to aid me with his knowledge in the disposition of the Bones, and he is now determining the analogy of the feet of this Animal & the Elephant.

Having now given a detail of what I conceive to be most interesting on this occasion, I shall only add that it is my intention to explore other places as soon as I have leisure and season and opportunity shall be most favorable. Having borrowed some money from the Philosophical Society, which with what I collected elsewhere was sufficient to pay all my expences, this I am fully satisfied, will be returned to me as soon as the exhibition of this Skeleton is opened, when I shall be enabled to fulfill all my engagements. Therefore with the present prospect it is not necessary to gain other pecuniary aid. My Museum under its present visitations supplies the common exigencies of the family, and a little more by our frugality to enable me to persue some of my plans of Emprovements that are not very expensive. Therefore permit me to return you my most cordial thanks for your kind intention of serving your much obliged friend

and Humble Servant
CWPeale[11]

When the expedition returned, on September 19, 1801, Peale found passports for all of South America awaiting him, with a promise of further cooperation. No matter. Now the mammoth was everything holding all his attention. The preliminary work of reconstruction alone would take three months. In this he gave credit not only to Dr. Wistar's expert knowledge but also to the guesswork of others. The rough zest with which the bones at Masten's had been dragged from the pit had created many puzzles.

Fixing the ox chains, perhaps, to one of the tusks broke the upper part of the head to pieces, and the under part of the upper Jaw is the only part that could be connected, which extends from the middle of the socket of the tusk through the orbits of the Eyes holes to the hind head. The tusk was also broke into three pieces, but the fractures being put together gave the true curve and twist of this enormous tusk, 11 feet in length. The fractures also of the several pieces of the head, fitting nicely together, produced the true form, but they could not be found out but [by] numberless tryals of puting first one piece, then another, together, and turning them in every direction. The most expert anatomist could not have found the fitting of a fracture better [than] those of the least knowledge, as was exemplified by the fact that Moses Williams fitted pieces together by trying, [not] the most probable, but by the most improbable position, as the lookers-on believed. Yet he did more good in that way then any one among those employed in the work . . .

The leg bones being put together with hinged joints, and a strong bar of Iron passing through the vertebrae of the back and neck, [this was] then connected with the head, and the ribs put in their several places. . . . [12]

The identity of the two skeletons was kept intact, and lacks in one were replaced by carved replicas based on the other. The Masten skeleton was given a wooden lower jaw copied from Rembrandt's specimen, found on the Millspaw land. Peale fashioned the top of the head of papier mache, working from an elephant's skull, and painted a horizontal red line around it to indicate that all above was conjectural. The work was done in the family parlor at the Hall, which, 15 feet high and 26 feet long, had very little space to spare.[13] As finally mounted, the skeleton stood 11 feet high at the shoulder, 9 feet at the hips; the chest 5 feet, 8 inches wide and the body 17 feet, 6 inches long from tusk to tail. Though the height of the animal was somewhat exaggerated, the effort of all concerned to achieve an authentic reconstruction had been sincere. Two years later, over Dr. Wistar's protest, Peale would add "cartilege" between the bones, an increase in size for which he felt he had scientific justification.[14]

Now, however, debts and personal expenses close to two thousand dollars must be met—the society's loan to him was overdue—and these the mammoth must be made to pay.[15] A "Mammoth Room" was created in the southeast chamber of the Hall, at a separate admission charge of fifty cents. Members of the society were invited to its opening on the evening of December 24, 1801. Handbills made all that could be made of a Shawnee legend of the thundering monster of "ten thousand moons ago," and the versatile Moses Williams dramatized that idea, wearing a feathered headdress and riding through town on a white horse with a trumpeter going before. The populace flowed in, and none was disappointed. There it stood, ghostly and tremendous, "the LARGEST of terrestrial beings"—"the ninth wonder of the world!!!"[16]

All this ballyhoo brought a roar of laughter from the younger DePeysters; it was good fun that would help bring back the money they had advanced. But added publicity was scarcely needed, for the

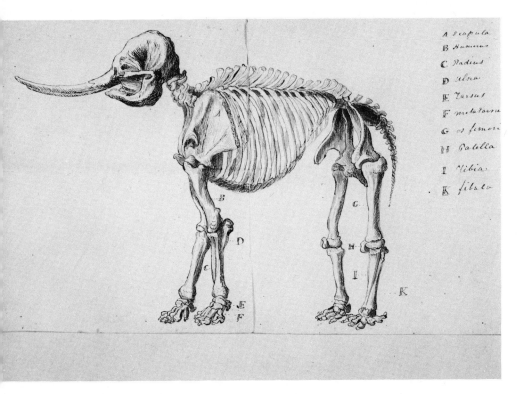

A scapula
B Humerus
C Radius
D ulna
E Tarsus
F metatarsus
G os femori
H Patella
I Tibia
K fibula

MOUNTING THE GREAT SKELETON
Putting the mastodon bones back into their natural form
posed many problems. Rembrandt Peale's drawing of 1801
was intended as a guide in this work. (American
Philosophical Society.)

great skeleton was one of those sudden revelations of a remote past,
like "King Tut's" tomb, which capture both popular fancy and
scholarly attention. Peale had won a permanent niche in the history
of paleontology, while for the populace around him this new marvel
of American bigness stirred every heart into a quicker, prouder
beat. The word "mammoth" had burst into the language just as
"atomic" was to do in a later day. A Philadelphia baker began
selling "mammoth bread." In Washington, a "mammoth eater"
devoured 42 eggs in 10 minutes; and the ladies of Cheshire,
Massachusetts, sent a "mammoth cheese," weighing 1,230 pounds,

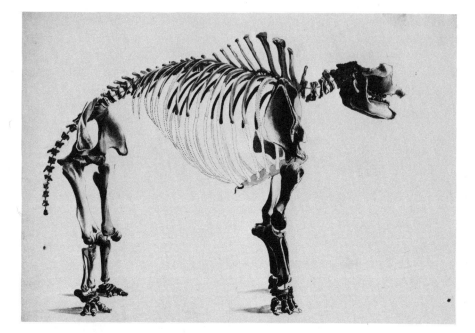

AFTER TWENTY YEARS
Top: In 1821, after returning from the West and beginning his
professional career at the Museum, Titian Peale made this new study of
the mastodon skeleton. (American Philosophical Society.)

TUSKS AND HEAD
Right: Rembrandt Peale's Historical Disquisition on the Mammoth,
or Great American Incognitum *(London, 1803), clear and logical in*
a youthful tone of authority, not only misjudged the teeth to be those of a
carnivore but also erred in the position of the tusks. He first turned them
upward (correctly) but then decided that "This position was evidently
absurd; and there is infinitely more reason in supposing them to have been
placed like those of the Walrus, and probably for a similar purpose."
Edouard de Montulé's lithograph of the Peale reconstruction in his
Voyage en Amerique, en Italie, en Sicile et en Egypte, pendant
les années 1816, 1817, 1818 et 1819 *(Paris, 1821) shows the*
acceptance of Rembrandt's theory and also the reconstruction of the head.
His father painted a red line around the head to make clear where the
original ended and conjecture began.

Titian Peale's drawing of the skeleton, made in 1822, when he
began regular employment at the Museum, indicates that the placing of
the tusks was corrected at that time.

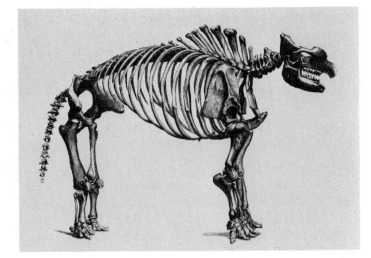

THE WORK COMPLETED

*Engraving after a drawing by Rembrandt Peale (1807), from
Andreas Coenraad Bonn's* Verhandeling over de Mastodonte, of
Mammouth van den Ohio *(Amsterdam, 1809). David Baird of
Princeton has pointed out that Rembrandt's drawing of 1801 has all
the appearance of a "paper reconstruction," whereas this version depicts the
actual mounting and shows the skeleton's one conspicuous lack, the frontal
bone of the head. This rendering was the source of Baron Cuvier's folio
plate in his* Les Ossemens Fossiles des Quadrupedes *(1812).*

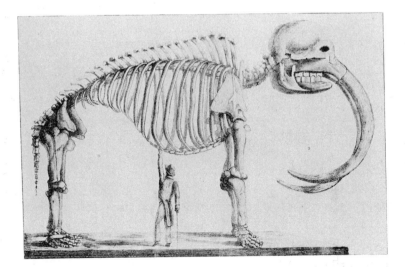

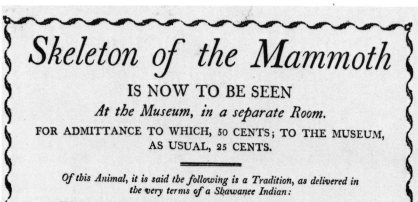

Skeleton of the Mammoth

IS NOW TO BE SEEN
At the Museum, in a separate Room.

FOR ADMITTANCE TO WHICH, 50 CENTS; TO THE MUSEUM,
AS USUAL, 25 CENTS.

Of this Animal, it is said the following is a Tradition, as delivered in the very terms of a Shawanee Indian:

" TEN THOUSAND MOONS AGO, when nought but gloomy forests covered this land of the sleeping Sun, long before the pale men, with thunder and fire at their command, rushed on the wings of the wind to ruin this garden of nature----------when nought but the untamed wanderers of the woods, and men as unrestrained as they, were the lords of the soil-----a race of animals were in being, huge as the frowning Precipice, cruel as the bloody Panther, swift as the descending Eagle, and terrible as the Angel of Night. The Pines crashed beneath their feet; and the Lake shrunk when they slaked their thirst; the forceful Javelin in vain was hurled, and the barbed arrow fell harmless from their side. Forests were laid waste at a meal, the groans of expiring Animals were every where heard; and whole Villages, inhabited by men, were destroyed in a moment. The cry of universal distress extended even to the region of Peace in the West, and the Good Spirit interposed to save the unhappy. The forked Lightning gleamed all around, and loudest Thunder rocked the Globe. The Bolts of Heaven were hurled upon the cruel Destroyers alone, and the mountains echoed with the bellowings of death. All were killed except one male, the fiercest of the race, and him even the artillery of the skies assailed in vain. He ascended the bluest summit which shades the source of the Monongahela, and roaring aloud, bid defiance to every vengeance. The red Lightning scorched the lofty firs, and rived the knotty oaks, but only glanced upon the enraged Monster. At length, maddened with fury, he leaped over the waves of the west at a bound, and this moment reigns the uncontrouled Monarch of the Wilderness in despite of even Omnipotence itself."

[*Carey's Museum, December,* 1790,—*page* 284.]

Ninety years have elapsed since the first remains of this Animal were found in this country----they were then thought to be the remains of a GIANT: Numerous have been the attempts of scientific characters of all nations, to procure a satisfactory collection of bones; at length the subscriber has accomplished this *great object*, and now announces that he is in possession of a SKELETON of this ANTIQUE WONDER of North America; after a long, laborious and uncertain enterprize. They were dug up in Ulster county, (State of New York) where they must have lain *certainly* many hundred years-------no other vestige remains of these animals; nothing but a confused tradition among the natives of our country, which states their existence, *ten thousand Moons ago ;* but, whatever might have been the appearance of this ENORMOUS QUADRUPED when clothed with flesh, his massy bones can alone lead us to imagine; already convinced that he was the LARGEST of *Terrestial Beings!*   C. W. PEALE.

NB. *The Mammoth and Museum will be exhibited by lamp light, every evening, (Sunday evenings excepted) until* 10 *o'Clock.*

[*Printed by John Ormrod.*]

Skeleton of the mastodon at Philadelphia. From Child's First Book of History *(1831).*

as a gift to the new President of the United States, who welcomed it as "an ebullition of the passion of republicanism in a state where it has been under heavy persecution."[17]

Federalists mocked and jeered, but their opponents were riding high. Rembrandt Peale devised his own ebullition as a send-off for his tour abroad with the second skeleton: a farewell dinner of thirteen gentlemen seated under the great skeleton in Philosophical Hall, followed by patriotic and political toasts downed to the music of John I. Hawkins' Patent Portable Grand Piano. On this note, he and Rubens took their "pet" to New York for a showing that would pay their passage to England. Rembrandt, though, enjoying the hoopla to the full, meant nonetheless to win whatever he could of the learned world's more temperate acclaim. Having shared in the discovery, he intended to stand as an authority and, in the main, carried out his intention well.

Dr. Mitchill's *Medical Repository* made the formal announcement of Peale's accomplishment.[18] Peale himself thought of bringing out a definitive exposition with plates, but Rembrandt, a year later, would do that in London. Then he thought to revive the Museum catalogue with a whole chapter on the mammoth, but Rembrandt's London debts would forestall that. In any event, Peale had too much on his hands, too many more prestigious authorities around him, and his mind was too firmly fixed on his ultimate goal, a national museum.

Jefferson was one of several who came forward at this time with offers of help, particularly to verify the form of the head. Their efforts brought from the West a huge skull that, though it turned out to be from a totally different, oxlike monster, warmed the Peale heart with an urge to explore new sites. Beauvois and Geoffroy were in touch with him again, and Cuvier was eagerly awaiting casts which Peale had promised to send. An eminent German naturalist, Johann Christian Daniel von Schreber of Erlingen, sought correspondence and exchanges through French introductions.[19] That strange little roving naturalist, Constantine Samuel Rafinesque, Turkish-born of French and German parents, was then in Philadelphia and forwarded to Peale the four volumes of Francois Marie Daudin's charming new treatise on birds, with the author's request for an exchange of specimens.[20] Philippe Rose Roume, French scientist who had been on a political mission to the West Indies, was now in Philadelphia, and in his contacts with government officials warmly and boldly commended Peale's plan for a national museum like that of France.[21]

Peale, facing the future with his own exuberance, meant to ride the wave. He saw and sensed excitement everywhere, saw it touching the new seats of state and national power, Lancaster and Washington. As ever, he was ready with a plan, a new one, but tested by experience.

He had the help of one good friend, Benjamin Henry Latrobe, America's first professional architect. Latrobe, who had been present at that special meeting on July 24 when the Philosophical Society had voted to become a partner in the exhumation, now drew preliminary designs for a museum building to extend the entire length of State House Yard on the Walnut Street side. Here was a tangible, full-scale objective for all to see. The Legislature would be asked to authorize a lottery to finance its construction, and the building would belong to the state but be managed by the Museum. The public would gain a handsome edifice, and the Museum a home intelligently adapted to all its purposes.

Privately, Peale could see the arrangement also as a commitment to continuing public support. His concept of a museum reached beyond state boundaries. It would be a national benefit. A scientific institution did not reach an acceptable level and stop there; it lived by growth, and growth meant increasing overhead costs. He understood this, and so did the President of the United States. He wrote to Jefferson, January 12, 1802:

Dear Sir,

The labourious tho' pleasing Task of mounting the Mammoth Skeleton being done, gives me leisure to attend to other Interests of the Museum.

The constant accumulation of articles not only of this but also of other countries—increasing my imbarresments to know how to dispose them for exhibition and public utility—these difficulties I expect will be greatly encreased after my Sons have visited Europe and made the exchanges of subjects of Natural History contemplated.

Things huddled togather as I am now obliged to put them, loose much of their beauty and usefulness. They cannot be seen to advantage for study.

I have long contemplated that by Industry such a variety of Interesting subjects might be collected in one view as would enlighten the minds of my countrymen and demonstrate the importance of diffusing a knowledge of the wonderful and various beauties of Nature more powerful to humanize the mind, promote harmony, and aid virtue, than any other School yet imagined. That in the end these labours would be crowned in a National Establishment of my museum— Here I must observe, and it ought never to be forgotten, that the collection which now constitutes my museum is but a *part* of an Establishment which, in becoming National, should embrace the *exhibition of every article* by which Knowledge, in all its branches, can possibly be comunicated.

Mr. Latrobe has made a design for a Building extending from 5th to 6th Street, the south side of the State House Garden, which I mean to offer for the consideration of the Legislature of this State now in session (the substance of which I enclose you) that some grant will be made to erect such a Repository to preserve this museum.

Before making my application I wish to know your sentiments on this subject, whether the United States would give an encouragement and make provision for the Establishment of this Museum in the City of Washington.

The income by visitations to a museum *there* would be far short of what may be had in any of our larger Cities, for many years to come. Yet if some funds were provided to make up such deficiencies, the donations which would naturally flow in would amply repay the expence.

I need not attempt a detail of the benefits of a well organized museum—or how it might be conducted to enhance its value to the Public. Your knowledge of the subject is superior to any thing I can suggest. I can only say, for the preservation of animal subjects, the mode I practice, I have good reason to believe, is much superior to those in general use in Europe.

I should not have chosen the time of the Session of Congress to intrude on your precious moments, but that it is of consequence that my application to the state Legislature should not be delayed. I hope my apology will be accepted.

The Mammoth Skeleton is admired by numbers—and many encomiums are bestowed on my labours of puting it together. I long for the favour of your visit, which will be highly gratifying to

your obliged Friend
CWPeale[22]

The President replied at once:

Washington, January 26th, 1802

Dear Sir:

I received last night your favor of the 12th instant. No person on earth can entertain a higher idea than I do of the value of your collection nor give you more credit for the unwearied perseverance and skill with which you have prosecuted it, and I very much wish it could be made public property, but as to the question whether I think the U.S. would encourage or provide for the establishment of your Museum here? I must not suffer my partiality to it to excite false expectations in you, which might eventually be disappointed. You know that one of the great questions which has decided political opinion in this country is whether Congress is authorized by the constitution to apply the public money to any but the purposes specially enumerated in the Constitution? Those who hold them to the enumeration, have always denied that Congress has any power to establish a National Academy. Some who are of this opinion, still wish Congress had power to favor science, and that an amendment should be proposed to the constitution, giving them such power specifically. If there were an union of opinion that Congress already possessed the right, I am persuaded the purchase of your Museum would be the first object on which it would be exercised, but I believe the opinion of a want of power to be that of the majority of the legislature.

I have for a considerable time been meditating a plan for a general university for the state of Virginia, on the most extensive and liberal scale that our circumstances would call for and our faculties meet. Were this established, I should have made your Museum an object of the establishment, but the moment is not arrived for proposing this with a hope of success. I imagine therefore the legislature of your own state furnishes at present the best propsect. I am much pleased at the success which has attended your labors on the Mammoth. I understand you have not the frontal bone. If this be so, I have heard of one in the western country which I could and would get for you. On this I need your information. I shall certainly pay your labors a visit, but when, heaven knows. Accept my friendly salutation and respect,

Thomas Jefferson[23]

As far as the nationalization of Peale's Museum was concerned, Jefferson had stated his position, and would stay with it. Strict interpretation of the constitutional powers was a fundamental principle of their party. Any deviation from it pointed to new Alien and Sedition Acts, vast military forces, secret agencies, and other Old World instruments of tyranny. And as far as a constitutional amendment was concerned, Peale now knew very well what opposition and delays that would encounter. His reply to the President, on January 21, is one of courteous acquiescence but also shows clearly that he attributed the refusal to political expediency rather than principle.

"With respect to the application to Congress," he wrote, "your communication has satisfied my mind, that at least from the diversity of opinion, if not from the present nature of the Constitution, it would be an unproductive one."

He was right, and would later see Jefferson ready to sponsor direct Congressional support of an educational project that held a fair promise of bipartisan support. Peale understood but yielded nothing of what he believed should be done, and must be done eventually. Without waiting for "the grand plan you have in contemplation for your native state," he was turning to his own state with the plan for a building on State House Yard. He enclosed his draft of a formal proposal to be made first to Pennsylvania. If rejected, it would go to other states, "or the United States." In it he offered two alternatives: first, "a suitable building," or, alternately, "Purchase the Museum in toto & provide for its maintenance and perfection by suitable Regulations and appropriations, and thus lay the foundations of an establishment which the wisdom and policy of all nations have encouraged."[24]

Peale's old friend Andrew Ellicott was back in Philadelphia, preparing his survey of the Florida boundary for publication, and the two had a long talk together on hopes, doubts, and chances. Would Pennsylvania vote "Yea" or "Nay"—dedicate some site in the city to natural history or "disinherit the child of her bosom"? Where could he turn then? "Every exertion in my power for 16 years" had brought the Museum to "considerable maturity"; yet how many others would look forward to the day when it would have "13 professors, men of conspicuous talent, giving lectures in the various branches of science"?

Back at his desk, he poured out continuing thoughts in a letter to Ellicott. Now he had changed his mind about giving the

Museum the subtitle "Temple of Wisdom." He did so with regret. "Altho' I like the word Temple, I must give it up for some name more humble and appropriate." Holding and revealing such abundant proof of the Creator's wisdom, he would never yield to specious popular attractions as his imitators had.

> I neglect many little contrivances which might serve to catch the Eye of the gaping multitude, but I rather prefer a steady perseverence to gain experience to execute such improvements as may tend to give a scientific cast, as being most effectual to make deep and lasting impressions on those who come to study the subjects of the Museum, and although this direction of my labour may not be immediately so productive of funds, yet it will ultimately be more important to the Institution and honorable to me.[25]

Nor did he need such "little contrivances" when he had the mammoth towering over all. The fact now was that the Peale proposal of building and lottery had a good chance of success—and one which reputable citizens of Philadelphia, among them many Peale friends, were beginning to view with alarm. There was a danger of losing the town's only true park, "State House Garden." It was quite within the power and thrifty mood of the Assembly not only to authorize the Latrobe building but to sell all the rest of the square for homes or shops. Strong recommendations came from the City Councils and Philosophical Society that the Museum be granted use of the State House, and no more. That would keep the Yard intact, menagerie and all; Peale would be happy, and the Museum become more than ever a municipal attraction.

This time there was no delay. By a joint resolution of March 12, 1802, Peale was granted use of all the upper floors of the main building and tower. He could also have the east room below (scene of the signing of the Declaration of Independence), provided that it be available, as always, on election days.[26] He was profuse in his thanks to all concerned, and hopeful still of much more. The members of the Assembly (not all of whom had voted for the resolution) would receive free Museum tickets, and their names would be inscribed and prominently displayed. The City Councils were extolled for supporting not only "an ornament to the City, but a foundation of a great national school of universal knowledge of which the present Museum is but a part."[27]

Work began at once. Partitions were taken down and

reerected, so that the old Assembly Room on the east, where Peale had sat as a member in 1779–1780, was cut in half to make a 100-foot main gallery, the whole length of the Chestnut Street front. This would be the heart of the Museum; here the great collection of birds would be arranged along the wall facing the tall windows, all in "classical" arrangement from Rapaces to Rasores, vulture to dove, and Grallatores to Natatores, the water birds, gallinule to grebe. The birds, below, and portraits, above, would have a softer light from the windows on that wall. Between the windows he would set up special collections, and, center, the music (harmony of sound, harmony of Nature), a small organ loft with a really fine organ as soon as he could afford it. Here, too, he placed Hawkins' newly invented silhouette tracer. John Isaac Hawkins was planning a return to England to exploit another invention, the polygraph, a device by which two or more pens moved on the paper in unison. He made Peale a gift of the "physiognotrace" rights and appointed him the American agent for the polygraph—though their expectations for the two inventions would be reversed: profiles became a popular fad, but the polygraph had only a limited sale.

Space did not yet permit complete departmentalization, but it seemed to be coming within reach. There was a good-sized entrance lobby, where Peale placed his electrical apparatus ready for demonstration, an apt introduction to a scientific scene. Two other large flanking rooms, each forty feet in length, were devoted to quadrupeds and marine life. The initial installation was quickly achieved, but after that the work moved slowly through the next two years and more.

> I have more subjects now ready to put into the Museum than I ever had at one time, and really am overwhelmed with Labour—besides the difficulties which are daily increasing for want of Room, at least to put things in their proper places—and I am determined not to exhibit any thing which shall not be nearly in classical arrangement.[28]

Glass chandeliers above and a new catalogue framed in beaded gilt for each group of exhibits added "a neatness, nay elegance, to the whole appearance."[29] As for a designation of the entire complex, it still wavered between "American Museum" and "Philadelphia Museum." Its newspaper announcements would be headed simply "The Museum," in fine contempt for burgeoning rivals. Over the main door on the Chestnut Street side, a sign now read:

MUSEUM
GREAT SCHOOL OF NATURE

For those entering from the Yard, there was a more succinct

SCHOOL OF WISDOM

beneath which some lines from *Injur'd Innocence* were inscribed:

The Book of Nature open
—explore the wondrous work,
an institute of Laws eternal.

Finally, as one approached the State House stair, a sign invited "Whoso would learn Wisdom, let him enter here."[30]

"School" . . . "Temple" . . . his mind still moved longingly from one to the other. "Temple" could not be risked, even though study may be seen as a first approach to worship. Publicity must be a link to the student as well as a summons to all. He wrote to Rubens and Rembrandt in England, on August 20, 1802, of his plan to buy a printing press. Handbills could be turned out readily—though that, he confessed, savored "of Bowen's plans to make money. No matter, provided I do not disgrace the Character of a Naturalist by too much puffing." They all remembered Daniel Bowen, seafighter of the Revolution who had been in and about with a waxwork show after the peace, intent upon making his fortune. He had bought up Robert Edge Pine's paintings and at the same time branched out into natural history, with some help from Peale. Rather than compete with a friend, Bowen had taken the show to New York, then Boston, where his Columbian Museum was now a fixture—the earliest freewheeling imitation of Peale's.

"The Museum Press" was at least a step toward a publication program like that of Paris. Labels, too, could be printed on it, along with framed catalogue pages, the Museum *Guide,* and all this tied in with Peale's thought—Benjamin Franklin in mind—of making one of his younger sons a printer. His letter to the boys in England is full of cautionary advice, news of Beauvois, Geoffroy, Cuvier, Daudin, and high hopes for new acquisitions by exchange. An ornithologist in Antwerp, Louis Wellens, had sent a consignment of birds; perhaps this could be balanced by birds the boys had brought with them for exchange. Dr. Woodhouse had gone abroad with letters of introduction from Peale and was back with a gratifying report. "Dr. Woodhouse speaks in raptures of Paris.

Of grains are Mountains form'd.

To advance the intereſt of the Muſeum, or Repoſitory of Nature and Art, is indirectly conducing to the public benefit; permit me therefore, to join my aſſurances of obligation for any aſſiſtance you may render the inſtitution by

And ſince it is from the ſcience, zeal and liberality of individuals that we muſt be indebted for the developement of Nature's boundleſs ſtores, as well as the ingenuity of art; it ſhall be my endeavour ſo to diſpoſe of them as may inſure their preſervation and public utility.

Sir, with reſpect,

Muſeum, Philadelphia,   180

In conjunction with expansion of the Museum into the State House in 1802, Peale designed this formal gift acknowledgment.

Their museum is splendid—and it is flattering to me that he thinks mine superior to what he saw in London, and in some respects little inferior to any."[31]

When this word reached them, however, the boys were encountering difficulties. They had landed at Brighton—Rembrandt, aged twenty-four, with Eleanor and their two baby daughters, and eighteen-year-old Rubens. The New York exhibition had netted two thousand dollars and they could afford to linger in pleasant surroundings before moving on to London for the season. Unluckily, the war with France would prevent a tour of the Continent, and in England there was little interest in fossil remains when Napoleon was threatening invasion. They toured the country collecting minerals and were in London from September 1802 to June 1803. Their father's introductions to Benjamin West and Sir Joseph Banks opened doors. Rembrandt entered the Royal Academy classes, but was expelled for misbehavior—a prank played on West. Rubens attended the lectures of Dr. John Heaviside, owner of an anatomical museum, and of the anatomist Sir Everard Home, brother-in-law of Dr. John Hunter, whose museum had just been transferred from government ownership to the Royal College of Surgeons.[32]

Sir Joseph invited the young men to the library breakfasts at his mansion in Soho, bringing them into informal contact with scientists and scientific thinking. He arranged passes for them to the then closely restricted British Museum. It was all a maturing experience, as one can see from the succession of Rembrandt's writing on the mammoth—progressively more temperate and knowledgeable—the broadside he issued in New York, the London pamphlet of October 1802 (dedicated to Sir Joseph), and finally his *Disquisition* of July 1803, with its dedication fully acknowledging the credit due his father. Throughout, Rembrandt did cling to his theory that the beast had been a carnivore, a point on which others remained skeptical.[33]

A tour through Bath, Bristol, and Reading showed the provinces to be as apathetic to American wonders as London had been, and with the coming of autumn the little party embarked for home, bringing with them their principal creditor, a London bookseller, as an immigrant. Their father, meeting this new debt, consoled himself with their presence and the meager collections they had brought back, chiefly minerals and fossils. Rubens had left thirty-two birds with Dr. John Latham, author of the *General Synopsis of Birds,* for which others were to be sent in exchange, and had arranged an exchange of birds and insects with an obscure and transient scholar, Leopold von Fichtel.[34] It came to very little beside all the paternal visions at the outset—triumphal tour, direct rapport and exchange with all the great museums, financial success crowned by a sale of the skeleton to France for a smashing sum. "But," Peale reflected, "they are good boys and I have no doubt will do well."[35]

Poulson's of November 22, 1803, had picked up the news of their return from the *New-York Morning Chronicle,* a facetious item:

> MAMMOTH'S RETURN.—We are happy to hear of the safe arrival of our great fellow countryman, the Mammoth and *suite.*
>
> Various reasons have been given for his abrupt departure from Great Britain, some say that he was expelled as an *Alien,* others that Mr. Peale was apprehensive he might be seized as a war horse for the first consul, and others again, that Mr. P. had heard of the voracious appetite of the French soldiers, as also of their late invention of extracting soup from *bones,* and feared his precious skeleton might be stewed down into a kettle of "bone soup" for to refresh the army, after the *grand expedition.*

Rembrandt and Raphaelle took the second skeleton on tour through the South that winter. Rubens attended lectures on mineralogy and botany at the University, and was urged by Dr. Wistar to become a physician, the basic training of so many naturalists. Museum management was becoming his goal, however, and his father was trusting him with more and more responsibility. At eighteen, Sophy, with Betsy's cheerful, careful training, had taken over much of the management of home life at the Hall, including two noisy, intractable half-brothers Lin and Frank, little Sybilla Miriam, and two other infants, the last of Betsy's brood. A second Titian Ramsay Peale had been born in 1799, and two years later Betsy's feeling for family namesakes was satisfied with an Elizabeth DePeyster.

Now another child was due soon after Christmas. The time came and passed, in mounting anxiety. "Ah, Charles, if I live I shall be a better wife to you than I ever have been." Betsy died in childbirth, February 19, 1804, and the child too was lost.

Betsy had had much to contend with in a large family, with menagerie and museum attached. When once asked in an emergency to take tickets at the door, she had made it quite clear that a lady born and bred was not to be seen in such a situation. To keep house in the Philosophical Hall was enough. She acquiesced, however, when her husband, who occasionally favored a phrase from his soldiering days, advertised the Museum as a haven to which lost children could be brought and commissioned her "Mother General." That had been in the summer of 1802, the time when Sophy had accidentally spilled a pot of boiling syrup on the Mother General's foot. The head of the house had his own sovereign remedy for burns, cold water. Cold water brought on a catarrhal fever, but that in turn yielded to treatment in the Patent Portable Steam Bath. When it was over, Peale congratulated himself upon having resisted the urgings to call a doctor. Too many people were dying of their "mercurial treatments."

But now, in spite of all that Dr. Wistar, Dr. Shippen, Dr. James could do, she was gone. They had shared alike a love for neatness and order. "Here in this room," the widower confided to his diary pages, "in that clothes press she kept part of her clothes, also an hundred little matters in such neat and pretty order that she could direct anyone to get the minutest article. She could even in the darkest night lay her hand on whatever she wished to take out. . . . Rest, dear shade, in peace."[36]

Chapter Six

HIGH TIDE (1804–1810)

Shaken, facing a future both clouded by doubts and bright with promise, Peale's life suddenly seemed short, but time more precious and work, more than ever, a solace. He was in his sixty-third year, the Museum beginning its twentieth. In this mood, one week after Betsy's death, he wrote again to the President of the United States:

> Viewing the uncertainty of human life, and wishing my Museum a permanent and important school of useful knowledge, I still continue to exert all my powers to put it into such a situation that those into whose hands it may fall, will have little trouble to put the increase of articles into their proper places. Linneus's classification of animals is framed in the Rooms. The name of each genus and the various specimens numbered, and the Lattin, English and French names placed over each case, so that no visitor ought to expect any attendant to accompany them through the Rooms. This is now nearly compleated in three of the orders, and on almost every other subject is the English name. I am making a new disposition of the Minerals, and as soon as possible I will enter on the general collection of Fishes, what is now done is only a few subjects accidentally obtained, and shortly after this I hope to put together my observations on the most interesting subjects, as a companion to the Museum. When this is done, I may then dispose of my time in any manner that promises to promote this great object. The Museum must be great, as mediocrity will stamp no value on it.[1]

He had enlisted his sons, he added, in a plan to illustrate all the mechanical arts with models, drawings, and explanations. Trades thought difficult would be found easy. Farmers in their off-seasons could turn a profit or amuse themselves. This would open to everyone, in short, an escape from those terrible "pains of ennui," that dreadful sense of unproductive mind and hands.

Jefferson's reply was friendly, with wishes for success in the new plan "as in everything else you undertake. By the immense collection of treasures contained in your Museum you have deserved well of your country, and laid a foundation for their ever cherishing your memory."[2] But more than this was needed fully to restore the Peale resilience. It was coming.

The Louisiana Purchase, doubling the size of the nation, was a triumph for Jefferson that no Federalist could deny, and its first anniversary, on May 12, 1804, was celebrated in Philadelphia with vernal festivity. A great parade came thumping and blaring through the streets, "the young men of Democratic principles" at its head with a huge emblematic banner—a Peale creation beyond any denial—Rembrandt, Raphaelle, Charles Willson, or James, or, likely as not, all together. It showed Liberty enthroned under a palm tree while "an aborigine" representing the United States raised "an aborigine" representing Louisiana from the ground and Minerva soared across the sky above them, symbolic of the wisdom of peaceful expansion.[3] The Museum was illuminated that night, and a transparency painted by Rembrandt Peale, *Apotheosis of General Washington*, filled the great window by the stairs.

Flags were still fluttering in the breeze, General Washington still ascending to Heaven at the Museum, when Friedrich Heinrich Alexander, Baron von Humboldt, stepped ashore at the wharves, home-bound after five years of exploration in South America—a dashing fellow of thirty-five, dark hair, bright blue eyes, radiant health, radiant zest for life and science. Here was great learning, sound sense and laughter all at once, nobly-born, gay, loquacious, informed. His speech was a rapid flow of fact and anecdote, English with a German accent, words and phrases in German, French, or Spanish bubbling along in the current. He had two traveling companions, Aimé Bonpland, a botanist of the National Museum in Paris, and Don Carlos Montúfar, a young gentleman of Quito, Ecuador—two envoys, as it were, one from the world headquarters of natural science, the other from the world's most fertile field for its study.

FRIEDRICH
HEINRICH
ALEXANDER,
BARON VON
HUMBOLDT
*Museum silhouette, 1804.
The great naturalist's
enthusiastic endorsement of
Peale's plan for a national
museum marked the high
tide of that hope. Peale
had a number of profiles
made for presentation to
friends when he brought
Humboldt to Washington
to meet President Jefferson.*

The Prussian baron was a cataract of information and energy, right on the forefront, commanding the future. He was delighted with the Museum, charmed by the Museum's proprietor, and, as he was shown from room to room, became an enthusiastic champion of the national museum idea.

Humboldt had found mammoth bones in South America, "perfectly distinguishable," as Rembrandt Peale reported with satisfaction, "by the great carniverous teeth."[4] However this may be, his tour of the Museum with the Peales began, of course, with the famous skeleton, still at Philosophical Hall. After acquisition of the State House, the Hall had become a three-room annex to the whole, its "Arts and Antiquities" segment. Here the "Mammoth Room" was entered by a door dramatically framed with the jawbones of a whale. A protective rail surrounded the monster where it stood, its size accented by some bones of *Megalonyx jeffersoni,* the giant sloth discovered in Virginia. The more complete *Megalonyx* in the museum at Madrid was shown in engravings on the walls. The skull of a fossil peccary given by Dr. Samuel Brown to the society was also here and, for comparison to the mastodon, a series of smaller skeletons: monkey, greyhound, parrot, ibis, and on down to the smallest, a mouse.[5]

The "Antique Room" and "Model Room" at the Hall held exhibits of archaeology and ethnology, relics of the past as remote as Herculaneum and Pompeii and the South American cultures, costumes and artifacts of American Indians, the Pacific, China, East Indies, and Peale's wax figures of the races. This led on to historical relics such as Oliver Cromwell's inkstand (a gift from Mrs. Washington) and, more importantly, to drawings, paintings, and models of recent inventions. It was becoming a curious and fascinating jumble such as delighted the public but offended Peale's sense of order.

Crossing to the State House past the clamorous menagerie in the Yard, the newcomers climbed the tower staircase to the areas above, where for the first time a consistent scientific arrangement had become possible. From the lobby with its electrical apparatus, they stepped into the "Quadruped Room" of nearly two hundred specimens; the larger were set on pedestals protected by wire screens from careless handling, and the smaller were in glass cases with landscape backgrounds. To Bonpland, with the Paris museum in mind, the American bison would be the only unfamiliar mounting, but there was a decided novelty in the natural attitudes and groupings of all. Turning the corner into the "Long Room," this feature was more strikingly evident in the birds, covering one wall, 100 feet in length and 12 feet high, within 140 cases ("the insides of which are painted to represent appropriate scenery, Mountains, Plains or Waters, the birds being placed on branches or artificial rocks, &c."). This was Peale's most complete representation of one form of life and his nearest approach to what he hoped eventually to have for the whole, in complete Linnaean classification.

Above the birds was the long double row of uniform-size portraits of "the Animal Man." Opposite, between the tall windows, upright cases extended into the room. In one alcove 4,000 insects were shown, with the smaller specimens mounted under microscopes (Jotham Fenton's specialty) adjusted for examination. In another were the minerals, with due emphasis on the beauty of crystals and precious stones but ample representation also of metals and ores and of the native and foreign clays used for porcelain and pottery. Yet another held shells and fossils, and beyond that was another with a miscellany of coins, small objects, and such curios as a tress of the beautiful hair of the albino Miss Harvey, given to Rubens Peale in England. While in the Long Room, the baron paused to have his silhouette taken by Moses at the physiognotrace, in addition to a handful of extra cuttings for friends. Around another turn was the "Marine Room," with its two huge Chama shells, the giant oyster of the eastern tropics (to satisfy the American craving for size perhaps), hammerhead shark, swordfish, and an array of other varieties glistening with varnish, as well as corals, sponges, shells, amphibia, and finally the serpents, living and preserved. All this had begun in that "rocksome height" at Third and Lombard, echoed here in artificial rockwork at the tops of the cases.

It was all fresh and new, glittering glass and fresh paint, brought into coherence by the framed catalogues in each room (frames gilded by Sophy, she and Rubens adding Latin to their French studies in order to master the scientific names). During the tour, Peale had little to say of what was already present, but much of what was to come: "Room! Room! I must have more room." His thoughts were already on adding a second story to each of the State House wings and spreading out on either side.[6] The baron approved. This was a firm foundation for a national museum.

Humboldt met the gentlemen of the Philosophical Society and was eager to meet its president also, then in the White House at Washington. A party was formed to make the journey and introduction: Peale and his steadfast ally Nicholas Collin, an English physician Dr. Anthony Fothergill, with the baron, Bonpland, and Montúfar. It was a happy journey, Humboldt's chatter ranging through every sort of people from jungle tribesmen to European aristocrats. The Prince of Parma? He could tell how His Highness had come to Spain to marry one princess, then had fallen in love with another, and how the switch had been arranged for him by Godoy, the queen's lover, ennobled as the "Prince of Peace."

Humboldt's chatter still has some of its freshness in Peale's diary pages. He told of his interview with the king of Spain, requesting permission to explore South America, and the monarch's astonishment that he would have any reason to do so, at his own expense and suffering "the want of all the necessaries of life" among "a miserable set of mostly savages."

> He says that the King is a good-natured man of tolerable natural powers, yet fond of nothing but Bull baiting and hunting, that he does not trouble himself with any concern

about his government. His prime minister (the Prince of Peace) has the direction of every department of it. The King being a perfect good man has no Idea of the incontinancy of his queen, who enjoys her favorites.

The King is so simple, or rather devoid of suspission of her loose conduct, that he one day asked an old Bishop of Rome if he did not think her child was like the Prince of Peace. The old Priest deliberately put on his spectacles and, exam[in]ing the features of the Child, replied that he thought it was like the Prince of Peace.

This same Prince of Peace was lately elected a member of the American Philosophical Society, altho' by the Baron's account of him he does not possess a single spark of Philosophy, and is quite an unlearned man, not even knowing the french Language.

Peale, embarrassed, suspected John Vaughan had brought up the name to please the Marquis Yrugo, the Spanish ambassador. He himself had given his vote innocently thinking the title must be a new one of the Prince of Parma.[7]

En route, Peale brought the party to his daughter's home in Baltimore. Earlier, in a mood of unusual asperity, he had characterized his son-in-law as a "miserable half-witted blockhead." The "blockhead," who looked upon the Museum as a family disgrace, would now have a chance to see natural history in a more socially acceptable light. Mr. Robinson responded well, playing an amiable host and taking them in his coach to visit the sights of his city. Though affable to the nobleman, he was afterward as cool to museums and museum men as he had been before. His father-in-law shrugged it off. "Alas, poor Aleck!"

On June 4, as recounted in Peale's diary, the six travelers dined with other guests at the White House: "a very elegant dinner at the President's, and what pleased me much, not a single toast was given or called for, or Politicks touched on, but subjects of Natural History, and other improvements in the conveniences of Life. Manners of different nations described, or other agreable conversation animated the whole company."

Secretary of State Madison, with whom Peale had been keeping in touch about his hopes for a national foundation, dined and wined them the next day. Jefferson and Madison alike were as delighted with their guest of honor as everyone else had been, and Humboldt responded with information and advice of value on the exploration of the new western territories. Captains Lewis and Clark had just moved out from St. Louis up the Missouri River on the exploring expedition which Jefferson had planned and held deeply at heart.

On the evening of the Madison dinner, the President and the baron had a private talk, noted in Peale's diary:

> As usual I went to bed before the rest of our company because my habit of rising early rendered it necessary to do so, but shortly the Baron came to my room & told me that he had been conversing with the President about me and my Museum, that he wondered the government did not secure it by a purchase [of] it—for such opportunity of getting so complete a collection of natural subject[s] seldom occured. The President replyed that it was his ardent wish and he hoped that the period was not far distant & he thought that each of the States would contribute means and thus it might be made a National Museum. The Baron seemed pleased with the subject of their conversation & altho he could not relate all that passed, yet he assured me that the President was very much my friend.[8]

One is left with a surmise that Jefferson may have said more than he wished Humboldt to repeat. His concern was sincere, but this was not a matter like the Louisiana Purchase, for which he had brushed constitutional doubts and political opposition aside, sure of the ultimate approval of every citizen. A large sum paid out and a continuing expense for vast corridors, collections, and lecture halls of natural history was quite another matter.

For the baron and his entourage it was a three-week holiday. They drove out to Mount Vernon in two hired hacks. While the others viewed mansion and estate, Peale sat in a cabin in the slave quarters talking with old Billy Lee who had been Washington's body servant through the war, a cripple now—past adventures recalled, and present needs for the preservation of health. They were back in town to dine with the jovial painter-poet-horseracer William Thornton, with Gilbert Stuart equally loud and lively among the guests, and Mrs. Thornton holding their attention, bright-eyed, as she played and sang. Dinner again at the White House and, on the return journey, an interval on Nathaniel Ramsay's plantation by the Chesapeake. The Colonel's cash crop was fish from the bay, and Peale urged him to send any unusual varieties to Philadelphia. "I hope my Museum will embrace generally the American Fishes, which will stamp an immence value on this Repository in the Eyes of Foreign Naturalists, as heretofore no one has much extended the knowledge of what we possess."[9]

Home once more, Peale painted the baron's portrait for the Museum gallery. He had not touched brush to canvas for six years, and to find his hand as sure as ever brought a wave of elation. He must paint a great series of new portraits and go beyond portraiture into subject pieces appropriate to the Museum. He would travel . . . would become an explorer-collector . . . visit Paris . . . tour Europe setting up a chain of cooperation among museums, as he had hoped to see Rembrandt and Rubens do.[10] When the Baron called on June 30, on the French frigate *La Favorite,* he carried letters in this tenor to Geoffroy and Daudin, accompanied by gifts of unusual specimens to underline the proposal.[11] What had begun so fortuitously, he told Ramsay, had now become "a national work—whether I shall live to see my country make such an Establishment I cannot say, but I believe it very probable that I shall gain credit, honor and profit for what I yet can do."[12]

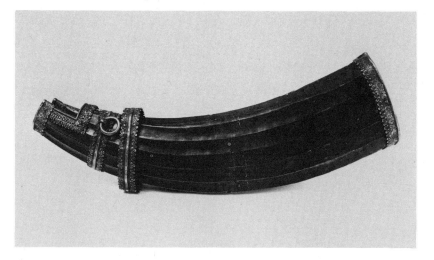

"CANTEENS OF IVORY AND BUFFALO HORN"
These pieces were part of a large gift from George Harrison in 1804. "Embossed helmets" and a coat of fish-scale armor, "covered with crimson velvet richly studded with gold, . . . the Dress of an Emperor or Commander-in-Chief" of India or Persia, came to the Peale collection also and have survived at Harvard (though now in poor condition). Harrison, a young diplomat of the Revolution and

He could now leave Rubens in charge and give all his attention to larger and farther issues. He was in New York in July. A French naturalist, Delacoste, was there with a collection of some five hundred pieces he was offering for sale. Dr. Perrein (he of the rue J'adore L'egalité, Bordeaux) was present also. Delacoste had been welcomed by the scientific community in New York and had himself sent Jefferson a proposal for a national museum.[13] In this instance, the President's reply had been entirely negative. "Abortive attempts," Jefferson wrote, retarded rather than advanced this favorite study of his. Museums in Boston and New York had fallen short of distinction. "In Philadelphia alone has the attempt succeeded to a good degree. It has been owing to a measure of zeal and perseverence in an individual rarely equaled, to a population, crowded, wealthy, and more than usually addicted to the pursuit of knowledge. And, with all this, the institution does not maintain itself."[14]

There, precisely was the crux of the matter. Scientific method,

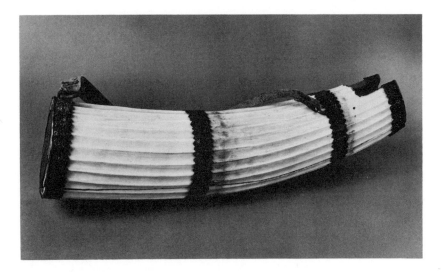

later Navy Agent at Philadelphia, "the most elegant man in American Society," according to Joshua Francis Fisher, shared natural history interests with Peale and made many gifts to the Museum, beginning with South Sea artifacts in 1788, from a voyage of his own. "The Eastern Armour" was a featured display of July 4, 1805. (Peabody Museum, Harvard University.)

maintenance and growth ran to costs far beyond income as a place of amusement. Peale returned from New York with nothing but more fish from the market, a few Delacoste duplicates, and a determination to persevere. "I repeat," he wrote back to John DePeyster, "the old tale of the Museum undergoing improvements. When will this work end? Not while it is under my care."[15]

On this trip, and again in a jaunt to Washington with Rembrandt that winter, Peale was promoting Hawkin's polygraph. He was to smooth out some mechanical difficulties and pay the inventor a royalty of 10 percent on sales. Just such a good copier was needed in the business world, but this one required delicate adjustment and care beyond the ability of the ordinary counting-house clerk. Peale lost out in this venture, though posterity would gain the great mass of Jefferson, Peale, and Latrobe letters from 1803 onward. When father and son called on Gilbert Stuart during their stay in the capital, the old punster greeted them loudly, "So! You have come to take off a few heads of the members of Congress, and to give them a brush, which is much wanting." They took Stuart's head for the Museum gallery. As for Congress, Rembrandt added those of two friends of the Museum, William Findley and Albert Gallatin. Great care was always taken that only primates of distinguished character or scientific interest should appear on the Museum's walls, but this honor was also used to bring influential persons into the circle of its friends and promoters. The two travelers returned home in February, the children crowding happily around them. They had managed so well in his absence, their father told them, that he thought it would be "to his interest to go again abroad."

"Oh! No, dear Papa. Do not leave us. We cannot part with you. If you leave us, we shall certainly run away from the Museum!"[16]

The Washington stay had at least advanced Rembrandt's career as a portrait artist. Rembrandt now had the advantage of a studio on the ground floor of the State House, the "Declaration Chamber," reserved for state use only at election time and used by the Museum itself only for an occasional special exhibit or some other temporary purpose. This summer of 1805 brought also the founding of the Pennsylvania Academy of the Fine Arts, in which both father and son were active participants. Rembrandt was sure that history would credit him with being "chief instigator" of the institution, just as he continued to imagine himself the primary discoverer of the mammoth.[17] His father would always feel a special tenderness for this son, whose laughing boyhood gaiety had been yielding more and more to exalted visions of the glorious profession. It would reawaken the older man's youthful feeling for his art to see his own early aspirations realized in this son. With Rembrandt, he saw only a matter of bringing recognition to obvious talent. With Rubens, management of the Museum was laying the foundation for a career. The problem was Raphaelle.

Raphaelle was all laughter on the surface, a marvelous tavern companion, raconteur, ventriloquist. He could set the table in a roar by making the fowl or fish he was about to carve plead for its life in sepulchral tones. Raphaelle and Patty McGlathery Peale had four children now, Eliza, Sophy, Charles Willson and Edmund, but their father was much away from home, a roving painter and silhouettist. Hawkins had given the Museum free use of his physiognotrace, but Raphaelle extended that privilege to himself, roaming the country from Charleston to Boston, taking profiles by the thousand. When he was at home Patty had much to contend with, though her quick, shrill Irish temper brought her little sympathy. Raphaelle had genius, as his father knew, but was smothering it in alcohol, awakening in sorrow and pain, softly promising better things, then laughing away the failure. He nursed a quiet bitterness toward the Museum, holding it to blame for his crippled arthritic hands—due, he thought, to long immersion in the arsenic solutions.

The father meanwhile, harassed by worries, was seeking a new mate, new wife and mother. He traveled through Maryland in the search as he had done before, and, as before, found her instead on returning to the Museum. Benjamin Latrobe sent the news to the White House:

> Peale is again married I find. This is his third ticket in the lottery of marriage. Prudence would not have advised this risk, for DeMoivre is clearly against him. The last he drew [was] a prize of the first magnitude, and I am told his first was a good one. He has now a fry of five or six little uneducated children about him to whom his daughter Sophonisba was a mother and an excellent and accomplished instructress. However, he is a boy in many respects and unfortunately also in this: that he has saved nothing. It seems not unlikely that he will have a fourth family to provide for—for, in his benevolence he has taken two small *fine* children by adoption to his house.[18]

SOPHONISBA AND COLEMAN SELLERS
Museum silhouettes, 1805.
(Author's collection.)

The third ticket was Hannah Moore, a Quaker maiden lady, aged fifty, and, as the groom frankly described her, "A Person of suitable years to me, a *friend* and uncommonly chearful for her time of life although as plain as any amongst friends."[19] The wedding was performed by a rural justice. Marriage "out of Meeting" was not taken lightly among Friends. Hannah was able to make her peace with the Society, and Peale, who in the past had cast many aspersions on "fanaticks" and "enthusiasts," was able now to express his admiration for the Society's principles of amity and forbearance. This informal wedding in August was followed by another in September—Sophy's to Coleman Sellers, a ruddy-haired, placid young manufacturer, endeared to his father-in-law by his strong mechanical bent and love for the romantic poets and novelists.

The identity of the two adopted children mentioned by Latrobe is unknown. They may have been placed elsewhere, for surely Hannah had a handful enough with Betsy's brood of five, all of them less docile than Rachel's. Trouble signs from the surly, unruly eldest, ten-year-old Linnaeus, may have awakened Peale's fears for the fate of his Museum if a division of his estate should take place. He was writing anxiously of that to Hawkins and others, and

Hawkins's news from London struck a disturbing note: the final dispersal of the Leverian at auction, in May and June, 1806. Some specimens from the sale came to Peale, probably by exchange with Thomas Hall.

Museum dispersal in London . . . museum silence from Paris . . . but a stir of great deeds and promise from far and farthest West, and from Washington. A large consignment of natural history objects from the Lewis and Clark expedition had reached Jefferson in 1805, and at the end of the following summer the explorers themselves returned from the dangerous unknown into which they had disappeared three years before, and were hailed as heroes of the trail they had blazed across the Rocky Mountains to the Pacific shore. What they had sent and brought back held interest and value equal to the moon rocks of a later day. The President wrote to Peale, on October 6, 1805, to tell what he had received and how he was dividing it. The minerals he was sending to the American Philosophical Society. "There are some articles which I shall keep for an Indian Hall I am forming at Monticello." This was the large square entrance hall of the mansion, one side of which would display paleontology, and the other, Indian relics. To Peale he was sending animal skins and skeletons.

THOMAS JEFFERSON'S INDIAN COLLECTION

The President sent many objects from the first official exploring expeditions to Peale's Museum. Others came to the Museum in 1828, after the sale of his Poplar Forest plantation.

WOMEN'S DRESSES, CREE INDIANS

These animalskin garments were obtained by Lewis and Clark from a large band of Cree who had come down the Saskatchewan River to Fort Mandan in November, 1804. That on the left is decorated with blue and white beads and brass buttons (probably obtained from Hudson Bay Company traders), while the hemline has tin pendants and a fringe of deer hair. The dress at right is painted with red and black symbolic figures; blue and green beads are shaped into disks on the bosom and brighten the lower border of the skirt. (Peabody Museum, Harvard University.)

THE PAINTED BUFFALO ROBE, 1797
This Indian warrior's account of a battle is first recorded in the invoice of articles sent
to Jefferson, on April 7, 1805: "1 Buffalow robe painted by a Mandan man,
representing a battle which was fought 8 years since, by the sioux & Ricaras, against
the Mandans, Minitarras & Ahwahharways." Hung by Jefferson on the wall at
Poplar Forest, it is the earliest such painting presently conserved and the most
important relic of the Lewis and Clark exploring party. (Peabody Museum,
Harvard University.)

BIGHORN SHEEP, OR AMERICAN ARGALI

In 1805 Jefferson sent to Peale skins and skeletons brought back by the Lewis and Clark expedition, and with great excitement he reconstructed the hitherto unknown animals and mounted the head of one bighorn to send back to Monticello. Always alert to any possible domestic interest in his attractions, Peale also exhibited the sheep's wool at the Museum. Thomas Doughty drew this plate from the Museum's male and female specimens for his Cabinet of Natural History and American Rural Sports *(1830–34).*

PRAIRIE DOG

The Museum's first specimen of this animal was sent by Lewis and Clark to President Jefferson, and then by Jefferson to Peale in 1805. To Lewis and Clark this was the "Braro, or burrowing dog of the Prairies," and to their guides, "Le Petit Chien des Voyageurs." The men of Pike's expedition called it "Wistonwish," and to Thomas Jefferson it was the "Louisiana Marmotte." George Ord made the first scientific classification, Arctomys ludovicianus. *Watercolor by T. R. Peale (c. 1821). (Private collection.)*

HORNED LIZARD

This was the earliest of the nondescripts sent by President Jefferson to the Museum. Peale replied, on July 24, 1804: "I am greatly obliged to you for the curious Lizard of Louisiana, which it certainly, is, and not a Toad. It shall not be exhibited untill the Osage Indians are on their return. I have not yet had time to examine the Authors to know if it has ever been described; if not, I mean to give a drawing of it to the Philosophical Society." He made the drawing. (American Philosophical Society.)

BIRDS FROM THE LEWIS
AND CLARK EXPEDITION
*Left and right: In gratitude for the
gift of the birds, Charles Willson
Peale made these drawings in May,
1807, to be used as illustrations if
Lewis should publish his journal of
the expedition.* Right: *Mountain
quail.* Right, below: *Lewis
woodpecker.* Left: *Louisiana
tanager.* (American Philosophical
Society.)

PRONG-HORNED ANTELOPE
Working with badly damaged skins and bones, Peale
was able to make this mounting of the newly discovered
species sent by Lewis and Clark to Jefferson in 1805.
This was long the only known example in the East.
From Doughty's Cabinet of Natural History and
American Rural Sports *(1830–34).*

FROM THE PACIFIC COAST
This Chinook woman's skirt of
cedarbark fiber was probably among
"some articles of dress" sent by Lewis
and Clark to Jefferson in 1805. The
basketry hat came from the Nootka
Sound Indians, and a basket of
twined weaving, from the Wasco
Indians of the Columbia River area.
These are described in the Peale
accession list of articles received from
Lewis and Clark as "Hat made by a
Catsop Woman, near the Pacific
Ocean," and "A bag prepared of grass
by the Pishquilpahs on the
Columbia." Meriwether Lewis
(November 21, 1805) mentions
buying hats from the Catsop women
"made of Splits & Strong grass, which
was made in the fashion which was
common in the U States two years
ago," and (February 22, 1806)
purchasing "a parsel of excellent hats
made of Cedar bark and ornamented
with beargrass." (Peabody Museum,
Harvard University.)

HUNTING SHIRT
*Painted and ornamented with porcupine quills, this may be
the piece identified by a Peale Museum label as "Indian
Hunting Shirt made of Buffalo skin. This was formerly
owned and worn by Capt. Clark in his Exploring
Expedition. Presented to Peale's Museum by Capt. Lewis
and Clark."* (Peabody Museum, Harvard University.)

Below: CALUMET, OR PEACE PIPE
*This is possibly one of several Indian pipes sent to Jefferson
from the Lewis and Clark expedition. The two clusters of
feathers represent the male and female elements—the lower
being the female, and the upper (eagle feathers decorated
with tufts representing scalps taken in battle), the male.*
(Peabody Museum, Harvard University.)

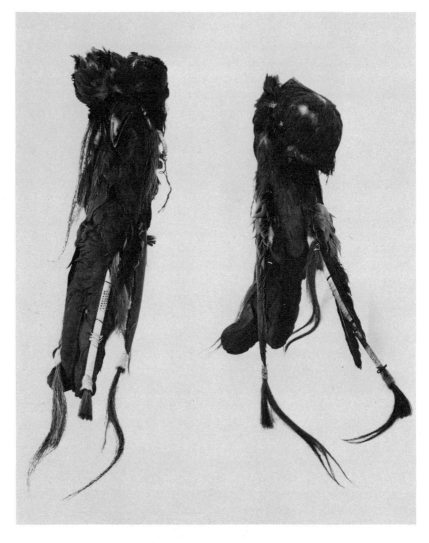

POLICE OFFICER'S BADGE OF AUTHORITY
*These raven feather items were worn by a Sioux Indian
when appointed by his chief to maintain order. According to
Lewis and Clark: "They seem to be a kind of constable or
sentinel, since they are always on the watch to keep
tranquility during the day and guard the camp at night.
The short duration of the office is compensated by its
authority. His power is supreme, and in the suppression of
any riot or disturbance no resistence to him is
suffered. . . . In general he accompanies the person of the
chief and when ordered to any duty, however dangerous, it
is a point of honor rather to die than to refuse obedience.*

*Thus when they attempted to stop us yesterday, the chief
ordered one of these men to take possession of the boat; he
immediately put his arm around the mast, and, as we
understood, no force except the command of the chief would
have induced him to release his hold. Like the other men,
his body is blackened but his distinguishing mark is a
collection of two or three ravens' skins affixed to the girdle
behind the back in such a way that the tails stick out
horizontally from the body."* In this example, the larger
piece was so worn at the back of the belt; the two others were
attached at the elbows. (Peabody Museum, Harvard
University.)

OMAHA TOBACCO POUCH
This quill-decorated otter skin tobacco
pouch of the Omaha tribe was also
part of the Poplar Forest collection.
(Denver Art Museum.)

Below: CROW INDIAN CRADLE
Sent to President Jefferson from one of
the Western exploring expeditions, this
intricately beaded cradle was added to
his Poplar Forest collection. (Peabody
Museum, Harvard University.)

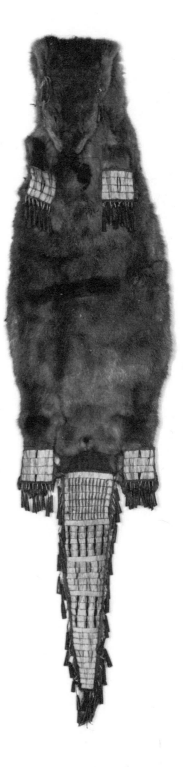

184

*FLUTE AND
WAR WHISTLE*
The flute is probably
Winnebago; the bone
war whistle is an
artifact of the Mandan
Indians. Both came to
the Museum from
Jefferson's Poplar
Forest plantation.
(Peabody Museum,
Harvard University.)

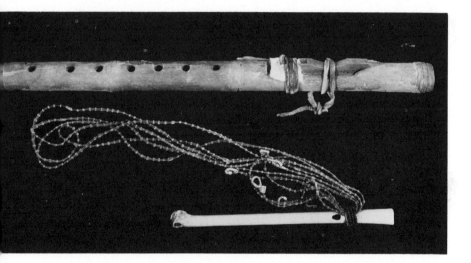

Skins and skeletons, mostly in poor condition, inevitably went to Peale's Museum, since no one else was ready and able to preserve and mount them. The skins at Monticello, buffalo robes, pouches, and clothing, already showed signs of damage by insects, and Peale responded to the President's concern with directions on safeguarding them from further deterioration. A little prairie dog, alias "Marmotte" or "Louisiana Badger," came to the Museum alive and good-natured, but sleepy as winter approached, and Peale acknowledged this gift as the small creature dozed at his side. Skins and skeletons included a variety of squirrels, a "burrowing wolf," a white hare, a weasel, and two large and important new species: the *Argali,* or bighorn sheep, and male and female specimens of a nondescript antelope. Peale mounted one bighorn for the Museum, and the head of another for the wall at Monticello. Wool from the sheep came also, recognizing the Museum's past promotion of such native textile materials as bison's hair.[20]

Peale, always an advocate of plain descriptive names, suggested "forked horned antelope" for the creature which did become known not long afterward as the "pronghorn." It had been a difficult mounting, but he thought the labor worthwhile. It might be long before an undamaged skin or a living animal could be obtained. He presented a paper on the subject to the society, accompanied by a drawing. His nomenclature met with objection. "But, sir, that is not a scientific name." Bridling, Peale turned to his friend in the White House with a sour word for those "who must be humored with high-sounding names made from the dead languages." What would Jefferson suggest to please them? Why not find it in the Indian languages?[21]

Two large magpies reached Philadelphia alive from the West. Also received were the Lewis's woodpecker (now at Harvard's Museum of Comparative Zoology), Clark's crow (or nutcracker), the Louisiana or Western tanager, and a head of the huge California condor. Peale planned to contribute illustrations to the explorers' journal as a grateful return for their gifts to the Museum. Lewis was in some financial difficulties, and this gesture, Peale hoped, would "give considerable profit to the bold adventurer." Three drawings have survived: mountain quail, Western tanager, and horned lizard. George Ord, the naturalist most warmly a friend and partisan of the Peales, remembered a drawing of a partridge also.[22]

There was a closer relationship, somehow, between the Philadelphia artist and the moody, self-doubting Lewis than there would ever be between Peale and the loud-laughing, red-headed extrovert Clark. The lists of Lewis and Clark expedition material entered in the Museum accession book in 1809, and published in *Poulson's American Daily Advertiser* on March 1, 1810, are not wholly complete, but they do show that besides such esoteric things as the bread and roots of Indian diet a good collection of weapons, utensils, and costumes illustrating the life of the tribesmen had come to the Museum. All the material of exhibition quality had not been kept at Monticello. While Clark kept everything of interest that he had brought back for his Indian museum in St. Louis, his partner in the adventure may have given nearly everything of his to Peale. Certainly, the most interesting mementos of all to the Museum came from Meriwether Lewis: the peace pipe and ermine-skin mantle from Cameahwait, chief of the Shoshoni nation in Idaho.[23]

The Shoshonis had contributed enormously to the success of the expedition, and Lewis and Clark's meeting with them had been highly dramatic. Each side was at first suspicious of the other—the Shoshonis especially so since they were in immediate fear of attack by their enemies, the Blackfeet, who like these newcomers were armed with guns. Full cordiality prevailed at last when Sacajawea, the young Indian woman who helped guide the exploring party, recognized Cameahwait as her brother and approached him with tears and strange gestures of affection. Captured as a child by the Minitaris many years before, she had now, unexpectedly, been brought home. Speech replaced sign language as Sacajawea translated from Shoshoni to Minitari, her trapper husband translated this into French, and yet another brought his French into English.

With the feather-decked peace pipe and princely ermine-skin mantle, Peale created an exhibit he hoped would perpetuate that mutual amity felt at Cameahwait's village in August 1805. It was a wax figure of Lewis, wearing the mantle and holding the pipe, as history's lesson for Indian visitors of the future and their white brethren no less—a plea for peace among men. "My object in this work is to give a lesson to the Indians who may visit the Museum, and also to show my sentiments respecting wars," Peale wrote to Jefferson on January 29, 1808. "The figure has its right hand on its breast, and the left holds the Calmut which was given me by Capt. Lewis." A label described the meeting of Captain and Chief, and then added:

> This mantle, composed of 140 ermine skins, was put on Capt. Lewis by Comeawhait, their Chief. Lewis is supposed to

say, "Brother, I accept your dress—it is the object of my heart to promote amongst you, our neighbors, peace and good will—that you may bury the hatchet deep in the ground never to be taken up again—and that henceforward you may smoke the *Calmut* of Peace and live in perpetual harmony, not only with each other, but with the white men, your brothers, who will teach you many useful arts." Possessed of every comfort in life, what cause ought to involve us in war? Men are not too numerous for the lands which we are to cultivate, and disease makes havoc enough amongst them without deliberately destroying each other—If any differences arise about lands or trade, let each party appoint judicious persons to meet together and amicably settle the disputed point.

"I am pleased," the artist concluded, "when I give an object which affords a moral sentiment to the Visitors to the Museum."[24]

Other wax figures were made at this same time: one for the splendid East Indian armor given by George Harrison, another to represent Cameahwait. A life mask was taken for that of Lewis, who posed also for a gallery portrait on canvas. All this was happily discussed over Dr. Wistar's dinner table, where Lewis, newly appointed governor of the Louisiana Territory, was guest of honor—a bright evening long to be remembered in contrast to his lonely and mysterious death in the wilderness, two years later.

But on May 5, 1807, writing to Hawkins in London, Peale was still full of the triumphs of the expedition, his own plan to illustrate its journal, and the musical evenings at the Museum, with Rubens learning to play and Sophy enjoying her Hawkins piano (so much richer in tone than the tinkling common sort). The Academy of Fine Arts' new building was to open soon with paintings by Benjamin West from Robert Fulton's collection. Fulton and Joel Barlow were then both in town, and their portraits had been added to the Museum gallery. The future had begun again to glow with promise.

Barlow, poet and diplomat, had been some years abroad, as had his close friend, the artist and inventor Fulton. Barlow's was the liberal mind most closely in tune with Peale's and Barlow had come home with a proposal which would bring that vision of a national museum alight once more. Establish, he suggested, the national university for which George Washington had left a bequest in his will, but let it be upon a modern model that he and Jefferson could approve. What Washington had urged in his Farewell Address and provided for in his will would surely receive bipartisan support. Jefferson, reading Barlow's prospectus for a "National Institution," was warmly favorable. The model was French, the purpose both teaching and research. The President asked Congress, in December 1806, to initiate a constitutional amendment extending its powers over education and to anticipate passage by providing a land-grant endowment.[25]

Peale, with Franklin, Paine, Rittenhouse, and other friends, had subscribed in 1787 to Barlow's *The Vision of Columbus*. Now the poet's expanded version of his patriotic epic had just appeared, and *The Columbiad* was on exhibition in the Museum as a major landmark in American literature and bookmaking. Peale had written Jefferson on July 4, 1806, urging the Museum's inclusion in Barlow's project, and again on December 13 of that year to express pleasure because the way was at long last being opened for "a great national school."[26]

In that hopeful spring of 1807, the "National Institution" bill was in committee—but there, alas, it would remain. Labor so freely given, faith in the future so cherished, again came to nothing.[27]

"Never mind." Peale turned away from Washington. His own city was, after all, the capital of American arts and sciences. The University of Pennsylvania had land enough for a building of the size he desired but lacked the funds. Let the University give the land, and the State Legislature buy the collections and house them. But at what price? It is here that the chief concern of the younger generation emerged. His sons had convinced Peale that it must be a sum which would draw interest equal to Museum receipts at the door.[28] They saw the Museum as a business property, and its value determined by its profits. For them, public benefit did not enter in. In line with this thinking, income turned back, as before, into strengthening the collection only diminished its worth. A national museum might hold to the old ideals, but a private one could not.

Public money to such a sum was unlikely indeed, but Peale clung to the lottery idea. That would bring a great building, the thing most needed. The President's grandson, Thomas Jefferson Randolph, was a student at the University through 1808 and 1809, and made his home with the Peales. Jefferson had chosen Philadelphia for the boy's education because of triple advantages "not to be found elsewhere": the Woodlands garden for botany, Peale's Museum for natural history, and the Medical School of the University. It made the Peale-Jefferson tie more intimate than ever,

but the President's two terms were ending, and the future of the Museum was still in doubt.[29]

Only by public endowment could the ideal of a living museum for public benefit be maintained. Rubens, in charge of the everyday running of the Museum, and Rembrandt, eager to share in its profits, were urging their father to retire. The father felt as young as ever at sixty-six, yet felt the weight of a dream unrealized, and had a new burden as well in Raphaelle's young family. Delirium tremens had brought this errant son to the hospital, from which his father took him into the country, for long walks and painting together, and more promises that would not be kept. In 1807 both Rubens and Rembrandt had gone afield, to Boston and New York, looking for museum opportunities unobstructed by parental ideals. Their father, alone at the Museum, confided his feelings to Angelica:

> All my children as well as other friends agree in oppinion that I have done so much, as to entitle me to rest. It is not in my natural disposition to be idle, I only wish to be indulged to pursue such labours as will turn out to best account, to improve and extend my museum; such as painting interesting Pictures, not only Portraits but also some of historical subjects &c—and in writing on the various subjects in each branch contained in the Museum and the necessary correspondence with the Professors of Natural History in the like Institutions in Europe & elsewhere to which I am invited by letters often received indeed from almost every part of the Globe, for this Museum is now known everywhere, and the subjects of America, it being as they call it, a new World, are much coveted.[30]

Rubens, home once again, stayed on at the Museum, but Rembrandt came up with a new plan: he would himself visit Paris, would establish contacts with the Muséum d'Histoire Naturelle,

CAPTAIN MERIWETHER LEWIS
Watercolor by C. B. J. F. de Saint-Memin, 1807. Lewis wears the ermine-skin mantle given him by Comeahwait, chief of the Shoshone nation. The costume was afterward presented to the Museum, where it was displayed on a wax portrait figure of Lewis, posed not with a rifle but with the pipe of peace smoked by the Shoshones and the captains of the exploring party. (The New-York Historical Society.)

THE MUSEUM SILHOUETTES

This drawing of John I. Hawkins's newly invented "physiognotrace" was sent to Jefferson by C. W. Peale on January 28, 1803. A is a sliding board adjustable to the height of the sitter, who rests his cheek against the projection D. As the brass gnomon is guided around the profile, it is traced in reduced size on the paper fastened at top, d. The silhouette would then be scissored out by the skillful hand of Moses Williams. Amies' Dove Mill banknote paper, twice folded, was used in making the four copies, to which the embossed stamp of the Museum was added. (Jefferson Papers, Library of Congress.)

and for himself draw inspiration from the great art treasury of the Louvre, Napoleonic loot from the wars in Italy. It was agreed, both father and son fired by the prospect. To finance it, the Museum would purchase from Rembrandt portraits of French savants at $100 each. Jefferson compiled a list. As many as fifty were planned, though only half as many would actually be painted during Rembrandt's two trips, first in the summer of 1808 and then, with his family, from August 1809 to December 1810.

It was a plan of rapport, the science of Old World and New, a lustre of great names greater than had ever reached the gallery walls before: Cuvier, Geoffroy, and Beauvois, of course; the American inventor Benjamin Thompson, now Count Rumford of the Holy Roman Empire; Jefferson's friend Du Pont de Nemours; André Thouin of the *Encyclopédie Méthodique* (a reference work in constant use at the Museum); the chemists Berthollet, Chaptal, Guyton de Morveau, and Vauquelin; the mineralogist Haüy, the botanist Jussieu, the astronomer Delambre, and the agricultural theorist Lasterie du Saillant; the engineer and bridge builder Prony; and Denon, Napoleon's Inspector General of Museums. Bernardin de Saint-Pierre had a double affinity as an ardent disciple of Rousseau and Intendant of the Jardin des Plantes. And of course, there were artists: David, Houdon, Gérard. They on their part warmed to the distant seat of science emerging across the sea, and to its young artist, to Saint-Pierre "mon cher Philadelphe, le Rembrandt de L'Amérique," as Saint-Pierre called him.

Some would doubt the value of this investment, but not the proprietor of the Museum. The paintings were well worth the cost as a record of "the present age . . . a time of great discoveries, more prolific than in 10 of the former centuries." He knew very well the strong popular appeal of the portrait gallery. Typical of many, Supreme Court Justice Joseph Story, who visited the Museum in the spring of 1807, found "natural curiosities arranged with genera and species upon the Linnaean system" admirable, but worth only a glance in contrast to the portraits. "These were to me a feast. I forgot birds, beasts, fishes and insects, to gaze on man. I was engaged in etching the outlines of genius, when, perhaps, I ought to have been surveying the impalpable down of an insect, or the variegated plumage of a bird." Rembrandt would now add new luster, a gallery truly worthy of a national museum.[31]

Peale wrote to President Madison, then only a month in the White House, and to Joel Barlow also, on the "National Institute" plan. But even as he learned that all hope had ended there, a new competitive enterprise threatened the Museum's tenure in the State House. A group of manufacturers was petitioning for its use as "a Factory Hall," a mechanical exhibit of a kind made popular by Peale's Model Room. In the Museum that feature had been a success from the start. Peale had picked up the idea from his friend clockmaker Robert Leslie, the father of Charles Robert Leslie, popular genre painter of Victorian England. He had had plans for its expansion in 1802, and again in 1804, when he wrote of it to Jefferson. The plow invented by Jefferson was there, along with Peale's wooden bridge and the iron bridge invented by his friend Thomas Paine.[32] The manufacturers would pay rent, which Peale did not.

Looming beyond this threat was another, the impending transfer of the State House from state to city ownership. The city planned, in that event, to add wings to the building for offices. Backed by citizen support and architectural plans, Peale petitioned the Legislature to erect fireproof offices for city and county use, but with all the upper level secured to the Museum in perpetuity. This proposal was referred to a committee of the House of Representatives, whose report of March 5, 1810 was favorable to the idea. The language of the legislators in approving the establishment of a museum unhampered by "Aristocratic rules," as was "the magnificent museum of London," and rivaling in grandeur that of Paris is revealing evidence of growing acceptance of the Peale concept of a popular museum of science.

> Here may at all times be open the most instructive school for the naturalist, botanist, mineralogist, chemist, anatomist, artist, mechanist, manufacturer, agriculturist, antiquarian, and lover of the fine arts—here may the curious and inquiring mind obtain ample gratification from the view of ancient costumes, arts and arms, and from the exhibition of every quadruped, bird, fish, amphibious animal and insect, each in its own kind, so perfect a link in the great chain that connects the whole; and here may be examined the different species of earths, stones, minerals, metals and gems, so useful in society, and capable of becoming so much more so, if generally understood—and amongst the other objects claiming particular attention, may be found a gallery of paintings, comprehending portraits taken from life, of all the principal sages and heroes to whose wisdom and valour the people of America are

indebted, under heaven, for the blessings they have enjoyed, and for the perpetuity of which such confident hopes may be entertained—here may be seen, in short, an epitome of the works of a beneficent Creator, calculated to inspire the minds of all beholders, a sublime conception of his greatness, and an hallowed gratitude for his boundless goodness.

The report concluded with "respect and applause" for him who had "devoted the best part of his existence, with singular industry and taste, to raise the museum to its present state of value, splendor and usefulness," and added a recommendation that State House Yard be made into a botanical garden, following the lead of the state of New York in purchasing the garden of Dr. Hosack.

In due course, a bill was introduced, backed by a petition signed by 570 Philadelphians. Peale lobbied for it happily, painted Governor Snyder's portrait for the gallery, and even made an artificial hand for a back-country member. But all in vain. The back-country members, particularly, were giving nothing away. The bill was defeated by six votes, 42 to 36, on March 5, 1811.[33]

By that time, Peale had retired to his farm, and Rubens was left in charge. Belfield (first called "Farm Persevere") had been recently purchased with the proceeds from the sale of city lots which Peale had acquired at a tax sale many years before and which were now far more valuable than their owner realized. He won the amused contempt of the business community by asking for them only a sum equal to the price of the farm. Rubens had taken over the Museum on generous terms, January 1, 1810: its entire management was his in return for quarterly payments of $1,000 to his father.[34] The commitment was based on Ruben's expectations of increased income, but the elder Peale had no intention of exacting the whole sum in adverse circumstances, and it is doubtful whether the full amount was ever paid. The father, too, had expectations of high income, both as a farmer and as a promoter of American manufactures using the waterpower on his farm.

Annual income at Philosophical Hall, from 1795 to 1802, had averaged $2,200; and in the years of both Hall and State House, 1802 through 1809, an average of $4,700.[35] The terms Rubens offered for his father's retirement reflect his confidence that he could double that figure again—and so indeed he would, for a time. He had served a long apprenticeship, and during this period of dual control the Museum had moved firmly into a significant place and influence of its own in American life. The Assembly's "value, splendor and usefulness" describe its status moderately well. Though imitations were rising everywhere, there was still nothing else like Peale's Museum. Nevertheless, it had been proved that wealth of material and fidelity to an ideal would not of themselves attract sufficient endowment. Rubens, and Rembrandt too, had absorbed much of their father's ideal in these years, though they were more ready to compromise for profit—indeed, had almost no other choice. To Rubens, keeping the Museum preeminent among its rivals was a matter, as his father quoted him, "of science, fashion and taste."[36]

Rubens added interest and attractiveness to the evening "illuminations." Simply to be among company in a brightly lighted room was an unusual experience in this primitive age. There was a magic, as Rembrandt recalled long after, in the flood of light pouring out from those great windows over Chestnut Street, an allure in the movement, voices, and music within that brought strollers from street or garden in to join the throng.[37] With its daytime attendance, the Museum could barely survive; its success came by night.

Music was there from the first, to emphasize the harmonies of Nature. In 1807, at a cost of $1,000, a new organ was purchased to replace the one acquired from Hawkins in 1803—an organ of eight stops made to order by John Lowe and installed in the small organ loft in the center of the Long Room by David Jones, the sentimental Welshman who did all the family and Museum cabinetwork. Lowe had been working on another organ for St. Paul's, but Peale insisted on priority for the Museum: "where it would be heard by more than an hundred to one than in a common church." Organ recitals followed, with concerts by The Amateur Society, a group of Peales and Peale friends.[38]

On other evenings, science prevailed. Since 1799 the static electricity machine had been generating a bolt of lightning that knocked a miniature house to flinders, and performing other wonders, including tests of its medical value. Now chemistry suddenly came to the fore with new and more subtle excitements—like the astonishing transformations of a magician's show, but with all the force of scientific truth and impending practical applications. Both father and son took up its study with intense interest, Rubens as lecturer and experimenter. It was a science that appealed to women as well as men; two of the most popular texts of the time were by women. Dr. Woodhouse's lectures at the University had established its popularity and importance, and James Cutbush's series of articles on "Application of Chemistry to Arts and Manufactures," running in *Aurora* in 1808, were a helpful accompaniment to the Museum evenings. Rubens enlisted other performers. Joseph Cloud, assayer at the Mint, who had made a simplified version of Dr. Robert Hare's new blowpipe for the analysis of ores, lectured and demonstrated with it at the Museum, then donated the equipment as well. Reuben Haines, a talented amateur of science, joined Rubens in a less abstruse but equally astounding demonstration, soap bubbles detonated by electricity. All in all, the public experiments drew well, and on Tuesday and Thursday evenings the Museum lobby, now filled with banks of seats facing a lecturer's table, was a crowded scene.[39]

Increased income freed the Peales themselves from routine but did little to provide expert staff. Jotham Fenton seems to have left about 1805, when he presented his collection of minerals to the Museum. He had been joined in 1802 by a young Welsh immigrant, James Griffiths, who became an even more expert taxidermist and a close friend of Peale. James returned to England, from 1807 to 1810, to care for his mother, and he left Philadelphia permanently for other museum work in 1815. These helpers were given lodging and salaries of from $300 to $500 a year. Their headquarters was the "lodge," a room added in 1803 on the second floor of the State House tower. There the work of preservation and mounting was done. From it one could see approaching visitors and step out into the little ticket office at the head of the stairs. With a thoughtfulness touchingly in line with his own temperament, at the stairway's foot Peale rigged a turnstile which rang a warning chime of bells above, thus saving his employees from "the fatigue of idleness." Large preparation work could also be done in the chamber below where Rembrandt had his studio. Part-time doorkeepers and cleaning help completed the staff, both male and female, elderly and amiable. The regulars all seemed to have a weakness for the bottle in spite of their employer's insistence that perseverance and industry thrived best without it—Fenton, Griffiths, Moses, and yet another Welshman, Samuel Jenkins, who was on the scene from 1803 to about 1807.

There had been one promotion of sorts among them. Moses Williams, who had been in from the beginning, was now a concessionaire and doing very well. He had been given custody of the Hawkins physiognotrace in 1802 and remained a constant presence with it at the west end of the Long Room. The machine was designed to be self-operating—you placed your cheek against it

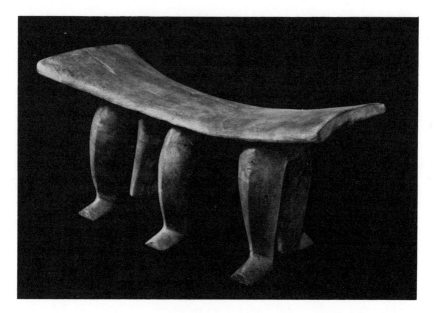

"WOODEN PILLOW FROM THE FEEGEE
ISLANDS"
*This artifact from Melanesia was presented to Peale's
Museum by Messrs. Fanning and Coles of New
York, along with others and an offer to collect
whatever else might be desirable. In his reply of June
6, 1808, Peale added directions for the preservation
of natural history specimens. It was an important
opportunity for the Museum, since Edmund Fanning,
the "Pathfinder of the Pacific," and his brother
Henry were at the height of their adventurous career.*
(Peabody Museum, Harvard University.)

and ran a brass gnomen about your head to trace an indented line of
the profile on paper—but for a charge of 8 cents Moses would
perform the whole operation, including the scissors work. He
became extremely proficient at this and soon had the whole in hand
as a profitable business. A good quality of banknote paper from the
Amies Dove Mill was used. Folded twice for the machine, the
cutout gave the purchaser four silhouettes. Deferring entirely to
Moses' expertise, Peale himself cut none and was only amused when
a Southern gentleman recoiled from its being done for him by a
Negro. The rage for these little likenesses was immediate and
long-lasting. Moses cut 8,880 of them in his first year. He saved the

inner cutouts ("blocks," or his "blockheads," as he called them) and stored them at home in barrels. Each finished product was marked with the Museum's embossed stamp, and small frames were for sale. Occasionally one of the younger Peales or an artist friend would sit nearby coloring the profiles. Moses is last glimpsed as a man of property, married to the Peales' white cook, who in a former day had refused even to sit at the same table with him.[40]

The proprietor was almost always part of the Museum scene, watching for visitors with scientific interests, possible donors, old friends, and at the same time intent on preserving decorum. Anyone noticeably intoxicated was to be refused admittance, and should a dispute arise, Peale himself would administer a reproof "comporting with their rank in life." Those who stood on the upholstered benches for a better look into the upper cases he would rebuke after they had stepped down by silently dusting with his handkerchief the place. One impulse of departing pranksters was forestalled by a sign, "None but the Rude and Uncultivated ring the Bells going down." The habit of touching everything and of scratching names in the great *Chama* shell in the center of the Marine Room seemed beyond cure.[41]

Most technical problems had been solved by the time of the expansion into the State House. Clear glass for case fronts remained difficult to obtain, and glass eyes were now being imported rather than made—helping to explain why native glassworks were receiving Museum display space and encouragement. Preservation techniques had benefited from advice of the chief of the Paris museum's laboratory, but that tended to confirm Peale's confidence in his own system. His earliest mountings were as good as ever after twenty years: "Time cannot alter them, so that if my system is pursued this Museum cannot fail of becoming in time the best Museum in the world."[42]

Thomas Jefferson had lent Peale a small volume on the Paris museum, *Promenades au Jardin des Plantes, à la Ménagerie et dans les Galeries du Musée d'Histoire Naturelle* by J. B. Pujoulx (Paris, 1803), and this suggested a similar work of his own, "A Walk With a Friend Through the Philadelphia Museum," composed at intervals through the winter of 1805–1806.[43] He bought a font of long primer type for its printing at the Museum Press and set to work, steel pen in hand, to describe everything as he would to a friend strolling at his side. From a full mind and heart, it became entirely too discursive, dwelling at length on the birds as he had done in his lectures.

Rubens, backed by Rembrandt, called a halt. This was entirely too expensive a substitute for their eight-page *Guide to the Philadelphia Museum,* first issued from the Museum Press in 1804 and reprinted as needed thereafter to be given out to every ticket purchaser. The *Guide* accompanied the visitor from ticket office to lobby, with a nod to the electrical machine, then on through the Quadruped Room, down the Long Room, and into the Marine Room with a concise listing of the contents of each, and of the three rooms in Philosophical Hall. By the summer of 1807 Peale was still hoping Rembrandt would put the "Walk" into shape for publication. The Museum Press must be expanded, and the full catalogue of the collections at long last printed. He wrote to London for information on the stereotype process, talked still of building out over the State House wings, proposed lighting the whole with carbonated hydrogen gas, which figured now in the chemical experiments, and began in earnest to assemble a Museum library. Joseph Dennie, suave and amiable editor of the *Port Folio,* dropped in that summer to see what was going on and went away impressed. Like many another, he had always dismissed natural history as an amusement for children. He now reprinted the *Guide* in his magazine with a prefatory word of admiration, avowing that the Linnaean classification gave "order, grace and beauty" to collections of great and increasing value.[44] From this the *Guide* found its way into other periodicals, and Rubens continued sounding his own horn and advertised even in the *Tickler,* a new Philadelphia sheet in a lighter vein.

From the parental viewpoint, the best publicity lay in newsworthy acquisitions and in cooperation with the great foreign museums. Exchanges with Paris, so eagerly welcomed, had been disappointing. Peale had sent specimens with Humboldt and more recently, in 1807, by the roving naturalist Louis Théodore Leschenault. No acknowledgment had come back and, as he reminded both Geoffroy and Cuvier in writing of Rembrandt's mission, it had been with mixed feelings that he had learned of their safe arrival only through one of the Paris museum's publications.[45] When James Griffiths returned to London, he took with him Alexander Wilson's list of British birds needed for comparison in the collection of Peale's Museum. In America there were exchanges with Edward Savage, now at the museum in New York, and in the South with gentleman-naturalists Augustus Gottlieb Oemler and Stephen Elliott, Elliott coming to Philadelphia for the purpose and spending a week at the Museum.[46] Not until many years later would the Museum issue a printed field guide for collectors, but Peale was always ready with personal directions to any who were willing to help:

It is difficult for me to point out any particular articles desireable from the Native Islands in the Pacific Ocean—but I shall mention generally that the utensils and weapons &c which serve to give a knowledge of their customs may be useful as well as curious. Subjects of natural History, such as snakes, Lizards and Insects (except Butterflies), can be preserved in Rum & thus easily brought here to be afterwards displayed; a single bottle may contain a multitude of different subjects. But if any Quadrupeds were attempted to be brought (except they were of the smallest kind which might also be put into spirits) [let them] take the skins, leaving in them the bones of the Head and feet. Soft soap will preserve them better than salt. However, seamen accustomed to long voyages know very well how to preserve skins.[47]

Among the Peales themselves, collecting of every sort went on. Even Sophy, up to the time of her marriage, had been out with her brothers, "shooting with the little Fuzee," and they all made it a rule to keep bottle and box in pocket, ready for unusual insects.[48]

Unhappily, all this purposeful collecting has no consistent record. The catalog begun in 1788 is lost, though much material in the lectures and the "Walk with a Friend" was drawn from it. The Record Book at the Historical Society of Pennsylvania tells more of what random donors thought a museum ought to be than what it actually was. This volume was opened in 1803 as a guest book in which visitors could inscribe their names and sentiments. Here we read:

I love the study of Nature, for it teacheth benevolence.

CWPeale

followed by Hawkins's—

Let us live for truth,

and truculent Thomas Cooper's vigorous—

Knowledge is Power.

Little Constantine Rafinesque, newly arrived in America, had a sentiment close to Peale's:

L'Histoire naturelle est la plus belle des sciences—c'est elle qui nous montre tous les jours dans les Oeuvres de la Création la toute puissance du Créateur.

And handsome Stephen Sayre, home again after his strange adventures as a secret agent of the Revolution, must have had his eye on the Museum's proprietor as he wrote,

I have never known an idle man to be a happy one.

Medical students, however, sent to the Museum as part of their course, began to add sentiments of their own, less lofty ("The noblest work of God—Woman"), and the book was withdrawn, to be used thereafter as a roster of gifts and donors.

As such it is nearly, if not wholly, complete. Gifts of value and trivialities were entered without fear or favor. The book shows with what ease a collection of surprising oddments could be brought together. Children often brought a gift, to get thereby a free admission, such things as "a wooden chain of 16 links without an end cut out of a solid piece of wood presented by the maker, Joseph Griggins, a mulatto boy," so recorded in both book and published accession list. Hair balls from the stomachs of cattle abound. Roderick Mackenzie's fragment of tapestry from the bedroom of Mary Queen of Scots brought a right-minded rebuke from a citizen against the filching of historical souvenirs—and started a rash of hoaxers sending in scraps of cloth attributed to other bedrooms, including those of Marie Antoinette, Louis XVI, and Peter the Great, all faithfully acknowledged in the Record Book. Yet the book would continue until 1842, a major source on the Museum's holdings.

Although trifles abound in the Record Book they do not appear in visitors' descriptions, since the Peales knew very well what damage such stuff could do to the Museum's reputation. Rather, with Rembrandt's support, Rubens pressed hard toward that trinity of science, fashion, and taste. Income for 1807 was low, but plans and activity high, and in the next year it was trebled, $2,195 to $6,686. Space was found for accumulating objects not shown before, mostly minerals and a miscellany of artifacts from the South Seas.

Rubens continues to improve the arrangement of articles, miscellanious as well as Minerals &c. Instead of those long horizontal glass cases which held such articles formerly, we have now perpendicular cases, the shelves of which [are] inclined to present a greater surface to the Eye in proportion to the height of each shelf, with ledges to keep the articles from sliding down, and all the shelves are covered with fine carded cotton. Each of these cases stands on a base with panneled doors, within which are keept all our duplicate articles, also such as cannot be immediately displayed.[49]

The Mammoth Room was now dramatized by a large background scene comparable to the landscape backgrounds in the glass cases, with the smaller *Exhumation* (now at the Peale Museum in Baltimore) to illustrate the drama of its discovery. Rembrandt and Rubens were urging that the great skeleton and all else at Philosophical Hall be brought to the State House, to make a more spectacular and lucrative unit. Their father temporized; his whole feeling was for expansion rather than contraction. Besides, he would first have to find a new home, for under the terms of lease he could not continue to live at the Hall without the Museum. He watched Rubens at work through 1807 and into 1808, neatness and polish everywhere—"entirely overhauled," he told the friendly and understanding Hawkins, "the walls and ceiling whitewashed, upwards of 2450 feet of glass cleaned, the Paintings cleaned &c. &c. All this has made a wonderful difference in the appearance of the Museum."[50]

With the move to the State House the birds, more than ever, dominated the whole—the largest and most complete department and, thanks to small size and the hundred-foot length of the Long Room, the best arranged. They also underlay the first and best scholarly work to be based on the Peale collections, the *American Ornithology* of Alexander Wilson.

It is a strange story, this of the poor Scottish weaver with an authentic poetic voice, imprisoned in Scotland for his bitter verses of social protest and now a refugee in America, a taut, melancholy temperament, quick to anger, a lonely, eloquent spirit aspiring to some great work, some path of his own to immortality. He was teaching at a small school near Bartram's Gardens on the Schuylkill River when, in the spring of 1804, he had come upon Rubens Peale, an early morning hunter in the woods. Rubens was marking with sticks an unusual flower he had found, a double anemone. The birds he had shot were spread on the ground. Wilson looked down at them and chided the stranger for having killed a songbird that had sung at his window nearby. Rubens responded with an invitation to the Museum. Wilson commemorated the meeting with a poem, "The Wood Robin." Later, the poet brought a nest of young hummingbirds to the Peales for advice on rearing them and soon, with warm encouragement from the William Bartram family

ALEXANDER WILSON, 1766–1813
Rembrandt Peale's portrait is of the Scottish poet, moody and intense, who was inspired by the Museum's collection to make the study of birds his lifework. Wilson's American Ornithology *(1808–1814), continued by Charles Lucien Bonaparte (1825–1833), is a classic of both science and literature, which did much to establish scientific method and nomenclature among other naturalists. Wherever possible, each entry was keyed to the Peale's Museum specimen, and many of the illustrations were drawn from Peale mountings.* (American Philosophical Society.)

and from the Scottish engraver Alexander Lawson, dedicated himself to the study that was to fill the remainder of his short life. A letter of Charles Willson Peale to Geoffroy, April 21, 1808, tells of his approval and pleasure:

> A frind of mine, Mr. Alexr. Wilson is about to publish a work of the birds of North America, which will rectify many errors of authors on our birds & he will also give plates of many that have not been noticed before. This gentleman is indefatigable in his researches to acquire a knowledge of the manners and habits of our birds. He has aided me considerably, for he is active with his gun at all seasons, and correct in his observations. The first volume will shortly be put to the press.

Wilson had all the admiration of the Peales, but his extreme sensitivity set him apart from them. He ignored Charles Willson Peale's preference for plain descriptive names unencumbered with Latin, and his work did more than any other to establish the use of scientific nomenclature in America. He meant his work to be, as it is, an independent and unimpeachable personal monument. He was both aloof and cooperative, drawing on Peale's knowledge of bird behavior and citing the Museum catalogue numbers so that his readers would have not only description and plate, but a type specimen. The Wilson formality appears in a note to Rubens, 1811:

> A. Wilson's compts. to Rubens Peale, encloses the names of such birds of the *Third* Volume as have not yet numbers from the Museum. Would thank Mr. Peale to put down the Numbers when convenient—many of them are *new,* these A. Wilson will point out and will present Mr. Peale with the skins. Perhaps the venerable founder and father of the Museum. Mr. C. W. Peale could furnish an anecdote or two of some of the birds for the Amer. Orn.—will Mr. Rubens be so obliging as to show these names to his father[?].

There follows a list of thirty-one birds, eight marked as new to the collection.[51]

Years later, a Peale grandson remembered having heard talk of his grandfather's experiments with Wilson "to get at the true sustaining power of the bird in its flight." Wilson "roundly asserted that the sustaining force of the bird in the air was due to its force in starting or getting under way, its angle or inclination in the air, and its power of maintaining its velocity, that Wilson used to cite the powerful muscles in legs and web feet of the duck, the angle it starts from the water in rising, the running of the wild goose to get its start." An ancient crossbow had come into the Museum, and the two shot "weighted winged arrows" of different forms to test the relationship of weight to wing, "as well as the shape of the wings to take advantage of what they called the eddy in the air caused by the flight."[52]

Wilson's work in nine volumes, with Charles Lucien Bonaparte's continuation in three more, became the leading stimulus in the growth of the bird collection. Peale had been working toward "a comparative view of each genus of birds of the old and new world," and Wilson encouraged this effort. The addition of Samuel Parrish's collection from the Malabar coast reinforced it, along with a purchase in 1806 of 34 birds from South America, with only one duplicate (*le diable enrhumé*), and Philip DePeyster's specimens from the West Indies in 1807. A major addition of 160 birds, American and foreign, came in 1809, and by 1810 the Long Room arrangement exceeded a thousand, "including many nondescripts."[53]

With quadrupeds, Buffon's controversial theory of the degeneration of American species had given special interest to all points of comparison. The Australian platypus acquired in 1807, the first in America, was doubtless viewed by our citizens as a pure freak of nature. The hippopotamus had been represented only by a tooth until 1805, when the friendly Monsieur Soissons donated skull and jaws along with native artifacts and living birds from Africa (scarlet ibis, crown heron, widow birds, Senegal finch). Most of the animals, even the strange and dangerous like the "jaguar of Buffon" from Dr. Edward Stevens of St. Croix, came in alive, but the first lion was an unhealthy cadaver purchased for $50 from a showman. "Never mind"—it soon stood nobly with the lesser felines round about.

Grizzly bears, more ferocious even than the hyena, dominated the Museum zoo. The first seen in the East was brought by a French trader in 1803. It grew large and fierce, broke out of its cage, and was killed. A haunch was sent to President Jefferson. The President reciprocated in 1808 with two grizzly cubs, male and female, brought to him by the explorer Zebulon Pike. They were described as "tame," but not for long. One tore off the arm and shoulder of a monkey which had come too near. Then, one night it broke out of its cage and entered the Peale kitchen in the basement of the Hall.

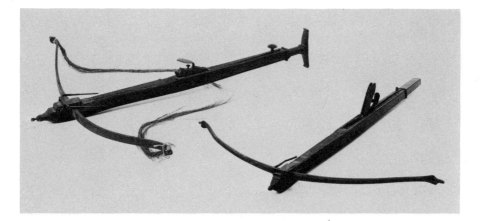

EXPERIMENTS IN FLIGHT
With one of these two crossbows, about 1812–1813, Peale
and Alexander Wilson shot winged darts in an effort to
determine the sustaining power of different wing forms.
(Peabody Museum, Harvard University.)

With the family in terror, Peale barricaded the animal in, then entered in the morning, gun in hand, and shot it. Its mate also was killed, and the two were mounted together.[54]

Other specimens followed the same route or were mounted from skin and skeleton: great anteater, Madagascar bat, llama, peccary, sloth, Indian musk ox, kangaroo, and elephant, leopard, and beaver seals from the DePeysters' sealing voyages, and many more. In 1810 the Museum boasted "Twenty-One specimens of Simia or the monkey tribe." Monkeys, always available in abundance, in 1808 brought an exhibit which may be attributed to Raphaelle Peale and which, with additions and variations, would long remain a popular feature. It began with a group of three, costumed and posed as "Poet, Painter and Sitter," followed by a monkey blacksmith shop and then monkeys at other occupations. The monkeys shown at trades are mentioned often in visitors' recollections, and twenty years later the New England Museum in Boston, Daniel Bowen's successor, was making a major feature of the idea.[55]

A visitor coming to the Museum at this time with any of the current books on four-footed creatures would have found nearly all

THE FAMOUS GRISLY BEAR,

hitherto unseen in the inhabited countries, and entirely unknown untill the celebrated A. MACKENZIE gave some account of that extraordinary animal, having met him in the neighbourhood of the Rocky Mountains, by 56. degrees N. L. in his ever memorable expedition to the Pacific Ocean, through the north-weſtern continent of America.

THIS ANIMAL was born in the spring of the year 1802. not far from the sources of the river Missoury, about 4500. miles from Philadelphia, in a country inhabited by an indian nation called the Cattanahowes. He is the firſt of his specie that ever was seen, and seems to be a separate class of White Bear, which differs from those known to and described by the naturaliſts, as well in point of colour, as in point of inclinations. His hair is a kind of straw colour or light sorrel, neither hard nor stiff, but somewhat like wool. His inclinations are so ferocious, that he follows the tracks of men, and attacks them with undaunted fury. Mackenzie's own expressions respecting that extraordinary beaſt, are as follows: " We perceived "along the river, tracks of large bears, some of which were nine inches wide "and of a proportionate length. We saw one of their dens, or winter-quar-"ters, called wattee, which was ten feet deep, five feet high, and six feet "wide; but we had not yet seen one of those animals. The Indians en-"tertain great apprehenſion of this kind of bear, which is called the GRISLY "BEAR; and they never venture to attack it but in a party of at leaſt three "or four".

By the ſize of this one, who has hardly attained the third part of his bignefs, by the length of his claws, when yet so young, one may form an idea of the powerful ſtrength of that dangerous animal, which may be conſidered as the moſt formidable wild beaſt of the continent of America.

During the short time he will remain in this place, the GRISLY BEAR may be seen at every hour of the day, at *the museum*

The price of entrance ~~is half a dollar.~~ *25 cents & half*

price for children NB. I gave the refrnch-man liberty to exhibit the Bear two weeks in the Hall of the Stah-House. 24013

THE FIRST GRIZZLY
Its ferocity made the young grizzly a notable attraction of the Museum zoo—and a very unwelcome intruder in the Peale kitchen. Peale sent this broadsheet description to President Jefferson, on March 18, 1804. (Jefferson Papers, Library of Congress.)

PIKE'S GRIZZLIES

As cubs, the two bears from Zebulon
Pike's exploring expedition were docile
and playful, but were too dangerous to
be kept long when mature. Titian
Peale's watercolor of the Museum
*mounting is inscribed "*MISSOURI
BEAR. ursus horribilis: *Ord.*
Specimens col'd. by Lt. Pike, presented
to C. W. Peale." (American
Philosophical Society.)

present, with the exception of the largest. In contrast, fish and insects ran well beyond the published descriptions. Fish were still limited in number, though Peale had long felt an impulse to collect them as he had the birds. Not only was this a vast area to be explored, but he was moved by an empathy with the creatures in it hardly characteristic of icthyologists. The fish, like the birds, had beauty, joy of life, and, he felt sure, domestic tenderness:

> . . . In every little stream may be seen numbers of little happy beings that sport through their watery element in sportive mazes, seeming sometimes to contemplate each other's beauty, and in an instant dart like lightning to another quarter as it were to contemplate some other object. Then on the bottom, less active beings in coats of shell armor to defend them, of infinite variety of form, ornamented with pearl and other colours. These lessor objects must excite the admiration of the attentive beholder, but if he turns to the immensity of beings that inhabit the ocean, every drop of which contains multitudes of living beings, the food of other beings! in gradual progression from the smallest to the largest whales, they bring forth their young living and protect them under their fins. . . . [56]

The insects taught similar lessons. They were moved to the State House newly arranged and keyed to a general label by number, the smallest mounted under Fenton's rotating magnifiers. In 1804 they were remounted in vertical cases, and three years later the whole exhibit was again enlarged and rearranged. Insects were also often sent in alive—important for those such as spiders which were difficult to preserve.[57] But for all Peale's effort to present the spell of beauty in minute forms, his public found a more compelling attraction in the "Black Bugs" presumed to have been cast up from a Maryland lady's stomach—a distinctly human story. It had been admitted to the Museum because of medical interest, which the inquiring reader of today may find set forth in Dr. John Redman Coxe's *Philadelphia Medical Museum* (vol. 2, 1806, p. 410). In entomology the representation was worldwide, with insects from India, China, South America, and Europe joining the North American collection assembled mostly by the Peales themselves—in all, by 1810, nearly 4,000.

Minerals, like insects, had their focal points of beauty. Here too was a wide area open to exploration, but with the additional lure of a conspicuous place in the wealth of the nation. Mineralogy stood close to chemical science and shared its popularity. Gifts in this area came more from interested and knowledgeable persons than from the random sort of donor. Abbé Réné Just Haüy, discoverer of the geometrical law of crystallization and Napoleon's professor of mineralogy at the Muséum d'Histoire Naturelle, sent a collection of minerals accompanied by copies of his own works, a grateful return for a replica of his portrait painted for the gallery of this distant museum. Popular interest was enormously stimulated by the "fireball" that had streaked thunderously down upon Weston, Connecticut, on December 14, 1807—the first falling meteorite seen by white men in America. Benjamin Silliman presented one of the fragments to the Museum, as he and Dr. Woodhouse, under whom he had prepared for his professorship at Yale, confronted the public and the learned world with competing analyses.[58]

Silvain Godon, a professor of mineralogy from Paris, was in town in 1808. Peale was delighted to give him a room at the Hall in which he delivered a lecture course from Museum minerals. Rubens attended, and then joined Godon on field trips through the countryside with a smaller group: Reuben Haines, Elisha Kent Kane, Benjamin Kugler, Robert M. Patterson, son of the Museum's early promoter, the brothers Benjamin and Thomas Say, and Charles Wistar. Near Baltimore they discovered a source of chrome yellow pigment, in which both Rubens and his mentor invested with high hopes. Several tons were mined. With all of the Peale's emphasis on practical applications of natural science, it was inevitable that they would become entrepreneurs themselves, but with uniform ill fortune. The Museum's proprietor set out to demonstrate the value of the new pigment and learned, the hard way, its worthlessness. For Godon, serious financial reverses led to mental breakdown—a sad ending to a career that had promised to become the Museum's first professorship.[59]

The incident of the chrome yellow was typical of others at this time and later, both within the Museum circle and beyond. Peale's friend Archibald Bruce figured in the discovery of rare mineral deposits in New Jersey in 1810, in which Mahlon Dickerson, William H. Keating, and David G. Seixas were also involved. Seixas gave a collection of these minerals to the Museum in hope of stimulating the search for a native source of plumbago, needed by American brassfounders. The promotion of manufactures and inventions was an essential Museum activity and a very personal Peale interest—pouring out to Hawkins, for instance, the exciting news of Simon Willard's washing machine, or sending Rembrandt

PEALE'S MUSEUM.

—

THE
JUBATA; Or,
GREAT ANT-EATER.
First of the kind ever seen in this country.

THE moſt extraordinary and wonderfully formed creature now offered to the inſpection of
the public, makes an intereſting addition to many
other curious ſubjects that have lately been depo-
ſited in the Muſeum.

The Great Ant-Eater, or Ant-Bear, is a native
of Africa and South-America. The preſent ſpeci-
men is among the largeſt known, and is in a fine
ſtate of preſervation. It is 7 feet 7 inches in
length : being 4 feet 6 from the noſe to the inſer-
tion of the ta.l, and thence to the end of the bruſh
3 feet 1 inch more. The tongue, which is ſingu-
larly formed, is about 2 feet 6 inches in length, extremely ſlender, and lies, when at reſt, in a double
fold within the mouth. Altho' the Ant-Bear has
no teeth—the nature of his food requiring none :—
yet he may be ranked among the moſt formidable
Quadrupeds of the foreſt. Armed with claws of
uncommon ſize and ſtrength, and poſſeſſing great
muſcular powers, this curious animal, tho' naturally inoffenſive, when undiſturbed, is terrible in his
wrath. His food conſiſts entirely of Ants. Theſe
he entraps in the following manner : Extending
his long ſlender tongue, which is coated with a
viſcous ſubſtance, he introduces it among the Ant's.
Either alarmed at the intruſion, or attracted by the
quality of the clammy matter, the inſects ſoon cover the tongue with their bodies, and thus fall an
eaſy prey.

In ſhort —The Ant-Eater, if not the moſt ſingu-
lar animal in the world, may juſtly claim a place
among the moſt curious Quadrupeds of the animal
kingdom.   October 24

to paint a gallery portrait of Colonel David Humphreys of Connecticut, not as General Washington's aide and secretary or as a poet, but in recognition of production of American cloth. The museum's founder was taking this interest with him into his approaching retirement, for his farm was planned from the first to include a mill seat. He meant to stay with the advancing times: "The spirit of manufactures will progress throughout the United States. The advantage of labour-saving machinery is all-important to this country."[60]

The year 1810 would bring with the founder's retirement a new era for the Museum. In the preceding decades, each failure to receive the expected recognition and endowment had emphasized the dependence on admission fees, and had widened the rift between an institution run for profit and emerging groups such as the dedicated young amateurs of Dr. Barton's American Botanical Society of 1806 (afterward the Linnaean Society). When in that same year the Royal Asiatic Society had given the Philosophical Society the skeleton of an elephant, Peale urged that Dr. Wistar make a comparative study with the mammoth. His colleagues at the Hall agreed to a comparative exhibition, but with a cool admonition: "Mr. Peale . . . perfectly understands that it is not to be advertised."[61]

Against such snubs, Peale could only look forward to his faculty of professors in the still-imagined future. All that vision of public service, of a national museum, would go with him to the farm, leaving it to Rubens the while to carry on, restricted by the balancing of profit and loss. Now the younger generation was taking over from the old; yet somehow, youthful élan seems more on the side of the father.

As part of his tidying-up farewell activity he would fix upon the mammoth the distinctive new name given it by Cuvier in 1806: "Grand Mastodonte." This, Peale had found on inquiry, was approved by Jefferson. But after three years it still had no popular currency whatever. "Mammoth," noun and adjective, had become a part of the American language; something must be done to shake it loose. Peale thought of the famous farewell dinner set up by

Description of "The Jubata; Or, Great Ant-Eater," a new attraction at Peale's Museum, from Claypoole's American Daily Advertiser, October 28, 1799.

Rembrandt before leaving for England with his skeleton; music and toasts within the mastodon itself. That had made a tremendous splash, and something like that would be the thing. He wrote to Rembrandt, in Paris, calling for "an appropriate song to be sung with clarinets" which would be set to new music composed by Duponceau Lafoie, again for thirteen hilarious diners in the shadow of the bones. It would take place on the coming July 4.[62] It did not, however. Perhaps Rembrandt's muse failed him this time, or perhaps it was just that so much else was going on. "Mammoth" would remain "mammoth" for many years to come.

Still there would be time enough. After all, at the age of sixty-eight, as scientifically reckoned, a man had come no more than halfway—in Peale's conviction—if he kept Nature as his guide. He was painting new gallery portraits for the Long Room, to make a complete double row from end to end, 96 in all, and he topped it off with likenesses of two more hardy oldsters copied from engravings in Sir John Sinclair's *Code of Longevity*—one reputed to be 185 years old, and the other ten years younger—and hung them with a motto underneath, right for both subjects and painter:

> The Blessings of Temperance are Health, Spirits and Long Life.

CHAPTER SEVEN

RUBENS AND REMBRANDT (1810–1827)

Rubens Peale had been born in 1784, the year when it all began. He and the Museum had grown up together, and when he took over its management at the age of twenty-six the spirit of imaginative inquiry had become a part of his being. He had no illusions, however, as to natural history's changing the course of civilization or lengthening the life of man. For him it was a popular and beneficent form of entertainment. Scientific probity must be maintained, but with a shift of emphasis from the "rational" to the "amusement." It was a business—profit, or perish.

Nearby, Philadelphia's Washington Museum was thriving with its lurid assembling of all the Peale elements: paintings, waxwork, "artificial" and "natural curiosities," profiles, evening illuminations and music. But Peale's had the great and famous collection. Rubens knew the importance of growth and change, and during his decade as "Director of the Philadelphia Museum" gifts would be recorded scrupulously; specimens exchanged with museums in New York, New Haven, Vienna, Leipzig, Zurich, and no doubt others as well; and though not an ardent hunter himself, there would be trips afield by James Griffiths and members of the family. From mineralogy he went on to take a course of lectures in botany and helped to make his father's farm in Germantown something of a botanical garden. Rubens, the shy brother with the thick spectacles, blossomed out in his new role, an eligible bachelor whisking through the streets of the town in a flashy one-horse rig, though still with that careful, serious air of the Museum's lecturer and scientific experimenter.

Rubens took full advantage of the departure of the paternal dynamo. By December 1811, the mastodon and all else at Philosophical Hall had been brought to the State House, forming a compact collection in which new objects could appear but expansion was impossible. The Marine Room became the Mammoth Room, with other fossils and the anthropology from the Hall, and a new Marine Room of sorts was created in the tower, up a narrow flight of stairs from the lobby. To that dimly lighted spot were added also the costumed monkeys, the "anatomical preparations" and freaks which his father had sedulously kept out of sight, making it something of a chamber of horrors. There was a tattooed human head never to be forgotten. Snakes lay coiled and threatening; one was shown swallowing a toad, the hindquarters protruding pitifully. Reptilian shapes and human and animal fetuses gleamed in their jars of alcohol. Even the monkeys at their trades took on a demonic air, the smithy blowing the bellows over a tinsel fire and the carpenter, cooper, and shoemaker, a shoe between his knees, all grinning evilly from ear to ear.[1] There was nothing like this down below—with the single exception of Raphaelle Peale's realistic masterpiece of many years before, "The Great Gray Wolf with Bloody Fangs," tearing the body of a lamb, its papier-mâché entrails protruding.

It should be noted that in general, in his long career as a museum man, Rubens would eschew freaks. Instead, he showed a penchant for human prodigies, starting in 1811 with Zera Colburn, a six-year-old mathematical genius from Vermont. Rubens, who knew the value of decorous special exhibits and events, gave first attention to his evening lectures and experiments, varied with the music of another amateur group of his own, the Harmonic Society, with Thomas Sully and other friends participating.[2] Among incidental diversions a weighing machine was installed, dignified by the name "Santorian Chair," the ancestor of millions of penny scales to follow.

The Leverian had been spoken of as London's "fashionable lounge," and to create a fashionable lounge, particularly for the evening affairs, was the goal of Rubens in these years. Brightness and polish were maintained, and the settees were more comfortably upholstered. The framed catalogue was taken down; Bible texts, prettily framed, attracted more attention. The Museum experience at the beginning of Ruben's regime is pleasantly described by

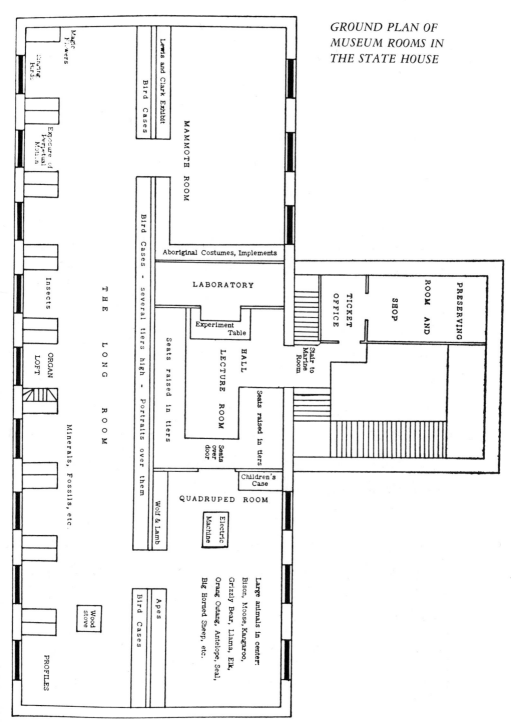

*GROUND PLAN OF
MUSEUM ROOMS IN
THE STATE HOUSE*

Magic Flowers

Moving Birds

Lewis and Clark Exhibit

Bird Cases

MAMMOTH ROOM

Exposure of Perpetual Motion

Aboriginal Costumes, Implements

Bird Cases - several tiers high - Portraits over them

LABORATORY

Experiment Table

Insects

THE LONG ROOM

Seats raised in tiers

HALL

LECTURE ROOM

Stair to Marine Room

TICKET OFFICE

SHOP

ROOM AND

PRESERVING

ORGAN LOFT

Seats raised in tiers

Seats over door

Minerals, Fossils, etc.

Children's Case

QUADRUPED ROOM

Wolf & Lamb

Electric Machine

Large animals in center:
Bison, Moose, Kangaroo,
Grizzly Bear, Llama, Elk,
Orang Outang, Antelope, Seal,
Big Horned Sheep, etc.

Wood Stove

Apes

Bird Cases

PROFILES

MUSEUM TICKETS, 1813 and 1814
C. W. Peale designed and etched a new admission ticket when his son Rubens took over the management of the Museum. Birds are shown at left, and mammals at right; the marine life in the lower center features the paddlefish, "1st Article of Museum, 1784." (Massachusetts Historical Society.)

Bottom: Rubens, however, preferred a more formal bank-note style. Over the tree at top center is inscribed the motto given him by Benjamin Franklin, "Perseverantia." (American Philosophical Society.)

Catherine Fritsch, one of a party of black-clad, tight-bonneted Moravians who came to the great city from Lititz, near Lancaster. A wall surrounded the State House garden then, and they entered dramatically through a tall gate:

> . . . Many people were there, either strolling in the walks or lounging on the benches. An angular space formed by the main building and one of its wings, enclosed and entered through a gate, held a large collection of beautiful flowers in pots, or boxes, and also a few living animals. Two great bears amused us exceedingly by their clumsy play, or as they drew from the recesses of their den vegetables—mostly asparagus—and eat them. On the top of the bears' house two parrots, apparently quite contented, chatted together; in the next cage an eagle sat right majestically on his perch—above his head a placard with this petition on it: "Feed me daily for 100 years"; and next to it there was a monkey, who kindly showed us his whole assortment of funny capers and wonderful springs.
>
> Over the lower door leading to the museum we observed this good advice: *Whoso would learn Wisdom, let him enter here!* At the foot of the stairway each of us paid ¼ dollar, and on the second floor we were shown into a large hall which was filled entirely with animals, finely mounted and in natural positions. In this room was located the *Oracle*—a lion's head: had I talked into it I should have fancied myself a priestess of a heathen temple; but we knew not where the sound outlet was, and it was only after we had gone through three rooms that I discovered it. Then Mr. Steinman at the lion's head and Christel at the other end of the tube, quite a distance apart, talked together; but the novelty of it caused them, and us, to laugh so immoderately that they could hardly ask or reply to any questions.
>
> I went about the room with my spectacles on under my bonnet, so that I could read the finely written labels; and in that way whenever I found anything remarkable I would call my companions to come and see it. Here we could observe abundant instance of the wisdom of God in His creation, as we viewed it, with astonishment, the many different animals, birds and fish, and the infinite variety of exquisite butterflies and insects. The latter two exhibits in large, but shallow, glazed cases, were preserved from the effects of light by covers

of heavy, marbled pasteboard, hinged at the top, over each pane of glass: lift up a cover and you see the butterflies!

I took much pleasure in reading whence all these curiosities came, and who had presented them: indeed, here "the inquisitive one" was in her element; for years she had wished that she might see this museum, and always she had honored the name of Mr. Charles Willson Peale: but now more than ever—since he has hung on the walls scripture texts—in oval frames—beautifully engrossed—as silent reminders to the unthinking that there is a God who has created all things. On the door leading up to the organ were affixed the rules of behavior for visitors.

Two live snakes in a large receptacle having sides and top of glass, and filling a window recess, attracted our interested attention. The large one lay coiled fast asleep; the smaller one was gliding through the green grass on the bottom of the box. Above them a little yellow bird hopped from perch to perch singing cheerfully all the while. Poor, innocent thing, thought I, you are happy despite your imprisonment with the most disagreeable of creatures . . .

In one of the rooms a man was making silhouettes. Polly coaxed me to have mine cut for her, but I couldn't think of it—with my big nose! Only Mr. Steinman and his daughter had theirs made. Here, too, were the Magic Mirrors, which afforded us much amusement—you might take your choice of a giant face, or a dwarf's, or have seven heads![3]

Such delights contributed to the doubling of Museum income in that first year, and the patriarch out at Belfield made good use of his liberal share—clearing and planting his acres, building his fabulous unspillable milk cart along with other inventions. Few seventy-year-olds have had so active a retirement, on hill and field from dawn to dark, returning in the twilight glow to be fed and praised, rubbed and petted by Hannah. A month or more might go by without even a brief return to the Museum. It was, however, by no means forgotten. He seemed to approve Rubens's changes without losing assurance that his own original goals remained intact. Rubens only needed more space. If the State House could not be enlarged, a new building must somehow be found.

That last campaign for state support had ended with the Museum and city in adversary positions, each in need of more room. At Fifth Street stood City Hall, the former Supreme Court

ELECTION DAY AT THE STATE HOUSE, PHILADELPHIA, 1816
This animated occasion in front of the home of the Museum from 1802 to 1827 shows
the newly erected wings for city offices that joined the three buildings into one, leaving
the Museum an unwelcome tenant at the center. Painting by John Lewis Krimmel.
(Historical Society of Pennsylvania.)

building, and at Sixth was the Philadelphia County Court House, formerly Congress Hall. In between stood the State House, now overflowing with natural history. In 1812–1813 the city built the connecting offices it had planned entirely for public use. The Museum would gain no more space. Looming over all was a likelihood that the State would put the whole square up for sale, a matter of grave concern to Philosophical Society as well as city.

In the meantime a woebegone Rembrandt Peale had begun to eye museum operation as a career preferable to painting, or at least one way of freeing an artist from total bondage to portraiture. He had returned from Paris with his portraits of French savants, with an African collection donated to the Museum by Beauvois, and with his technique and style greatly improved and his young ambition soaring into dreams of high poetic art—"haunted day and night," as his friend John Neal put it, "by magnificent spectres of genius."[4] He had transformed a stable on Walnut Street opposite the present Washington Square into "Rembrandt's Picture Gallery" (later,

221

"The Appolodorian Gallery"), displaying his life portrait of Napoleon, his *Napoleon Crossing the Alps,* his *Roman Daughter,* and other adventures into high art.

This was the year of the Russian campaign, and his Napoleonic adulation incensed the Russian artist Paul Svinin, who started a malicious rumor that the *Roman Daughter* was not an original composition. The implication was false, but it spread. Profoundly depressed on the one hand and stirred by Rubens' success on the other, the young Rembrandt put forward a proposal for the future of the Museum in which he would have a major part. His father rejected it as unfair to his other children.[5] Rembrandt then betook himself to Baltimore, the commercial and cultural rival of Philadelphia, and there raised the necessary capital to establish a museum of his own. In two more years it would be a reality—the first legitimate offspring of Peale's Museum, in the first American building designed and built for that purpose. Rubens, grateful for a move which left him still in full control, helped liberally with duplicates. The patriarch at Belfield watched, first with grave forebodings and then with fond complacency, aware that this would be no "Great School of Nature," but a resort of artistic taste with a dash of science thrown in, another "fashionable lounge" for daytime browsing and social evenings.

Rembrandt's handsome edifice on Holliday Street, designed by Robert Carey Long and still, as "The Peale Museum," very much a part of the life of Baltimore, was nearing completion in September 1814. A British fleet was in the harbor, British troops were at North Point, and the ruins of Washington were smouldering behind them. True to his father's testimony for peace, Rembrandt refused to shoulder a gun and spent the night of the rockets' red glare in a windowless museum with his pregnant wife and seven youngsters, hoping it would pass as a residence and so be spared from the burning.[6] Baltimore afterward held none of this against him, and he had his share in the commissions for civic portraits of the heroes of the defense.

His half-brother Linnaeus, dedicated at birth to the great naturalist, was another matter. Lin, who had rebelled against becoming a printer, had run away to sea, swaggering in from Rio de Janeiro (October 1812) with a monkey on his shoulder ("living horned sapajou") as a peace offering to the Museum. In 1813 he was a privateersman, saw a bit of France, saw his ship burned and beached after a battle on the New Jersey shore, joined the crack "Washington Guards," disgraced himself in a fight with a comrade,

REMBRANDT PEALE'S BALTIMORE VENTURE
Rembrandt Peale's Baltimore venture was located in America's first building designed
and erected as a museum (Robert Carey Long, architect). It opened in 1814, the year
of the British assault on the city. After many vicissitudes, it houses a present-day
municipal museum of history and art. (The Peale Museum, Baltimore.)

and then enlisted in the light artillery, regular army—at war with
his father, too. The rattling weapons and martial bravado that
delighted his sisters were anguish to the master and mistress of
Belfield.

The master of Belfield was himself preoccupied with erecting
monuments to peace in his formal garden, with the work of the
farm, with the manufacture of decay-proof false teeth, with plans
for his textile manufacturing center, and with a storm-resistant
windmill that would harness the power of the air for him and
perhaps pump water for the entire city at a trifling cost. That idea

REDHEFFER'S PERPETUAL MOTION
*The Peales' delight in presenting new advances in science
was matched only by their eagerness to expose a fable or a
fraud. When an obscure mechanic "discovered" perpetual
motion, they were the first to detect the imposture. This exact
replica was built for the Museum in 1813, when the
excitement was at its height, as a demonstration to end all
the controversy.* (The Franklin Institute.)

met with no favor, but great was the excitement when another citizen of Germantown, Charles Redheffer, announced his discovery of—perpetual motion! There it stood, an elegantly built, busy little machine, admission one dollar. Bets were laid. Typefounder James Ronaldson wagered $200 against Robert M. Patterson's sneer of "imposture." But it was Coleman Sellers who noted that cogs supposedly driving were in fact being driven—sure evidence of a hidden power source. To clinch the matter, Isaiah Lukens, a machinist and steady friend of the Peales, built a duplicate for the Museum, both as an exposure of the fraud and as a puzzle: what *did* make it work? The versatile Moses Williams was placed in charge of its operation. The Redheffer furor was at its height in October 1813, but the Museum model would remain a popular attraction—still to be seen twenty or thirty years later, next to "the magic flowers and the singing birds, to the left of the optical illusion in which a hat or a hand could be placed between the eye and the object without cutting off the view."[7]

Inevitably, the Museum had assumed a patriotic cast. New heroes of the war joined the portrait gallery, with reminders of the Spirit of '76 as well in James Peale's spirited painting of Colonel Allen McLane fighting his way out of an ambush by British dragoons, George H. Miller's bust of Franklin, and William Rush's of Benjamin Rush. Rubens Peale published his *Historical Catalogue of the Paintings in the Philadelphia Museum, consisting chiefly of Portraits of Revolutionary Patriots and other Distinguished Characters* in 1813. Historical relics appeared: Major Eli B. Clemson's gift of the pipe smoked by British trader Robert Dickson when he brought the Sioux out on the warpath with the enemy; the manuscript of John Andre's satire on Anthony Wayne's soldiers, "The Cow Chace"; Talleyrand's oath of allegiance to the United States; "portable soup" of the British army, 1775; and other like digressions from natural history.[8]

War's end was celebrated at the Museum with transparencies in the tall front windows: an eagle descending from on high with a scroll of "PEACE," and similar designs. All at the Museum knew, however, that the end of the larger conflict would signal a return to the wrangle over tenancy in the State House. Peale brought his concern, as he had done so often, to Jefferson on May 2, 1815. "I have ten children, five of them married. I am now in my 75th year, and it is my wish to settle my worldly affairs in the best manner I can." The demands of his heirs could bring a sale of the Museum like that of the Leverian. Also evident was his concern that it be

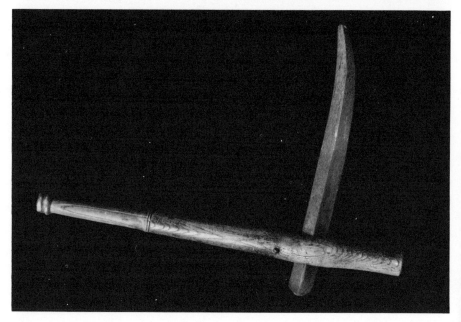

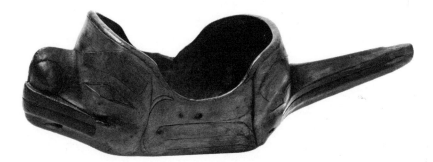

INDIANS OF THE NORTHWEST COAST

EYAK CARVED THROWING STICK

Left, top: Thomas Robinson, a famous sea captain who in later life commanded the U.S. frigates John Adams *and* New York, *gave the Museum in 1813 a collection of objects from China, Hawaii, and the Northwest Coast, including "3 darts & apparatus for throwing them." One end of this finely carved piece from southern Alaska represents a raven or eagle with folded wings; at the other, two small figures are huddled against the body of a wolf.*

CANOE MODELS

Center: *Model of war canoe, probably Haida, from gift of Captain Robinson, 1813.*
Below: *Kayak model from the Aleutian Islands, presented by F. Thompson, 1812.*

"SLAVE KILLER" CLUB

Nootka, Kwakiutl style, in the western Waskasan tradition. This was probably the "war club" presented by F. Thompson in 1812.

WOODEN BEAR-AND-MOSQUITO FOOD BOWL

Probably Haida. This wooden bowl was presented by George Campbell in 1820 as "carved to represent the sea otter." The effigies at the ends are now identified as the Bear, left, and the Mosquito, right. (Peabody Museum, Harvard University.)

made secure, and soon, against the decadence that commercialization was sure to bring. He again had a lottery in mind, the revenues from which would endow the Museum, preferably as government property under "a President and Directors."[9]

His friend at Monticello had no answer. John Vaughan, librarian of the Philosophical Society, proposed a tontine as more attractive to subscribers, but Peale was revolted by a plan in which one gained by others' deaths; besides, public rather than proprietary ownership was the thing. The patriarch took charge of the Museum that summer while Rubens was on vacation, pondering the problem as he painted backgrounds in the cases for new birds brought back by James Griffiths from the seashore. "I cannot do better," he told Rembrandt at last, "than to give it in trust to the Corporation of the City, in order to prevent its division in case of my death, reserving the income of it for my family, under certain regulations. This measure will secure it to the City of Philada. and may be an inducement to the Counsils when it becomes necessary to make some appropriations for more extensive apartments."[10]

It was his hope that one step toward public ownership and support might lead to another. He had found encouragement in a decision that both the Philosophical Society and the Museum would be exempted from Federal taxation. He had already agreed with Rubens that a modest rental to the state would be preferable to continuing responsibility for repairs to the State House, and it had been set at $400 a year. Rubens, in that winter of 1815–1816, was planning a costly improvement: to replace the once sensational argand lamps with something far brighter and entirely free from smoke. His father's friend James Trenchard, the engraver, made regular trips abroad, bringing back messages from Benjamin West and news of London affairs, including the lighting of a London street by gas in 1807. Peale had at once thought of introducing this new illumination at the Museum. It had been suggested again in 1814 by Dr. Benjamin Kugler, one of Rubens's companions on the mineralogical walks with Godon. The young man, with Frederick Accum's *Practical Treatise on Gas-Light* (London, 1815) as guide, now set out to accomplish it. Rubens, as his father once observed, "disregards labor when in prospect of any profit," and here the prospect was good.[11] To demonstrate the potential of gas by lighting a large public building for the first time in America not only would keep the Museum securely in the forefront of scientific advance, but would be in itself the greatest evening entertainment yet.

Rubens soon ran into difficulties, but Dr. Kugler and his brother Charles came to the rescue with an improved system of their own.[12] Their progress was watched from all sides with excitement, trepidation, and not a little hostility. The gasworks up under the tower rafters, tubes and tubs and pipes and fierce blue flame, bore a threatening aspect, to say the least. Some 500 feet of soldered tin pipe were laid from the source to elegantly designed ceiling fixtures in the rooms, and many people, seeing flame at each end of the system, concluded that flame also filled the pipes. Dealers in candles and oil became loud in warning and complaints. Yet the Peales marched on, with the ever-eager old man working along with the young, as they triumphed over leaky pipes, bursting tanks, and public enmity, forward at last to the accomplishment: a new light that could be adjusted at pleasure from the merest pinpoints of flame up to a brilliance many times grander than ever enjoyed before. The five great burners in the Long Room, glistening with cut glass, far outshone all the old patent lamps. Late in April, it was done. Rembrandt came to see and found the rooms thronged as never before. The expense had been staggering—$5,000—but by May 5 the concourse of visitors had very nearly repaid it.[13]

In Baltimore Rembrandt was prompt in following suit, again with the Kuglers and their system. And here, once more, it was a brilliant success, crowned in the center of his large gallery by a "magic ring," composed of a hundred flames that could be brought up from mere pearls up to a gloriously luminous blaze by a valve in a corner of the room. This was followed in June by the organization of the Gas Light Company of Baltimore to light the streets, chartered on February 5, 1817.[14] In Philadelphia the municipal councils had appointed a committee on the practicality of lighting the city by gas, but the hopeful aspects became submerged in controversy arising from the Museum experience—fear of fire or explosion from the gasworks in the steeple, along with the conspicuous fact that this dangerous operation would be making a great deal of money for tenants occupying public property on favored terms.

Just as Peale arrived at his decision to bestow his creation on the city, and just as carbureted hydrogen gas was about to brighten his proposal in more ways than one, a new turn of events suddenly altered whatever receptive mood the town fathers might have entertained. On March 11, 1816, the State authorized sale of the entire State House area, giving the city an option to buy at $70,000; this was accepted on April 11, only days before the

THE WONDER OF CARBURATED HYDROGEN GAS

Writing to his daughter Angelica in 1816, Peale is surer than ever that his Museum "will be the admiration of the world" and explains how its latest triumph was achieved. Gaslight would transform city life and open a new era. Citizens crowded to the illuminated spectacle, but fear of fire or explosion forced removal of the gasworks in 1820 and delayed its general acceptance. (American Philosophical Society.)

populace began streaming in to experience the new wonders of night-become-day. Two members of each council, with Mayor Robert Wharton, were to fix a rental for the Museum, and when Rubens told them, with some pride, how its earnings had leapt forward, they set the sum at $2,000 a year.[15] This figure plainly spelled disaster as far as the Museum's educational purpose was concerned. Only by following gaslight with more novelties and more popular entertainment could it survive.

Once more the aging proprietor called upon politicians and friends to support a museum of natural history as it should be and could be, for the city and for the nation. He had a core of public-spirited well-wishers strongly in favor of a city museum of natural history on the foundations he had laid. The majority, however, were only moved by the argument that a famous and popular museum was good for business. Good enough, but let it stand on its own feet. "Diffusion of knowledge" had nothing to do with it. Peale stood firm. Earlier, in seeking relief from taxes, he had told how "the madness to establish a great National Museum had seized my imagination," how he had brought it to prominence as "a scientific museum" and scorned to increase income by "catchpenny shows." In short, he had declared, the Museum must be seen as "a public benefit" on the same terms as "seminaries of learning or places of worship."[16] In the State House it was already stifled by overcrowding. He needed a new building—perhaps a new city. In this resolute spirit he took his proposal to the public, on July 18, 1816, in the Academy Hall on Fourth Street, with seats reserved for the gentlemen of the Select and Common Councils—very few of whom, however, deigned to appear. Undaunted, his prepared speech was very soon out in pamphlet form, *Address delivered by Charles W. Peale to the Corporation and Citizens of Philadelphia.* Here he told again the story of what he had done, the plan for public enlightenment, the successive appeals for public support, and the present crisis and opportunity. He touched on the fate of the Leverian. "It was the most splendid museum in Great Britain. What has now become of it? Wanting a good foundation, it is lost; it was divided, it was sold, and it is scattered abroad; and some of its articles are now in my Museum."

Would the Philadelphia Museum remain in Philadelphia as a "national ornament" or be driven "from the place of its nativity to some more liberal or opulent city, in search of the patronage and support which had been denied to it by its countrymen?"

Under these circumstances of embarrassment, I have
chosen to address the more enlightened portion of my fellow
citizens, and to solicit the aid of their talents and advice, in
devising some plan by which the Museum may be rescued
from its difficulties, and which, at the same time, may insure
its advancement to perfection, and perpetuate its usefulness to
the city and to the world.[17]

Promptly, too, he drafted an appeal directly to the councils
but then, on the advice of friends, withheld it. Better, they said, to
let the petition come from a group of concerned citizens. A meeting
was held at the University, and a memorial sent to the councils
urging that the city accept title to the Museum, retaining the Peale
arrangement but with a fixed ratio of its income assigned to
continuing improvement. Autograph collectors have clipped names
from the surviving document, but it still attests the character of the
Museum's support in the city. Charles Biddle, successful merchant
and politician and the father of banker Nicholas Biddle, was
chairman. Nicholas Collin, that most faithful friend, was there,
along with the Museum's first donor, Robert Patterson, and his son
Robert M., Joseph Hopkinson, James Milnor, old Bishop William
White, naturalists George Ord and Thomas Say, lawyers William
Tilghman and Joseph Reed Ingersoll, and Doctors John Barnes,
Thomas Billings, and William Currie. The learned Rabbi Emanuel
Nuñes Carvalho, a newcomer to Philadelphia, was present as
renewed evidence of the Jewish community's approval of Peale's
accomplishment. Among the professional men, there were a
number such as economist Tench Coxe and merchants Samuel
Hodgson and Samuel Alexander to represent the concern of
commercial interests.[18]

This intervention did not sit well with the councils, however,
who deemed it a precipitate interference in their deliberations. In
the newspapers "A Friend to Propriety" and another anonymous
citizen took the Museum proprietor sharply to task for his
pretensions. What if the Museum *was* worth $100,000? Other men
had accumulated as much or more in the same time. Donations to
the Philadelphia Museum could not honorably be taken elsewhere;
and, anyway, every city able to support a museum already had one.
Peale replied promptly, apology to the councils, and defense of his
own position.[19]

The councilmen were friendly in private conversation, but
hostile as a body. They took no action, and Peale allowed eight

months to go by before venturing a formal proposal—a plan for a "City Museum." Philadelphia would own the collections, guarantee use of the State House, and open new space over the wings. Peale and his heirs would retain management, pay $800 a year for this privilege, invest at least $400 in improvements, and receive all surplus income for their services. To stabilize the family control, it was to be organized as a stock company, with 100 shares and a total valuation of $100,000. A committee of the councils met at the Museum on April 16, 1817. Peale was ready for them with architectural plans and legal opinions. Still waiting for a decision, he poured out the whole story to Jefferson on May 20, bemoaning the probability that his offer, so promising for the general welfare, would be blocked by councilmen lawyers who wanted space in the wings for their offices. Blocked it was, as he learned the next day.[20]

In the days of the Revolution, like many another idealist-patriot, Peale had declared himself a "citizen of the world." That spirit was with him still. New York was a rising power, where science had always found encouragement. He would look into prospects in New York and, if that failed, in Washington. On May 23, with Hannah at his side, he set out for the north.

New York, he soon found, was not prepared to take over the Philadelphia collection but was itself setting an example he could well wish for Philadelphia to follow. The former Alms House on City Hall Park had been granted for ten years to The New York Institution, an association of cultural organizations encompassing the American Academy of Fine Arts, the Lyceum of Natural History, the Literary and Philosophical Society, and the New-York Historical Society, together with the Institute for the Deaf and Dumb and some other agencies. Samuel Latham Mitchill was prominent in this milieu. He introduced Peale to a meeting of the Lyceum of Natural History as "the father of natural history in America" and sponsored his membership at the Historical Society; the gentlemen of the Literary and Philosophical Society also did him honor. There would be no encouragement, however, for a move from Philadelphia to New York, for an entire wing of the former Alms House had been assigned to the old Tammany–Gardiner Baker collection, now called "The American Museum" under the management of John Scudder. It had just moved in from Chatham Street and was nearly ready for its formal opening, announced as "unrivalled by any similar institution for splendor, correctness and scientific arrangement."[21]

Scudder owed much to Peale, even the phrase "a world in miniature." His installation even included an imitation of Peale's former mossy "bank," real ground with trees and animals. Peale admired the neatness of it all but found much to criticize: the birds and beasts were mounted only for show, poses unnatural, muscle form not preserved. Natural history was further diluted by waxwork and "cosmorama." Concerts would be a popular attraction; but better, there would be what Peale had so long desired, regular lectures illustrated by museum specimens and delivered by men of established authority.

In June, Peale was back at Belfield with no immediate impulse to look into opportunities in Washington. The New York Institution had impressed him. Given a worthy building—not an abandoned alms house—Philadelphia could do far better. In fact, what he had seen and what he could imagine in his own city were all part of a cultural change more significant than he realized. A new generation of younger, dedicated scientists, more specialized than its elders, was bringing with it the beginnings of a network of learned societies. They scrupulously avoided popularization, which the commercial museums had brought into bad odor. The marriage of the scholarly New York Institution and Scudder's American Museum would not be a happy one.

In Philadelphia, the Academy of Natural Sciences, founded in 1812, was coming to maturity. It had its hall in Gilliams Court in Arch Street, the seat of a learned and active group, among whom Zaccheus Collins, Reuben Haines, Dr. Richard Harlan, the geologists William H. Keating and Gerard Troost, the brilliant artist-naturalist Charles Alexandre Lesueur, the dour and scholarly George Ord, and the entomologist-conchologist Thomas Say were particularly close to the Peales. The Academy had begun laying the foundation of its modern museum of today, but Peale's Museum would long remain a major resource of its members.

At the State House both types of museum men may be seen in contrast: Rubens Peale, scientific showman, and his youngest half-brother Titian, a naturalist. Both Franklin and Titian had rebelled against the careers in textile manufacture planned for them and had come to the Museum as assistants. Franklin's training had at least laid a good foundation in mechanics. He could do well at the evening demonstrations in the Lecture Room. Rubens had carried these beyond chemistry, using the magic lantern to illustrate astronomy and other sciences, and even showing pictures in motion. (His boats sailed well, but his galloping horses were less convincing.) Franklin, for his part, could be equally clever, while giving the evenings a more studious cast.

Titian, aged seventeen, wanted no part of cotton spinning, nor did he find allure in the manufacture of porcelain false teeth, as laboriously developed by his father. But he was a keen hunter, an excellent taxidermist, and a meticulously accurate painter. He attended Dr. Wistar's lectures on anatomy at the University, began a study of entomology as if to continue what his namesake brother had begun, and at the age of eighteen was elected to the Academy of Natural Sciences. This was just at the time when William Maclure, wealthy Scottish geologist, became its president, launched the publication of its *Journal,* and opened an era of productive activity. The Academy now had all the elements of stability and influence Peale had so desired, which an association could attract and maintain, but a proprietor could not. He had long received a correspondence far larger than he could reciprocate, with all else he had to do, but the Academy had faithful corresponding secretaries such as Reuben Haines, drawing responses from an informed membership—a link to other institutions much closer than was possible for Peale with his exchanges of specimens.

In the winter and spring of 1818, Titian was in Georgia and Florida on a collecting expedition with Maclure, Ord, and Say. It involved disciplined hard work and danger, shooting alligators, opening an Indian mound, avoiding hostile Indians, and eventually returning with trophies that made his father sigh again for lack of museum space, though glowing with pride in the presence of this son, tall, discreet, and studious.

This was all good preparation for what was to follow in the next year: Titian's appointment as assistant naturalist on the government expedition commanded by Major Stephen Harriman Long, ordered to explore the country between the Mississippi and the Rocky Mountains. This prospect sparked Peale's long-delayed trip to Washington, and a little party set forth in November 1818: Charles Willson and Hannah Peale, with James Peale's daughters, Anna Claypoole and Sarah Miriam. Anna, at twenty-seven, was a decorous painter in miniature. Sally, a willful and delicious eighteen, was just crossing the threshhold into her long career as a portraitist in the large.

Secretary of War Calhoun handled their business with smooth efficiency: Titian's appointment, a revolutionary pension for James Peale, bounty land for soldier Charles Linnaeus Peale. Calhoun's portrait was painted for the Museum gallery at this time, as were those of President Monroe, Vice-President Tompkins, Secretary of State John Quincy Adams, and others, including the lively centenarian and former slave Yarrow Mamout. In Adams, Peale recognized a probable future President, and one who would be friendly to learning and the arts.[22]

Calhoun readily agreed that the collections from the Long expedition should be deposited in the Philadelphia Museum. Here was another step toward national status, but Peale's efforts to impress Congress with the need for a national museum were rebuffed even more flatly than before. Democratic Congressman Adam Seybert put it plainly. Seybert, a physician who had studied mineralogy with Abbé Haüy in Paris and then followed Woodhouse as professor of chemistry at the University of Pennsylvania, was also a political realist and chief authority on government expenditure. Such a bill would never pass, he said, and when Peale turned from Seybert to others for opinion, the point was amply confirmed. "The time will come when they shall be sorry for having let it slip through their fingers," he confided to his friend at Monticello. "Having laid aside all other pursuits except what may tend to the improvement of the Museum, I hope I may live long enough to place it on a permanent mount."[23]

This was the end of the national museum dream, but it came on a gay note, with some of the accolade that the long effort deserved. Peale was entertained everywhere as a celebrity, with music, dinner, and dance climaxed by the White House receptions in the sparkle of candlelight, crystal, and court dress, Sally shining to her elderly uncle's pride and delight and, proudest, Hannah in her plain Quaker dress, with her plain face and gentle air of pleasure, was singled out for special attention by Mrs. Monroe, to stand beside her at the center of the scene.

And so home again with the first touches of spring in the air, picking up a new wonder in Baltimore on the way, a European invention, the bicycle, or "fast walking machine"—no pedals, propel yourself by your feet and then lift them to coast. Here was a new delight for all at Belfield, whisking along the garden paths—and "downhill," as Lin wrote to the absent explorer Titian, "like the very devil"—while plowing and planting began, and another big elk went to its treadmill to pump water for the garden beds on the hill, the fields and foliage green once more. Once again, alas, the city councils dampened the ardor of scientific advance, for they forbade the dangerous practice of "fast walking" in the streets.

To help pay its rent to the city, "catchpenny shows" had

"THE FAST-WALKING MACHINE"
This precursor of the bicycle was also known as a "Pedestrian's Hobby-horse," or the
"Draisiana," after its inventor Baron von Drais. Drawing by C. W. Peale, 1819.
(American Philosophical Society.)

already invaded the Museum. One of the most popular—with everyone but the proprietor—was the "Pandean Band" in the person of one Signor Hellene, who, by plying hands, elbows, and knees, played the Italian viola, Turkish cymbals, and tenor drum, at the same time blowing on a set of Pandean pipes affixed to his head and chiming in with a frame of Chinese bells worn as a crown. It was grotesque, but it drew well and, at a cost of only $5 a night, showed a good profit through many return engagements.[24]

Perhaps in appreciation of this effort, perhaps to discourage it, the city reduced the Museum rent to $1,200, which was less than either of the two lower rooms might have brought in rental. The building must be insured by the Peales for $10,000, but their premium could be deducted from rent. The councils expressed strong disapproval not only of the gasworks but also of the crowded workroom Peale had built over the tower stairwell and which had become an essential part of the museum operation. Faced by the financial panic of 1819, Rubens delayed removing the "gas factory"

BUFFALO HUNT, MAJOR LONG'S EXPEDITION, 1820
This convincing action drawing is by Titian R. Peale, who had acquired his own
skill with bow and arrow from the Indians. (American Philosophical Society.)

in the tower (a fire risk of the first order) until the summer of 1820.
He had been married to pretty Eliza Burd Patterson that March and
was living nearby in the pleasant house Rembrandt had used before
moving to Baltimore; but the Museum rental was in arrears, and he
was also in danger of losing his home. In November his father
published an offer to exchange Belfield for a suitable museum site in
town, but it brought no response. Then, on December 11, he
deeded the Museum to his sons, reserving the right to all proceeds
during his lifetime and an annuity for his widow.

Formal incorporation as The Philadelphia Museum Company
followed on February 1, 1821. It became a stock company of 500
shares valued at $200 each, and its stockholders (with himself
currently the only one) were annually to elect a board of five trustees
to run the institution. By charter, no part could ever leave
Philadelphia without a payment of twice its value to the city, the
assessment to be made by the trustees.[25]

It had finally become, therefore, a city museum, though independently administered. Its future, however, lay with the stockholders rather than the trustees. The Pennsylvania Academy of the Fine Arts was doing well as a stock company, but the Academy's shareholders were a large group of public-spirited persons with no expectations of profit. All depended upon how well the Museum's future owners would reflect the viewpoint of its founder.

Responding to the act of incorporation, the city cut the rent in half, to $600, conditioned on removal of Peale's workroom and some other changes. Unpaid arrears must be met, and this was done by a bank loan, an initial concern of the trustees for some years to come. Since a workroom was essential, application was promptly made for rental of the East Room below—the Declaration Chamber, no less.

A public foundation of sorts had at last been achieved. Curiously, the long campaign for a national establishment had a brief, belated revival. In 1820 Congress had granted 20 acres of District of Columbia land to the Columbian Institute for the Promotion of Arts and Sciences, a concession due largely to John Quincy Adams's interest in the institute and its objective of a national museum. Burgess Allison, Mahlon Dickerson, Benjamin Latrobe, William Thornton, and other Peale friends were institute members, and on September 1, 1821, Thornton moved that Congress be asked to purchase the Peale collection for $100,000, or to authorize a lottery for that purpose. The motion was tabled, probably because of others' awareness of the Museum's recent incorporation.[26]

Belatedly also, Peale now moved to replace the "fashionable lounge" of Rubens' creation with his own concept of thirty years earlier, an American version of the Muséum d'Histoire Naturelle. He named his five trustees: Pierce Butler, Zaccheus Collins, Robert Patterson, Rubens Peale, and Coleman Sellers. They first met on April 11, 1821, and the first business given them was the election of a faculty of professors. Young Dr. John Davidson Godman, soon to become the husband of Rembrandt's daughter Angelica, was given the chair of physiology; Thomas Say, that of zoology; the spruce young Dr. Richard Harlan, comparative anatomy; and the amiable Dutch geologist Dr. Gerard Troost, a founder and first president of the Academy of Natural Sciences, mineralogy.

Senator Butler, though absent on his Georgia plantation, was elected president of the board. The wealthiest and most prestigious figure, he was the son of a British baronet but had been an American since 1773—a Federalist, but of a freewheeling sort. He was a Germantown neighbor of the Peales, and his daughter had married Dr. James Mease, a Peale friend prominent in the city's scientific and literary affairs. (Dr. Mease's children took the name Butler, and one of them later married the actress Fanny Kemble.)

That summer brought a return of yellow fever, with all business in abeyance. The epidemic reached Belfield near its close, and both Peale and his gentle Hannah were stricken. She, under a doctor's care, died on October 10, 1821. Peale, stubbornly following his own treatment, recovered, though weakened and woebegone. It was the end of the happy Belfield years. He was taken to Rubens' house in the city, for a slow convalescence but close again to the Museum.

On October 25 the councils confirmed a two-year lease of the State House at the reduced rent, but Rubens was making other plans. Rembrandt had lost heart with his "elegant rendezvous for taste, curiosity and leisure" in Baltimore, and Rubens was ready to take over. Debt-ridden as it was, there would be no trustees, faculty of professors, or parental ideals. He would be his own man. With Rubens' resignation and the death of Pierce Butler, two new members joined the Museum board: Joseph Parker Norris, of an old Quaker family and president of the Bank of Pennsylvania, and Henry Pratt, the well-to-do son of artist Matthew Pratt. On April 26, 1822, they elected C. W. Peale as manager, with 25 percent of income as his remuneration, and whatever assistants he might choose.

Assistants he had aplenty. Best of all, Titian had returned early the year before—rosy-cheeked, tall and straight as an Indian, a professional naturalist who would compromise on nothing to win popular applause. He brought new verve, fresh as the West, and with it quadrupeds, birds, fish, and reptiles, in all nearly a hundred mounted exhibits, as well as botanical specimens and over a hundred drawings—all duly entered in the Record Book as held on deposit for the War Department of the United States. Portraits of five of the scientific corps were now hanging in the gallery: Major Long, commander; Lieutenant Augustus Edward Jessup, geologist; Dr. William Baldwin, physician and botanist, who had not survived the hardships of the trail; Thomas Say, zoologist; and Titian himself. The civilian members are shown in their specially designed uniform, though in the field that was replaced by leather hunting shirt, breeches, and moccasins.

Ottoes. may 1820)

INDIAN MOTHER WITH BABY IN CRADLE
This drawing of an Indian encampment, dated May 1820, was made by Titian R.
Peale during the Long expedition to the Rocky Mountains. (American Philosophical
Society.)

Titian had had his full share of adventures: he had moved out
with small detachments of the main body to explore a tributary
river or open a lonely aboriginal burying ground said to contain the
remains of a pygmy race; had learned to face danger and
near-disaster in strange places; had smoked a fraternal peace pipe
with Chief Long Hair of the Pawnees; had pursued buffalo with the
Indians and become expert with bow and arrow as well as gun; had
devised a wolf trap for night prowlers (three prairie wolves and one
black wolf were mounted now in the Quadruped Room); and had
hunted and fished to his heart's content. For Titian, science and
adventure had blended into one. His heart leapt at the thought of
sailing as naturalist with Commodore Charles Stewart's Pacific
Squadron. Stewart was a fellow Philadelphian and a friend of the
Museum, bringing gifts from every voyage. He bore the same
popular name as the ship in which he had first won fame, "Old
Ironsides"; back from the Mediterranean, he had strode into the
Museum in 1821 with an Egyptian mummy head and a mummified
small animal. But love intervened, and the ships sailed without a
naturalist. Titian was married the next year to little Eliza Cecilia

AMERICAN
WILD TURKEY
This is the original Muse-
um mounting from which
Titian Peale drew a plate
for Charles Lucien Bona-
parte's continuation of
Alexander Wilson's
American Ornithology.
Titian had brought the
bird back from Major
Long's expedition; it is
shown, unmounted, in the
foreground of his father's
large self-portrait of 1822
(frontispiece). (Museum of
Comparative Zoology,
Harvard University.)

Laforgue—in the Roman Catholic chapel—over his father's somber protests but with the festive cooperation of all the younger Peales.

Marriage and family responsibility enforced routine work in the Museum, where Titian spent all his time preparing and arranging the collections, but disdaining the Lecture Room with its taint of popular flummery. The evening demonstrations and entertainments were still essential to income, and here Franklin, a young man chastened by adversity, stepped into Rubens' place and kept these affairs both amusing and informative. Franklin, also married against his father's will, now had a small daughter and an insane wife. The two brothers, if not entirely congenial at work, shared alike the Peale love of music and, when in a social circle of like-minded friends, raised their voices happily together in song.

Franklin had inherited a Lecture Room assistant from Rubens, a small Peale grandson named Escol Sellers. For Escol the Lecture Room was the heart of it all, and excitement was highest when he himself would be given a part in the show—a stir of people everywhere, lights shining on the Long Room promenade of "gay

RED FOX AND PRAIRIE WOLF
A fox whelp (above) was mothered by a cat and kept as a pet near the Museum's ticket
office, at the head of the State House stairs. The cat was the chief of many mourners
when the little creature slipped through the bannister and fell to the floor far below.
The wolf (below) was brought back from Major Long's expedition, where Titian Peale
many times matched his ingenuity against the cunning beasts before he could trap a
living specimen. Drawing by Charles A. Lesueur for J. D. Godman's American
Natural History *(1826).*

bonnets and cashmere shawls," and then suddenly a bell would
tinkle and the seats begin to fill. At the hollow table, it might be
Uncle Rubens or Uncle Franklin, Dr. Robert Hare with his great
voltaic coil, or Dr. Thomas P. Jones, Dr. John Kearsley Mitchell,
or some other friendly volunteer.

Sometimes the front of the table was removed and the great
electrical machine trundled in, and all the electrical experiments of that period shown, including dancing dolls, lightning flashes over glass plates sometimes arranged to display

GEORGE ESCOL SELLERS
A future member of the board of
directors, this silhouette of Sellers
was made when he was boy
assistant with the "Magic
Lanthorn." Museum silhouette.
(Author's collection.)

portraits—the cloud made of a couple of oil flasks covered with tin foil suspended to an electric charged trolly wire, drawn by a silk cord over a many-jointed and hinged house, with a lightning rod to its chimney. The clouds would rise when passing over the pointed rod, until it was capped with a brass ball. Then the cloud would descend to send its lightning flash into the ball. The cork would blow out of the gas bottle and with its thunderclap the house would fall to pieces. These electrical exhibitions closed by firing the brass gas cannon.

Sometimes, too, when Uncle Rubens had one of his headaches, Escol and his older brother Charles had been asked to run the whole magic lantern show themselves. Escol "did the talking," but the boys loved it best when they could bring in Uncle Raphaelle for that. Raphaelle when sober was an excellent ventriloquist and would keep the audience in a roar when comic pictures were shown, and some of his sleight-of-hand and mechanical tricks were very good.[27]

No faculty of professors could compete with this. Of the trustees' four appointments, Godman responded most warmly; the young physician was filled with the hectic, fretful, affectionate energy of the doomed consumptive. He and Gerard Troost lectured together in the spring of 1821; their formal introductory lectures were held in the Declaration Chamber, the others in the Lecture Room above, with Godman's physiology scheduled at five and Troost's mineralogy at eight. The magic lantern rounded out the week on Saturday evenings. Neither Godman nor Troost repeated his course, though Godman, now married to Rembrandt's daughter

MAGIC LANTHORN

WILL be exhibited THIS EVENING, at eight o'clock, in the PHILADELPHIA MUSEUM, and will continue to be exhibited every Saturday evening.

Admittance, as usual, 25 Cents—Children half price, under 12 years.

oct 27   stf

Angelica, remained close to the Museum and based his *American Natural History,* published in three volumes in 1826, almost entirely on its collections. Troost, who had lectured both from the Museum's minerals and his own, had accumulated a rich natural history collection that, in his later years at the University of Nashville, would form one of the most authentic and valuable of the western museums.

Harlan and Say never got around to giving their courses in comparative anatomy and zoology, though Harlan compensated for this lack by gifts and the loan of a comparative anatomy exhibit. His donation of the skeleton of a gigantic horse with a human skeleton mounted on it dramatically illustrated both skeletal structure and the famous Benjamin West theme of "Death on the Pale Horse." Say's election as professor of natural history at the University in 1822 prevented his appearance, but he made some amends by bringing out his *American Entomology* under the imprint of the Philadelphia Museum.[28]

Poor attendance had discouraged the lecturers, and Peale tried to encourage them by appearing himself with a survey of natural history's beneficent influence. Raphaelle and Dr. Godman helped to polish his style, but his discourses of April and May 1823 were, as he confided to Jefferson, a failure. So indeed they were, when one considers that this was the time of the rise of the lyceum movement, when lectures of every sort were popular. Perhaps the new Franklin Institute was following the lead of the Museum when, in spring of the next year, it created a similar faculty of volunteer lecturers in a sharp departure from the usual pattern of self-education in the mechanics' institutes of the period. That program was an immediate success. Robert M. Patterson and William H. Keating spoke on chemistry and mineralogy to large audiences, and even Godman talked on natural history, in spite of the fact that his subject was marginal to the institute's basic purpose.[29]

One may also hear a derisive echo of the Peale efforts of 1822-1823 coming from Second and Market streets, where the Washington Museum was sponsoring lectures by "Mr. Adrian, Professor of Philosophic Legerdemain," and where, in contrast to the decorous art of the Peales, one saw Adolph Ulrich Wertmüller's *Venus, Bathing Figure, Wood Faun,* and titillating *Danaë and the Shower of Gold,* not to mention Dr. Joseph Chiappi's compositions in wax, *Queen Dido on the Funeral Pile,* and *Death of General Packingham at the Battle of New Orleans.*[30]

Advancing age might be apparent in the fumbling revival of early ideals, but with brush in hand the old man was all he had ever been, and more. His *Retreat Across the Delaware* was a lesson on peace for the Museum walls, suggested by Thomas Sully's *Washington at the Delaware.* But Peale's was a nocturne showing the beaten army seeking safety across the firelit river, a scene he had watched himself and which stood in memory as holding all the horrors of war. In gentler spirit, an altered copy of Charles Catton's *Noah and His Ark* was painted for his own and visitors' pleasure. In 1822, when the trustees voted a self-portrait of the Museum's founder, Rembrandt had patronizingly advised his father to go to New York to see Sir Thomas Lawrence's full-length of Benjamin West, a good model. Not for the old man. This work must top everything he had ever done. He would defy models and conventions by placing the light behind the figure rather than in front—the deeper symbolism in a life's monument, unique and bold.

Trustee actions at this time were largely in response to the founder's wishes, tempered by thoughts of financial accounting and foresight. They had been prompt in voting a return to the published accession lists, and *Poulson's* of August 30–31, 1821, carries the "Additions and Donations" of the previous three years. The lists encouraged donations, but also showed how much dross had to be accepted to bring in one truly appropriate object. Rubens, with the museum man's casual handling of round figures, had estimated the total collection at 100,000. One of his handbills issued from 1818 to 1820 cites 212 animals in the Quadruped Room (apparently no change since 1810), 1,240 birds, together with 180 portraits overhead, 121 fishes, 148 snakes, 112 lizards, 40 tortoises and turtles, 1,044 shells, corals, and so on, and the mineral collection rounded out as 8,000.[31]

Only one scientific marvel on a par with the Weston meteorite had occurred during Rubens' tenure, but when his father took over again, "the celebrated Sea Serpent" of Gloucester, Massachusetts, was already slipping into a half-world of doubt and derision. While the reports of its sighting were receiving serious attention, the Museum had acquired a panoramic painting by John Ritto Penniman of Boston showing its great length, the protuberances on its back, and the threatening "shovel" head thrust up above the waves.[32] This could be seen alongside a real marine marvel, a huge turtle, "*Testudo Mydas,* of Linnaeus," which gained national publicity; brought in alive it was nearly six feet long and of such weight that four men could barely lift it.[33] The awesome, gargantuan devilfish of 1823 outdid the turtle in a special exhibit in the Declaration Chamber. Abovestairs, soon after, Peale got rid of the costumed monkeys and restored the Marine Room to its former senses with a "classical" arrangement of fishes of the world.

In January 1824, he launched another feature of his ideal museum, a journal. Volume 1, Number 1 of *The Philadelphia Museum, or Register of Natural History and the Arts* was to be both popular and scientific. Rembrandt Peale was there in prose and verse. A short article by Franklin Peale, "On Magnetism," reflected his current interest in a magnet capable of lifting great weights and was later expanded for the *Journal of the Franklin Institute.* If well received, *The Philadelphia Museum* was to be published twice a month from the Museum Press. No other issue followed—another family effort dying even more quickly than the lectures.[34]

Through the city fathers' formal celebrations marking Lafayette's return—General of the Revolution, hero wounded in battle, patriot soldier of French and American liberty—every effort was made to keep natural history out of sight, only to be defeated by the one old man's recognition of the other. Peale must stand at Lafayette's side throughout the reception in the Declaration Chamber, and they all must tour the collections afterward. When the gallery portrait was pointed out, others laughed at the lack of likeness in the boyish face, but the "National Guest" declared stoutly that no better picture of him had ever been painted.

From France, too, young Titian Peale now had a distinguished friend. Just turned twenty-one, short, black-eyed, and alive with Latin enthusiasm, Charles Lucien Jules Laurent Bonaparte, Prince of Musignano, had caught the excitement of the Museum and was determined, with what help he could find, to complete the *American Ornithology* of Alexander Wilson. Had his uncle, the Emperor, recognized the legitimacy of his birth, he would have stood second in the line of succession to the imperial throne. He had married his first cousin, Zénaïda, daughter of the exiled king of Spain now living in royal grandeur at nearby Bordentown, New Jersey. But Charles Lucien had no interest in politics and was making conquests of his own as the only scientist among the warlike clan. Titian was painting illustrations for the new volumes, collecting, dissecting, identifying.

John James Audubon had come to town in April to launch his career as a professional naturalist. Unfortunately, he also launched that controversy between his admirers and Wilson's which persists to this day. It began when Dr. James Mease introduced him to the Peales, Harlan, Leseuer, Bonaparte, and Ord, and brought him to a meeting of the Academy of Natural Sciences. Shown some of Titian's meticulously accurate drawings for Bonaparte, Audubon at once criticized them sharply from the point of view of his own style, with its pictorial qualities of animation and variety. This as quickly aroused the ire of George Ord, the stoop-shouldered sophisticate and "Father of North American Zoology"; his resentment grew as Audubon's inaccuracies and his slurs on Wilson appeared. Harlan, conversely, became Audubon's friend and partisan, as admirers of the aggressive bird-painter lined up against those of the dead poet-naturalist. Bonaparte stood fast with Titian, whom he sent on a collecting tour to South Carolina and Florida at the end of the year.[35]

Titian was not openly hostile, though thirteen years later when Audubon's work was in publication he did decline an invitation to contribute to it a study of the geographical distribution of North American birds. Another visiting lion of 1824 would also become a Wilson-Peale partisan. This was the vigorous and lively British naturalist Charles Waterton, whom Titian had encountered in the Museum that summer and brought home to meet his father and enjoy a cup of tea. Waterton had developed a taxidermy technique of his own, as well as a method to prevent the fading of birds' plumage, and shared these with the Peales. He disapproved of their method of showing every beast with open jaws, because he said it gave an unnatural grinning aspect to the whole array. The Philadelphians conceded that point but defended the need to show tooth structure. Waterton brought their first direct contact with European practices since the visit of Dufresne, director of the conservation of birds and quadrupeds at Paris, in December 1817. Waterton went on his way after a hunting trip through the New

Jersey countryside with Titian, carrying pleasant recollections back to his English estate: "Mr. Peale has now passed his eightieth year, and appears to possess the vivacity, and, I may almost add, the activity of youth. To the indefatigable exertions of this gentleman is the western world indebted for this splendid museum. . . . The skeleton of the mammoth is a national treasure. I could form but a faint idea of it by description, until I had seen it. It is the most magnificent skeleton in the world. . . ."[36]

Also in this year, Rubens decided he had had enough of Baltimore and the 8 percent payments due on Rembrandt's building. His creditors persuaded him to continue the exhibition under a manager, but he himself moved to New York. There, on October 26, 1825, the gala day of the opening of the Erie Canal, "Peale's New York Museum" began its career at 252 Broadway, facing the park and City Hall. "The Parthenon," he called it, perhaps taking his cue from William Bullock's London Museum and Pantherion, whose catalogue had been sent him by a friend. Part of the military parade of that day, in the presence of the

LEG RATTLE, LOWER CREEK OR SEMINOLE INDIANS
The original Peale label reads "Rattle made from Turtle shells, worn by the Florida Indians during their war-dance." War dances were performed during Titian Peale's earlier visit to Florida, but this piece was probably obtained in the winter of 1824–1825, when he was painting Florida birds for Prince Charles Lucien Bonaparte. (Peabody Museum, Harvard University.)

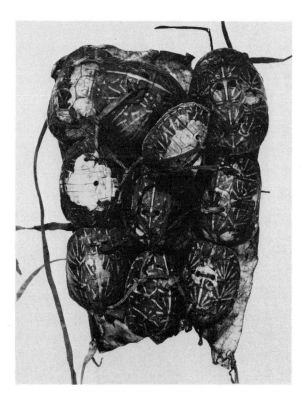

Corporation of the City, filed through the new museum's rooms and fired a salute from among the statuary adorning its rooftop terrace—an official blessing upon this new bastion of science and art. Here Rubens would preside for more than a decade, as a popularizer of scientific discovery, but with a Lecture Room that yielded more and more to purely theatrical attractions.

Baltimore and New York, the direct offspring of the Philadelphia Museum, had each begun with a compromise toward the "fashionable lounge" idea. But in Cincinnati, a city whose growth was stimulated at many points from Philadelphia, a new museum unlike the many random imitations of Peale's had come into being, in 1818–1820. This was the Western Museum Society of Dr. Daniel Drake, dedicated to making that city a scientific capital. It had good community support in the framework of a stock company: a $50 share brought free admission to the holder, and the general public was admitted for 25 cents. Dr. Robert Best was chief curator, and John James Audubon was in charge of mounting birds and fish. The collections grew well, but these were years of financial depression, and disaster struck in 1823. Everything was offered for sale but found no buyers, and the whole, as with Tammany and Baker, fell into the hands of a remaining curator, Joseph Dorfeuille. He agreed only to honor stockholders' admission. After only three years, the time for compromise with popularity had come.

Drake had been a medical student in Philadelphia in 1805–1807, when the State House collection was newly arranged and catalogued. Dorfeuille had held an annual ticket to the Philadelphia Museum in 1808 and was listed as a donor in 1809 and 1810. Drake was an earnest promoter of cultural advance over a wide range. Dorfeuille, said to be a nephew of the Duchesse de Richelieu, had come to America from travels in Europe and the Orient. A slight figure with a long nose and small mouth, he was lively and witty. He gave organ recitals. He was compiling a work on the insects of Louisiana. He had, in short, one eye on science and the other on his need for a supportive popular attraction—out of which came that long-famous marvel of the West known as "Dorfeuille's Hell," the waxwork and mechanical spectacle that owed so much to the ingenuity of young Hiram Powers.[37]

Portrait painter and Peale friend James Reid Lambdin opened a museum in Pittsburgh in 1827, encouraged by Rubens Peale in New York and reinforced by Indian materials from General William Clark's collection in St. Louis. It was a serious effort, bringing contacts also with the Philadelphia Museum, but a digression away from art which Lambdin came to consider the great mistake of his life.[38]

Rembrandt Peale, too, had had some regrets, though from first to last he would value museums only as they supported his career in art. There may have been some truth in Raphaelle's belief that museum arsenic solutions were the cause of his deformed hands and the internal pains he could only drown in alcohol. Raphaelle, master of still-life painting and founder of that art in America, all laughter, all sorrow, succumbed at last in March 1825, reduced at the end to writing happy little verses for a baker to put into cakes.

Of all the Peale sons, Linnaeus was the least in touch with natural history; a stout, loud young man, he was married now and lived at Belfield till the place was sold in 1826. He was in politics in 1824, a Jackson man, calling on the voters to break the "chains of foetid corruption, . . . nail their flag to the staff and rally round the standard of Enlightened Democracy." Then away he went to fight for Bolivar as second officer of the frigate *La Plata,* leaving his wife to get along by taking in boarders just as Raphaelle's long-suffering Patty had been obliged to do. Back again with roaring Latin cronies in his wake, for lack of anything better to do he drifted into taxidermy and other museum work with Rubens in New York. His father rarely heard from him. "He knows," the old man said, "my dislike of man killing and privateer robbing." They met briefly, however, when Lin was back in town during a new transition period for the Philadelphia Museum.

In 1826 a way had been found to end the conflict with the city and to put the Museum once more on the forefront of modernity. An office building, something new to America, had been projected with John Haviland as architect. It was patterned after London's new Burlington Arcade, and would stand on the north side of Chestnut Street between Sixth and Seventh, only a block west of the State House. It was to have a frontage of 109 feet and a depth of 150 feet. Two stone-paved walkways lined by shops would lead through from Chestnut to Carpenter (now Jayne) Street, lighted by a glass roof above the upper levels. The second floor would hold offices, and it was proposed that a third be added to extend the Museum, giving it five large, well-lighted rooms. This was not all the space its founder wished, and there would be no room for further expansion, but the advantages gave promise of a period of security. The Philadelphia Arcade's cornerstone was laid on May 3, 1826, for completion in the summer of 1827.[39]

Stimulated by this prospect, the aging sole stockholder

purchased 150 rattlesnakes from Luzerne, Pike, and Wayne counties and the best collection of Indian costumes, weapons, and utensils ever seen in Philadelphia. The serpents, "well secured in boxes," were given a special showing at the Masonic Hall in June 1826.[40] The Amerind collection was acquired in September at a cost of $200, and in a mysterious way.

The mystery is worth inquiry, and even conjecture. Peale announced the acquisition in *Poulson's,* on September 22, as "an extensive and very complete collection of the dresses, arms, implements, pipes and instruments of music, &c. of the Sioux, Shienne, Aricaree, Mandan and Osage nations." There were dresses of men and women, "ornamented in their peculiar manner with dyed porcupine quills, and is in some of the specimens extremely beautiful. One of the SKIN LODGES used by them is placed in such a manner as to exhibit its use." Also, "their arms, consisting of bows and arrows, war clubs, &c. and a buffaloe skin upon which is painted a record of the fight of Colonel Leavenworth with the Aricaree Indians executed by themselves, their flag, shield, &c . . . In short, this collection contains all their Dresses of War, Ceremony and the Dance, and is the most complete that has ever been exhibited."[41]

Two days later, Peale explained in a letter that he had made the purchase from "traders" who were bringing the Indians for exhibition in Europe. Of this plan the braves and squaws had no inkling until they reached the coast. Learning of it then, they had wisely decamped for home.[42] Conjecture begins with a supposition that the traders, having recouped by selling their theatrical properties, then went back to assemble another cast and try again. If that be the case, the rascals' identities are known. For in the next year, one David Delaunay, with two other St. Louis traders, Tesson and Loise, assembled another group of Indians and this time took them downriver to New Orleans, where they got a part of the group at least aboard a ship bound for France. Delaunay was a Frenchman who had held the rank of major in the territorial militia. In uniform he could deceive the Indians into believing he was officially bringing them to visit the Great White Father in Washington.

Actually, he had the Great White Father in Paris in mind and had concocted a story of Indian loyalty to France inherited from an earlier generation of the tribe. His forlorn little group, introduced as chiefs and princesses, created a tremendous sensation from the moment of their arrival at Le Havre, were received by Charles X at his palace, and toured Europe with great (but waning) éclat. When the attraction ceased to be profitable, Delaunay abandoned the

MEDICINE BOW

George Catlin's drawing of a Blackfoot medicine man approaching his patient with jumps and yelps—"horrid grunts, growls and snarls of the grizzly bear"—while shaking his rattle and brandishing his "medicine spear or magic wand" explains this object better than the original Peale label: "Medicine Bow, which formerly belonged to the Mohawk Tribe of Indians." (Peabody Museum, Harvard University.)

troupe. Kindly persons, among them Lafayette, rescued and returned them to their homes.[43]

Was it Delaunay who came to Philadelphia with his still unsuspecting charges in 1826? One account gives New York as his embarkation point, suggesting an earlier attempt. If so, Peale may have had some part in warning them of the imposition, for the Indians would probably have learned the truth from someone speaking French, the more familiar language on the upper Missouri. Such a happening is possible, though Peale does not mention it.

He was lonely. It had been five years since Hannah died. He had brought the manufacture of porcelain teeth to perfection, molding and firing them himself, and was eager to spread their benefit to others. He began to visit New York that winter to court Miss Mary Stansbury, a teacher of the deaf and the daughter of an old friend. The greatest kindness he could offer her was a new set of teeth, and Miss Mary, though reluctant as to marriage, was grateful. But she never received the set. His heart was strained by carrying his trunk through the cold on the journey home. It was a new kind of illness that he did not understand, oppressive, with so much waiting still for him to do. His hope of finding a companion faded. "I am now very much depreciated in my own opinion," he wrote to Hannah's sister. "I can be of no value to anyone, and I cannot desire to give trouble to the Fair Sex, who will ever be high in my estimation."[44]

Escol stayed near him to help, and remembered how his mind was full of memories of Rachel and of times gone by. This was the end, coming slowly in the rhythm of the years, chords of love and kindliness, of valor and hope, of new discovery and destiny, and with a thin high note of the absurd rippling through it here and there. But that final statement in the Museum self-portrait was true; he had indeed lifted a curtain revealing to the people of his America the wonders of nature. Whatever the perversions of scientific truth in those manifold museums the country over, he had nonetheless opened to the New World an awareness of all life that otherwise would never have reached so many. Science was the stronger for it, and science for the multitude would have a stronger renaissance because of what had come before.

Death came to Charles Willson Peale in the night of February 22, 1827, in his eighty-sixth year. Obituaries said little of the Museum; the long funeral procession was for the artist and soldier of the Revolution. Quietly now, the Peales and their friends took in hand that teeming storehouse of forty years' accumulation.

CHAPTER EIGHT

TITIAN AND FRANKLIN (1827–1845)

In his children and grandchildren and in generations beyond, one branch or another of the patriach's career is relived again. Raphaelle and Rembrandt were professional artists in contrasting measures of genius and success. Titian was the naturalist, accurate, painstaking and adventurous, and Rubens the exponent of "rational amusement." Franklin was the mechanic and inventor, and one who would be praised for the beauty of his machines. All drew or painted except, apparently, Linnaeus, the soldier and politician, the most strikingly variant sprig. There was even a grandson in dentistry, Harvey Lewis Sellers, whose practice ranged from the Mississippi River towns to the capitals of Europe, who painted miniatures on the side and was married three times, and whose memory is treasured by the author of this chronicle in a large lithograph portrait of Lola Montez, dancer and courtesan, "uncrowned Queen" of Bavaria, inscribed by her to Harvey.

Their names too—just as those of the first generation show the shift in emphasis from art to science, so one can read in the later their excitements and loyalties—two little Bertrands, for instance (sons of Titian and of Elizabeth DePeyster Peale Patterson), both born in 1823, the year of Alexandre Bertrand's work on "animal magnetism's" powers of hypnotic suggestion—or Titian's little Florida, born after his return from the South—Lin's Simon Bolivar, Izabella Carapaba and Hercules Tescier—Rembrandt's Michael Angelo—and the Angelicas, Sophonisbas, Charles Willsons, in every generation.

These were the heirs. There was no will. There was no estate, other than the Philadelphia Museum Company's 500 shares of stock, valued at $200 each and now divided neatly into a nominal $10,000 for each of the ten inheritors. Five went to Rachel's surviving children (Angelica, Rembrandt, Rubens, Sophy) and to Raphaelle's children; and five to the DePeyster group (Linnaeus, Franklin, Sybilla, Titian, Elizabeth). One of Raphaelle's seven, another Sophy, had married the artist–bank clerk James Peale, Jr., bringing that branch of the family into the picture. Raphaelle's son Edmund would figure, in his own way, in Museum history. It is not known from what romantic drama or poem this name had come, but the youth may well have patterned his life upon Robert Traill Spence's *Edmund the Wanderer,* impassioned and forlorn.[1] He was now aged twenty-two and had already survived a woebegone attempt at suicide, followed by a plunge into South American adventure, capture by a Spanish warship, and a death cell in Havana's Morro Castle. Led out to execution, he had leapt into the sea and been picked up by an American schooner outbound for Baltimore.

The Robinsons still remained aloof, but Rembrandt in Boston and Rubens in New York were very directly interested. Sophy's Coleman Sellers was in a central place, both as a trustee and as administrator of the estate. Franklin's marriage had been annulled, leaving him with the care of an infant daughter. Sybilla Miriam, now Mrs. Andrew Summers, and Elizabeth, now Mrs. William Augustus Patterson, both had slender means and growing families. William Augustus, pioneering as a sheep farmer in the back country, was jubilant. He had heard that the Museum was taking in $80 a day, and felt sure of dividends of at least $500 a year.[2]

That the Museum had a profit potential was clear, but trustees and management were of no mind to abandon the founder's purpose of an educational institution. As early as June 20, 1826, they had foreseen the hazards of "a floating stock."[3] Growth must be maintained, the public attracted by valid scientific features only, and pressures from stockholders resisted. Parsimony could bring slow deterioration, and an effort to achieve financial security by expansion could bring (as it did at the end) disaster. But as of February 1827, the stock had all the appearance of a sound investment. Museums were a going business everywhere. This was the oldest and largest of them all, about to move into a new building redesigned in order to receive it, on fashionable Chestnut Street with the Shakespeare Buildings and the new Chestnut Street

Theater alongside, a perfect setting to draw in the devotees both of science and of "rational amusement."

At the first trustees' meeting after the founder's death, on June 27, 1827, both Rembrandt and Rubens presented themselves as charter members, with Rembrandt presiding over the informal reorganization. Coleman Sellers, John Bacon, and Robert M. Patterson made up the five. Bacon had come in in 1824 after the death of Robert Patterson, father of the other new member. He was a former city treasurer and was taking a leading part in negotiations with the Arcade Company. They elected Franklin Peale manager and Titian Peale curator, at salaries of $1,000 each (later, as incentive and safeguard, this was changed to a percentage of income), adopted bylaws as advised by Chauncey and Binney, the city's most prestigious law firm, took a long look at their funds in hand ($12.06½ in cash and $546.15 due from the founder's estate), and confirmed the lease of the Arcade's upper floor for ten years at $1,500 a year.

In January the first stockholders' election returned Patterson, Bacon, and Sellers, and brought in George Ord and James Peale, Jr. A behind-the-scenes conflict is discernible. Ord would represent a nonprofit ideal, whereas James stood with Linnaeus for higher dividends than the 1 percent which the trustees were then willing to allow.[4] Both left at the end of that year, but the election of 1829 brought a good group. Robert Eglesfeld Griffith, merchant and amateur naturalist, was active in the Philosophical Society and a nationally known authority on conchology. Reuben Haines made a strong link with the Academy of Natural Sciences. Daniel B. Smith, a founder of the College of Pharmacy, the Apprentices' Library, and the Philadelphia Savings Fund, would also be a founder in 1833 of Haverford College and later head its faculty. Coleman Sellers, named president, and John Bacon, treasurer, completed the five-member board.

But ominous signs were present. Haines was the nominee of Rembrandt Peale, who had borrowed heavily from him to finance an extended trip abroad, leaving his Museum stock as security, with the expectation that dividends would cover interest. Haines would also exercise voting rights on the stock, and Rembrandt wanted no mistake: "Believing it to be the duty of every Stockholder to keep in view the *present,* as well as the *future* Interests of the Museum, which has grown up a *private* establishment, and *must* be considered a *money-making Institution,* conducted, however, always in a manner to insure its respectability, its permanency, and usefulness as a

Depository of Scientific objects." Rubens Peale strongly endorsed this view, declaring that every member of the family concurred.[5] The emphatic tone of both at least implies that a contrary opinion existed. Rubens, who was eager to tie Philadelphia in with his New York and Baltimore interests and create a regular circuit for his entertainment features, would find the trustees often unwilling to accept his standard.

While the proprietary museums wrestled with the conflict between quality and profits, those of the professional associations were gaining strength. The Academy of Natural Sciences had now been publishing its *Journal* for a decade and had a library of nearly 3,000 volumes, 2,500 minerals, 5,410 fossils (rather touchingly classified as "American," "British," and "Foreign"), 1,000 shells, and 106 reptiles; only its collection of birds, greatly overshadowed by Peale's, was a minor feature. All this was now open to the public without charge, protected from abuse by a rule that visitors must present a card signed by a member.[6]

In the sultry heat of August 1827, the Museum moved into its new environment of modern grandeur behind the Arcade's tall arched facade of Pennsylvania marble in John Haviland's impressive design. Its wide expanse of floor was broken by the long open wells with walkways below and skylights above. Down the center was a colonaded hall 130 feet in length and 26 feet wide, with a gallery above, and one of the first-floor shops had been rented as a workroom. In these commodious quarters the Museum would remain for the next ten years.

The great mastodon skeleton stood on a raised platform at the heart of it all, set off not only by Peale's painting of the exhumation but by a large background scene of the site, dramatized by the skeleton of a mouse posed at its foot and by other attendant beasts large in size yet nonetheless upstaged by the monster. The skin and skeleton of the performing elephant "Columbus" were added in 1829, a rhinoceros in the next year, and later an acquisition long desired, the "cameleopard," or giraffe.[7]

The new arrangement was eyecatching, breathtaking to many. New accessions poured in, some by chance, some eagerly purchased by the young curators. In 1828 Lieutenant George Christian Hutter stopped by with an American Indian collection of some thirty-five unusual pieces and a smaller group of minerals from the West, the gift of his father, Christian Jacob Hutter, newspaper publisher and Democratic party chief in northern Pennsylvania. No one at the Museum was aware, nor would it be discovered until 150 years

THE PHILADELPHIA ARCADE
The Arcade's spacious upper floor was the home of Peale's Museum from 1827 to 1838. Designed by John Haviland; engraving after a drawing by Charles Burton.

259

later, that these had come from Thomas Jefferson's Bedford County estate, Poplar Forest. Among them was the great buffalo robe battle painting from the Lewis and Clark Expedition.[8] Dr. Marmaduke Burrough, home from his study of the Inca mounds of Peru, came stumping in with his big gold-headed cane and sold the Museum a major collection of South American quadrupeds. William Whiteman Wood, son of Philadelphia's popular actor William Burke Wood, had sketched and painted with the young Peales, worked at the Museum as a boy, then with Rubens in New York and Baltimore, and was now off to the Far East with the trustees' authorization to purchase specimens in Australia, the East Indies, and China. Six cases of insects arrived from him in November 1831, to be followed by much more. Bill Wood lingered in Canton as publisher of China's first English-language newspaper, printed on type sent him by his friends at the Arcade. Other gifts and purchases flowed in: African material from Governor Joseph Mechlin of Liberia, shells from Professor Ravenel in Charleston, minerals from Maine and New Hampshire. The exchange program flourished once more, with the National Museum of Peru, Sir Charles Lyell of the Geological Society of London, and, again, the Muséum d'Histoire Naturelle.[9]

Rembrandt Peale was in Paris in 1830 and found the National Museum greatly enriched in Cuvier's department, comparative anatomy, since his previous visit twenty years before. But the vast collection of insects had been destroyed by insect ravagers, and the stuffed animals he found poorly mounted: "The *Philadelphia Museum,* with the skill and taste of my brother, *Titian Peale,* has greatly the advantage; the insects, being perfectly preserved between perpendicular plates of glass, inaccessible to the *dermestes,* are seen on both sides; and the quadrupeds and birds, preserved with the knowledge of an artist in drawing, modeling and anatomy, by a method improved upon Waterton's, possess all the beauty and character of the living animals."[10]

In a European view of the same time, Prince Maximilian of Wied-Neuwied, a roving naturalist, found only one American collection worthy of serious attention—". . . the museum of Mr. Titian Peale, which contains the best collection of natural history in the United States. There is the fine large skeleton of the Ohio elephant (*Mastodon,* Cuv.), and likewise most of the animals of North America, pretty well stuffed. Among them I noticed, especially, the bison, the bighorn or wild sheep of the rocky mountains, the prairie antelope (*Antilocapra Americana,* Ord), the

Trials in lithography
Philad^a

"TRIALS IN LITHOGRAPHY"

Titian Peale here tries his skill at a new process in which the artist's
drawing was reproduced without going through the hands of an engraver.
It had first been used in America for scientific illustration by his friend
Charles Alexandre Lesueur in 1822. (American Philosophical
Society.)

elk (*Cervus major,* or *Canadensis*), the grisly bear (*Ursus ferox*) and others. . . . There are likewise many specimens of foreign animals; for instance, a rhinoceros; and the collection of Indian dresses, utensils, and arms is, I think, the most important I have yet seen. . . . Mr. Peale's collection deserves precedence above all the public museums in the United States, for its more scientific arrangement, and because fewer trifling nicknacks have been admitted into it."

The rhinoceros had been bought in 1835 for $50, apparently the going price when a showman had a dead beast on his hands. When in that year stockholders objected to Titian's museum-supported hunting expeditions, he could report that the deer and wolf sent to Prince Maximilian at a cost of $46 had brought specimens worth at least $500 in exchange. He pointed out that other accessions—birds of New South Wales, birds and insects of Cuba, and a collection of woods—all had cost only his own and an assistant's labor in preparing equivalents for exchange. "If properly continued," he told them, "such work will enable us to hold our superiority over all other museums on this side of the Atlantic."[11]

Maximilian had supposed the Museum to be entirely Titian's; and, in a basic, essential way, so it now was. He was all his father could have wished. He gave care and long hours to his work and found ample compensation for poor pay in the collecting trips to Maine, up the Susquehanna, or to New York in a search for a new mastodon skeleton. In 1831, to encourage others, he published the *Circular of the Philadelphia Museum: Containing Directions for the Preservation and Preparation of Objects of Natural History,* with twenty-nine pages and five engraved plates, a concise little manual for collectors. In 1829 the trustees had appropriated $600 to send Titian up the Missouri River, but then abandoned the plan because of Indians on the rampage. But when, the next year, New York merchant Silas E. Burrows offered free transportation for an expedition to the jungles of Colombia the board eagerly accepted, taking only the precaution of a $5,000 insurance policy on its curator's life. Titian, with his friend and assistant William McGuigan, returned in February 1832 with a wealth of new birds, shells, and other objects.[12]

Purposeful collecting was still less well recorded than gifts, so that growth statistics are hard to estimate. In 1830 Dr. Mease listed 250 quadrupeds and 1,310 birds. The guidebook *Philadelphia in 1830–1* gives us 274 quadrupeds and 1,284 birds, adding:

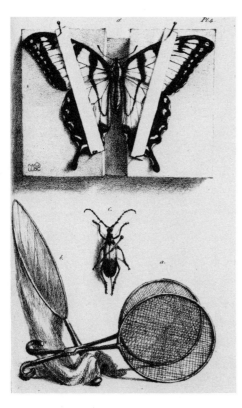

THE INSECT COLLECTOR
Lithographic illustration for
Circular of the Philadel-
phia Museum: Containing
Directions for the Prepara-
tion and Preservation of
Objects of Natural His-
tory. By Titian R. Peale,
Professor of Zoology and
Curator of the Museum
(*Philadelphia, 1831*).
(American Philosophical
Society.)

The system of Linnaeus has been adhered to in the arrangement of the mammalia and birds; . . . that of Cleaveland in mineralogy, the cabinets for the display of which contain about 1,700 specimens, some of which are very beautiful. Lamarck's system has been the guide in conchology, the cabinets of which contain more than 1,000 specimens.[13] The corals, &c. are arranged according to this system, and are also numerous.

The Museum, besides the above departments, contains a large collection of fossil reliquiae of this country, and of Europe, at the head of which is the mammoth, so remarkable for its great size and perfect preservation. . . .

An already numerous cabinet of fish is continually increasing, among the most remarkable of the specimens in which is one of the genus raga, or ray, commonly called the "devil fish," which has been lately added to the collection; it measures twelve feet in length by fifteen in breadth, and weighed upwards of two thousand pounds.

Steamer Libertador
Stranded near Buenavista
Pielro Honda, the head of navigation
of the Magdalena River, New Granada.
JR Peale 1830

STEAMER LIBERTADOR, *NEW GRENADA*
Titian Peale's 1830 drawing shows the paddlewheel vessel stranded at the head of
Colombia's Magdalena River, during the Museum's South American expedition
financed by Silas E. Burrows of New York. (The American Museum of Natural
History.)

Cabinets of reptiles, comparative anatomy, &c. and a
numerous collection of miscellaneous articles, of works of art,
implements, dresses, arms, antiquities, &c. from every part of
the globe, occupy different situations in the rooms.

The collection of the dresses, implements, arms, &c. of
the native tribes of America, is full and complete in all that is
illustrative of the customs of this interesting, and fast
decreasing people.

Insects were arranged in geographical divisions, with the
Lepidoptera (butterflies and moths) most prominent. Two hundred
portraits and thirty-eight other paintings are mentioned and
attention is called to the "laboratory" for popular lectures and
experiments in chemistry and "natural philosophy."[14]

Franklin, as manager, and Titian, as curator and naturalist,
were working well as a team, with equal salaries. In the social life of

the city Franklin, with his sweet tenor voice, was a leading light of the Musical Fund Society, with Titian at his side. Franklin, in turn, marched out to the targets with Titian's United Bowmen. The young explorer had returned from the Indian country with a passion for archery and in 1829 had brought fellow enthusiasts together in this elite corps, dashingly romantic in their uniforms of white and green.

At the Museum, model machinery was Franklin's forte, notably a miniature railroad built for him by Matthias Baldwin— historic, too, as it marked the beginning of the Baldwin Locomotive Works, giant of the industrial revolution in America. Begun in the old Model Room of the 1790's, machinery displays had been on a rising wave of popularity. By 1833 Philadelphia's "Hall of Industry" had a train in competition with Franklin's. Kimball's

LOCOMOTIVE FROM THE MODEL ROOM
This model, dated about 1832–1835, is identified by John H. White, Jr., of the Smithsonian Institution as "an inside cylinder engine with a counter-shaft for conversion to outside connection to the rear driving wheels," a device evolved by the Mohawk & Hudson Railroad to accommodate the pivoted forward truck which was needed, as engines grew in size, on curved track. Length, 15½ inches; width, 6¼ inches. (Courtesy of Dr. R. Sloan Wilson; photograph by Greer H. Lile.)

Boston Museum followed with a "pneumatic" railroad—though the popular museums in general ran to automata of various sorts, the fascination of the robot.[15] Interest was not enough; only wonder would do. Then came the "mechanics' fairs" of Philadelphia, Boston, and other cities, sponsored by associations such as the Franklin Institute and carried far beyond the earlier commercial shows. Philadelphia reached its summit in the Centennial of 1876, essentially a mechanics' fair—down a long road from the little display at Philosophical Hall eighty years before.

Franklin's activity in the Museum and in serious research brought him an appointment as assistant assayer at the United States Mint in 1833. He was sent abroad at once to make a study of European mints, returned in 1835, and would thereafter be with the Museum only as a member of its board. In 1831 Titian had been given the honorific title of professor of natural history, but a board resolution of two years later, when Franklin was leaving, that he lecture once a week on the subject points up his distaste for the evening demonstrations. Each brother had a foothold in a professional society: Titian as a curator of the Academy of Natural Sciences since 1827, Franklin at the Franklin Institute. Both were elected to the American Philosophical Society in 1833.

The growing professional societies tended to diminish the Museum's use by mature students, but for the young its usefulness and popularity increased, bringing it closer to that major function of the municipal science museums of today. It was now offering schools an annual admission for $7.00, and some fifteen or twenty had subscribed, bringing problems of unruly youth, but nonetheless a reinforcement of the Museum's educational standing.[16] Charles Godfrey Leland, folklorist and popular poet of the "Hans Breitmann" ballads, brings us a small boy's view of the Arcade scene—revealing, too, that lighting had again become a problem:

> I owe so very much myself to the old Peale's Museum; it served to stimulate to such a remarkable degree my interest in antiquities and my singular passion for miscellaneous information, and it aided me so much in my reading, that I cannot pass it by without a tribute to its memory. How often have I paused in its dark galleries in awe before the tremendous skeleton of the Mammoth—how small did that great elephant seem beside it—and recalled the Indian legend of it recorded by Franklin. And the stuffed monkeys—one shaving another—what exquisite humour, which never palled upon us!

No; *that* was the museum for us, and the time will come when there will be such collections made expressly for the young. . . .

Never shall I forget one evening alone in that Museum. I had come with Jacob Pearce's school, and strayed off alone into some far-away and fascinating nook, forgetful of friends and time. All the rest had departed homewards, and I sought to find them. The dark evening shades were casting sombre tones in the galleries—and I was a very little boy of seven or eight—and the stuffed lions and bears and wolves seemed looming or glooming into mysterious life; the varnished sharks and hideous shiny crocodiles had a light of awful intelligence in their eyes; the gigantic anaconda had long awaited me; the grim hyaena marked me for his own; even deer and doves seemed uncanny and goblined. At this long interval of sixty years, I can recall the details of that walk, and every object which impressively half-appalled me, and how what had been a museum had become a chamber of horrors, yet not without a wild and awful charm. Of course I lost my way in the shades, and was beginning to speculate on having to pass a night among the monsters, and how much there would be left for my friends to mourn over in the morning, when—Eureka! Thalatta!—I beheld the gate of entrance and exit, and made my latter as joyously as ever did the souls who were played out of Inferno by the old reprobate of the Roman tale.[17]

Moses Williams had long before retired on his earnings as a profile cutter, but silhouettes were now the established museum souvenir, and he was succeeded by others: Elizabeth Hampton in 1827, Eliza Meigs in 1834. With Franklin's departure the program of lectures and experiments languished, and the equipment fell into disrepair. Popular as lecture courses were becoming throughout the nation, the Museum's faculty was still almost wholly inactive. When Dr. Richard Harlan, professor of comparative anatomy, proposed a course of lectures in that field on March 11, 1829, the trustees loftily refused him permission to do so; he, striking back, withdrew the various loans he had made to the collection. His *Fauna Americana* of 1825, in which he cites a number of the Museum holdings, had been attacked by young Dr. Godman as largely a plagiarism from Demarest's *Mammologie*—a doubtful charge, since the work freely acknowledges its debt to the French author. Harlan's enmity may have contributed to the failure of the lecture program and may be linked to his partisanship for Audubon and against Peale, Ord, Waterton, and other naturalists in the Museum circle.[18]

As for special exhibits, Titian brought in occasional live animal shows as they became available—the two boa constrictors of 1833, for instance, or the giraffe of the following year. Fancy glassblowing, a popular exhibit at all the museums, had a showing in 1834, and a model "Italian Village" was rented at $100 a year over a long period. On becoming a trustee, Reuben Haines had offered the use of his solar microscope, an eighteenth-century device adapted to demonstrations before an audience. Rubens' recommendations were occasionally accepted, bringing in 1829–1830 the Siamese twins and the "Big Children" (a pair of jolly outsize girls from Poughkeepsie), along with Mr. And Mrs. Canderbeck, "lately arrived from France," he with violin, she with harp, and the voices of both raised in song. Some features came by chance. Black Hawk drew such a crowd in the summer of 1833 that he was allowed to return for a private showing.[19]

Another income source was taxidermy, William McGuigan's department. Jonathan Harrington of Boston, ventriloquist and prestidigitator, built up a museum of his own in the 1830's, containing a respectable group of McGuigan mountings plus random curiosities. He had been sent to Philadelphia by Rubens, and the one performance he gave there may have been in part payment for the specimens received—ventriloquism for natural history. The holdings of Harrington's Museum were sold in 1842, after it was unable to compete with Moses Kimball's new and larger Boston Museum.[20]

In 1829 the trustees had turned their attention to the production of a Museum Medal, a numismatic rarity today, struck off in copper, as an admission token, in silver and gold as a recognition to benefactors.[21] Portraits could no longer be used, as of old, to engage the support of prominent persons. A portrait of Isaac Hull by Sully had been voted in December 1827, but was never carried through. After that the gallery appears only in trustee minutes as it was guarded against would-be copyists. Whatever dignities the Museum might assume, there would remain that need for special—undignified—exhibits to supplement income. The fact comes out plaintively in the report of a "Committee to Devise Means to Further the Interests of the Museum," regretfully advising that salaries be kept minimal "in the hope that the measures adopted by the trustees will so increase the income of the museum that the percentage insisted upon by the stockholders will be equal

CAMELEOPARD

A SPLENDID specimen of that rare and singular animal, the GIRAFF, or CAMELEOPARD, has been received from the interior of Africa, and will be exhibited for a few weeks at the
PHILADELPHIA MUSEUM.
Admittance as usual 25 cents, Children 12½.
oct 1-tf

to the compensation which the Manager and Curator have heretofore received."[22]

Stockholders would continue their pressure, but the early trustees were of a sort to resist. They were "liberal," as George Ord put it at the time, and committed to policies which "will meet the approbation of all true lovers of science,"[23] Haines died in 1831 but was replaced by Professor Keating of the University, now also recording secretary of the Academy of Natural Sciences. Samuel P. Griffitts, Jr., elected in 1833, was the son of a well-known Quaker physician, a druggist in a day when druggists were equally men of science and of business. He was not markedly successful in either, but was a friend of Titian Peale and one of Titian's United Bowmen,

269

a strongly fraternal group. Desperately, the trustees grasped at semiscientific straws to keep their ship afloat. In 1835 they had "Dr. Welden" demonstrating his "Oxy-hydrogen microscope"—presumably the same "G. Welden, magician" who at Rubens' stand in New York had been displaying the "Coffin of Mahomet" and the "Cardbox of Beelzebub" and permitting "any gentleman" to fire a pistol at his breast, he catching the bullet in his hand.[24]

But amid these diversions new problems loomed, and the board changed character with them. The Arcade was deteriorating, both the building and the neighborhood. As early as 1829, leaking skylights had caused damage. By 1834, protests notwithstanding, there was damage with every rain. Offices and shops no longer attracted the best tenants. Titian reported "a bawdy wax Venus" on street level, bringing the Museum into disrepute.[25] As early as December 28, 1830, the trustees were considering the erection of a new building, and in 1833, sure of ample grounds to break their lease, they appointed a committee to work on financing it.

Coleman Sellers was not returned in the election of January, 1834. Franklin Peale, divorced from his insane wife, had had to deposit security with a trustee guaranteeing her support. Sophy had lent him her stock for the purpose, and the trustee, lawyer James M. Broom, had voted the shares against her brother. Andrew Summers, Sybilla's husband, came in as sole representative of the family. Elhanan W. Keyser, a lumber merchant, together with Bacon, Griffith, And Griffitts, made up the five board members for that year. In the next year, only Summers was continued, with four new members who were all strong proponents of expansion: James M. Broom as president, Rubens Peale, Alfred Harrold, and George Escol Sellers.

Escol, who had been in England in 1832–1833 studying British papermaking methods, had returned to marry his Philadelphia sweetheart, Rachel Parrish, and then, with Coleman Sellers' sudden death on May 7, 1834, had taken over the business in partnership with his brother Charles—iron and brass foundry, papermaking machinery, fire engines, locomotives for the Philadelphia and Columbia and the Allegheny Portage railroads.[26] Alfred Harrold, with his long nose, sad eyes, and earnest mouth, was an English businessman who had married a daughter of Coleman Sellers in 1832. Looking about him with favor on the American scene, he had invested heavily in Museum stock, an optimism perhaps derived from and certainly shared by his new brother-in-law, Escol.

Escol owned only eight shares of stock, but he now moved to obtain a court order establishing his mother's right to vote her own shares, whoever held them in trust, and to obtain proxies from Rubens, Angelica, and others of the family. In September 1835, he replaced Andrew Summers as treasurer of the company. Board minutes tell us now of "the Virginia Dwarfs" engaged to appear in the Museum's "lecture" hall, while giant plans for expansion were in the making.

A rising wave of financial euphoria was carrying these ambitious plans along. The Academy of Natural Sciences, the American Philosophical Society, and the Franklin Institute were all intent upon new and more imposing edifices.[27] Money could be borrowed on expectations alone, and the Museum trustees imagined a double advantage—an institution of learning like the others, but also a business. On June 2, 1835, they appealed for donations, in effect museum memberships graded from $20 to $100. All would carry admission privileges, and the higher categories would include donors' names "inscribed upon marble in a conspicuous situation." No rush of subscribers followed, and on July 17 the board authorized a loan of $200,000. A printed announcement to the public listed past annual income ($11,032.78 in the first year in the Arcade, now down to $5,053.50) and argued for $150,000 as the total value of the collections, rather than a mythical "offer" of $100,000 said to have been made to Charles Willson Peale.[28] The new building would have a superb lecture room, a diorama room, a panorama room, and a skylighted picture gallery 60 feet square. The rental of eight stores on its ground floor would help to sustain the whole.

A charter revision authorizing new issues of stock under a board of directors increased from five to nine was hurried through the Legislature in December, and on January 7, 1836, the new board met: James M. Broom, Joseph Cowperthwaite, Nathan Dunn, Isaac Elliott, John K. Kane, Robert A. Parrish, Franklin Peale, and George Escol Sellers. Cowperthwaite, a boyhood chum of Escol, had gone on to become cashier at Nicholas Biddle's Bank of the United States, thus in a position, and ready, to advance the desired loan. Parrish was Escol's father-in-law. Elliott was a conveyancer who has a place in the early history of the Pennsylvania Railroad. John Kintzing Kane, a lawyer, had represented Philadelphia in the Legislature, served as city solicitor, and had been active in the Philosophical Society since 1825. He would later become attorney general of the state and a Philadelphia judge—a career overshadowed by that of his son, Dr. Elisha Kent Kane, the Arctic explorer. Escol now engineered the election of Nathan Dunn as president of the board. The ousted Broom would resign from the board soon after, and William D. Lewis, cashier of the Girard Bank, would take his place.

Escol Sellers and Nathan Dunn stand out as contrasting and controversial characters on this tragicomic stage, each with a strange career. In the winter of 1808 Coleman and Sophy Sellers had fixed upon the name George for their second son. But on the night of his birth, a Quaker neighbor had dreamed a dream of the brook Eshcol and the grape clusters gathered by the Children of Israel. This portent came as an imperative in naming the child, and the kindly parents agreed. George Escol became a young stalwart of his grandfather's museum and his father's firm. Inevitably, it was by the unusual name that he came to be known, and that name heaped trouble and sorrow on the sorrows that beset him in middle life.

Those who have read Mark Twain's collaboration with Charles Dudley Warner, *The Gilded Age,* particularly the first edition, may be inclined to prejudge Escol unfairly. With a novel about a shifty inventor-promoter in mind, the two humorists needed a name. It was Warner, groping back in memory, who put the question: Could anyone with a name as ludicrous as Escol Sellers still be alive? Impossible, they decided, and "Colonel Escol {later Mulberry} Sellers" went on into a best-seller and popular play. But when "a college bred gentleman of courtly manners and ducal upholstery with a libel suit in his eye" appeared at Hartford, Warner, at least, expressed profound regret. There was no libel suit, though from Escol's career before the book's publication in 1873 one can understand how damaging it was. His Philadelphia firm had failed in the panic of 1837. In the 1840's he was operating the Globe Rolling Mills in Cincinnati, and in 1850 went south as a mechanical engineer for the Panama Railroad, where grade-climbing locomotives of his invention were crossing the isthmus to shorten the route to California. He was next at "Sellers Landing" on the Ohio River in southern Illinois, operating the Saline Coal Company for a group of Philadelphia capitalists. Soft coal was to be sold to the river steamers, but the rivermen proved slow in converting their machinery from wood, thereby leaving Escol, already enmeshed in tragedy with the death of his wife and children, trying desperately to make the venture pay by developing other industries. At a later day, others would profit from his patents, notably a process for making paper from marsh reeds. As

Escol struggled in his lonely post, Philadelphia stockholders were complaining, and young Warner was listening.[29]

Escol holds a respectable place in engineering history. The only fault linking him to the "Colonel Sellers" of the story was a generous share of his grandfather's optimism. The optimism was with him in 1835 as he sought to place the Museum at long last upon a secure foundation. His first notion was of a new stock issue based on admission rights rather than dividends: a $50 share giving perpetual admission to the owner, and a $100 share extending the same privileges to his family. Lawyer Charles Chauncey promptly headed the $100 subscription. Escol had $10,000 subscribed in short order, while Jacob Broom, brother of the president of the board, as easily booked another $40,000. The subscriptions were not to be binding until $100,000 could be realized. The plan was similar to the scholarship endowment schemes that by the 1850's would bring weal and woe to many colleges. But it was at this point, in examining museum sites and possibilities, that Escol bethought him of what Nathan Dunn might do as a member of the enterprise.[30]

Contemporaries would take two views of Dunn, seeing him as either a benign philanthropist or a cynical plutocrat. There is evidence for both. He had come from a New Jersey farm in 1802, aged twenty, properly commended by a certificate of removal to the Philadelphia Monthly Meeting, and had launched ambitiously into the dry-goods business. Thirteen years later he was bankrupt and disowned by the Society of Friends for having favored some creditors above others. In 1818 he took ship for China, and was in Canton for another thirteen years, prospering there steadily in tea and other articles of trade, still a Quaker in dress and speech and given favored standing because of his refusal to join in the opium traffic. He kept in touch with Philadelphia, lent a Chinnery landscape to the Academy of Fine Arts in 1828, was elected a corresponding member of the Academy of Natural Sciences in 1820, and certainly learned much about the Museum from William Wood. Then at last, in 1832, he was back in the city, as one of its wealthiest citizens, comfortably settled at 3 Portico Square. A first act had been to entertain all his old creditors at dinner on the anniversary of his disownment; under the plate of each was placed a check for the amount of his debt with interest in full.[31]

Dunn had brought with him a huge and carefully assembled collection illustrative of almost every aspect of Chinese life, and it was Escol's thought that the Museum and Dunn's Chinese

PHILADELPHIA

Museum.

FOUNDED BY C. W. PEALE, 1784,

Incorporated 1824;

Now permanently arranged in the Great Hall, built expressly for its accommodation at the corner of

NINTH AND GEORGE STREETS,

And is open every **DAY** and **EVENING.**

Admittance, 25 Cents.

Stock for sale by the Treasurer at $100. per share. A share admits the holder at all times, or entitles him to 25 transferable admissions annually.

The Treasurer attends at the Museum daily.

collection could be housed together to mutual advantage. Dunn agreed. He was a man for prompt action, and ready to back it with capital, of which the Museum had none. He brushed aside Escol's financial plan in favor of a straight 6 percent preferred stock. Cowperthwaite, with the resources of the Bank of the United States at his command, felt confident of a syndicate that would take up to $100,000 of it. Dunn approved and moved as swiftly to secure the land that Escol saw as the best site.

The site chosen was at Ninth and George (now Sansom) Streets, and the purchase agreement was signed on January 20, 1836, with Dunn making the first payment of $20,000.[32] Escol also decided on the new building's architecture. Designs had been drawn by John Haviland, William Strickland, and John Notman. Titian and Franklin favored Haviland's, though Escol afterward described it as "a showy thing" which "would have been some big beastly Egyptian affair, not unlike his N.Y. Tombs." An Englishman, Isaac Holden, had been ignored by the others, but Escol supplied him with the basic functional needs. Holden's plans, simpler and less costly, were accepted on July 23, 1837, with Holden himself as builder, at a basic cost of $80,000.

There would be no panorama, diorama, or grandiose picture gallery, but the essential museum space was there, with preserving room and curatorial offices larger and more convenient than ever before and a lecture hall with an exterior entrance. The upper of the two storeys (till the age of electricity always preferred for better natural light) would hold the Museum, 238 feet by 70 feet and almost as high as wide, with surrounding galleries adding another level of exhibition space. The ground floor, leased to Dunn for ten years at $1,600 a year, was shorter, 163 feet, since the Museum auditorium with a capacity for a thousand spectators on rising semicircular tiers was also placed at street level.[33] The bulding was opened with due fanfare on July 4, 1838. Passing mention might be made of the arrival in America, only a few weeks later, of the ship *Mediator,* bringing a half-million in gold, the bequest from James Smithson which would in time, amid mingled protest and acclaim, give reality to Charles Willson Peale's dream of a national museum.

Again the great mastodon took central place, dominating the Museum's main hall (now always deferentially spoken of as "the Saloon"). A stage for an orchestra rose at one end of the room, and a huge scene painting, very distantly and romantically suggestive of the skeleton's ancient habitat, dramatized the entire area. This last was the work of Russell Smith, a landscapist and friend of the Peales, noted for his theater curtains.[34]

The scene is vividly brought back to us by a foreign observer who stepped into it at just this time. James Silk Buckingham had been ordered out of India for exercising too freely his Englishman's right to describe what he saw as he saw it. A sympathetic Prince Albert had encouraged him to tour the United States. A new book, friendly but candid and thorough, the Prince advised, would offset the hostility of other British travelers and promote friendship between the two nations. With his wife and teen-age son at his side, Buckingham did just that and filled four volumes with fluent and careful description. They arrived in Philadelphia in February 1840, to find the Museum pristine in its new revival. It was a lecture tour, and Buckingham spoke six times in the "Saloon" of the new edifice, about lands of the East from Arabia to India. Undisturbed by the appearance there of a rival attraction in "Master Hutchings, the Lilliputian Wonder, aged 5 years, delineator of character and vocalist," Buckingham praised the collections:

Museums in the United States are on a totally different footing from Museums in Europe, and are in general so full of worthless and trashy articles, that they are scarcely worth a visit. In Europe the Museums are either the property of the State, and enriched by annual grants from the crown or parliament, to purchase such additions as may be thought desireable; or they are attached to some literary or scientific institution, and great care is evinced in the choice, preparation and arrangement of the articles, so as to make them at all times worthy the inspection of persons of the first rank in knowledge and taste. In America, on the contrary, Museums are almost always the property of some private individual, who gets together a mass of everything that is likely to be thought curious—good, bad and indifferent—the worthless generally prevailing over the valuable. The collections are then huddled together, without order or arrangement; wretched daubs of painting, miserable wax-work figures, and the most trifling and frivolous things are added; and there is generally a noisy band of musicians, and a juggler, belonging to the establishment, to attract visitors. Such Museums are more visited in the evening than in the day-time, and especially by children; and mere amusement, and that of the lightest and most uninstructive kind, is the only object sought in visiting them.

The Philadelphia Museum is an exception to this description, and well merits a place of distinction, not only as being the very finest, if not indeed the only really good Museum in the United States; but as being quite equal to many of the best in Europe. The great saloon, which extends the whole length of the upper story or first floor of the building, is 230 feet in length, by 70 in breadth, and about 50 in height, a most noble and imposing hall, as its dimensions will sufficiently show. On both sides of this room, and at one end, are galleries, extending round three of its sides, which galleries occupy the midway of the whole length, about 25 feet from the floor and ceiling, and are about 12 feet in breadth. In the space corresponding to this breadth of the galleries, on the lower floor of the hall, are placed large glass-cases, going across the breadth, and leaving an ample recess between each, leaving, therefore, a central promenade up and down the great saloon of 230 feet by about 45. In these glass-cases are arranged all the well-preserved animals, birds, reptiles, and fishes, of which there is a very large and fine collection; and at the bottom of the hall, the entire end is left without a cross gallery, for the purpose of exhibiting there the gigantic skeleton of the fossil mammoth, the largest in the world. In the galleries above are arranged the shells, corallines, minerals, fossils, and insects, of different seas and countries; and here also are many articles of costume and weapons of war, from the aboriginal tribes of American Indians, and from the islanders of the South Seas, with antiquities from Mexico and Peru, armour and arms from Persia, Turkey and other countries of the globe; and both here and around thr frieze and cornice of the great saloon are portraits of from 200 to 300 of the most remarkable public men of America and France, including not merely political, civil, naval and military characters, but men of science, art and philanthropy. The whole of the saloon is lighted by gas, and in its general form, arrangement, and effect, it may be pronounced to be one of the finest rooms in the country.

Among the articles which particularly attracted my attention, as being either very remarkable for their rarity or beauty, or worthy of praise for their fine state of preservation, the following deserve mention. The devil fish, *cephalopterus*

THE DEVILFISH
Titian Peale's drawing of a specimen of Cephalopterus vampyrus *captured off Cape May, New Jersey.* (American Philosophical Society.)

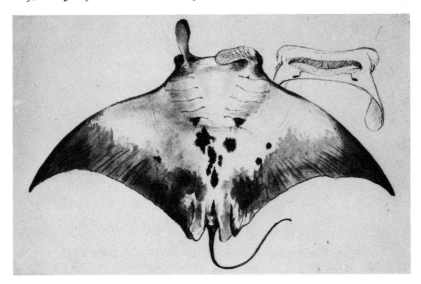

vampyrus, caught off Cape May, of the coast of Pennsylvania. This singular monster of the deep is lozenge-shaped; its whole form being an oblong square, placed diagonally, and its dimensions being about 12 feet in length by 8 in breadth, the skin perfectly smooth, of a light brownish colour; and the thickness of the fish, which was a flat one, like a turbot or flounder, being about 2 feet in the centre. It was altogether the strangest creature I had ever seen; and only one of its kind had ever been caught on these shores. Another of the finny tribe which attracted our attention was the globe sun-fish, *tetrodon mola.* It was nearly circular, being in diameter, from head to tail, about 4 feet, and from back to belly about 3 feet; but while it had no fin projecting from its hind part to act as a caudal or tail, it had a high perpendicular dorsal fin, standing erect like an obelisk, and a deep ventral fin going perpendicularly downward, each at least a foot in length, and making the creature look considerably higher or deeper than it was long. This also is a fish rarely seen, and, like the former, most probably inhabits chiefly the depths of the sea, from whence perhaps individuals are occasionally driven by submarine eruptions, currents, or other causes, and are then thrown on the coasts and taken.

Among the reptiles there were some finely preserved specimens of the iguanas of South America: and the cayman, or *crocodilus acutus,* with whole tribes of lizards, the family to which these belong, from the smallest little creeping things up to the great alligator itself.

The birds were very numerous, and many of them beautifully preserved. A revolving case of humming birds, from New Grenada, and the countries bordering on Mexico and the Isthmus of Darien, exhibited all the richest tints of the most bright and glowing gems. The ruby-crested, the emerald-bosomed, the sapphire-backed, the amethyst-necked, the cinnamon-winged, and many other kinds, well deserved their names; and, indeed, it was difficult to believe that so much of dazzling brilliance in colour and hue could be produced from a feathered surface only. There was also a large variety of eagles and hawks; a fine collection of sea-birds, from the albatross of the ocean to the flamingo of the lakes, and every variety of form and every tint of plumage that the imagination could conceive; the ostrich in his plumes, the peacock with its expanded tail, and owls and parrots of every size and kind. But the prince of all the feathered tribe was the Argus pheasant, from Malacca, the most surprisingly beautiful creature, in all the majesty of its expanded wings and plumage, that the eye could dwell upon, and forming certainly the gem of the cabinet.

A rich collection of the butterflies of France, Germany, South America, China, and Japan, is preserved in the gallery, the two latter countries furnishing the largest and most gorgeously coloured of the whole. In this department also are the marine productions; the madrepores and corallines of which, all presented by a lady, Mrs. Hyde, are unusually fine. In the same place, among the antiquities and curiosities, are seen the real head of a New Zealand chief, ornamentally tattooed, and preserved after death; busts and whole-length figures of native Indian braves, with their painted faces, war-dresses, weapons, and ornaments of the claws of the grisly bear, and other barbarous trophies. Close by these are the mummies of a family of the Incas of Peru, preserved by embalming, like the mummies of the ancient Egyptians, and, like them, wrapped in cloths saturated with the embalming substances.

But the most striking picture in the Museum is that presented at its remote end, where a fine delineation of tropical scenery, in mountain, sea, architecture and foliage, including the banian tree, the palmetto and other productions of the South, occupies the entire surface of the wall, in breadth about 40 feet, and in height about 50. In the foreground of this picture stands the skeleton of the huge mammoth, dug up in the interior of the State of New York, with its immense head and lofty curved-up tusks, rising to a height of 20 feet at least, and making the figure of a very tall elephant and a large rhinoceros, which stand on either side of it, quite diminutive by the effect of contrast, and filling the beholder with awe, as he sees standing before him the identical frame-work of the huge creature that once ranged the prairies and forests of the West, whose very race is now extinct, as every other will probably become in its turn, before the final course of created things shall be terminated.

This Museum . . . is open, on a very moderate fee, to the inspection of the curious, from morning till sun-set; and in the evenings the central part of the large saloon is usually occupied for the performance of concerts, delivery of lectures, or any other description of public entertainment that combines instruction with amusement. Its . . . noble edifice, good management, and the admirable order and neatness of everything connected with it makes it an acquisition of great value to the institutions of Philadelphia.[35]

Buckingham enjoyed the Museum, but his surprise and delight with Dunn's Chinese collection were even greater. He visited it repeatedly and describes it in detail. There was nothing like this in England.

> I felt a longing desire to have it transferred to London, where it would gratify ten times the number of persons that it can here, and where the visitors would, I think, feel more pleasure, from the more sensitive and ardent temperament of Europeans generally, compared to the coldness and indifference of the Americans.

Here, he reflected, was an exposition of the true character of a people, better even than words in promoting mutual understanding—a profound deterrent to such measures as the Opium War then in progress, "bombarding their towns, and burning, sinking and destroying their ships and boats, so as to compel them to receive this curse and abomination against their own laws and edicts."[36]

Quaker Nathan Dunn agreed with Buckingham. He chose not July 4 but Christmas Eve as appropriate for the opening of his collection; in the interim he employed Titian and William McGuigan to install it for him. Diarist Sydney George Fisher was there for the occasion, a man with a jaundiced eye, yet here all admiration:

> . . . certainly nothing could be more interesting or more splendid. Mr. Dunn is a bachelor of large fortune, which he has accumulated during a long residence in China, and whilst there he amused himself by collecting this vast and magnificent assemblage, which cost $50,000 there, and $8,000 to put it in order for exhibition. It now forms a part of the Museum, and a permanent ornament & honor to our city, and is a spectacle unique in its kind and I suppose unequalled in any country. It exhibits a perfect picture of Chinese life. Figures of natural size, admirably executed in a species of fine clay, all of them portraits of individuals, are there to be seen, dressed in the appropriate costume, engaged in their various avocations and surrounded by the furniture, implements and

material objects of daily existence. The faces are expressive, the attitudes natural, the situation & grouping well conceived, and the aspect of the whole very striking and lifelike. Mandarins, priests, soldiers, ladies of quality, gentlemen of rank, play-actors and slaves; a barber, a shoemaker and a blacksmith employed in their trades; the shop of a merchant with purchasers buying goods, the drawing room of a man of fortune with his visitors smoking and drinking tea & servants in attendance; all sitting, standing, almost talking, with the dress, furniture and accompaniments of actual life. Some of the costumes are of the richest and most gorgeous description. Models of country houses and boats, weapons, lamps, pictures, vases, images of Gods, and porcelain vessels, many of them most curious and beautiful, and in number, infinite. Mr. Dunn was in the room himself and explained to us the nature and uses of many things.[37]

But all this splendor was in a red dawn. Financial panic had been running wild for a full year, business houses failing, specie payments discontinued, and stock issues all but worthless. It may have been with relief that the directors of the Philadelphia Museum Company granted a leave of absence to Titian. Two years before, he had been appointed to the scientific corps of the Navy's first exploring expedition; now, after delays, uncertainties, careful planning, high hopes, and acrimonious debate, the squadron was about to sail. The Company, in its new mood, wanted Titian's salary more than they wanted a resident naturalist. Had William McGuigan sailed also as the expedition's taxidermist (a post later eliminated), it would have left the directors entirely free to concentrate on music and light drama.

But for Titian the four-year cruise gave promise of salvation through adventure. There was no mistaking the threat posed by the grandiose new building. Museums were turning into theaters. Here was a chance to reverse that trend or, if that were impossible, to save himself. For the great United States Exploring Expedition was bringing into view his father's dream of a national museum, recognized at long last as inevitable.

It was coming about, however, not at all with that smooth and sure inevitability which his father had imagined. The Age of Reason had gone by. The Enlightenment had vanished under waves of that "enthusiasm" so despised by Peale, Paine, or Jefferson, under a return to the ever-present God of camp meetings, the voices of prophets and popular frenzy. This was the Age of Jackson. William Miller was uttering his "Midnight Cry" of a Second Coming computed with mathematical accuracy. Science had its visionaries too, among them John Cleves Symmes, Jr., who from St. Louis, in the Missouri Territory, on April 10, 1818, had issued his pronunciamento to the world: "I declare that the earth is hollow and habitable within; containing a number of solid concentric spheres, one within the other, and that it is open at the poles twelve or sixteen degrees. I pledge my life in support of this truth, and am ready to explore the hollow, if the world will support and aid me in the undertaking. . . ." His thesis caught on, argued so persuasively in scientific terms that Congress was flooded with petitions for an expedition to discover the verdant, happy realms below. After all, Columbus had sailed with an odd notion too, and had found America. Faith in "Symmes' Hole" faded away at last, but the excitement of impending discovery lived on, sustained by the genuine need for a charting of the seas roamed by American ships.

Andrew Jackson brought to the presidency an aggressive no-nonsense view of the matter. Too many of our ships had been lost on unknown reefs or cannibal islands of "the great Southern Ocean." The United States must stand in the forefront, a peer of the older nations in exploration. The American Philosophical Society, the Academy of Natural Sciences, and other learned bodies were consulted. Titian Peale came to the White House, as bearer both of institutional advice and of a recommendation of himself as "a general zoologist, a natural history painter and a taxidermist" whose "superior, if his equal, cannot be found in the United States." It was a picturesque confrontation: an old man with the thunder of battle still in his ears, warming to the presence of this younger fellow, sure shot with rifle or bow, keen for the forest, prairie or mountain—and a birthright Democrat as well. "Old Hickory" talked of the future, of scientific gains far beyond the former expeditions, and of massive collections to be assembled and preserved. He spoke of "the legacy of an English gentleman, James Smithson, who had bequeathed a sum of money to the United States to found an institution for the increase and diffusion of knowledge, which seemed to indicate the foundation of a museum," in which Titian could expect to have an important part.[38]

To Titian, and equally to many others, the Smithson bequest was pointed toward a museum in his father's pattern. But whether the Philadelphia Museum could be absorbed into the new institute was doubtful. It was certain only that the scientists of the expedition would be gathering specimens by the thousands and that these must be preserved somewhere until a Smithsonian bill could be maneuvered through Congress. Long delays followed. Jackson's term ended and Van Buren came in, but Titian had his appointment and the squadron was at last making ready to sail. When James Barton Longacre, painting a portrait of Secretary of War Poinsett for his *Gallery of Distinguished Americans,* found his sitter in agreement that the Philadelphia Museum would be the best depository for the expedition collections, he passed on the word to Museum director Kane. Kane acted promptly. So it was that only a week after the gala opening at Ninth and George, just in time for the order to be transmitted to the ships, Van Buren's newly appointed Secretary of the Navy ordered all collections to be sent direct from the squadron to the Philadelphia Museum. They would be held on deposit, "subject to the orders of the U. States," but the board in its confirming resolution was careful to reserve a right to exhibit any part. [39]

Titian sailed in the sloop-of-war *Peacock* from Hampton Roads, on August 17, 1838. Two other members of the scientific corps were aboard with him, Horatio Emmons Hale, a philologist, whose *Ethnography and Philology* of 1846 would be the first and best of the published reports, and the mineralogist James Dwight Dana, whose *Zoophytes* appeared that same year. Other vessels carried Dr. Charles Pickering, a physician and naturalist prominent in the Academy of Natural Sciences; Joseph P. Couthouy, a seafaring conchologist; William Rich and William D. Brackenridge, botanists; and Alfred T. Agate and Joseph Drayton, artists. [40]

Titian, at thirty-nine, was a senior member of the corps—indeed, of the entire force. Hale had been a Harvard undergraduate at the time of his appointment. Pickering, at thirty-three, regarded himself as Chief Naturalist, a rank fully justified by his Harvard M.D., experience, and knowledge, but stiffly resented by Titian. Titian was a museum man with a Peale family education: French language and knowledge picked up in reading and in the field, all impelled by family enthusiasms rather than disciplined instruction. He had been assigned the fields of mammalogy and ornithology, but his duties included overseeing the preservation of specimens, and assembling, packing, and shipping all the collections. Thus he would know precisely what deposits were coming to the Philadelphia Museum, and was in a good position also to collect for the Museum and for himself.

The squadron was composed of the flagship *Vincennes,* the

Peacock, the supply ships *Relief* and *Porpoise,* and two small pilot boats for use in the marine surveys, the *Sea Gull* and *Flying Fish.* In command was Lieutenant Charles Wilkes, Jr. (he of "the *Trent* Affair" in the Civil War), a young officer well qualified to direct the surveys but a martinet of the first order, touchy, temperamental and vindictive, quick to rebuke and punish, constantly on the watch for cabals against his authority. Desertions would be many, and when their two-year enlistments ran out, his men would be bullied into signing on again, with a cat-o'-nine-tails as the ultimate persuader.

It was Titian's good fortune that the *Peacock* was commanded by a contrasting character. Lieutenant William H. Hudson was affable and easygoing, a steady and courageous sailor, as well versed in wind and wave as he was innocent of the mysteries of hydrography. The small space assigned to the scientists for their work was so wet and dark it could not be used. Most of that had to be done in harbor, but Hudson was not averse to giving up the captain's cabin to it when needful, and at other times his quarters served as a social center, a sort of clubroom brightened by music and amateur drama.

The little squadron would swing first across the Atlantic to Madeira and the Cape Verde Islands, then back across again to Rio de Janeiro, south to Rio Negro, south again around Cape Horn and up to Valparaiso, with a taste of the Antarctic (and perhaps a passing thought of "Symmes' Hole") in between, then from Lima west to the Tuamoto Archipelago, Tahiti, and the Society Islands, with an interval of civilized relaxation in Sydney and the Australian countryside. Wilkes left his scientists behind when he sailed to his discovery of an Antarctic continent, Wilkes Land, picking them up again at Bay of Islands in northern New Zealand. Proceeding north then, there was a bloody rencontre with the cannibals of Fiji, in vengeance for the loss of two young officers clubbed to death while ashore on survey.

Navy men gave the charts priority, with only contempt at first for the poking mumbo-jumbo of the "scientifics." Gradually, the scientists won cooperation and respect. With all his faults, Wilkes was a tireless worker, driving himself as he drove the others. There was no scientific idling. Titian stood out among them all as the best marksman in the squadron, and this included such duties as peppering the legs of threatening natives with mustard-seed bird shot, and at Tarawa—"Drummond's Island" in the Gilbert group—he had been called upon to pick off the chiefs of a warrior band (standing, as they thought, at a safe distance) who had enticed a seaman into their village and murdered him.

"PAPEETE, ISLAND OF TAHITI"

This on-the-spot study bears descriptive notes for possible enlargement in a painting: "2" is the Peacock, *with the masts of the* Flying Fish *seen nearby at "8"; "3" is the whaler* Charles Carroll, *noted as "too large"; "4" is "the Queen's Palace, white with thatched roof"; and "5" is a "hill covered with Guava bushes."* (The American Museum of Natural History.)

From island-hunting and new discoveries in Micronesia, eastward to Hawaii, east again, and then the *Peacock* wrecked on the uncharted Oregon coast. There was no loss of life, but natural history specimens deemed too valuable to be entrusted to other vessels went down with the ship. Titian and his shipmates traveled adventurously south by land, exploring and collecting along the way, to rejoin the *Vincennes* at San Francisco. Westward then to the Philippines, on a homeward journey around the world, arriving ultimately in June, 1842.

As the explorers had sailed away in the summer of 1838, Rembrandt Peale returned to Philadelphia to begin his career as professor of "Graphics" at Central High School. Central, a high school which for a time awarded the bachelor's degree, still maintains its record of distinguished alumni and teachers. Rembrandt had written his own textbook, expounding his theory that handwriting is a key to other artistic skills. It was another transitorydigression from painting, but it brought him close once

TITIAN PEALE ON "PEALE'S RIVER"

The Peacock *arrived at Rewa in the Fiji Islands on May 16, 1840. The diary of F. D. Stuart, her captain's clerk, records that on the next day "a couple of Boats were dispatched under Comd. of Lt. Budd & P. M. Davis with Mr. Peal as assistant and phillips as guide up the river on a surveying excursion to be gone 3 or 4 days." The men drank ava with the natives but kept "arms and accoutrements in readiness," aware of cannibal treachery. Drawing by T. R. Peale.* (American Philosophical Society.)

DEATH ON DRUMMOND'S ISLAND

Facing page: A relaxed atmosphere prevailed on the Peacock *when unaccompanied by the flagship. At Drummond's Island (now Tarawa) in the Gilberts, her commander stepped ashore, confident that "there is no harm in these people." Provocative women and noisy warriors surrounded his small party. The dying scream of a sailor who had been lured away was heard. Confronted by a wild mob shouting defiance, "Mr. Peale, the best shot of the party," was summoned to pick off its leaders in the onset of a bloody punitive foray on April 3, 1840, which—whatever else it accomplished—added more native artifacts than at any other site to their scientific collections.*

Above: *Melanesian warriors in coir armor and porcupine fish helmet, armed with sharktooth spears.* From Charles Wilkes, Narrative of the United States Exploring Expedition *(Philadelphia, 1845).*

Below: *Armor of woven coir, with a spearhead. The high backpiece was to protect the wearer's head from an enemy's war club.* (Peabody Museum, Harvard University.)

WILD GOOSE CHASE IN CALIFORNIA
*Shipwrecked off Oregon in 1841, members of the Wilkes expedition traveled south by
land to rejoin the rest of the squadron at San Francisco. Drawing by Titian R. Peale.*
(American Philosophical Society.)

more to Museum affairs, and in December 1838 the directors had invited him to deliver the first lecture in their new auditorium.[41]

Serious discourse, however, was not what they saw as the
primary need, and they were investing recklessly in light entertainment. Talented Francis Johnson's Negro band, lively and sophisticated, drew well. The concerts of Miss Sheriff and Mr. Wilson were
"rapturously received." Edward L. Davenport, a front-rank actor,
appeared in his Yankee impersonations. But then came the "Belgian
Giant," the Hungarian Minstrels, the sleight-of-hand artists, the
Automaton Chess Player and Automaton Musical Lady, and,
cheapest to produce, "The Dissolving Tableaux" on the magic
lantern. This was on a par with the American Museum at Fifth and
Chestnut, whose lecture room had become a "Scientific Saloon"
with tightrope walkers, a mechanical panorama of the Treaty of
Ghent, and the like.[42]

In the face of deepening depression and heavy debt, all this was seen as the important aspect of museum operation, and directors Dunn and Cowperthwaite, seeking a replacement for Titian, recommended a secretary-treasurer at a salary of $2,000. He was to be in charge of "exhibitions," that is, a stage manager, though the term was avoided. Two-man committees would oversee everything else. Franklin Peale and Robert M. Patterson would take "Natural History and Miscellaneous Collections." That would cover the shipments soon to be arriving from the exploring expedition—and in a quantity which would tax available storage space. Kane and Sellers would have "Portraits and Pictures": Franklin Peale and a new member, John Jay Smith, Jr., the "Library of the Museum." Dunn and Franklin Peale would have oversight of the building. To John Jay Smith, librarian of the Library Company of Philadelphia and hereditary trustee of the Loganian Library, went the salaried post of secretary-treasurer.[43]

Smith, the new chief executive—high forehead, Roman nose, and in character a foretaste of his more celebrated grandson, the essayist Logan Pearsall Smith—had grown up with the young Peales as friends and the Museum as a boyhood delight. Apprenticeship to a druggist had given him a foothold in science, but he had gone on into partnership with a printer, then to editorial work on *Waldie's Select Circulating Library*, a publishing venture based on America's freedom from international copyright; and since 1835 he had been editing Littell's similar *Museum of Foreign Literature, Science and Art*. He was a member of the Academy of Natural Sciences and a founder of the Athenian Institute, a popular lyceum. He was, in short, a man from whom "rational amusement" of high quality could be expected. His salary was more than double what he had received from the Library Company, and Museum duties required only an hour a day at the office there. Rembrandt had established young Edmund Peale as agent for the new issue of stock, valued at $100 a share, and had Smith's assurance that Edmund would speedily "sell stock enough to satisfy the Bank debt & make dividends to Stockholders of at least 6 per cent, besides the personal privileges. And he is confident the Stock next summer will readily sell for 120 or 125 dollars pr share." This was the euphoric hopefulness that comes from, and prolongs, depressions. By November, Smith was ready to resign his treasurership.[44]

The Bank of the United States, which had so freely advanced the money for the new building, was now in trouble. As payments fell due, only Dunn was there to meet them. Edmund Peale confided to his mother that the Museum stock was "precariously situated and has made no dividend nor never will." Edmund did make a profit for at least one investor. He sold a share to James Forten, one of Philadelphia's successful Negro businessmen, assuring him (correctly) that it carried admission privileges in the evenings as well as by day. The directors, shocked at the prospect of a Negro appearing at their evening affairs, must needs buy it back at well above par.[45]

The museum function meanwhile was held together by Titian's friend and assistant, William McGuigan, and he was made curator in 1841, though with no increase in his $600 salary. George Campbell, another librarian, had succeeded Smith as treasurer (salary, $1,000) and was now replaced by Griffitts as manager (5 votes to 4 over Rembrandt Peale), at a salary of $800. But the turn of the year, from 1840 to 1841, brought also two climactic events. First came a subsurface eruption exposing all the Company's devious ineptitude, and then, hard on the heels of that, events in Washington which destroyed the last frail hope of its ever becoming a United States National Museum.

Franklin Peale was now happily married to a niece of millionaire Stephen Girard and secure in his position at the United States Mint. One can sense a reaction against the whirlwind course set by Dunn in his motion, on January 15, 1841, that an investigating committee be appointed. The committee, comprising Elliott, Parrish, Rembrandt Peale, and an elderly affable Quaker merchant, Joseph Parker, gave long hours to its task and found ample cause for concern. A devastating report came on February 3. The purchase of land had never been formally completed. The building had cost more than $30,000 beyond the contracted figure of $80,000, and with finishing and furniture had totaled $139,238.63. "Your Committee were no little surprised and astonished, that so great a responsibility should have been assumed by those who must have been aware that not One Dollar (Comparatively speaking) was in the Treasury, and further that a building so costly and Magnificent should have been erected on a lot to which the Company had no title whatever." Outstanding debts were then itemized to a total of $120,341.42. A personal claim of Joseph Cowperthwaite to $41,585.24 was held open to question.

The Committee, "without unkind feeling toward anyone," presented a situation "so irregular" that it could not pass unnoticed. The Company had no title to the property but was receiving rent from Dunn, its "apparent owner." No regular stock books had been kept before January 1, 1841. On top of this confusion, the vast and spreading debt "has given your Committee much Solicitude, and although the prospect is so very gloomy, they are still not without a hope, that by reasonable indulgence of creditors and a proper appeal made by our fellow citizens on behalf of the noble Institution, long the pride of Philada., we may yet be extricated from the difficulties which surround us."

Smith was found to have paid himself a salary after resigning as treasurer. On threat of a lawsuit, the money would be returned in payments to Dunn. Dunn was at the center of it all. The report reflects a changed attitude toward men of business: as hard times hardened, their leadership was discredited, leaving only the anger and distrust that had fallen first on Nicholas Biddle, then on bankers and moneyed men in general, one of whom was Nathan Dunn.

Beginning in the spring of 1839 and continuing through all this ominous internal turmoil, scientific collections had been arriving from the squadron—boxes, barrels, bales, and bundles sent back by ships encountered at distant ports. This was Franklin Peale's responsibility, and he and McGuigan opened and examined them, made lists and receipts. How much was placed on exhibit is not known. Most of it—minerals, seeds, skins of animals of all sorts—was not exhibitable. At Titian's suggestion, Wilkes had sent back a request from Rio de Janeiro, on December 25, 1838, that containers be undisturbed except to make sure that specimens preserved in alcohol did not need refilling. Franklin took this to mean a general oversight of everything, since skins might need preservatives also. Secretary Paulding agreed to pay for the work, with the needed whiskey, corrosive sublimate, and arsenic, and it was done.[46]

Beyond the formal agreement of 1838 to receive, store, and exhibit the materials, the Company minutes make no mention of these matters. Its board was too busy with music, magicians, and financial wizardry. But in Washington the expedition's future had been much discussed, both in Congress and among men of science. The vast collections, the reports and studies to follow—here was the making of a museum-centered learned society, with the Smithson money lying ready for its support, still unassigned. On May 7, 1840, Joel R. Poinsett, soon to retire as Secretary of War, brought together a group of statesmen and government officials, all with a knowledgeable interest, to discuss the need for "a Cabinet of

Natural History." John Quincy Adams, a supporter of the old Columbian Institute and now chairman of the Smithsonian Bequest Committee of the House, was present. There emerged "The National Institution for the Promotion of Science"—an undertaking strong enough to absorb the Columbian Institute, receive Congressional approval as custodian of government collections, and a supporting grant of $5,000. Everything depended, or seemed to, on the collections. As one member put it, as soon as those were held "by right" rather than "by Permission," assignment of the Smithson endowment must follow as a matter of course. Poinsett then persuaded Paulding to order all expedition shipments to Washington rather than Philadelphia.[47]

Paulding sent Franklin Peale a brief note, February 5, 1841; its message was that the National Institution was now prepared to receive everything, from Philadelphia and from the squadron. His order to the Commandant of the Philadelphia Navy Yard to make immediate transfer from the Museum had gone out the day before. Commandant John Gwinn reported on February 6 that about 150 crates and barrels were en route. Here was a sudden death blow to the Museum's last hope of national status. William McGuigan's consternation is evident in his warning against any handling of the material by inexperienced persons: "Death might be the result," due to "the immense quantity of Arsenic and Corrosive Sublimate."[48]

Franklin did not answer until February 16, when he mentioned a box of seeds his brother hoped could be distributed among the botanists of Philadelphia. His request was promptly denied from Washington, where the National Institution group, intent on creating a de facto museum as quickly as possible, was commandeering museum material from government offices wherever it could be found. They had ample space. Secretary of State Daniel Webster had made the Patent Office's new edifice available, with halls and rooms beyond the wildest dreams of the Peales. Gifts from private donors were pouring into the prospective National Museum. John Varden, running a little museum operation in Washington, sold out to the new behemoth and joined its curatorial staff. The National Museum must be open free to all, and he could not compete with that.[49]

Half-filled containers in the shipment from Philadelphia aroused suspicions that the first shipment direct from the squadron confirmed. Colonel John James Abert, chief of the Corps of Topographical Engineers, a naturalist and a founding father of the

National Institution, wrote to Poinsett on May 6, 1841, telling bluntly what the Institution's curator, Dr. Henry King, had found:

Since you left us 20 tons more of the collections from the Exploring expedition have arrived. . . . Nearly one fourth of the whole is marked as private, and from an examination of one case, the most choice articles are so marked. If such a course should be sanctioned, it would be destructive of the collection. We have therefore, that is [Peter] Force, King & myself, determined to represent these facts to the Secretary of the Navy and recommend that all such marks be disregarded, the same being destructive to the objects of the expedition and opposed to the instructions. We have no doubt that our recommendation will be adopted. The cases and specimens so marked are from Peale & no doubt intended for his museum, but it would be a shocking outrage of propriety to countenance the idea that this Expedition was got up, and these naturalists paid, by the U.S. for private benefit.

If these 20 tons had gone to Phila. and been allowed to lay there as those previously received, all this "private property" would have been abstracted, as with the cases previously received. For among those we found large cases with but few articles in them & the void filled with shavings—now we doubt if shavings were an abundant article with the Squadron, and still more, that large cases would have been sent so great a distance with so little in them. In one case, of those lately received, were ten smaller ones, & six of these marked private, as I have just understood from Dr. King. He also said that the four intended for the public contained merely common corals & shells. But we have no doubt that this will be corrected, as soon as we can make the representation to the Secretary, and that he will authorize King to disregard the private marks.

There may be some apology for Peale in the impression at first entertained that the U.S. was indifferent about the collection & intended to distribute it. Yet however he should have allowed the U.S. to have made the distribution. There may be no serious objection to a distribution of the duplicates, but it should first be known what these are & what can be obtained in exchange, and also I think, even for such a distribution, some authority should be obtained. That clause in our Smithson bill will settle the power in such cases.[50]

A year later Abert would find Dr. King "selfish & intriguing," and intrigue, however well intentioned, characterized this whole plan to capture the Smithsonian name and fund. It was fostering jealousies and putting all concerned in doubtful relationships to one another. Henry King, a geologist employed in the Ordnance Department, was holding a position for which Titian, on his return, would be the most conspicuous candidate. Later, when a rival Smithsonian party appeared, King would try to keep a foot in both camps.

Back in Philadelphia, the loss of the government deposit was followed by another and far more devastating withdrawal. First, the entertainment program hit rock bottom. On July 6, 1841, Manager Griffitts reported that the engagement of Miss Wyman, "the Lady Magician," had been totally unproductive. His request for a leave of absence to take an ailing Mrs. Griffitts to the seashore was granted. Mr. Dunn's request that the Chinese buffalo sent from Canton by William Wood be placed on loan in his collection was granted. Then, six days later at a special meeting, Dunn struck a decisive double blow, presented in writing. First: He had determined to take his Chinese Museum to London. Since some directors had complained of the length of lease and the amount of rental, he felt sure there could be no objection. Second: The Museum building must therefore be sold, and with this he enclosed a letter from Herman Cope, superintendent of the Suspended Debt and Real Estate Department of the United States Bank, demanding immediate settlement of the Museum's obligations.

Nathan Dunn, as usual, was acting promptly. Packing and removal of his Chinese collection began at once. His fellow directors were alert enough to notice that their buffalo had gone with the rest, and Griffitts had to dash over to New York to retrieve it. Dunn may have had his move in mind when, six months before, on Christmas Eve of 1840, he had called the board of managers of Haverford College into a special meeting to receive his gift of $20,575, made in appreciation of the fact that this was the "only institution in the United States at which youthful members of the Society of Friends can get a liberal education under instruction of members of the Society," and that improvement of the mind is "an auxilliary to its religious duties." Haverford's treasury was then as bare as the Museum's and its prospects were almost as bleak. Dunn, who had declared from the first that profits from the Chinese museum were to be assigned to charity, had thus removed some of the onus of a second departure leaving financial chaos behind.[51]

Furthermore, he was leaving with a plan in mind for the rescue of the Museum—though as matters came out, it would only enlarge the anguish and disaster. The city now owned all of Independence Square with the exception of Philosophical Hall, and in 1835 it had offered to purchase that. Referees were to agree on a price, and the society was anticipating a move into some greatly improved situation. Dunn, who had been elected to membership in January of 1836, at the time he had assumed the presidency of the Museum, now offered the Museum building and land for $37,250 and, swift and persuasive, was able to close the deal on August 5, 1841. Robert M. Patterson, acting for the society, then laid down the terms on which the Museum might remain; a $2,400 rental and "the premises to be used only for the exhibition of the Museum collection." In short, no theatricals, and the voice of the society only to be heard. Under existing conditions, this would have forced the Museum into the arms of the society, and such may have been Dunn's beneficent intention. His move to London would not only recover his own position but bring the Philosophical Society and the Museum together, resulting in an enlarged home for the one and a true institutional foundation for the other.

It was at this point in the continuing business depression that the city withdrew its offer to buy and thus plunged the society into a crisis which very nearly stripped it of Hall, library, scientific collections, everything. In London the while, Dunn was finding it just as James Buckingham had predicted—his "Chinese World in Miniature" was an immediate success, praised on all sides, visited by the Queen, commended by the Duke of Wellington, and bringing in an income of over $50,000 a year. Word came back to the Philosophical Society that he had written into his will a bequest relieving his fellow members of their burden. At his death three years later, however, the debt to Dunn remained uncanceled, and his executors brought suit for its recovery, so that only a strong rallying of its membership saved the society from ruin.[52]

This was the situation to which Titian returned in June 1842. All the bright hopes of four years before were gone, and worse would follow. The explorers had expected a hero's welcome; instead, they met disapproval or indifference. Many people saw the long cruise as a pleasure jaunt at taxpayers' expense, while John Citizen bore the brunt of hard times. A Whig administration was cool to what Jackson men had begun. The new Secretary of the Navy informed the "scientifics" that their pay and employment had ended on landing. Wilkes, who had ordered some of his officers

TITIAN PEALE,
COLLECTOR
The personal collection made by
Titian Peale on the Wilkes
expedition included this
"Palaua," a neck ornament of
the ancient Hawaiian royalty,
and a fly whisk of Tahiti with a
small grotesque figure carved on
its handle. (The University
Museum, University of
Pennsylvania, Philadelphia.)

court-martialed, was court-martialed himself for false statements, punishments without trial, and overfree use of the cat. Titian and others, obliged to appear as witnesses in New York, watched as the expedition's accomplishments sank into further disrepute.

As for the scandal regarding the collections, little more was heard of it. Titian had collected on his own, sure of his right to do so. Abert's is the strongest insinuation of wrongdoing, and his "one fourth of the whole" would have been five tons, an obvious exaggeration. Other crewmen had collected in a small way: Midshipman William Reynolds, who had brought back two suits of native armor from the affair at Drummond's Island, gave one to Titian for the public collections and planned to send the other to the museum in his home town, Lancaster, Pennsylvania. It was only as the ships neared home that Wilkes had ordered not only all journals but all objects given up. Titian, writing to Franklin Peale from Bay of Islands, New Zealand, on April 5, 1840, refers to collections of birds and butterflies given him by friends in Sydney which, "with two trunks of my own," had gone in the barque *Shepherdess* to Boston. Franklin was to look out for these and store them at Titian's house. Invoices show that at Bay of Islands on the same day the ship *Lydia* had received a consignment for Boston including three boxes of ornithology from Titian and "Native Manufactures of New Zealand" from Horatio Hale. The freight on the *Shepherdess*, Sydney to Boston, was receipted by Franklin Peale on December 26, 1840, while that from the *Lydia* went to Washington.[53]

Titian later recovered some "private" objects in Washington, and it is significant that the meticulous Wilkes, then in charge of the Washington collections, recommended him warmly as a Smithsonian curator. Wilkes, often in Philadelphia, must have known of the personal collection Titian eventually gave to the Academy of Natural Science, where it was described in 1915 as "one of the best collections of Polynesian ethnica anywhere in the world." Yet, actually, that which stayed in Philadelphia fared better than the rest in Washington, where the crash program to mount birdskins, clean shells, and set up prettified exhibits of every sort under a mixed medly of paid and volunteer help brought damage, loss of identifications, and a growing confusion. Ignorant haste was followed by ignorant neglect, neglect by irreparable damage, as seen at last in 1899 when the remnants were dug out from under a coal bin in the Smithsonian cellar.[54]

But Titian had returned to find his own institution in sorry straits. The entertainment program had failed utterly, and neglect of natural history had brought daily attendance down to the lowest on record. McGuigan, laboring in the summer heat, did effect a brief and, in its way, memorable revival. Barnum was riding high in the spring of 1842 with his most celebrated hoax, "the Feegee Mermaid," which Kimball in Boston had bought from a sailor there and which Barnum played up with banner publicity and fake scientists delivering fake lectures of authentication. It was easily identifiable as a conjoined monkey and fish, and when William McGuigan promptly acquired a matching specimen of his own, from "a gentleman of this city," one may suspect that he, the expert taxidermist, had made it himself. His, however, he advertised only as "a wonderful creation of man's ingenuity . . . being the handy work of the Japanese," contrived with "the most remarkable skill and address in the mode of joining the two apparent bodies, . . . and, as a matter of curiosity, may rival any mermaid ever exhibited in this country." This it did, attracting crowds and cutting short the fanfare built up in New York by Barnum.[55]

Adversity had at last brought the Philadelphia Museum Company to a mood of repentance for past neglect of its true function. Titian, welcomed as a redeeming angel, could only point to accessions still unprocessed (perhaps including some Expedition material), and suggest that these might put a new face on everything if money could be found for the purpose. Much of the business of the Company was now in the hands of its Committee of Investigation, two of whom, Rembrandt Peale and Joseph Parker, addressed the stockholders on January 1, 1843, in a *mea culpa* of past sins and slender hopes:

> At the time the present Board came into office the Institution was still suffering under the injurious effects resulting from the morbid excitement produced by a series of entertainments catered to the public taste in 1839 & 1840 & at a subsequent period continued in, on a more reduced scale both as regards the means employed & the receipts realized. Public opinion, at all time & under all circumstances Omnipotent, has decided that the departure from the legitimate objects of the Company could not be sustained and the converting into a concert room of a receptacle for the works of Nature and Art and for which purpose alone it was reared and nurtured by its illustrious founder was sufficient cause for the withdrawal of the patronage formerly so liberally bestowed by our most influential citizens. . . .

Amidst all of this gloom and despondency your Board take unfeigned satisfaction in announcing the reinstatement of Mr. Titian R. Peale as Manager, leave of absence having been granted him, during the period he was engaged as a member of the Scientific Corps on the U.S. exploring expedition. Of the talents & high attainments of this gentleman & his perfect knowledge and experience in the well conducting and improving of a scientific collection it is useless to enlarge: Your Board have full confidence that under his direction the resuscitation of the Institution may confidently be hoped for. All that is now required to obtain this wished for result is means sufficient to mount & arrange for exhibition a large collection of Specimens (valued at $30,000), the property of the Company and which the want of funds alone has prevented being placed in the Saloon. This being accomplished, we fervently trust that the Museum may be placed in its original firm position unaided and unaffected by any entertainment foreign to its objects and the intention of its founder. . . .

No one knew better than Titian the intention of the founder. Titian alone had inherited the ideals and hopes of his father, and he also must bear the full anguish of what the others had brought about. Titian was a field naturalist, a hunter and collector, yet could hold his own well among the emerging specialists in natural science. Lepidoptera was one chosen point of concentration, and in the precision and charm of his drawings of butterflies and moths one can see the ideal of scientific clarity, his father's delight in the beautiful, and can sense a greater depth of dedication, an extension in himself of the hand and eye of his lost half-brother and namesake.

The directors had reinstated Titian as curator on November 1, 1842, William McGuigan stepping aside with only an expression of friendship and pride in his fifteen years' service. McGuigan had at least a small livelihood as a taxidermist. With his departure the Museum Record Book entries cease—the last, on October 28, being for a collection of butterflies presented by Master C. Sellers. No funds were in sight with which to process the $30,000 worth of exhibits in storage. But Dr. Pickering had been given a small salary as curator for the National Institution, and soon after the turn of the year he begged Titian to join him there "to review, arrange and label"—in short, to bring some order out of the confusion. Titian was aghast at what he found, his months of painstaking shipboard work undone:

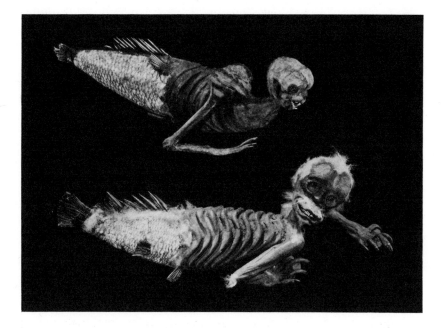

THE RIVAL MERMAIDS
Bottom, *the famous "Feejee Mermaid," which Moses Kimball of the Boston Museum lent to Barnum in 1842. Barnum gave it a tremendous publicity buildup, including a frock-coated lecturer to prove its authenticity. The public's astonishment suddenly evaporated when William McGuigan, a taxidermist at the Philadelphia Museum, produced his "Japanese Mermaid" (above) and advertised it as a "wonderful creation of man's ingenuity . . . composed entirely from different species of fish, and, as a matter of curiosity, may rival any mermaid ever exhibited in this country."* (Peabody Museum, Harvard University.)

One hundred and eighty specimens of birds which *I* collected are missing, including some new species:—the aggregate of all other branches of Nat. history, and the collections of others which are not in my register, I leave you to infer.

It is really sickening, but I suppose there is no remedy for what is passed; I have about 60 Species of new Mammalia and Birds, which I am now preparing an account of; they will form a very pretty volume, if completed; after that I shall be pennyless, and out of employment unless my friends will help me look out for some new "berth."—so much for enterprise!—after five years exile, with my children running wild for want of paternal presense—I can only expect to be rewarded with poverty, and a broken constitution.[55]

He went back to Philadelphia, wholly discouraged. There, on May 1, 1843, the Museum building was sold at sheriff's sale, with the directors holding firm in their contention that its contents remained by charter inviolate, never to be sold, never to leave the city. Isaac Brown Parker, the purchaser, permitted the collections to remain at an annual rental of $10,000; all receipts at the door were to go to him in payment. This was the end of the Museum for Titian. He had a family of five to support, and he brought them to Washington, where a resumption of his Navy pay had been promised. One child had died while Titian was at sea; a new baby, Louis Bonaventure, born that summer, lived less than a year. Their mother would die of consumption in February 1846; and Florida, of the same disease, a year later. That would leave only two, Francis Titian and Sybilla Miriam, as their father labored to complete his "pretty little volume," the expedition's report on mammalogy and ornithology. At least the struggle and discontent were shared by others of the scientific corps. Only Wilkes seemed able to stay on top. His five-volume *Narrative,* compiled from all the explorers' journals, sold well. He succeeded Pickering at the National Institution, and ran the Patent Office setup with quarterdeck order and authority. And it was Wilkes who, when Titian's work was completed in 1848, took offense at an imagined slur upon the Navy in its preface, found fault with the contents, suppressed the small edition, and then raised ample funds for another to rewrite it. As Titian bitterly protested, such faults as it had would not have appeared had he himself been given the same freedom and support.[56]

He had been sustained in part by his hope of a chief curatorship at the Smithsonian, but that too was disappointed. So also were the founders of the National Institution, when their plan was defeated by the very magnitude of their collections and the enormous cost of housing and maintaining so much. There was a museum clause in the Smithsonian Act of 1846, but Joseph Henry, as first secretary, approached it with marked caution and some distaste. Another decade would go by before fretting Patent Office officials were relieved of the vast congestion of "natural and artifical curiosities" in their midst and our National Museum became a reality under the aegis of the Smithsonian.

BUFFALO HERD
This oil painting of 1854, made by Titian Peale from earlier studies, reflects his pride in having had a part in the exploration and opening of the American West. (The American Museum of Natural History.)

Titian, after completing his book, accepted a post as assistant examiner at the Patent Office, where, if no more, he had the achievements of the great expedition in sight around him. He found a more congenial environment at the Saturday Club, a group of Washington scientists, and became a founder of the Philosophical Society of Washington. He painted, pioneered in photography, continued his study of Lepidoptera, and published articles also on American Indian archaeology and on his experience in the great expedition. Four years after Eliza's death, he married Lucinda MacMullen, who joined him in the filiopietistic labor of arranging his father's papers for publication. He retired in 1873 and returned to Philadelphia among old friends and memories, active again among his collections at the Academy of Natural Sciences. The spirit of the past was with him still, though touched by sadness.

Friendships warmed his last years. The great humanitarian reformer Dorothea Lynde Dix, aging too, sent butterflies for his collection and questioned him about birds. "As for leisure," he wrote, four years before his death, "it is a synonym for idleness, the 'root of all evil.'" He was busy to the end, but when he looked back it was as an explorer that he saw his life's accomplishments:

> Now at the age of 81, I feel blessed by good health, and not oppressed by poverty or wealth— . . . afloat in the world, after spending the best half of my life in the service of the government, helping to found a bureau of *Hydrography,* a *National Museum,* a *Botanic Garden,* and an *Astronomical Observatory,* at Washington, the proceeds of the expeditions:—besides exploring the way to a vast interior, and a west coast for our people who followed there, and now count by millions.[57]

Hard times in the flashy, unstable 1830's and in the roaring 1840's had taken their toll of museums. Only Barnum in New York and Kimball in Boston continued to thrive. Kimball was finding stability in legitimate drama, and Barnum in the sheer weight of gaudy and tawdry fantastics. Kimball was cautious; Barnum, combative, expanding, eager to outsmart and outlive all rivals. He watched the decline at Philadelphia, ready to move in—Baltimore, too.

Rembrandt Peale's handsome building of 1814 had been Baltimore's City Hall since 1830; a century later it would be restored to its original dignity as the Peale Museum of today, dedicated to Baltimore history and arts. Its museum collection had been moved in 1829 to the corner of Calvert and Baltimore Streets, and five years later it had come under Edmund Peale's management.[58] Edmund was a Barnum imitator if not disciple, concentrating upon theatrical entertainments in the Lecture Room.

But Rubens' New York "Parthenon" was the first to fall to the legendary showman. The panic of 1837 had been too much for Rubens' combination of light entertainment and honest science. His sincere effort to bring mesmerism before the public as a new wonder of medical science was no match for Barnum's fake demonstrations, which never disappointed an audience.[59] His natural history collections were not large, but Rubens had been at pains to keep them authentic, supported by John Bell, whom he had trained himself, and with help from William Wood and Charles Atkinson of Philadelphia. His exchange program had reinforced Lambdin's Pittsburgh museum, and with Linnaeus as assistant he had launched Comfort Butler's museum in Utica.[60]

Rubens hung on desperately till 1842 and refused Barnum's offers. A group headed by Dr. John Hoskins Griscom, Rembrandt's son-in-law, had tried to take over as "The New-York Museum of Natural History and Science," pledged "to sweep away all this rubbish which so disgraced the name of the museum, and to render the establishment worthy of the patronage of the learned, the scientific, of teachers, parents and guardians, and of youth."[61] In vain. Rubens yielded up everything to the owner of his building, for rent due. Comedian Yankee Hill had the place for a short span. An English promoter, Henry Bennett, ran it hard as a competitor to Barnum, freak against freak. By January 1843, Barnum had it and was jubilantly running it as a sham rival to his sprawling American Museum.[62] A month later he was writing in his exuberant, nearly indecipherable scrawl to his friend Moses Kimball of the Boston Museum, chortling over this success and looking forward to more:

> . . . I have concluded to have no kind or sort of performance at Peales, nothing but the [gypsy?]. She at $5 per week—lady doorkeeper at $3.50 per week, boy to sweep out at $3.50 per week—advertisements $3.50 per week, fuel $1, Gas $8, Rent $25—total $47. . . .
>
> Tom Thumb left for Philadelphia today—yesterday was his adieu Farewell "Benefit." I took $280! Did you ever hear the like? The day previous took $90—odd. I had the Rocky Mountain wild [Indians?] this week. Give them half after deducting $400! . . . That is a leetle better than to give them two thirds à la Peales. . . .

He had been in Philadelphia the day before, looking for an exhibition hall for Tom Thumb, and had stopped in at Ninth and George. It may have been McGuigan whom he met there. Certainly it was someone with the Company's penitential New Year's resolutions in mind:

> A superintendent said that for a present or [for $?]000 he would not have the dwarf or any other living curiosity exhibited there. I tried to point out his folly when he replied that he knew all about it—that performances could serve [to] keep up the excitement more one year—that he once made

$40,000 in one year with that Museum and the next year lost half that amount. I told him he was a *liar* in saying that; and a fool in expecting me to believe it and left him in a rage.

When I went there he was sweeping out the Chinese Museum. I supposed he was some loafer—who he is I don't know, but I expect he is some fool that the stockholders have placed there confining him to those restrictions.

I engaged the Masonic Hall *front room first floor* for only $12 per *week* including *gas* and *fuel*. If I don't clear $1000 there, I shall for the thousandth time in my life be mistaken. . . . [63]

Barnum knew, as Rubens had, the advantage of a chain of museum lecture halls for his feature exhibits. Baltimore seemed ripe for plucking, but Philadelphia still the great prize he aimed for. Moses Kimball was cool to such further conquests. He had museum enough. His theater, once a mere lecture room adjunct, was becoming the primary thing. "I am half glad you will not want Peale's," Barnum wrote good-naturedly to his friend, on August 26, 1845. "I ought to buy it, for if the American should burn down I could not get Peale's probably short of $10,000 or $15,000 to replace my stock."[64]

The United States Bank was ready to sell, but the Philadelphia Museum Company clung desperately to the terms of its act of incorporation: nothing to be sold, nothing to leave Philadelphia. Then, behind the scenes, a way out of that was found. On September 23, 1845, Edmund Peale arrived with a proposal. Having just yielded the Baltimore collection to Barnum, he had capital for a fresh start in Philadelphia. If the directors would withdraw their claim of immunity from sale, he would make the purchase while honoring the commitment to remain in Philadelphia and continuing the stockholders' right of free admittance, "except when the same is exhibited in connection with other entertainments." The final entry in the Company's minutes postpones "further negotiations . . . for the present." After that, it would seem, silence gave consent.

George Ord sent the news to Charles Waterton in England:

. . . Poor old Mr. Peale thought by getting his pet Institution incorporated he would secure its perpetuity. The worthy virtuoso had yet to learn, that, in our free country, an act of incorporation is a nose of wax, *c'est ou camus ou aquilin ou retroussé ou comme vous voudrez.*[65]

CHAPTER NINE

FULL STAGE AND FINAL CURTAIN (1845–1854)

Nathan Dunn's sudden depart-
ure had brought in Rembrandt Peale as the last president of the
Philadelphia Museum Company—reminding us that he had also
presided over John Trumbull's American Academy of Fine Arts in
New York at its demise twenty years before. He had been in no way
responsible for that unhappy situation and got only ill will from it.
The Museum's dilemma was another matter, and his last-minute
contrition of no avail. He fancied himself a founding father of the
Pennsylvania Academy, and it may have been he who inspired a
newspaper editorial of November 5, 1845, calling upon "the ladies
of the Bazaar" to save the Museum as they had saved the Academy.
But that plea came only three days before the sheriff's sale, where
Edmund Peale bid in every lot at a total figure meeting what
remained of the Company's debt to the United States Bank—
$13,410.69, with interest from January 1, 1840.[1] He needed
capital for a fresh start, and it may be assumed that his agreement
with the bank's Mr. Cope included payments from earnings.

Edmund's romantic career of adventure and escape was now in
full flower, and he meant to make the best of it. He would
out-Barnum Barnum, and may have had his eye also on Moses
Kimball, whose Boston Museum was becoming a prosperous theater

with an adjunct of random curiosities. Barnum claimed credit for being the first to transform museum lecture room into playhouse in all but name, and it seems to have been at Rubens' old stand in New York that he did it. Museum business was show business now, all the way. So was art, if an American artist expected to get beyond portraiture. And here we can take leave of Rembrandt Peale, back in Boston in 1846 exhibiting his enormous (24 feet by 13 feet) *Court of Death* of 1820, "The Great Moral Painting," now to be viewed by gaslight, no less ("25 cts., season tickets 50 cts."), a spectacle of somber majesty very far from the moods his nephew was seeking to arouse at "Peale's Philadelphia Museum and Gallery of Fine Arts."[2]

Edmund had moved his acquisition into the former Masonic Hall in Chestnut Street above Seventh, a neat, shop-fronted building of fifteen rooms, including a banqueting hall and grand saloon. All was ready by January 1846, the collections filling upstairs and down, entries and stairwells. The mammoth stood center stage in one large hall, while at the heart of the whole the grand saloon had been turned into a fully equipped little theater. The theater had no regular company, but in between other engagements Joseph Jefferson, John Sefton, John E. Owens, and other of the best talents of the time were behind its footlights. When plays were lacking, a concert, "Ethiopian Harmonists," "The Mystic Temple of Witchcraft," or somesuch came on. John A. Ellsler, famous manager of later days, here began his dramatic career as Edmund's office assistant. As one contemporary remembered, it was "a moral bijou in all respects. It had neither seats for Cyprians, nor bars for drinkers."[3] Edmund was following Barnum's lead in this. The large public who saw theaters as highroads to hell and museums as educational must not encounter prostitutes or drunken rowdies. Only the naturalists held aloof, giving all their support now to the Academy of Natural Sciences or the Philosophical Society.

These were lean years for the drama, however, as for the country as a whole. By 1846 hard times had at least settled in long enough to be laughed at, and "Hard Times" was a popular song, sung "at the Philadelphia Concerts, with unbounded applause":

The bosses have no work to give their boys.
Who live upon nothing but riots and noise;
They have nothing to do but round hose-houses lurk,
And the times are so hard even *Physic* won't work.[4]

THE OLD MASONIC HALL
Here in 1845 Edmund Peale established his little "bijou" of a theater, with the
Philadelphia Museum collections spread out in the rooms around it. Drawing by
B. R. Evans, 1851. (Historical Society of Pennsylvania.)

These were the "Roaring Forties," and Barnum, controlling the
museum industry in New York and Baltimore, was moving in. He
had a strategy that combined cooperation with competition, and in
January–February 1848 we find General Tom Thumb, Barnum's
happiest star, at Peale's in the Masonic Hall, while the old stand at
Ninth and George was running "the greatest wonder of the age,
CHOC-CHU-TUB-BEE," an Indian chief who performed on "the
one-keyed Flute, Fife, Flageolet, Castanet and Saucepan!" his wife
accompanying him in song, and Signor Blitz following with feats of
magic.[5]

Desperation becomes evident at Masonic Hall with the
appearance of James Andrews's "Model Artistes," and it may have
been a ploy of Barnum's that brought Andrews' arrest for
"exhibiting these vile living figures of male and female sexes." The
exhibitor denied they were nude and got off with a reprimand. But
Edmund was in trouble, and there is reason to believe he was paying
debts in wampum and other small objects from the Museum. From
February 2 to March 4, he was billing the mammoth as a special
feature, suggesting a farewell appearance. A sheriff's sale was
scheduled for June 8, and a catalogue printed. The sale was deferred

until September 6, then deferred again, and it must have been here that the bank took possession of all the paintings.[6]

The mammoth is not listed in the catalogue. It had already been sent abroad for sale. London was not interested, but the French national museum agreed to a good price. Agreed, but could not pay, as the Revolution of the summer of 1848 intervened. It went instead, for a much smaller sum, across the Rhine to the Geologisch-Palaontologische und Mineralogische Abteilung des Hessischen Landesmuseums at Darmstadt, Germany. There, in today's West Germany, the old veteran may still be seen, more accurately mounted than of old and still intact despite wear and tear from war damage to the roof above.[7]

At the Masonic Hall, sans fine arts and skeleton, Edmund moved into a frenzy of plays and such specialties as "Ethiopian Mock Italian Opera" and John Rowson Smith's great panorama of the Mississippi. Then there was a lull in his advertising until the turn of the year, when we suddenly find him in direct and open competition with the Great Showman himself. Barnum had established himself nearby, in the new Swaim Building at Seventh and Chestnut, its red sandstone front towering five storeys with shops on street level, museum rooms above, a large theater over that, and offices under the roof—a monument to the success of Dr. William Swaim's patent panacea and purifier of the blood, the secret of which he had discovered, so the story goes, in his young days as a bookbinder, browsing through the pages as he stitched them.[8] Barnum broke the news jubilantly to Moses Kimball in Boston:

Philadelphia, April 3d, 1849

Friend Moses,

I have taken Swaimes Museum on a lease of ten years—privilege to quit it *when I please* by giving six months notice.

Do you know a good naturalist or two you can send me to help Guilledeau get the things ready to open here? Also do you know a man of *taste* who understands the arrangement of the cases &c and who can superintend the fitting up of this whole concern? Write me to New York & oblige as ever thine

P. T. Barnum

P.S. You know *Fenton* the portrait painter. He was once with you a little in the old museum. He offers his services to me. What can he do in a museum—what sort of man is he & what is he worth per week? Write immediately & oblige &c.

B.[9]

It is interesting to note that in Philadelphia "taste" in arrangement and expert naturalists were more needed than they had been in New York. So also is the appearance of Charles L. Fenton, a portrait painter with museum experience and a son, perhaps, of Charles Willson Peale's former right-hand man. Barnum was ready for the kill, and a week later he wrote:

Museum, April 10th

My dear Moses,

Thank you for your two letters. I have engaged Bell's brother, also a couple of other naturalists who with old Guilledeau will I think soon get things to rights. I guess after all I shall take your advice & alter the galleries at once, for I feel confident that the concern properly opened and managed *must* succeed. I'll kill the other shop in no time and give you a chance for the collection. . . . Your business is indeed *stunning*. It beats mine all hollow. I have only averaged $1850 per week. But *yesterday* we commenced picking up a little.

Receipts at the Museum . . . . $408.
Receipts for Col. Fremont's
Wooly Horse . . . . 176.50!! first day
_____
$584.50 all delighted &
astonished at this
*California Produc-
tion!*

Glory enough for one day!
Charity sends her compliments. She & my daughter Caroline go with me to Philadelphia today. I have written to Fenton.
Thine as ever
Barnum[10]

With the famous Wooly Horse (a creature which had never seen either California or Colonel Fremont) doing so well in New York, Barnum's Philadephia operation was being carefully tailored to his idea of that city's moral atmosphere: waxwork groups the "Temperate Family" and "Intemperate Family" balanced by another of "The Last Supper," and onstage the Quaker Giant and Giantess, along with Dr. Valentine's repertoire of eccentric characters complemented by "Scripture Statuary." Just down the street, Edmund was countering again with "Ethiopian Serenaders," varied by "Comic Vaudeville" and "the Burlesque of MENTAL ELECTRICI-TY," a satirical spectacle that would have distressed his Uncle

Rubens, now practicing hypnotic cures in the fastnesses of Schuylkill County, Pennsylvania.[11] On March 24, Edmund announced the closing of the museum collections to prepare for the summer season; but it took Barnum only till summer's end to "kill the other shop."

A "Grand Nautical Panorama" was announced on August 27, 1849, to continue through that week at the Masonic Hall. This was the last Peale's Museum advertisement. Barnum tells us only that he "purchased the collections at sheriff's sale for five or six thousand dollars, on joint account of my friend Moses Kimball and myself." It may have occurred in the summer of 1849, or later, since in April and May 1850 he settled bills for room rental at the Masonic Hall, presumably for storage of his purchases. Much of his share must have gone to New York, but probably more went to his Swaim Building operation nearby, where, according to an announcement of June 2, there were "301,000 CURIOSITIES to be seen." The Lancashire Bell Ringers were on stage to chime in as he gloated, "The collection of CURIOSITIES is, without controversy, the finest in the world."[12]

Since August 1848, apparently in anticipation of what was coming, Kimball had been running a newspaper blurb on his museum department along with the regular dramatic announcements, emphasizing a total of "nearly FIVE HUNDRED THOUSAND ARTICLES." Beginning on October 1, 1850, his Peale acquisition is proclaimed with the surprisingly restrained statement that it had swelled his "already immense collection to upwards of HALF A MILLION ARTICLES." We know that Barnum was in town at the time, for he delivered a lecture to the "Friends of Temperance" on October 5, and the two must have joined in mutual congratulations.[13]

But Barnum, like Kimball, was turning from museum work to theatrical management. It was in Philadelphia in February of 1850 that he signed his first contract with Jenny Lind, the beginning of a new high point in his career. In 1851 he sold out in Philadelphia for $40,000 to Clapp Spooner, a businessman of old Yankee stock, and Spooner carried the "Barnum's" of the Swaim building through to its dramatic and long-remembered finale.[14]

It came at the very end of the year. *Major Jones' Courtship* had opened on December 22 and was running well. In this delightful Christmas comedy—lock, stock and barrel American—the young major, having persuaded Miss Mary to hang up a very large "Crismus Bag" for a present to keep all her life, creeps into it

BARNUM'S PHILADELPHIA MUSEUM
*Gaudy posters adorn the facade of the building newly erected with the profits of
"Swaim's Panacea." Here, on the southeast corner of Chestnut and Seventh Streets,
with the old State House tower rising nearby, much of the Peale collection vanished in
a "Brilliant Pyrotechnic Display." Lithograph, about 1851.* (Library Company of
Philadelphia.)

himself in the night. The afterpiece which followed this was a
fantasy entitled *The Mystic Cross,* ending in "a brilliant Pyrotechnic
display." On December 30, a gray and stormy afternoon, the
matinee audience trooped out, down the stairs, through the
museum and down the stairs again, out into the cold. Audience and
actors had departed, but not the pyrotechnic display. Smoke was
seen, and the old State House bell nearby began to sound the alarm
of fire. As flames lashed upward from the third floor to the fourth
and fifth, citizens rushed in to rescue what they could of the
301,000 curiosities. The newspapers mentioned only the larger or
more conspicuous, the wax figure of General Zachary Taylor
"carried off by an ardent admirer of that deceased hero," the figures
from the Automaton Band, large paintings of *The Deluge* and *The
Death of Abel* torn out of their frames, and a procession of portraits
identified as from Joseph Delaplaine's collection, indicating that
they had been sent over from Rubens Peale's New York museum.

Within an hour the Swaim Building was a gigantic torch against the black sky, its walls crashing thunderously at last into the street below.[15]

The sheriff's sale catalogue of 1848 is the best guide we have to what comprised the Barnum-Kimball purchase. Even so, most was put down in job lots by room, with species given or not in a random way, and the collections can only be summarized in somewhat the same fashion:

BIRDS
A case of birds' nests and eggs.
A "stand and vase" of hummingbirds.[16]
Birds in lots, totaling 1,624, and including,

  1 albatross
  3 cranes
40 ducks
  8 eagles
  2 "game chickens"
  6 geese
33 hawks
12 ostriches
41 owls
  3 peacocks
20 pelicans
19 "pheasants and other birds"
32 pigeons
  2 snake birds
19 snipe
  2 "tropic birds"

INSECTS
  3 "stands"

MARINE LIFE
214 fish
  9 swordfish
12 "porpoises, seals, &c."
  1 jawbone of a whale
  2 cases of lobsters and crabs
13 cases of shells
  2 large [Chama] shells
  1 case of coral
  2 case of seaweed

MINERALS
11 cases of minerals[17]
Basalt from Giant's Causeway
Minerals from Giant's Causeway
"5 pieces stone and lead ore"

QUADRUPEDS
Anteater
American antelope
Indian antelope
5 antelope
Case of 28 bats, rats and mice
Case of 10 bears, dogs, weasels and squirrels
2 bears
American deer
Moose deer
4 deer
5 "bucks and fawns"
2 elk
56 deer horns
8 deer horns and tusks
2 stag horns
9 dogs, including lap dog and terrier
Dromedary
Elephant "Columbus"
"Grecian goat"
6 goats
"Wild hog"
3 leopards
Lion
Llama
58 monkeys
"Thibet ox" {Chinese buffalo?}
"Poncho, tapir and neki"
11 porcupines
Rhinoceros
"Horned sheep"
2 sheep
26 squirrels
Wolf and lamb group
3 wolves

[Making a total of 194 mounted animals, or 18 less than the summary of 1818.]

REPTILES AND MISCELLANEOUS
23 lizards
27 snakes
35 turtles
Groups of serpents
Group of 4 iguana
362 "preparations in spirits"
4 cases, "various curiosities"

WOOD
1 case

Even if we assume that most of the cases were large and crowded, there is still evidence that the collection had been shrinking. The "Framed Engraving of an Ear" seems to be a sole survivor of the anatomical display Dr. Harlan had arranged (then later removed his own additions). The platypus, which surely would have had a listing, does not appear. Natural history specimens would have been less likely to have drifted away than American Indian or other historical relics. Few would have wanted the "6 Casks of Skins" in the cellar, probably from Abraham DePeyster's sealing voyage of fifty years before. Small objects not itemized but of considerable value were what Edmund could use to meet occasional pressing needs. None of the Museum's historic manuscripts are entered, though at least two survive: Benjamin Franklin's letter to his brother (April 3, 1755) and John André's satirical poem of the Revolution, "The Cow Chace."[18] McGuigan's "Japanese Mermaid" went to Kimball who already had one. Both are still extant.[19]

In the field of general anthropology, the auctioneer's catalogue gives us:

AFRICA
1 case, "various articles."

AMERICAN INDIAN (Contents of the "Indian Room")
1 case, "Curiosities, Stone Pipes, Idols, &c."
1 case, "Indian Dresses, Bows, Arrows, Belts, Pouches, &c."
1 case, Indian pipes.
1 case, "Buffalo Dress, Arrows, &c."
1 case, "Wax Figure of Captain Lewis, and curiosities."
1 case, "Canoes, various."
1 case, Indian articles of dress.

1 case, buffalo robe, drum, scalp, &c.
Buffalo robe with "Record of Fight with US Troops."[20]
1 case, "Buffalo Robe, Moccassins, &c."
1 case, "Indian Buffalo Sioux Tent, Papoos, &c."
1 case, "Indian Dresses and Figure of an Indian."
1 case, "Female Dresses and figures of Idols, &c."
1 case, "Figures of Indian, Squaw, Quivers, Arrows, &c."
1 case, "Indian Curiosities, 100 Articles."
"Indian Table."
23 "various Articles on Wall above cases."
Stone Sundial.

CHINA
3 cases, "Chinese Curiosities."
"A Chinese War Junk."
"A Chinese Boat."
"A Chinese Pagoda."
12 Chinese fans and umbrellas.

NORTHWEST COAST, PACIFIC, AND EAST INDIES
1 case, dresses from New Zealand.
1 case, "Head of New Zealand Chief and various curiosities."
1 case, "Articles from the Fejee Islands."
1 case, "Articles of Bark Clothing."
1 case, "Dresses made from the Intestines of a Whale, &c."
1 case, "Articles from the Sandwich Islands."
1 case, "East Indian Curiosities, 23 Idols and other Figures."
"A Man of War and 9 Paddles."
"An East Indian Palaquin."
4 cases containing 98 "East India Figures."

SOUTH AMERICA
A Mexican saddle.
1 case, "Mexican Curiosities."
58 "Mexican and Indian Figures."
1 case, "South American Curiosities."
"Mummies of Inca Family, Man, Woman and Child, and various Peruvian Curiosities."

MISCELLANEOUS AND UNIDENTIFIED
3 "Frames containing Lenses and Lace Bark."
1 case, Persian armor and clothing, &c.

3 "frames containing Lenses and specimens of Minute Writing."
1 case, "various kinds of Shoes, Stockings, &c."
1 case, "Turkish Curiosities, Guns, Boats, &c."
"The Japanese Mermaid."
18 spears and hats.
30 arrows.
23 war clubs.
16 bows, arrows and bats.
"Case with 2 Wax Figures."

HISTORICAL RELICS
2 flags taken from the British.
Ancient carved chair, A.D. 1123.
Ancient chair once owned by Washington.
Washington's letter to the Grand Lodge of Pennsylvania.
1 case, "Washington's Sash & various curiosities."
"Model of Lafayette Arch and Helmets, 9 Pieces."
      Wooden model of a fortification.
"Anchor, Balls, and 11 Pieces of Iron."

The catalogue also lists the Museum library of about 370 volumes, a few museum furnishings, and a hodgepodge of paper-cutting, needlework, and wax flowers. These last must have been latter-day acquisitions, although as early as 1807 a Martha Ann Honeywell, born without arms, had presented examples of

WAR HORN OF THE BASSA TRIBE
This elephant tusk war horn was found on the battlefield after the attack on the Liberian colonists at Bassa Cove in 1835. Gift of Mr. Whitehurst to Peale's Museum, 1836. (Peabody Museum, Harvard University.)

KAFFIR SPOON, LADLE, FORK, AND COMB
An African comb had been given to the Museum in 1794, and a "wooden spoon and fork from Senegal" in 1813. However, those shown here may be from Mr. Etting's gift of 1827, which included a spoon, fork, and comb. One original label reads "Spoon named Kefoui, made by the Natives of Siania, Africa." (Peabody Museum, Harvard University.)

paper cut and sewing done with her feet, together with "the donor's diminutive shoes."[21]

As for Barnum's share of the purchase, it is anyone's guess what stayed in Philadelphia, only to be burned in 1851, or what went to New York to be lost in the American Museum's fire of 1865. The American Museum catalogue of 1852 gives much space in a random way to birds, and, at a chance meeting with Barnum, Escol Sellers remembered his dwelling on Philadelphia's "loss of the ornithological collection, and some of Wilson's work and original drawings. From this I infer that he valued even the rude original drawings and backing of cases." The catalogue says nothing of provenance but describes such objects as the "Great Sun Fish" which had caught Buckingham's attention, and there is an illustration of a Roman sarcophagus that seems to match one in an 1831 woodcut of the Philadelphia Museum interior.[22]

Barnum may have sold part of his acquisition on the spot or shipped parts to other museums. One large segment was acquired either from him, or much earlier in some arrangement with Edmund and the bank, by Montroville Wilson Dickeson, physician-chemist-geologist-showman-adventurer, a man of popular fame and some scientific repute. At the 1854 opening of the City Museum Theatre in Philadelphia, he was billed as the professor in charge of its "Museum Department," containing much natural history, archaeology, and an "Indian Cabinet" claiming to be "the most complete in this country," which he had collected during twelve years among the Indians. The City Museum Theatre, occupying a former Universalist church, went through various changes of fortune until it was completely destroyed by fire in 1868. Some part of its contents may have been rescued, for in the next year "a portion of the collection" of Professor Dickeson was sold at auction—"262 of which are from the Celebrated PEALE'S MUSEUM OF PHILADELPHIA."[23]

More than half of these items were historical relics, small freaks of nature and curiosities of little value, fragments of famous flags, bed curtains and the like, Washington's shaving brush and nightcap, Mrs. Washington's silver thimble and "fine lace mitts embroidered with gold bullion and cherry-colored silk." Charles Willson Peale's landscapes of Sedgeley and Lemon Hill had somehow gone to Dickeson with the rest. He also acquired the distorting and multiplying mirrors from the old museum, John Haviland's design for a new museum building, and the horn of James Galloway, the "Horn-breasted Man." With this miscellany, too, were objects from the heart of the collections: 18 from Africa, 6 Chinese, 26 from the Pacific areas, and 68 of American interest, which must have included some of the finest things from Peale's Amerind purchase of 1826—among them the "Great War Eagle" of the Mandan, costume and appurtenances of a Sioux warrior (taker of 10 scalps and 170 horses), the "Great Shield of a Comanche Chief" (scarred by bullets and with a javelin point embedded), the elaborately ornamented bed of a Comanche chief, the "Door of a Pawnee Lodge" adorned with beads, porcupine quills, and bear claws, a variety of "Big Physic Medicine Bags," weapons of all sorts, and more.

Barnum may well have been concerned, in the sales on January 24 and February 14, 1850, of "a quantity of stuffed birds" and "a beautiful collection of Preserved Birds" by Thomas and Sons, Philadelphia auctioneers.[24] In 1858 Harmon A. Chambers of

Carbondale, in northeast Pennsylvania, an "Amateur Collector of objects of Antiquity and Curiosity," printed a catalogue of items he wished to sell from his collection.[25] Numismatics fill the first fourteen of its twenty-three pages, and later he would turn up in Philadelphia as a dealer in old coins. In Chambers' catalogue American Indian material from Peale's Museum appears: axes, arrows, strings of wampum, some with donors identified. We find: "3327 to 3330. Four Arrows, beautifully made and highly finished. Belonged to an African Prince. From Peale's Museum"—recalling General Williams' gift of 1789, relics of Fort Motte during the Revolution. Twenty-five varieties of "Boots, Shoes, Slippers and Sandals" in Chambers' list may explain why only a few such seem to have come through from Philadelphia to Kimball's museum. No source is given for the forty-four cases of Chinese insects (each 12 x 16 x 1½—2 inches in size) containing 2,500 specimens; yet these are surely those received by the Peales from William Wood in November 1831. Collections of Chinese crustacea, fish, groups of corals, shells, fossils, and minerals are also described. The 500 minerals are noted as "very fine," but "I [Chambers] did not collect them and never was much interested in them." Also viewed by their owner with a lackluster eye were the "34 small boxes with one bird in each. The boxes have painted backgrounds and are fitted up with twigs, moss, &c., and are much admired by some"—early mountings, perhaps, from Third and Lombard or from Philosophical Hall.

As for Moses Kimball's share of the spoils, his catalog of 1847 shows that he already had 28 cases of quadrupeds, including elephant, rhinoceros, and platypus; 24 cases of birds; 27 of ethnology; 13 of marine life; and 1 of minerals. He was amply supplied with "Rare and Curious Boots and Shoes from all parts of the World," a popular form of tourist souvenir also well represented at Philadelphia. His broadsheet *Rhyming Catalogue,* printed soon after the Peale acquisition, lists a hippopotamus skull together with other objects that may have come from Philadelphia, but more than anything else, it reveals the owner's waning interest in natural phenomena. Museums were for children now. The play was the thing; live entertainers were much preferred over stuffed.[26]

As the Boston Museum's natural history collections sank into total neglect, the Boston Society of Natural History rose, eminent and authoritative, and in 1893 Kimball presented a major part of his collections to it. He allowed no time for second thoughts, perhaps aware that curator Alpheus Hyatt, breezy imperial on a

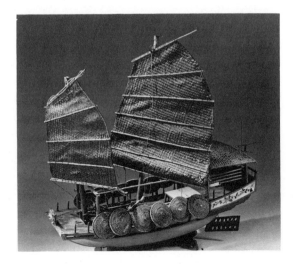

stout and balding head, was not a man to hesitate, while the society might. "The acquisition of this collection," Hyatt reported to his confreres on May 2, 1894, "was attended with certain difficulties. It had to be removed within three days, and as it included a number of large specimens, this obliged the Executive Committee to take the responsibility of accepting the gift and the expenses of the removal and installation without formal action of the Council. These expenses, including a large amount of taxidermist's work subsequently done, came to about one thousand dollars." Much was recognized as from the Peale Museum:

> The smaller elephant in a crouching position, now in our possession, came from this historical collection, and also most of the larger quadrupeds and birds. The giraffe, however, and the large elephant, and most of the game birds, were purchased by Mr. Kimball. . . . The leather-back turtles, also parts of the Peale collection, both came from the Delaware River, and were among the first ever captured and preserved. These and many interesting details of this collection have come to the Curator through the kindness of Mr. Kimball, and it is hoped that in the course of further work upon the specimens it may be practicable to obtain the history of most of them.[27]

This anticipated careful procedure did not, alas, prevail. The society's rooms were jam-packed, and one can sense a growing mood of impatience among the membership: "a Noah's Ark," in Professor

Hyatt's words, of animals saved from destruction "for the future use of science," but with no Ararat in sight. Moses Kimball died in 1895, and in 1899, after a fire had damaged his Boston museum, heirs divided what remained between the Society of Natural History and the Peabody Museum of Archaeology and Ethnology at Harvard. For Alpheus Hyatt it was indeed an embarrassment of riches, the more so since much of the last gift had been damaged by smoke and water. Many of the birds were soon after disposed of to the Newtonville barn of Charles Johnson Maynard, an ornithologist, taxidermist and dealer in natural history specimens. He was quick to recognize such Peale rarities as the Wilson types and the Washington pheasants. "It is quite easy," he told Witmer Stone of the Academy of Natural Sciences, "to recognize C. W. Peale birds by their fine condition. He was a good taxidermist."[28]

Damage and neglect followed once more, however, and it was another Bostonian, William Brewster, who intervened and restored the birds to the society's museum. There they were cleaned and studied by Jewell David Sornberger, who pursued the subject to Philadelphia and brought back voluminous notes on the history of Peale's Museum. In 1914 those specimens which had survived their many vicissitudes were transferred to Harvard's Museum of Comparative Zoology, where Sornberger was also employed. The next year that institution's *Bulletin* published Dr. Walter Faxon's article with the full history of the Boston Museum collections, from Daniel Bowen's 1797 show to Kimball's theater, and describing in detail the North American birds that had come to Harvard and relating a number of them to Wilson's plates and the Philadephia Museum. Unhappily, the Peale cases with their landscape backgrounds had all vanished long before, nor could any of the original mountings be restored until recently, when a pair of golden pheasants was remounted with the original label identifying them as Washington's gift.

At the MCZ's sister institution, the Peabody Museum of Archaeology and Ethnology, the 1899 gift of the Kimball heirs filled more than a thousand entries in its register, with many of them recording a Philadelphia provenance. Moses Kimball had acquired bits and pieces of former Boston museums back to Daniel Bowen's, and Jonathan Mix's of New Haven as well. How many Peale pieces survive in this mélange will always be in doubt, but one segment, the largest, holds a mystery of its own. Over 400 of the objects are from Pacific Ocean areas, totaling more than twice the number of the next largest group, the North American Indian.

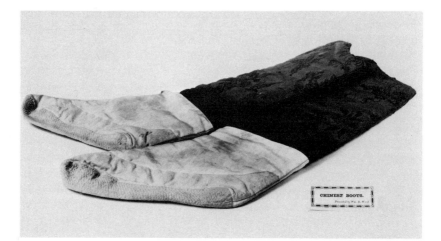

"VARIOUS KINDS OF SHOES"
Footwear from the world over was a popular travelers' souvenir, and the collections
accumulated in museums were always a popular attraction. These "Chinese Boots" (with
the original Museum label) were the gift of a leading actor of the day, William
Burke Wood, whose son collected for the Museum in Australia and the Orient,
published a newspaper in Canton, and wrote a book on Chinese life and customs. (Peabody
Museum, Harvard University.)

Advertising and other records of the Boston and Philadelphia
museums show no such preponderance of Oceanian material; yet one
or the other enterprise had acquired parts or the whole of a rare and
valuable collection of over 300 pieces, assembled about 1840—
1845, and of which a catalogue had been printed. Extensive search
has failed to locate any copy of that catalogue. It is known only
through clippings from it which have accompanied some of the
objects as labels. If it was a Boston Museum acquisition, it is
strange that Moses Kimball did nothing to publicize it. If it had
come by way of Philadelphia, it would have been in the last
desperate days of the Wilkes expedition deposits and the disintegra-
tion of the Museum Company.

One special piece, a mystery within the mystery, holds fragile
evidence of a Peale provenance. This is a small New Zealand figure,
its darkly frowning face scarred in a decorative pattern of threat and
defiance, and one hand clutching the small ceremonial club of the
Maori. It is carved in wood and inscribed on the back, "Depos:d by

324

J." Many years ago, someone at the Peabody became convinced that this was the monogram of Thomas Jefferson, marking one of his deposits in Peale's Museum. This is impossible. It more nearly resembles the identifying marks placed on shipments and bills of lading in early days. "Depos:d by" does point to a museum, however, and the words are written precisely as Titian Peale wrote them in the Museum Record Book. All in all, it is interesting but not convincing evidence. Moreover, this inscription was followed by a full name that has been erased almost beyond hope of recall, and the letter or monogram substituted. Another highly conjectural

WARRIOR'S HELMET FROM TUBUAI, AUS-TRAL ISLANDS *With its tall waving plumes and four-foot spread, this headgear was well calculated to overawe an enemy. It is a major and controversial piece in the Harvard collection still of undetermined provenance. The original label, a clipping from the printed catalog of the whole, is reproduced below.* (Peabody Museum, Harvard University.)

WARRIOR'S HELMET, AUSTRAL ISLANDS

Peale's Museum, ca. 1804-1822(?)

53611

269. Helmet, or Cap, from Tubuai, one of the Austral Islands, Lat. 24° S.; Lon. 149° W. "The crown ornamented with the dark glossy feathers of aquatic birds, towering two or three feet above the head, the front beautifully ornamented with the green and red feathers of a kind of paroquet, and pieces of shells and mother of pearl; the hinder part of the cap is covered with long flowing human hair, of a light brown, or tawny color, said to be human beard, fastened to a slight net-work attached to the crown of the helmet, floats wildly in the wind, and increases the agitated appearance of the wearer. This was a head-dress in high esteem, and worn only by distinguished warriors."

NEW ZEALAND EFFIGY
An early Maori wood carving of
great interest and value, this little
creature clutching his abdomen with
one hand and his small ceremonial
club with the other is guarding a
mystery all his own. An inscription
on the back reads: "New Zeeland
Idol/Depos'd: by J." A full name
has been erased, and the J (once
assumed to be "the sign manual of
Thomas Jefferson" on one of his gifts
to Peale's Museum) has been
substituted. The collector and
intended museum depository of this
carving, collected along with
hundreds of other objects in the
1830's, are still not clearly
identified. (Peabody Museum,
Harvard University.)

link to Titian appears in Franklin Peale's list of Wilkes expedition material received at the Museum, where "Box No. 10" carried a similar "J" as identifying mark—its contents covering the same range as the printed catalogue, from the Marquesas to New Zealand and New South Wales.[30] There is no New Zealand effigy mentioned, but a deposit for the Museum would not, of course, have been listed with the government collections.

As for the printed catalogue, that might have been made in Philadelphia, at the Boston Museum, or by the unknown collector. It includes artifacts from islands not visited by Wilkes's ships. This does not exclude a connection with Titian, for he and the others were buying articles and receiving gifts that had originally come from as far away as Japan. Sydney was a center for trade in curiosities, most of it routed from the Pacific islands to London. Clues from the catalogue's descriptions do make it unlikely that

Titian himself was the compiler.[31] Someone in Philadelphia may have been making a last desperate effort, after the withdrawal of the Wilkes deposits in February 1841, to restore the Museum's waning prestige. But against this supposition stands the simpler possibility that Moses Kimball had acquired this distinguished collection, one way or another, and was too busy at the time with his theater to do much if anything about it.

Amerind relics in the Kimball gift, if fewer than the Oceanian, make up for their numbers in interest. The Kaskaskian

BEAVER BOWL
This wooden bowl is inscribed on its side by Peale: "Indian Sculpture of a Beaver/presented by Judge Turner." In February 1797, George Turner also gave a similar piece to the American Philosophical Society, where it was recorded as "Kaskaskian sculpture of a beaver in wood. Used as a tureen." No other objects in the collection have been ascribed to the Kaskaskia, an Algonkian tribal group of southern Illinois. Thomas Barbour described this piece as "a treasure worthy to stand beside King Philip's samp bowl and the Sudbury bow." (A Naturalist's Scrapbook, *p. 93*). (Peabody Museum, Harvard University.)

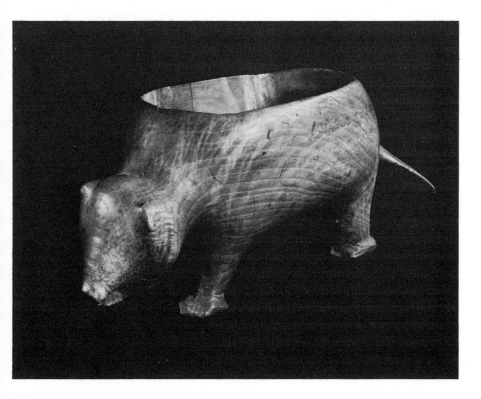

beaver bowl given by George Turner in February 1797 is a superb work of art of the greatest rarity. The similar piece given by Turner to the American Philosophical Society is now at the University Museum in Philadelphia, and both are the only known objects identified as coming from this Central Algonquin culture. Superb also is the collection surviving from the Lewis and Clark expedition, joined with other fine pieces that may be presumed to have come from Peale's purchase from the mysterious Europe-bound traders of 1826.

All the objects, from the Americas, Africa, the Orient, or wherever, have increased in value with time—an aspect dramatized by one of them which the Peabody staff of 1899 had not thought appropriate to its collections and had sent to a historical group in downtown Boston, the Old South Society, without troubling to accession it. In 1977, however, the Society saw fit to return it, Peale Museum label and all: *"Washington's Sash. Presented by Himself."* Here is the wide blue ribbon of watered silk, worn across the chest from shoulder to hip as insignia of the commander-in-chief, adopted by Washington's order at Cambridge in 1775 and continued until June 1780, when stars on the epaulettes were substituted. The Peabody people, as before, were unenthusiastic, but it can be pointed out in their behalf that Peale himself never had any thought of putting it into a museum of natural history. To him it was more malapropos than the cadaver of Washington's horse, which he had declined to receive. The first record of the sash's presence in the Museum is in 1832; it had probably been added by Rubens sometime after Lafayette's visit in 1824.[32]

Only at Harvard has any substantial part of the Peale collection survived, but the old Peale Museum had gone down slowly, a thin drift of flotsam and jetsam spreading around. Almost all the Peales had a touch of Museum fever, cherishing overflow from its stores and gathering new stores of their own. Charles Sellers writes to young Coleman, in April 1848, on ores and fossils, urging him to bring his tools for preserving birds when he comes. In Cincinnati at the same time, Ann Sellers writes to another Ann Sellers that Coleman's room is itself a museum and he in his spare time delivering lectures and performing experiments. Rubens' son, Charles Willson Peale, curator of the "Sharnokin Lyceum," writes begging the Academy of Natural Sciences for mineral specimens in 1855.[33] Fragments of unknown source have been around the writer of this history from childhood—a large Kwakiutl-Nootka fishhook of wood and bone, a Chinese Lady's tiny shoe, a seal picked up by

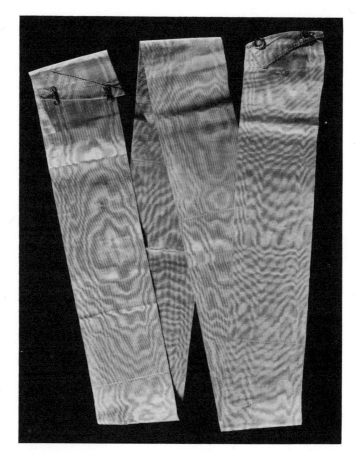

"WASHINGTON'S SASH"

At Cambridge, Massachusetts, on July 14, 1775, eleven days after taking command of the Continental Army, Washington recommended "to Officers and Men to make themselves acquainted with the persons of all the Officers in General Command" and ordered, "to prevent mistakes," that ribbons be worn across the breast between coat and waistcoat—light blue for the commander-in-chief, purple and pink for major-generals and brigadiers, and green for aides-de-camp. Light blue was the traditional color of the Whig Party, and this was still a civil war, Whig against Tory. The wide ribbons of watered silk continued as field officers' insignia until his General Order of June 18, 1780, substituting stars on the epaulettes.

This ribbon was given to Peale by Washington himself (as the original label states), probably with a complete uniform for use in his portraits. Peale, however, never thought of placing it in a natural history museum, and its presence there was first noticed, among other Washington memorabilia, in 1832. Similarly, the Harvard ethnologists of 1899 did not accession it, but sent it instead to the Old South Society in Boston, from where it was returned in 1978—again receiving a cool welcome. (Peabody Museum, Harvard University.)

one of Paul Jones's men when they raided the Scottish shore, and a silver-mounted spur that serves as paperweight, a slender, tarnished wishbone from forgotten battles won or lost.

It was a fever that spread far beyond the Museum circle, to be glimpsed here and there by chance. In 1810 Alexander Bryan Johnson, of Geneva, New York, recently married to a granddaughter of John Adams, came to stand in awe before the mammoth and attend the evening chemical experiments; impressed by it all, he went home a "scientific," a founder eventually of the Utica Lyceum. Joseph Henry, cool as he was to the Smithsonian's museum function, acknowledged that he had "almost from childhood conceived a desire to visit Philadelphia, especially that he might see Peale's museum, and the impression which the sight of this interesting collection made upon his youthful mind is still retained with a vividness which will be among the last to be obliterated by advancing years."[34] When the Museum was in its heyday, a Philadelphia boy caught the collecting passion so ardently that his mother had to make him outsize pockets lined with leather. This eager lad was William Wagner, who amassed a fortune in business while building up a museum of his own. He has left no explicit record of a debt to the Peales, other than that his Wagner Free Institute of Science, founded in 1855, was so close to what Peale had conceived but failed to achieve—a museum with its own faculty of teachers, bringing science to public and specialists alike.

In terms of survival, the Peale portrait gallery fared best of all. The credit for this should go to Herman Cope, who had taken early possession of the paintings to protect the interests of the United States Bank. The bank offered them first to the new Smithsonian Institution, whose board of regents was said to be favorable but needed an act of Congress to meet the cost of acquisition. Escol Sellers, then in Cincinnati, relayed this information to Charles Stetson of the Cincinnati Art Union. Although a price of $20,000 had been set, Escol believed that as little as $12,000 would take the whole lot. Stetson turned to public-spirited citizen Nicholas Longworth for help in founding a "National Portrait Gallery" at Cincinnati.[35]

Edmund Peale, acting as Cope's agent, brought the pictures to Cincinnati in 1851, and they were hung in a fireman's hall on Fourth Street for all to see. Longworth headed a stock company to raise a combined purchase price and endowment at $50 a share. The promoters hoped to sell a thousand shares, but would close the deal when they reached 300. Edmund remained there through the summer, as the first flow of interest slowly faded away. In September, while watching a parade with Escol's family, he was suddenly taken ill. Delirious, "a raving maniac," he died on the next day. He was found to be destitute; his only assets were a book of autographs and a gold brooch containing a lock of Napoleon's hair—both Museum strays. His landlord took the brooch in settlement of his hotel bill.[36] Escol adopted one of his children, a little girl who would remain with him for the rest of his life. Eventually the portraits went back to Philadelphia.

They were finally sold at auction, on October 6, 1854. In February of that year, the long-agitated consolidation of the old city with all its adjoining liberties and outlying county districts had at last been achieved. A mood of civic pride prevailed, and a group of citizens headed by Morton McMichael, editor of *The North American* and leader of the consolidation campaign, and by James L. Claghorn, an art collector and later president of the Pennsylvania Academy of the Fine Arts, had approached the United States Bank with an offer to buy the whole for the city.[37] Their offer was refused, and the sale was held, but with the city as the largest single purchaser. Many of the works went elsewhere, but a nucleus of 106 was hung in Independence Hall, and a catalogue of Philadelphia's "National Portraits" was published the following year. Thus this one invaluable segment of the old Museum, with its starting point back in the last years of the Revolutionary War, was continued as a living and growing entity. The establishment of Independence National Historical Park brought in fresh strength and resources, and in 1976 the collection, expertly restored and with valuable additions, was opened to the public in a gallery building of its own.

Thus Peale's Museum, built up with so much effort over so many years, passed out of sight forever. In retrospect it is like a book, once enjoyed by thousands, but of which only a few tattered leaves remain. For more than fifty years it had stimulated and supported the study of the natural sciences. Curiously, however, the methodology that made it in so many respects a counterpart of modern science museums was lost in the interval between its dispersal and the rise of the later endowed museums, in which similar experience was repeated and its techniques rediscovered.

Peale's original concept of an institution bringing authentic science to the populace at large and the research scholar alike may have retained a tenuous continuity, though this too was revived with the impact of a new discovery. He had planned a museum where all people would come face-to-face with nature and with themselves, attracted to it by the allure of beauty and surprise, by "rational amusement." Never before had there been such a "School of Wisdom," as he called it. The idea was American in spirit, born at the birth of the nation, yet reappears next in England, to be transmitted back to America as something quite new.

It is a strange story, at the heart of which was Peale's goal of a national museum. Only in this way could he be sure of wide and unrestricted use, continuing growth, and the permanence for which an artist or a collector yearns. How firmly the Peale concept had taken hold can be seen in the ten-year debate (1836–1846) over what should be done with James Smithson's princely bequest "for the increase and diffusion of knowledge among men." All sorts of institutional frameworks were put forward. But only one was well known and wholly American: a museum with an educational function, open to all, administered by experts, offering lectures, issuing publications. Every American had grown up with some of that substance and all of that ideal before him. Many of the politicians had heard the old man discourse on his vision of vast halls and perfect arrangement. Even the group attempting to capture the Smithson fund in 1840 with its "National Institution" was building on the Peale model.

One happenstance of the Peale pattern had been repeated in proprietary museums all over the country—the combining of natural history with pictures. After having started his portrait gallery of heroes of the Revolution, with science being superimposed, Peale continued the gallery to honor great figures of peace rather than war. Thus, in the act of August 10, 1846, creating the Smithsonian Institution, we have due provision for both natural history and art:

> . . . And be it further enacted that so soon as the regents shall have selected the said site, they shall cause to be erected a suitable building . . . with suitable rooms or halls for the reception and arrangement, upon a liberal scale, of objects of natural history, including a geological and mineral cabinet; also a chemical laboratory, a library, a gallery of art, and the necessary lecture rooms.

The regents and their executive officer were of another mind, however, and there would be no full-scale natural history museum until much later, and no art gallery until Harriet Lane Johnston's bequest of 1906.

The realization of the old ideal would come instead in such a setting as Jefferson had described as necessary in 1807, among "a population, crowded, wealthy, and more than usually addicted to the pursuit of knowledge." An editorial in *The New York Times* of March 18, 1868, two weeks after the burning of Barnum's museum had stated in plain terms the city's need for "a museum without any 'humbug' about it." A young naturalist, Albert Smith Bickmore, was ready. He had had experience with Agassiz at Harvard, had gathered specimens for Barnum, and the *Times* editorial expresses an ardent, long-standing ambition of his own. More, the time was ripe. The close of the Civil War had left the nation in a mood very similar to that of 1784. It would almost seem as if natural history assumes an especial significance in times of national expansion and renewal. New York's Central Park was being opened as an environment for cultural institutions of all sorts, and abundant supporting wealth, public and private, was at hand. The American Museum of Natural History came into being in 1869 with a broad educational function written into its charter. The assembling of collections began at once, its great building opened in 1877. Here, from the first, has been our foremost exemplar of the Peale plan—nature in popular and dramatic display, reinforced by lectures, publications, research scholarship and expeditions afield. To a generation in which the Peale experience had been forgotten this was the "first" museum "to make the public a founding partner, . . . the first to act as mediator and explicator between the research laboratory and the man on the street, . . . the first to seek out its audience and use new devices in putting across its message."[38]

That was the Peale concept precisely, and it would now take hold not only in New York but in all the rising museums of the post-Civil War era. But Albert Bickmore was not simply combining Barnum with Agassiz. The American experience with popular public museums was one factor in his success, yet his primary impetus was from England, whose "New Museum Idea" had become a wave of compelling force and concern. Sir Richard Owen, first to bring the British Museum's natural history collections into a setting of their own, had showed the young American his plans for South Kensington with their new emphasis on popular enjoyment and instruction. Through all the formative years of both institutions, the British Museum (Natural History) shared ideas and technical expertise with New York.

"The New Museum Idea" was British in origin and all its

elements of strength. An organized movement for education of masses had preceded passage of the First Reform Act of 1832. Gradually widening suffrage and political power had brought a demand for admission to the nation's museums, so long notorious for inaccessibility and languid management. As attendance doubled and redoubled, year after year, active and forward-looking curators and directors came in—men like Owen at the British Museum, or young Edward Forbes, whose lecture of 1853 *On the Educational Uses of Museums* was promptly republished in America. After 1859 the impetus of the movement was further heightened by the Darwinian controversy. By 1864, when John Edward Gray, Keeper of Zoology at the British Museum, gave the British Association for the Advancement of Science his definition of the new idea, it might have been Charles Willson Peale who was speaking: "First, the diffusion of instruction and rational amusement among the mass of the people, and secondly, to afford the scientific student every possible means of examining and studying the specimens of which the museum consists."

It might have been Peale, but was not. Peale's Museum had been well known in England, through the books of travelers, its exchange program, the correspondence with Sir Joseph Banks, the young men's tour with their mastodon skeleton, and more. It had had an indirect reflection in William Bullock's popular Liverpool and London museums. British response to the Peales had always been friendly, but there had been no eyes on America as a source of inspiration. Where anything like emulation appears, it is quite fortuitous and unconscious—popping up, for instance, in the oddest manner imaginable in the midst of Prince Albert's "Great Exhibition" of the Crystal Palace.

Fifty years had passed since the famous "Mammoth Dinner" of thirteen gentlemen seated inside the great skeleton at Philosophical Hall, topped off with musical toasts played on John Isaac Hawkins' Patent Portable Grand Piano. Hawkins had gone back to England in 1803, married, and settled in London as a civil engineer and patent agent. In the next generation we have Benjamin Waterhouse Hawkins, sculptor and anatomist, working with Richard Owen to create life-size reconstructions of antediluvian monsters for the adornment of a park near Crystal Palace. Upon Waterhouse Hawkins' invitation, December 31, 1853, Owen and twenty other scientists sat down to dinner inside the model Iguanodon, his largest dinosaur.

FEASTING ON "THE NEW IDEA" AT THE CRYSTAL PALACE
From the Illustrated London News, *January 7, 1854.*

There was music here, as there had been at Philadelphia. The life of the party was the genial, high-spirited naturalist Edward Forbes, and Forbes had composed the song for the occasion. Glasses and voices were raised together as they caroled,

> The jolly old beast
> Is not deceased,
> There's life in him again . . .

words which, all unbeknownst to the celebrants, spoke even more eloquently for an old idea caught up in a renaissance of its own.

NOTES

ABBREVIATIONS:

APS, American Philosophical Society
CWP, Charles Willson Peale
HSP, Historical Society of Pennsylvania
PMHB, Pennsylvania Magazine of History and Biography

Chapter 1

1 *CWP, autobiography, typescript, p. 107, Peale Papers, APS; Whitfield J. Bell, Jr., "A Box of Old Bones: A Note on the Identification of the Mastodon, 1766–1806,"* Proceedings of the American Philosophical Society, *vol. 93 (1949), pp. 171–72.*

2 *Autobiography, p. 108.*

3 *William J. Potts, "Du Simitière, Artist, Antiquary and Naturalist,"* PMHB, *vol. 13 (1889), pp. 351–75; Paul G. Sifton, "A Disordered Life: The American Career of Pierre Eugène Du Simitière,"* Manuscripts, *vol. 25 (1973), pp. 235–53.*

4 Columbian Magazine, *vol. 1 (1786–87), p. 109, describes a paddlefish found in the Allegheny River and mentions another, probably Peale's, taken from the Delaware, c. 1765.*

5 *Letter of Jeremy Belknap to Manasseh Cutler, Nov. 10, 1785, with his "account of a picture exhibition worth going 400 miles to see,"* PMHB, *vol. 37 (1913), p. 493; C. C. Sellers,* Charles Willson Peale *(New York, 1969), pp. 204–11, gives the full repertoire.*

6 Pennsylvania Journal, *July 27, 1785; George O. Seilhamer,* History of the American Theatre *(Philadelphia, 1889), vol. 2, pp. 165, 167, 169, 296–97; George C. D. Odell,* Annals of the New York Stage, *vol. 1 (New York, 1927), p. 232; Thomas Clark Pollock,* The Philadelphia Theatre in the Eighteenth Century *(Philadelphia, 1933), pp. 42–3, 136; CWP's accounts, 1785, Peale Papers, APS.*

7 Emilius; or, a Treatise of Education. Translated from the French of J. J. Rousseau, Citizen of Geneva *(Edinburgh, 1768), vol. 1, p. 1.*

8 *Laura M. Bragg, "The Birth of the Museum Idea in America,"* Charleston Museum Quarterly, *vol. 1 (1923); William Martin Smallwood,* Natural History and the American Mind *(New York, 1941), pp. 109–12.*

9 Address delivered by Charles W. Peale to the Corporation and Citizens of Philadelphia, of the 18th Day of July, in Academy Hall, Fourth Street *(Philadelphia, 1816), pp. 9–10.*

10 *"A Walk through the Philada. Museum, by C. W. Peale," Ms., p. 119, Peale Papers, HSP.*

11 *Letter to Rembrandt Peale, Sept. 6, 1814, Letter Book, Peale Papers, APS.*

Chapter 2

1 *CWP, "1st Lecture, 1801. The Theory of the Earth. Linnaean System of Animals, and moral reflections on Man," p. 31, Ms., Academy of Natural Sciences, Philadelphia, on deposit at APS.*

2 *Daubenton to Franklin, July 20, 1773, Franklin Papers, APS;* Columbian Magazine, *vol. 1 (1786–87), pp. 326–27; CWP copied "Directions for preserving*

Birds &c." into his Letter Book, 1787, Peale Papers, APS; Charles F. Jenkins, "Franklin Returns from France, 1785," APS, Proceedings, vol. 92 (1948), pp. 427–28, mentions three cats, "gifts from Madame Helvétius who had so many," and quotes W. Temple Hornaday's precept for taxidermists: "Do not take a cat for your first subject, for a cat is the most difficult of all small subjects to mount successfully."

3 John Coakley Lettsom, The Naturalist's and Traveller's Companion, containing Instructions for discovering and preserving Objects of Natural History (London, 1772); by coincidence, on Aug. 30, 1786, the Académie Royale des Sciences had authorized a study by the Abbè Manesse, Traitè sur la Manière d'Empailler et des Conserver les Animaux, les Pelleteries et les Laines (Paris, 1787), dedicated to Daubenton and with an explanatory foreword by the Marquis de Condorcet (a copy was given to the library of Peale's Museum in 1814).

4 CWP, Autobiography, typescript, pp. 109–10, 112; CWP to Thomas Hall, Oct. 12, 1792, Peale Papers, APS.

5 CWP to Washington, Feb. 27, 1787, Peale Papers, APS; New-York Daily Advertiser, March 12, 1787; the pheasants, now at Harvard University, are described by Elizabeth and Max Hall, About the Exhibits (Cambridge, Museum of Comparative Zoology, 2d ed., 1975), pp. 39–43.

6 CWP to John Beale Bordley, Aug. 22, 1786, Peale Papers, APS.

7 Peale Papers, APS; printed in Robert L. Brunhouse, ed., David Ramsay, 1749–1815. Selections from his Writings, APS, Transactions, n.s., vol. 55 (1965), p. 106.

8 Columbian Magazine, vol. 1 (1786–87), p. 653.

9 Autobiography, p. 272.

10 Peale Papers, APS.

11 Manasseh Cutler, Life, Journals and Correspondence of Rev. M. Cutler, LL.D. (Cincinnati, 1888), vol. 1. pp. 259–61; John Hall, Memoirs of Matthew Clarkson (Philadelphia, 1890), pp. 121–23.

12 CWP to Hazard, July 26, 1787, Peale Papers, APS.

13 Autobiography, p. 217

14 Ibid., p. 318.

15 Ibid., p. 218; Dunlap's American Daily Advertiser, Aug. 28, 1792.

16 CWP to Nathaniel Ramsay, April 5, 1805, Peale Papers, APS.

17 "A Walk through the Philada. Museum, by C. W. Peale," p. 96, Ms., Peale Papers, HSP.

18 Pennsylvania Packet, Sept. 3 and 11, 1787.

19 C. Edwards Lester, The Artists of America (New York, 1846), pp. 201–02.

20 Hall, Clarkson, pp. 119–20.

21 CWP, Diary, June 27, 1788, Fordham University.

22 Ibid., July 8, 1788.

23 Ibid., July 17, 1788; Charles B. Wood III, "Mr. Cram's Fan Chair," Antiques, vol. 89 (1966), pp. 262–64.

24 Ibid., Aug. 31, 1788; Diary, July 13, 1791, Peale Papers, APS; Pennsylvania Packet, Aug. 19, 1789; May 26, 1791; Jan. 23, 1792.

25 Diary, Nov. 14, 1788, Fordham University.

26 Derby to Joseph Anthony & Son, June 10, 1791, courtesy of Roger A. Derby,

Jr.; Dunlap's American Daily Advertiser, *Jan. 23, 1792;* Claypoole's American Daily Advertiser, *Sept. 14, 1796; CWP to Derby, Oct. 26, 1796, Peale Papers, APS.*

27 *Diary, Aug. 15, 1788, Fordham University; "Log and Journal of the Ship United States,"* PMHB, *vol. 55 (1931), pp. 225–58.*

28 *CWP to Washington, Sept. 27, 1787, Peale Papers, APS;* Pennsylvania Packet, *Oct. 4, 1787.*

29 *Diary, Fordham University; Harold S. Colton, "Peale's Museum,"* Popular Science Monthly, *vol. 75 (1909), pp. 22–38. Dr. Colton, founder of the Northern Arizona Museum of Science and Art, was the first to call attention to Peale's contributions to science and museology.*

30 *Diary, Aug. 24–25, Fordham University.*

31 Pennsylvania Packet, *Sept. 11, 13; Aug. 3, 1787; CWP, "Walk," p. 98 ("We name it the Minute Tern");* Pennsylvania Packet, *Sept. 15, 1788; advertisement, July 21 to Sept. 1, 1788.*

32 Recollections of Joshua Francis Fisher, written in 1864, Arranged by Sophia Cadwalader *(privately printed, 1929), pp. 177, 181ff; CWP, "Walk," p. 54.*

33 Pennsylvania Packet, *July 8, 1790, the only accession list of that year; other early lists appear Aug. 23, Dec. 11, 1788; Jan. 23, May 21, Aug. 19, 1789;* Massachusetts Magazine or Monthly Museum, *vol. 1 (1789), p. 54;* Dunlap's American Daily Advertiser, *Feb. 7, May 26, 1791; Jan. 23, Aug. 28, 1792.*

34 *CWP to Tobias Lear, March 23, 1792, Peale Papers, APS;* Dunlap's American Daily Advertiser, *Aug. 28, 1792 ("Otaheite" was a name then often applied to the whole of Polynesia); Ebenezer S. Thomas,* Reminiscences of the Last Sixty-five Years *(Hartford, 1840), vol. 1, pp. 42–4.*

35 *CWP, Broadside address to visitors, untitled, 1792, APS.*

36 *Museum Record Book, pp. 46–8, Peale Papers, HSP; Autobiography, p. 121, gives the name "Boleman"; H. U. Hall, "A Link with the Old Peale's Museum,"* University of Pennsylvania Museum Journal, *vol. 16 (1925), p. 64.*

37 *Diary, Aug. 1, 1789, Peale Papers, APS; CWP, "The Bow,"* American Museum, *vol. 6 (1789), p. 205.*

38 *Autobiography, p. 132;* Pennsylvania Packet, *Feb. 1, 1787, sentence of John McCrumm to seven years at hard labor for the Peale robbery and Elizabeth Emery to one year for receiving stolen goods.*

39 *Massachusetts Historical Society; Newspaper printing,* Pennsylvania Packet, *Feb. 3, 1790.*

Chapter 3

1 *Autobiography, typescript, p. 272, Peale Papers, APS.*

2 Pennsylvania Packet, *Feb. 28, 1787; David E. Swift, "Thomas Jefferson, John Holt Rice and Education in Virginia, 1815–25,"* Journal of Presbyterian History, *vol. 49 (1971), p. 45; CWP to Rembrandt Peale, June 4, 1815, Peale Papers, APS.*

3 Pennsylvania Packet, *April 26, 1790;* Dunlap's American Daily Advertiser, *Jan. 13, 1791.*

4 *Walter Barrett,* The Old Merchants of New York City *(New York, 1863), pp. 174–77; Robert M. and Gale S. McClung, "Tammany's Remarkable Gardiner Baker. New York's First Museum Proprietor, Menagerie Keeper, and Promoter Extraordinary,"* New-York Historical Society Quarterly, *vol. 42 (1958), pp. 142–69.*

5 *Diary, Aug. 10, 1791; CWP, Ms. account, Peale Papers, APS; APS, Minutes, Oct. 7, 1791;* National Gazette, *Oct. 31, 1791;* Universal Asylum and Columbian Magazine, *vol. 7 (1791), pp. 409–10. Similar cases noted in APS, Transactions, vol. 2 (1786), p. 392;* Nouvelles de la Republique des Sciences et des Arts, *Nov. 21, 1787;* Weekly Magazine, *vol. 1 (1798), p. 109; G. W. Corner, ed.,* The Autobiography of Benjamin Rush *(Princeton, 1948), p. 307. {Rush in APS, Transactions, vol. 4 (1792), pp. 289–92, attributes the condition to leprosy.}*

6 *George Escol Sellers to Coleman Sellers, May 15, 1887, Peale-Sellers Papers, APS; Whitfield J. Bell, Jr., "Nicholas Collin's Appeal to American Scientists,"* William and Mary Quarterly, *ser. 3, vol. 13 (1956), pp. 519–50.*

7 *CWP to Royal Academy, May 11, 1791 (the book soon became vol. 3 of regular correspondence); CWP to Banks, {Dec. 28}, 1800, mentioning previous correspondence, Peale Papers, APS.*

8 Pennsylvania Packet, *July 9–29, 1790.*

9 *CWP to Daniel Delozier, March 4, 1792, Peale Papers, APS, HSP.*

10 Dunlap's American Daily Advertiser, *Jan. 19, 1792; repeated at later dates and in a small broadsheet dated Feb. 1, 1792.*

11 Federal Gazette, *Oct. 29, 1788 and widely reprinted; L. H. Butterfield, ed.,* Letters of Benjamin Rush *(Princeton, 1951), vol. 1, p. 388; vol. 2, pp. 491–95.*

12 *Minutes of the Board of Visitors, Peale Papers, APS.*

13 *Peale Papers, APS.*

14 *Autobiography, p. 200.*

15 *Minutes of the Acting Committee, 1792, Smithsonian Institution Archives; CWP to Board of Visitors {June 3, 1792}, Peale Papers, APS; Visitors' meetings were announced in* Dunlap's American Daily Advertiser, *Mar. 16, Dec. 6, 1792; Mar. 6, 11, 1793.*

16 Pennsylvania Packet, *Dec. 11, 1788;* Dunlap's American Daily Advertiser, *Feb. 7, 1791.*

17 *Letter to the author, July 17, 1975.*

18 *Banks to CWP, Dec. 1, 1794; CWP to Banks, Dec. 28, 1800, Peale Papers, APS. The Library of the APS, catalogued by CWP, contained George Shaw's* Musei Leveriani explicatio, Anglica et Latina *(containing select specimens from the Museum of . . . Sir A. Lever) (London, 1792); this was elaborated in a communication from Rudolf Valltravers, May 29, 1795, APS Archives, no. 10.*

19 *Joseph P. F. Deleuze,* History and Description of the Royal Museum of Natural History *(Paris, 1823), pp. 67–70; P. A. Gratacap,* Le Muséum d'Histoire Naturelle. Histoire de la Fondation et des Developpements Successifs de l'Etablissement *(Paris, 1854).*

20 *Peale Papers, APS.*

21 *Autobiography, p. 202.*

22 *CWP to James Trenchard, Dec. 18, 1793, Peale Papers, APS; CWP and A. M. F. J. Beauvois,* A Scientific and Descriptive Catalogue of Peale's Museum *(Philadelphia, 1796), p. 32; CWP, Lectures, 1799–1800, no. 4, p. 19; no. 16, p. 22, Academy of Natural Sciences, on deposit at APS.*

23 *Lectures, 1799–1800, no. 2.*

24 *CWP to Gabriel Furman, Sept. 16, 1799, Peale Papers, APS.*

25 *C. C. Sellers,* Portraits and Miniatures by Charles Willson Peale *(Philadelphia, 1952), p. 108, and* Charles Willson Peale with Patron and Populace *(Philadelphia, 1969), pp. 67, 130.*

26 *CWP to Thomas Hall, Oct. 12, 1792, Peale Papers, APS; Autobiography, p. 221.*

27 *Valentin to René La Roche, Dec. 12, 1827, Peale Papers, APS.*

28 *Lectures, 1799–1800, no. 27, p. 2*

29 *Some of the acquisitions listed in* Dunlap's American Daily Advertiser, *Jan. 25, 1794.*

30 *CWP to Rembrandt Peale, Sept. 25, 1819, Peale Papers, APS.*

31 *Autobiography, pp. 213–14.*

32 *"Extract of a Letter from a person in Philadelphia to his friend in Maryland,"* National Gazette, *Sept. 4, 1793.*

33 Poulson's American Daily Advertiser, *July 17, 1828.*

34 *David John Jeremy, ed.,* Henry Wansey and His American Journal, 1794 *(Philadelphia, 1970), pp. 104–05.*

35 *"A.R." in* Dunlap and Claypoole's American Daily Advertiser, *May 2, 1794.*

36 *Frank Colliger, "Recollections of the Past. Peale's Philadelphia Museum &c.,"* Philadelphia Daily News, *Dec. 10, 1859, clipping in Poulson Scrapbooks, Library Company of Philadelphia.*

37 *James Hardie,* Philadelphia Directory and Register *(Philadelphia, 1794), pp. 230–32.*

38 *Peale Papers, HSP.*

39 Journal of the Senate of the Commonwealth of Pennsylvania, commencing on Tuesday the Third Day of December in the Year of Our Lord one thousand seven hundred and ninety-three, *vol. 4, p. 107.*

40 Independent Gazetteer, *starting March 8, 1794.*

41 Journal of the Senate, *p 121.*

42 *CWP to Nicholas Collin, March 20, 1794, Library of the Royal Swedish Academy of Sciences, Stockholm.*

43 Dunlap and Claypoole's American Daily Advertiser, *May 30, 1794 (Dr. Brown had been Dr. Michaelis's intermediary in commissioning Peale to make the mastodon drawings of 1784); ibid., Feb. 16, 1795.*

44 *Nassy to the Society, May 30, 1794, APS.*

45 Early Proceedings of the American Philosophical Society *(Philadelphia, 1884), pp. 221–22.*

46 Journal of the Second Session of the Fourth House of Representatives of the Commonwealth of Pennsylvania *(Philadelphia, 1794), p. 58, Sept. 22, 1794,*

authorizing *"a neat palisade fence, the breadth of the Philosophical Hall, and extending from the southwest end of it about half a square."*

47 Rubens Peale, *"Memorandums of Rubens Peale and the Events of his Life,"* p. 204, Peale Papers, APS.

48 *Autobiography, p. 219; removal was first announced in* Dunlap and Claypoole's American Daily Advertiser, *Sept. 22, 1794.*

Chapter 4

1 *CWP to Robert Leslie, July 26, 1795, Peale Papers, APS.*

2 *On Barton, CWP, Autobiography, typescript, pp. 201–02; Whitfield J. Bell, Jr., "Benjamin Smith Barton, M.D. (Kiel),"* Journal of the History of Medicine, vol. 26 (1971), pp. 202–03 *(CWP and Barton were both curators of APS, 1794–1800); on exchange,* Dunlap and Claypoole's American Daily Advertiser, *Dec. 30, 1793;* Pennsylvania Gazette, *Jan. 1, 1794; CWP to Thomas Jefferson, June 22, 1796, Peale Papers, APS.*

3 *Autobiography, p. 201.*

4 *François Alexandre Frédéric, Duc de la Rochefoucauld-Liancourt,* Voyage dans les États-Unis d'Amérique *(Paris, An VII), vol. 6, p. 330.*

5 *Médéric-Louis-Elie Moreau de Saint Méry,* Voyage aux États-Unis de l'Amérique *(New Haven, 1913), p. 378.*

6 *Michaud,* Biographie Universelle *(Paris, 1843), vol. 32, p. 15; E. D. Merrill, "Palisot de Beauvois as an Overlooked American Botanist," APS,* Proceedings, *vol. 76 (1936), pp. 899–920.*

7 *CWP to the Representatives of Massachusetts in Congress, Dec. 14, 1795, Massachusetts Historical Society; Memorial to Pennsylvania Assembly in* Dunlap and Claypoole's American Daily Advertiser, *Dec. 30, 1795;* Catalogue Raisonné du Muséum de Mr. C. W. Peale, membre de la société philosophique de Pennsylvanie. Redigé par A. M. F. J. Beauvois, membre de la société des sciences et arts du Cap François, île et côte Saint-Domingue; de la société philosophique de Pennsylvanie et correspondent du Muséum d'histoire naturelle de Paris. NATURE! les ignorans seuls méconnaissant tes bienfaits *(Philadelphia* [1796]). The author had been much distressed by a misprint on p. 11, "Kamschatka" for "Chama and Keto"; this is corrected in longhand in the French and in type in the English edition, which also adds names of donors and includes CWP as author. *A Scientific and Descriptive Catalogue of Peale's Museum, by C. W. Peale, Member of the American Philosophical Society, and A. M. F. J. Beauvois, Member of the Society of Arts and Sciences of St. Domingo; of the American Philosophical Society and correspondent to the Museum of Natural History at Paris *(Philadelphia, 1796)* [both editions end with catchword for the next, unprinted page]; CWP to Beauvois, June 10, 1796; to the Library Company of Philadelphia, Feb. 2, 1797, asking loan of books for continuing the catalog, Peale Papers, APS.*

8 *CWP, Diary, 1795, pp. 10–11, Peale Papers, APS.*

9 *Peale family record on flyleaf, Matthew Pilkington's* Gentleman's and Connoisseur's Dictionary of Painters *(London, 1770), Peale Papers, APS;* Early Proceedings of the American Philosophical Society *(Philadelphia, 1884), p. 238.*

Notes

10 *Autobiography*, p. 221; John Young, of Maryland, in his Experimental Inquiry into the Principles of Nutrition, and the Digestive Process (*Philadelphia*, *1803*), p. 27, adds, *"Mr. Peal informs me his Eagle never drinks during the cold season; and that he only gives it water in the hot summer weather, when it is fond of washing itself in it, and will then occasionally drink, but very sparingly."*

11 *CWP, Lectures, 1799–1800, no. 8, p. 20, Academy of Natural Sciences, on deposit at APS; John Byng, Viscount Torrington, The Torrington Diaries (London, 1954), pp. 239–40, describes an elk on exhibition in England, in 1790, with the "orifices . . . through which he breathes and snorts occasionally";* Dunlap and Claypoole's American Daily Advertiser, Feb. 7, 1795, announces *"an elegant DINNER at Secundo Bosio's Italian Coffee House, late Mr. Peale's Museum, corner of Lombard and Third Streets. The Dinner will consist of some excellent Turtle Soup, and part of the Elk lately kept by Mr. Peale.—Price for each Gentleman, One Dollar."*

12 *Dean Bashford, "A Reference to the Origin of Species in an Early Letter (1796) Signed by both Lamarck and Geoffroy,"* Science, n.s., vol. 19 (1904), pp. 798–800; the letter is discussed by Henry Fairfield Osborn, From the Greeks to Darwin: The Development of the Evolution Idea through Twenty-four Centuries (*New York, 1929*), p. 256.

13 *CWP to Mordecai Lewis, April 12, 1796, Peale Papers, APS;* Aurora, *April 21, 1797,* Claypoole's American Daily Advertiser, *April 27, 1979.*

14 *CWP, Diary, Feb. 23–25, 1799, Peale Papers, APS.*

15 *Rubens Peale, "Memorandums of Rubens Peale and the Events of his Life," p. 55, Peale Papers, APS.*

16 Claypoole's American Daily Advertiser, *June 18, 1796; July 15, 1797.*

17 Dunlap and Claypoole's American Daily Advertiser, *Feb. 16, 1795.*

18 *C. C. Sellers, " 'Good Chiefs and Wise Men.' Indians as Symbols of Peace in the Art of Charles Willson Peale,"* American Art Journal, *vol. 7 (1975), pp. 10–18.*

19 Claypoole's American Daily Advertiser, *July 15, 1797; George R. Loehr, "A. E. Van Braam Houckgeest, the First American at the Court of China,"* Princeton University Library Chronicle, *vol. 15 (1954), p. 185; Charles H. Carpenter, Jr., "The Chinese Collection of A. E. Van Braam Houckgeest,"* Antiques, *vol. 105 (1974), p. 338.*

20 Aurora, *Sept. 29, 1797 to July 25, 1798;* Porcupine's Gazette, *Oct. 3, 1797.*

21 *John Page to St. George Tucker, Jan. 20, 1795, on Tucker's invention of a telegraph, College of William and Mary;* Aurora, *Jan. 3, 1795.*

22 *Autobiography, pp. 234–35.*

23 *"In the winter of 1797 my son Raphaelle informed me of his invention of building a chimney within a chimney," entry at back of Board of Visitors' Acting Committee Minutes, Smithsonian Institution Archives.*

24 New-York Daily Advertiser, *Jan. 5, 1786. The brick stove invented by Francois Cointereaux was given wide publicity:* Claypoole's American Daily Advertiser, *Jan. 14, 1797;* Maryland Journal, *Jan. 30;* Virginia Gazette, *Jan. 3; by François Cointereaux was given wide publicity:* Claypoole's American Daily Advertiser, *Jan. 14, 1797;* Maryland Journal, *Jan. 30;* Virginia Gazette, *Jan 3; and elsewhere. Evening hours,* Claypoole's American Daily Advertiser, *Dec. 23,*

343

1796 to Jan. 31, 1797; Volney's oft-quoted remark, Dunlap and Claypoole's American Daily Advertiser, *Dec. 30, 1795, and CWP to David Hosack, June 29, 1805, Peale Papers, APS.*

25 Philadelphia Gazette, *Oct. 22, 1794;* Aurora, *April 10, 1794; James Fennell,* An Apology for the Life of James Fennell *(Philadelphia, 1814), p. 340; CWP on lectures,* Claypoole's American Daily Advertiser, *March 31, 1796.*

25A Titian's drawings are in the U.S. National Agricultural Library. The volume in the Museum library, "Merian's History of Insects," was probably her Histoire Generale des Insectes de Surinam et de toute l'Europe *(Paris, 1771). The author is indebted to Dr. John L. Heller of the University of Illinois for this explanation of Sybilla's christening.*

26 John DePeyster to CWP, April 15, 1794, Peale Papers, APS; Aurora, *Jan. 4, 1798; Frank Colliger, "Recollections of the Past. Peale's Philadelphia Museum, &c.,"* Philadelphia Daily News, *Dec. 10, 1859, clipping in Poulson Scrapbooks, Library Company of Philadelphia.*

27 CWP, Discourse Introductory to a Course of Lectures on the Science of Nature; with Original Music *(Philadelphia, 1800), p. 46.*

28 Aurora, *Jan. 2, 1797.*

29 CWP to the Prince of Parma, Feb. 21, 1799, Peale Papers, APS; the Parma list is in Smithsonian Institution Archives.

30 CWP to Beauvois, June 16, 1799, Peale Papers, APS.

31 Diary, May, 1799, Peale Papers, APS.

32 J. J. Rousseau, Emilius; or a Treatise of Education *(Edinburgh, 1768), vol. 1, p. 267, author's library.*

33 Keir Brooks Sterling to the author, Mar. 25, 1976.

34 Claypoole's American Daily Advertiser, *Apr. 13, 1799.*

35 CWP to the trustees of the University of Pennsylvania, Oct. 29, 1799, Peale Papers, APS and University of Pennsylvania Archives.

36 CWP, Introduction to a Course of Lectures on Natural History, Delivered in the University of Pennsylvania, Nov. 16, 1799 *(Philadelphia, 1800), p. 12.*

37 William Smellie, Philosophy of Natural History *(Edinburgh, 1790, 1799), 2 vols.; quoted in Lectures, 1799–1800, nos. 1, 2, 24.*

38 Nicholas Collin, "Remarks on the Utility of Mr. Peale's Proposed Lectures in the Museum. No. II," Poulson's American Daily Advertiser, *Dec. 18, 1800.*

39 Benjamin Smith Barton, A Discourse on Some of the Principal Desiderata in Natural History *(Philadelphia, 1807), p. 20.*

40 Lectures, 1799–1800, no. 4, p. 102; no. 30, pp. 1–2; no. 22, p. 27. "In this American Bittern I have dressed the neck feathers in the same form as those of Europe, in order that the difference of the plumage may be seen more distinctly by a comparative view," no. 25, p. 24; in no. 36, p. 4, CWP discounts Thomas Pennant's comparison of species.

41 Ibid., no. 38, pp. 4–10

42 Ibid., no. 8, p. 20.

43 Ibid., no. 7, p. 12.

44 Ibid., no. 6, pp. 13–14.

45 Ibid., no. 8, pp. 1–3.

46 Ibid., *no. 22, p. 6.*

47 Ibid., *no. 16, pp. 20–25.*

48 Ibid.; *ibid., no. 18, p. 2.*

49 Ibid., *no. 1, p. 10.*

50 Ibid., *no. 31, pp. 9–10.*

51 Ibid., *no. 13, pp. 22–25; CWP may have wounded some friends by declaring the use of discoverers' names "ridiculous and absurd. . . . It feeds the vanity of some naturalists without enlightening the science." "A Walk through the Philada. Museum, by C. W. Peale," Ms., 1806, Peale Papers, HSP.*

52 *Lectures, 1799–1800, no. 15, p. 3; no. 13, pp. 14–15.*

53 Ibid., *no. 1, pp. 18–19.*

54 Ibid., *no. 4, p. 9; no. 38, p. 11; no. 2, p. 22; no. 16, p. 14; no. 18, p. 12.*

55 Ibid., *no. 5, p. 22.*

56 Ibid., *no. 28, pp. 23–24.*

57 Ibid., *no. 11, pp. 33–34.*

58 *CWP*, Introduction to a Course of Lectures, *p. 13.*

59 *Lectures, 1799–1800, no. 18, p. 3.*

60 Aurora, *Jan. 27, Feb. 4, 1800;* Claypoole's American Daily Advertiser, Jan. 27, Feb. 10, 1800.

61 *Peale Papers, APS; Coxe Papers, HSP.*

62 *CWP to William Findley, Feb. 18, 1800, Peale Papers, APS.*

63 *CWP*, Discourse Introductory to a Course of Lectures, *p. 24.*

64 *Lectures, 1799–1800, no. 32, p. 2.*

65 *CWP, Lectures, 1801, no. 1, Academy of Natural Sciences, on deposit at APS.*

66 *CWP to James Madison, 1801, Peale Papers, APS.*

67 *CWP to the Marquis Yrujo, 1801, Peale Papers, APS.*

68 Medical Repository, *vol. 4 (1801), pp. 211–14.*

69 *CWP to "Victor Hughes," June 4, 1801, Peale Papers, APS.*

Chapter 5

1 *Museum Record Book, p. 6, Peale Papers, HSP.*

2 *CWP, Diary, Peale Papers, APS.*

3 *Philip DePeyster to CWP, Jan. 14, 1800, Peale Papers, APS.*

4 *George Turner, "Memoir on the Extraneous Fossils denominated Mammoth Bones; principally designed to shew that they are the remains of more than one species of non-descript Animal,"* APS, Transactions, *vol. 4 (1799), pp. 510–18; Read, July 21, 1797.*

5 *Samuel Ewing, "The Mammoth Feast,"* Port Folio, *vol. 2 (1802), pp. 71–72; reprinted in J. E. Hall, ed.,* The Philadelphia Souvenir *(Philadelphia, 1826), pp. 45–55.*

6 *CWP to his wife, June 28, 1801, Peale Papers, APS.*

7 *CWP, Diary, Peale Papers, APS.*

8 Early Proceedings of the American Philosophical Society *(Philadelphia, 1884), pp. 313–14.*

9 *CWP, Diary, Peale Papers, APS.*

10 Ibid., *May 30, 1799; CWP, Autobiography, typescript, pp. 265–66, Peale Papers, APS.*

11 *CWP to Jefferson, Oct. 11, 1801; draft in Peale Papers, APS; original in Jefferson Papers, Library of Congress.*

12 *Autobiography, p. 314.*

13 *CWP to Andrew Ellicott, July 12, 1801, Peale Papers, APS.*

14 *Rembrandt Peale,* Disquisition on the Mammoth, or, Great American Incognitum, an Extinct, Immense, Carniverous Animal whose Fossil Remains have been found in North America *(London, 1803), pp. 60–61; reprinted in Keir B. Sterling, ed.,* Selectd Works in Nineteenth Century North American Paleontology *(New York, 1974).*

15 *Benjamin Rush, who advanced money for the tour of the skeleton in England, stated on July 29, 1803 that CWP's costs in exhuming the bones had come to $2,000; Rush Papers, Library Company of Philadelphia. Rembrandt Peale in* Crayon, *vol. 1 (1855), pp. 82–83, gives the figure as $5,000.*

16 *CWP to John DePeyster, Jan. 18, 1802, Peale Papers, APS; broadside, "Skeleton of the Mammoth is now to be seen at the Museum . . .," APS and Yale University; Shawnee legend from* American Museum, *vol. 8 (1790), pp. 284–85.*

17 *John H. Powell,* General Washington and the Jack Ass *(South Brunswick, New York, and London, 1969), pp. 252–66.*

18 Medical Repository, *vol. 5 (1802), p. 83.*

19 *CWP to Schreber, Jan. 2, 1803, Peale Papers, APS.*

20 *F. M. Daudin,* Traité Elémentaire et Complét d'Ornithologie *(Paris, 1800), 4 vols.; CWP to Daudin, July 16, 1802, Peale Papers, APS.*

21 *Autobiography, p. 316.*

22 *CWP to Jefferson, Jan. 12, 1802, Jefferson Papers, Library of Congress (slightly altered from draft in Peale Papers, APS).*

23 *Jefferson Papers, Library of Congress.*

24 *CWP to Jefferson, Jan. 20, 1802, Peale Papers, APS. "The Substance of an address intended to be presented to the Legislature of Pennsyla. in 1802 by CWPeale," Jefferson Papers, Library of Congress.*

25 *CWP to Andrew Ellicott, Feb. 28, 1802, Peale Papers, APS.*

26 Poulson's American Daily Advertiser, *Feb. 19, 27; Mar. 24, 1802.*

27 *CWP to Councils, March, 1802, Peale Papers, APS;* Poulson's, *June 28, 1802, with announcement of removal to the State House; CWP to Hon. Samuel Wetherill, March 24, 1802, Peale Papers, APS.*

28 *CWP to Raphaelle Peale, Sept. 29, 1804, Peale Papers, APS.*

29 *CWP to Rembrandt Peale, Aug. 30, 1802, Peale Papers, APS.*

30 *"A Walk through the Philada. Museum, by C. W. Peale," Peale Papers, HSP; "Notes of a Visit to Philadelphia,"* PMHB, *vol. 36 (1912), p. 359.*

31 *CWP to Rembrandt and Rubens Peale, Nov. 3, 1802, Peale Papers, APS.*

32 *Rubens Peale, "Memorandums of Rubens Peale and the Events of his Life," pp. 7–8. Peale Papers, APS.*

33 *Johann Friedrich Blumenbach to Sir Joseph Banks, British Library, Add. Ms. 8099.*

34 Museum Record Book, pp. 6, 39.

35 CWP to Angelica Peale Robinson, Nov. 3, 1803, Peale Papers, APS.

36 CWP, Diary, June 21, 1804.

Chapter 6

1 CWP to Thomas Jefferson, Feb. 26, 1804, Peale Papers, APS.

2 Jefferson to CWP, March 1, 1804, Jefferson Papers, Library of Congress.

3 Aurora, May 14, 1804.

4 New York Herald, June 9, 1804.

5 Guide to the Philadelphia Museum (Philadelphia, 1806).

6 CWP to Rembrandt and Rubens Peale, Sept. 11, 1803, Peale Papers, APS.

7 CWP, Diary, May 30, 1804, Peale Papers, APS.

8 Ibid., June 5, 1804.

9 CWP to Nathaniel Ramsay, April 5, 1805; CWP to Presely Nevill, Aug. 5, 1804, tells of a plan to preserve all specimens coming to the New York fish market, then to extend the work "to all parts of the United States," Peale Papers, APS.

10 CWP to John DePeyster, March 19, 1804; to Thomas Jefferson, March 30, 1805; CWP, Letter Book VIII, pp. 56, 57, 69, 78, Peale Papers, APS.

11 Diary, June 28, 29, 1804, Peale Papers, APS.

12 CWP to Nathaniel Ramsay, April 5, 1805, Peale Papers, APS.

13 Diary, July, 1804, pp. 74, 76, 80–83; CWP, Autobiography, typescript, p. 350; CWP to David Hosack, June 29, July 17, 1805, Peale Papers, APS; Max Meisel, A Bibliography of Natural History: The Pioneer Century, 1769–1865 (Brooklyn, 1924), vol. 3, p. 365.

14 Thomas Jefferson to G. C. Delacoste, May 27, 1807, Jefferson Papers, Library of Congress.

15 CWP to John DePeyster, Nov. 22, 1805, Peale Papers, APS.

16 Autobiography, p. 354, Peale Papers, APS.

17 C. C. Sellers, "Rembrandt Peale, 'Instigator,' " PMHB, vol. 79 (1955), pp. 331–42.

18 B. H. Latrobe to Thomas Jefferson, Sept. 13, 1805, Latrobe Papers, Maryland Historical Society; Abraham Demoivre (1667–1754) was author of The Doctrine of Chances, or Method of Calculating the Probabilities of Events at Play.

19 CWP to Raphaelle Peale, Sept. 7, 1805, Peale Papers, APS.

20 Museum Record Book, Peale Papers, HSP; Poulson's American Daily Advertiser, *March 1, 1810.*

21 CWP to Thomas Jefferson, July 4, 1806, Peale Papers, APS. The antelope is described and illustrated from the Peale mounting in John D. Godman, American Natural History *(Philadelphia, 1826), vol. 2, pp. 321ff; CWP's paper was withdrawn in deference to the expected publication of the Lewis and Clark journal.*

22 Reuben Gold Thwaites, ed., Original Journals of the Lewis and Clark Expedition, 1804–1806 *(New York, 1959), vol. 6, pp. 121, 233; Paul Russell Cutright,* Lewis and Clark, Pioneering Naturalists *(Urbana-Chicago-London, 1969), pp. 241, 296–97; C. C. Sellers, "Charles Willson Peale with Patron and*

Populace," APS, Transactions, *n.s., vol. 59 (1969), pp. 36–38; George Ord to T. R. Peale, May 20, 1845, Peale Papers, APS.*

23 C. C. *Sellers,* Portraits and Miniatures by Charles Willson Peale *(Philadelphia, 1952), p. 127.*

24 *Peale Papers, APS.*

25 *Joel Barlow to Thomas Jefferson, Sept. 15, 1800, Jefferson Papers, Library of Congress; Message to Congress, Dec. 2, 1806, in John Carroll Brent,* Letters on the National Institute, Smithsonian Legacy *(Washington, 1844), pp. 13–14.*

26 *Peale Papers, APS.*

27 A. Hunter *Dupree,* Science in the Federal Government: A History of Policies and Activities to 1940 *(Cambridge, 1957), pp. 23–24; James Woodress,* A Yankee's Odyssey: The Life of Joel Barlow *(Philadelphia—New York, 1958), pp. 240–43.*

28 CWP to John I. Hawkins, Dec. 17, 1805, Peale Papers, APS.

29 *Thomas Jefferson to Caspar Wistar, June 21, 1807, Jefferson Papers, Library of Congress.*

30 *CWP to Angelica Robinson, Aug. 12, 1807, Peale Papers, APS.*

31 *CWP to Thomas Jefferson, April 20, 1808; to J. I. Hawkins, May 4, 1808, Peale Papers, APS; William W. Story,* Life and Letters of Joseph Story *(Boston, 1851), vol. 1, pp. 146–47.*

32 Journal of the Nineteenth House of Representatives of the Common- wealth of Pennslyvania *(Lancaster, 1808), pp. 168–69, 280; Robert Leslie, proposed museum of models, Pennslyvania Packet, Sept. 7, 1789; CWP to Timothy Matlack, March 15, 1802, Peale Papers, APS.*

33 Journal of the Twentieth House of Representatives of the Common- wealth of Pennsylvania *(Lancaster, 1809), pp. 652, 692–95, petition, Peale Papers, HSP.*

34 *Autobiography, p. 385; Rubens Peale, "Memorandums of Rubens Peale and the Events of his Life," p. 13, Peale Papers, APS.*

35 *Museum Account Books, Peale Papers, HSP; C. C. Sellers,* Charles Willson Peale *(New York, 1969), p. 348.*

36 *CWP to Angelica Robinson, Oct. 29, 1805, Peale Papers, APS.*

37 *Rembrandt Peale to the President and directors of the Philadelphia Museum Company, May 5, 1836, Peale Papers, APS.*

38 *CWP to J. I. Hawkins, May 5, Dec. 15, 1807; to Angelica Robinson, June 16, 1808, Peale Papers, APS.*

39 *CWP to Rubens Peale, Oct. 18, 1809, lectures on chemistry for ladies; Mrs. Jane Marcet's* Conversations on Chymestry *(Philadelphia, 1806) was in the Museum library, and probably also Mrs. Fulhame's* Essay on Combustion, with a View to a New Art of Dy[e]ing and Painting *(Philadelphia, 1810); CWP to Rembrandt Peale, Sept. 11, 1808, Peale Papers, APS; W. Edmunds Claussen,* Wyck: The Story of an Historic House *(Philadelphia, 1970), p. 45.*

40 *CWP, Letter Book IV, pp. 15, 25, 42, 53, 55, 60, 92; VI, p. 183; Auto- biography, pp. 319, 330, Peale Papers, APS; Aurora, Dec. 28, 1802; Poulson's* American Daily Advertiser, *April 22, 1807; C. C. Sellers, "The Peale Silhouettes,"* American Collector, *vol. 17 (1948), pp. 6–8.*

41 CWP, Letter Book X, pp. 95, 104, Peale Papers, APS.

42 CWP to Thomas Jefferson, Jan. 30, Feb. 2, 1806; to Stephen Elliott, Feb. 14, 1809; to J. I. Hawkins, May 17, 1807, Peale Papers, APS.

43 Manuscript, in Peale Papers, HSP. The "Walk" provides a useful listing of quadrupeds and birds, five years beyond that in the 1799–1801 Lectures.

44 CWP, Letter Book V, pp. 132, 140, 153; to J. I. Hawkins, May 17, 25, 1807; to Thomas Jefferson, Aug. 30, 1807; to Sarah Zane, Nov. 29, 1807; to Rubens Peale, Nov. 7, 1808; to Joseph Dennie, June 16, 1807, Peale Papers, APS; Port Folio, *n.s., vol. 4 (1807), p. 293. Dennie's previous view may have been derived from Maria Edgeworth, quoted in the* Philadelphia Juvenile Magazine, *vol. 1 (1802), p. 99, "Natural History is a study particularly suited to children . . ."; the 1804 first edition of the Guide seems to have survived only as reprinted in the* Literary Magazine and American Register, *vol. 2 (1804), pp. 576–79.*

45 CWP to Geoffroy St. Hilaire, June 8, 1807; April 21, 1808; to Georges Cuvier, April 21, 1808; to Rembrandt Peale, Sept. 11, 1808, Peale Papers, APS; Rembrandt Peale to D. B. Warden, Sept. 8, 1808, Maryland Historical Society; Muséum d'Histoire Naturelle, Annales, *vol. 1 (1802), pp. 251–53.*

46 Wilson bird list, May 25, 1807, Chicago Historical Society; CWP to J. I. Hawkins, May 14–25, Oct. 25, 1807, Peale Papers, APS; Record Book, pp. 6, 11.

47 CWP to Messrs. Fanning and Coles, June 6, 1808, Peale Papers, APS.

48 Letter Book IV, p. 43; V, p. 37; VII, p. 66, Peale Papers, APS.

49 CWP to J. I. Hawkins, Oct. 25, 1807, Peale Papers, APS.

50 Ibid.; to Angelica Robinson, June 16, 1808, Peale Papers, APS.

51 Rubens Peale, "Memorandums," p. 42; Rubens told the story of his meeting with Wilson in greater detail to his daughter: Diary of Mary Jane Peale, March 15, 1850, Peale Papers, APS; Robert Cantwell, Alexander Wilson, Naturalist and Pioneer *(Philadelphia–New York, 1961), pp. 120–21; CWP to Geoffroy, Peale Papers, APS; Wilson to Peale, Archives of the Smithsonian Institution.*

52 George Escol Sellers (1808–1899) to Octave Chanute, June 10, 1891, acknowledging receipt of Chanute's Aerial Navigation *(New York, 1891), Sellers Papers, APS; James Mease,* Picture of Philadelphia *(Philadelphia, 1811), p. 314, cites "an Ancient English bow gun" in the Museum.*

53 CWP to Samuel Latham Mitchill, July 26, 1803; Letter Book IV, p. 102; VI, p. 96; VIII, p. 63, Peale Papers, APS; Poulson's American Daily Advertiser, *Aug. 23, 1809;* Picture of Philadelphia, *p. 312.*

54 CWP to Thomas Jefferson, March 18, 1804, Peale Papers, APS; Record Book, p. 28.

55 Poulson's American Daily Advertiser, *Jan. 4, Aug. 23, 1809; Abel Bowen,* Bowen's Picture of Boston *(Boston, 1829), p. 196.*

56 Autobiography, pp. 271–72.

57 CWP to Rembrandt Peale, Aug. 30, 1802; April 26, 1804; to B. H. Latrobe, April 19, 1804; to Stephen Elliott, Feb. 20, 1807; to Joseph B. Harris, July 11, 1809, Peale Papers, APS.

58 Record Book, pp. 28, 37–39, 49–50; John C. Greene and John C. Burke, "The Science of Minerals in the Age of Jefferson," APS, Transactions, *vol. 68, pt. 4 (1978), pp. 24–26.*

NOTES

59 Letter Book IX, p. 88; X, pp. 17, 24, 91, 106; Rubens Peale, "Memorandums," pp. 44–45; Greene and Burke, Minerals, pp. 32–34.

60 Jeanette E. Graustein, Thomas Nuttall, Naturalist (Cambridge, 1967), p. 164; Edwin Eolf 2nd and Maxwell Whiteman, The History of the Jews of Philadelphia from Colonial Times to the Age of Jackson *(Philadelphia, 1957), pp. 331–32; David Seixas to CWP, undated; CWP to J. I. Hawkins, May 17, 1807; to Rembrandt Peale, Oct. 28, 1809, Peale Papers, APS.*

61 Early Proceedings of the American Philosophical Society *(Philadelphia, 1884), Jan. 17, 1806, p. 381; the request was again made and granted, Sept. 15, 1826, pp. 557–58. (The Museum later obtained a skin and skeleton from another source.)*

62 Muséum d'Histoire Naturelle, Annales, vol. 8 (1806), pp. 1ff; CWP to Thomas Jefferson, April 3, 1809; to Rembrandt Peale, May 14, 1809, Peale Papers, APS; George Gaylord Simpson, "The Beginnings of Vertebrate Paleontology in North America," APS, Proceedings, vol. 86 (1942), p. 150n.

Chapter 7

1 George Escol Sellers to Horace W. Sellers, May 2, 1895, Peale Papers, APS.

2 CWP, Autobiography, typescript, pp. 378–79; Rubens Peale, "Memorandums of Rubens Peale and the Events of his Life," p. 10, Peale Papers, APS.

3 A. R. Beck, trans., "Notes of a Visit to Philadelphia, made by a Moravian Sister in 1810," PMHB, vol. 36 (1912), pp. 346–61.

4 CWP to H. M. Muhlenberg, Dec. 16, 1810, Peale Papers, APS; Harold E. Dickson, ed., Observations on American Art and Selections from the Writings of John Neal *(State College, Pa., 1943), p. 18.*

5 CWP to Rembrandt Peale, July 27, Sept. 4, 1812, Peale Papers, APS.

6 Autobiography, p. 137; Rembrandt Peale to Rubens Peale, Aug. 22, 1814, Peale Papers, APS.

7 G. E. Sellers to H. W. Sellers, May 2, 1895, Peale Papers, APS; Rubens Peale, "Memorandums," pp. 13–17; Museum Record Book, October, 1813; Museum Expense Account, Nov. 24, Dec. 6, 1813, Peale Papers, HSP; Eugene S. Ferguson, ed., "Early Engineering Reminiscences (1815–40) of George Escol Sellers" (Smithsonian Institution Bulletin, 238, 1965), pp. 79–86, with illustrations of the machine now at the Franklin Institute, Philadelphia.*

8 Henry Bradshaw Fearon, Sketches of America *(London, 1818), p. 154, Museum Record Book, Peale Papers, HSP.*

9 Peale Papers, APS.

10 CWP to Thomas Jefferson, June 18, 1815; to Rubens Peale, Aug. 8, 1815; to Rembrandt Peale, Aug. 8, 1815, Peale Papers, APS.

11 Rembrandt Peale in The Crayon, *vol. 1 (1855), pp. 269–70; CWP to Angelica Robinson, Jan. 3, 1815; to Nicholas Biddle, Jan. 15, 1815; to Rubens Peale, Nov. 7, 1808; to Rembrandt Peale, June, 1823, Peale Papers, APS.*

12 CWP, Letter Book XIV, Peale Papers, APS; Rubens Peale, "Memorandums," pp. 10–12; Frederick Moore Binder, "Gas Light," Pennsylvania History, vol. 22 (1955), p. 361.

13 *Letter Book XIV, pp. 14, 17, 18, 21, 27, 30, 36–37, 41; "Upwards of $5,000," CWP to Common Councils, Dec. 14, 1820, Peale Papers, APS.*

14 The Crayon, loc. cit.; *J. Thomas Scharf,* The Chronicles of Baltimore *(Baltimore, 1874), p. 386.*

15 *Autobiography, p. 404.*

16 *CWP to Caspar Wistar on newspaper publicity, July 14, 1816; to the Commissioners of Public Revenue, Peale Papers, APS.*

17 Address delivered by Charles W. Peale to the Corporation and Citizens of Philadelphia *(Philadelphia, 1816), pp. 22–23.*

18 *Library of Haverford College.*

19 Poulson's American Daily Advertiser, *Aug. 14, 16, 19, 1816.*

20 *C. C. Sellers,* Charles Willson Peale *(New York, 1969), p. 381.*

21 American Monthly Magazine, *vol. 1 (1817), pp. 271–73, 455; New York Directory, 1817; CWP, Diary, 1817, Peale Papers, APS.*

22 *Diary, 1818, Peale Papers, APS.*

23 *CWP to Thomas Jefferson, Jan. 1, 1819, Peale Papers, APS.*

24 *George C. D. Odell,* Annals of the New York Stage *(New York, 1927), vol. 2, p. 541;* Poulson's American Daily Advertiser, *June 12, 1821.*

25 *Philadelphia Museum Company Minutes, Peale Papers, APS.*

26 *William Thornton, resolution, Peter Force Papers, Library of Congress; Minutes of the Columbian Institute, Sept. 1, 1821, Archives of the Smithsonian Institution.*

27 *G. E. Sellers to H. W. Sellers, May 2, 1895, Peale Papers, APS.*

28 *Record Book, May 5, 1821, p. 114; Thomas Say,* American Entomology *(Philadelphia Museum, Published by Samuel Augustus Mitchell, 1824, 1825, 1828), 3 vols.*

29 *Letter Book XVII, pp. 178–79, 213, 215–16, 221, 224–25, 230, 233, 244; CWP to Thomas Jefferson, Sept. 10, 1825, Massachusetts Historical Society. The manuscripts of the lectures are in Peale Papers, APS, "Natural History," "The Use of the Museum," and two based on earlier pamphlets, "Domestic Happiness" and "Health."*

30 Poulson's American Daily Advertiser, *April 2, 3, Oct. 5, 1821; J. T. Scharf and T. Westcott,* History of Philadelphia *(Philadelphia, 1884), vol. 2, p. 951.*

31 *Handbill, 1818, Boston Public Library and HSP.*

32 The True American, *Jan. 19, 1818, announces the Museum's acquisition of "the celebrated Young Sea Serpent."* Poulson's American Daily Advertiser, *Feb. 16, 1818, opens a list of accessions with the painting (9 feet by 19 inches) of the parent monster, together with J. S. Copley's pastel of P. E. DuSimitière and portraits by the Peales.* National Gazette, *July 13, 1826, reports a sighting between Newburyport Bar and Plum Island; naturalists had at first given some credence to the sightings, but that had passed by 1831 when* The Sea Serpent, or Harlequin in Gloucester *was playing on the Boston stage.*

33 *Precise measurements are given in* National Intelligencer, *May 30, 1815.*

34 *CWP to Rubens Peale, Aug. 25, Oct. 5, Nov. 30, 1823, Peale Papers, APS;* Journal of the Franklin Institute, *vol. 3 (1827), p. 1ff.*

35 *Anna Wells Rutledge, "Artists in the Life of Charleston," APS, Transac-*

tions, *vol. 39, pt. 2 (1949), p. 215; Record Book, pp. 131–32; Erwin Stresemann,* Ornithology from Aristotle to the Present *(Cambridge, Mass.–London, 1975), pp. 154–55; J. J. Audubon to T. R. Peale, Sept. 19, 1837, Houghton Library, Harvard University.*

36 Autobiography, *pp. 474–75; Record Book, p. 90; Charles Waterton,* Wanderings in South America, the North-West of the United States and the Antilles in the Years 1812, 1816, 1820 and 1824 *(London, 1825), pp. 264–65; Waterton's instructions are printed in Titian R. Peale,* Circular of the Philadelphia Museum *(Philadelphia, 1831).*

37 *Louis Leonard Tucker, " 'Ohio Show-Shop,' The Western Museum of Cincinnati, 1820–1867,"* A Cabinet of Curiosities *(Charlottesville, 1967), pp. 73–105.*

38 *James Reid Lambdin, Autobiography, Ms. Pennsylvania State Archives; Virginia E. Lewis,* Russell Smith, Romantic Realist *(Pittsburgh, 1956), pp. 22–25.*

39 *Philadelphia Museum lease agreement, 1826, Peale Papers, HSP; CWP to Rubens Peale, Sept. 24, 1826, Peale Papers, APS; Scharf and Westcott,* History of Philadelphia, *vol. 1, pp. 617–18.*

40 Poulson's American Daily Advertiser, *June 9, 1826.*

41 Ibid., *Sept. 7, 13, 1826; Record Book, p. 127.*

42 *CWP to Rembrandt Peale, Sept. 24, 1826, Peale Papers, APS.*

43 *Thomas Loraine McKenney and James Hall,* The Indian Tribes of North America, with Biographical Sketches and Anecdotes of the Principal Chiefs *(Edinburgh, 1933), vol. 1, pp. 44–49; Alice C. Fletcher, "The Osage Indians in France,"* American Anthropologist, *n.s., vol. 2 (1900), pp. 395–400; Carolyn Thomas Foreman,* Indians Abroad *(Norman, Okla., 1943), pp. 132–46.*

44 *CWP to Mrs. Rachel Morris, Feb. 9, 1827, Peale Papers, APS.*

Chapter 8

1 Minstrelsey of Edmund the Wanderer *(New York, 1810); romantic poems and prose with a background of the Navy, in which Edmund Peale vainly sought to obtain a commission.*

2 *Edmund Hayes Bell and Mary Hall Colwell,* James Patterson of Conestoga and his Descendants *(Lancaster, Pa., 1925), p. 198.*

3 *Minutes of the Philadelphia Museum Company, here cited by date, are held as follows: APS, March 5, 1821 to Oct. 11, 1827, with rough minutes of 1828 to 1835; Archives of the Smithsonian Institution, June 25, 1827 to Dec. 31, 1840; HSP, Jan. 8, 1841 to June 10, 1845, with rough minutes from 1841 to Sept. 23, 1845. {Each institution has a typescript of the whole, with index.}*

4 *James Peale, Jr., to Charles Linnaeus Peale, July 12, 1828, Peale Papers, APS.*

5 *Rembrandt Peale to Reuben Haines, Oct. 22, 1828; Rubens Peale to Haines, March 26, 1829, Quaker Collection, Haverford College.*

6 S. G. Morton, Report of the Transactions of the Academy of Natural Sciences of Philadelphia *(Philadelphia, 1829), pp. 11–16.*

7 *Charles Godfrey Leland,* Memoirs *(New York, 1893), p. 39, recalls* "Columbus" *on stage in* The Englishman in Siam.

8 *"These articles were collected by Lieut. Hutter, U.S. Army & pres. by his father," Museum Record Book, pp. 137–38, Peale Papers, HSP. An effort to authenticate the buffalo robe now at Harvard's Peabody Museum led at last to the solution of this puzzle. Charles C. Willoughby of the Peabody Museum, John C. Ewers of the Smithsonian Institution, and other authorities had judged it to be the one sent by Lewis and Clark to Thomas Jefferson in 1805. Yet Jefferson had not sent it to Peale, and twenty-three years later the Hutter collection contained a robe similarly described. Further search raised doubts that the lieutenant had brought this collection from the Indian country. The key was provided by Julian P. Boyd, both from his knowledge of the Jefferson Papers and his friendly association with the Hutter family, and the connection with Poplar Forest was confirmed by Eric Frank of the Jones Memorial Library in Lynchburg.*

9 *Minutes, 1829–31; Rubens Peale, "Memorandums of Rubens Peale and the Events of his Life," Peale Papers, APS;* Margaret Hunter Hall, The Aristocratic Journey, Being the Outspoken Letters of Mrs. Basil Hall written during a Fourteen Months' Sojourn in America, 1827–1828 *(New York–London, 1931), p. 143; Oriental and African gifts, Minutes, March 23–24, 1829; Sept. 14, 1830; B. F. Peale to T. R. Peale, May 5, 1831; William W. Wood to T. R. Peale, March 11, 1833; Wood to John Vaughan, Feb. 17, 1833, Peale Papers, APS.*

10 *Rembrandt Peale,* Notes on Italy . . . written during a Tour in the Years 1829 and 1830 *(Philadelphia, 1831), pp. 317–18.*

11 *Maximilian, Prince of Wied,* Travels in the Interior of North America *(London, 1843); reprinted in Reuben Gold Thwaites, ed.,* Early Western Travels *(Cleveland, 1907), vol. 22. pp. 69–70; T. R. Peale, Report to Trustees, June 18, 1835, Peale Papers, APS.*

12 *Minutes; Record Book.*

13 *Jean Baptiste Pierre Antoine de Monet de Lamarck,* Genera of Shells; partly copied from the London Quarterly Journal of Science, Literature & the Arts, & partly translated from the original *(Philadelphia, 1831).*

14 *James Mease,* Picture of Philadelphia *(Philadelphia, 1831), vol. 2, pp. 5–9;* Philadelphia in 1830–1; or, a Brief Account of the Various Institutions and Public Objects in the Metropolis *(Philadelphia, 1830), pp. 108–11.*

15 *Minutes;* Poulson's American Daily Advertiser, *May 18, 1833, where the announcement has a competing notice of "The Hall of Industry" at Fifth and Chestnut Streets; Minutes, Aug., 21, 1834, record the sale of the locomotive to James Reid Lambdin for his museum;* Boston Transcript, *May 16, 1842, on railroad. The Philadelphia Museum's emphasis on science is lost in a maze and blaze of phantasmagoria, magicians, and automatons. Record Book, Aug., 1840 records "the celebrated Automaton Chess-player, formerly the property of Mr. Maelzel. Deposited by a number of Gentlemen who united in its purchase," confident, no doubt, of doing a great thing for the Museum and themselves.*

16 *CWP to trustees, May 5, 1821; T. R. Peale, Report to Trustees, March 20, 1834, Peale Papers, APS.*

17 *Leland,* Memoirs, *pp. 38–39.*

18 *John D. Godman's copy of* Fauna Americana *at APS contains his accusatory marginalia; George Ord to T. R. Peale, July 19, 1835, HSP.*

19 *Rubens to Franklin Peale, June 28, 1829, Peale Papers, APS; Minutes, April*

6, 1830. (Susan Tripp, 205 pounds at age 6, and Deborah, 124 at 3.) Irving and Amy Wallace, The Two (New York, 1978), pp. 156–57.

20 766 items listed in Catalogue of Splendid and Rare Curiosities, consisting of Paintings, Engravings, Wax Figures, Busts, Animals, Birds, Fishes, Shells, Minerals, &c. to be sold at auction on Monday, July 11, 1842, at 9 o'clock, by N. A. Thompson & Co., at Harrington's Museum in Boston, comprising the whole of Mr. Harrington's rare and valuable collection, including cosmoramic views, Conflagration of Moscow, stage properties, &c. (Boston, 1841).

21 Minutes, Nov. 10, 1829; Jan. 24, May 2, 3, 9, June 17, 1833; Jan. 16, 1834; March 14, 1836.

22 Ibid., Feb. 3, 1829.

23 George Ord to T. R. Peale, Jan. 8, 1830, HSP.

24 T. R. Peale, Report to Trustees, May 2, 1835, Peale Papers, APS; Odell, Annals, vol. 4, pp. 44, 176, 585.

25 T. R. Peale, Report to Trustees, April 17, 1834, Peale Papers, APS.

26 George Escol Sellers, Early Engineering Reminiscences (1815–40); Eugene S. Ferguson, ed. (Washington, D.C., U.S. National Museum Bulletin, 238, 1965); John H. White, Cincinnati Locomotive Builders (Washington, D.C., U.S. National Museum Bulletin, 245, 1965); John W. Maxson, Jr., "George Escol Sellers, Inventor, Historian and Papermaker," The Paper Maker, vol. 38 (1969), pp. 40–57; the original model of his hill-climbing locomotive is at the Franklin Institute in Philadelphia.

27 Bruce Sinclair, Philadelphia's Philosopher Mechanics: A History of the Franklin Institute, 1824–1865 (Baltimore, 1974), pp. 221, 223.

28 Printed prospectus of "Philadelphia Museum Loan," August, 1835, Peale Papers, APS.

29 G. E. Sellers, clippings, etc., Peale Papers, APS; Harold S. Colton, "Mark Twain's Literary Dilemma and Its Sequel," Arizona Quarterly, vol. 17 (1961), pp. 229–32; Hamlin Hill, "Escol Sellers from Uncharted Space: A Footnote to The Gilded Age," American Literature, vol. 34 (1962–63), pp. 107–13.

30 G. E. Sellers to H. W. Sellers, Dec. 28, 1896, Peale Papers, APS.

31 Nelson B. Gaskell, "Nathan Dunn" (compilation of documents and narrative), HSP; Robert C. Smith, "Friend Dunn," Haverford College Publication—Horizons, vol. 67 (1969), pp. 9–13; Arthur W. Hummel, "Nathan Dunn," Quaker History, vol. 59 (1970), pp. 34–39.

32 Nathan Dunn, agreement to purchase, Jan. 29, 1836; deed to land, $170,000, April 6, 1836, APS.

33 Nathan Dunn, lease, Sept. 22, 1838, APS.

34 Virginia E. Lewis, Russell Smith, Romantic Realist (Pittsburgh, 1956), pp. 69–70.

35 James S. Buckingham, The Eastern and Western States of America (London–Paris, n.d.), vol. 1, pp. 539–44.

36 Ibid., vol. 2, pp. 42–43, 71.

37 Nicholas B. Wainwright, ed., A Philadelphia Perspective: The Diary of Sidney George Fisher (Philadelphia, 1967), pp. 65–66.

38 George Ord to the Exploring Expedition, Oct. 1, 1836, Academy of Natural

Sciences; T. R. Peale, "The South Sea Surveying and Exploring Expedition," American Historical Record, *vol. 3 (1874), p. 245.*

39 *J. K. Kane to J. R. Poinsett, Mar. 10, 1838, National Archives; Minutes, July 20, 1838; Resolution, July 21, 1838, signed by Nathan Dunn and Franklin Peale, transmitted to Paulding, National Archives; Ralph H. Aderman, ed.,* The Letters of James Kirke Paulding *(Madison, 1962), p. 290.*

40 *T. R. Peale, "Exploring Expedition," pp. 244–51, 305–11; Jessie Poesch,* Titian Ramsay Peale, 1799–1885, and his Journals of the Wilkes Expedition *(Philadelphia, 1961); William Stanton,* The Great United States Exploring Expedition of 1838–1842 *(Berkeley–Los Angeles, 1975).*

41 *Rembrandt Peale,* Graphics; a Manual of Drawing and Writing for the Use of Schools and Families *(New York, 1835).*

42 *Wainwright, . . . Fisher, pp. 69–70, 83;* Philadelphia Gazette, *Feb. 4, 6, 1840;* Public Ledger, *Sept. 17, 1839; May 19, July 1, Dec. 22, 30, 1840; Feb. 4 1841;* The Pennsylvanian, *Jan. 10, 1835.*

43 *Minutes, Dec. 20, 1838; Jan. 5, 12, 1839.*

44 Recollections of John Jay Smith. Written by Himself *(Philadelphia, 1892), pp. 208–09, 212–14; Rembrandt Peale to B. Wistar, Dec. 8 {1838} and {1839}, Quaker Collection, Haverford College.*

45 *Edmund Peale to Mrs. Raphaelle Peale, Jan. 8, 1839, Peale Papers, APS; Minutes, Jan. 10, 1840, on motion of Nathan Dunn.*

46 *Charles Wilkes to Franklin Peale, Dec. 25, 1838; Franklin Peale to Paulding, July 23, 1840; Paulding reply, July 28; Peale report on work completed, Sept. 23, 1840, National Archives; Franklin Peale, lists and receipts, National Archives and Smithsonian Institution Archives.*

47 *Stanton,* Exploring Expedition, *pp. 292–93; R.W.G., "National Institute,"* Southern Quarterly Review, *vol. 8, p. 382; J. J. Abert to Joel R. Poinsett, Nov. 9, 1842, Poinsett Papers, HSP.*

48 *Paulding to Commodore Charles Stewart, Feb. 4, 1841, in Aderman,* Paulding, *p. 294; Paulding to Franklin Peale, Feb. 5, 1841; John Gwinn to Paulding, Feb. 6, 1841, with William McGuigan letter, National Archives.*

49 *Franklin Peale to J. K. Paulding, Feb. 16, 1841; Paulding reply, Feb. 19, National Archives; Stanton,* Exploring Expedition, *p. 295.*

50 *Poinsett Papers, HSP.*

51 *R. C. Smith, "Friend Dunn," p. 12.*

52 *APS Archives; R. M. Patterson to Rembrandt Peale, {1841}; George Ord to T. R. Peale, Dec. 21, 1845, Peale Papers, HSP; William E. Lingelbach, "The Story of Philosophical Hall," APS,* Proceedings, *vol. 94 (1950), p. 51; Duke of Wellington to Nathan Dunn, July 26, 1842, HSP; A. W. Hummel, "Nathan Dunn"; Jacob Snider to George Ord, Sept. 11, 1845, APS. For Dunn in London see Richard D. Altick,* The Shows of London, *(Cambridge–London, 1978), pp. 292–93.*

53 *Journal of William Reynolds, Franklin and Marshall College; Titian to Franklin Peale, April 5, 1840, Peale Papers, APS; Papers of the United States Exploring Expedition, Smithsonian Institution Archives; Poesch,* Titian Ramsay Peale, *p. 167; Stanton,* Exploring Expedition, *p. 277.*

54 *William Churchill, "The Earliest Samoan Prints,"* Academy of Natural

Sciences, Proceedings, *vol. 67 (1915), p. 109. (Titian's collection is now at the University Museum, Philadelphia.)*

55 *William McGuigan, Curator's Report to Directors, June–Aug., 1842, Smithsonian Institution Archives;* The North American and Daily Advertiser, *Aug. 15, 1842; P. T. Barnum,* Struggles and Triumphs; or, Forty Years' Recollections *(Buffalo, 1873), pp. 129–30; Museum Record Book has no mention of the mermaid, indicating a McGuigan origin.*

56 *T. R. Peale to George Ord, Mar. 14, 1843, Peale Papers, APS.*

57 *The report was rewritten by John Cassin and published in 1858; estimates of the two versions appear in Poesch,* Titian Ramsay Peale, *p. 102, and Stanton,* Exploring Expedition, *pp. 327–29, 339, 356. (A reprint of Titian's original work was published by Arno Press, 1978.)*

58 *T. R. Peale to D. L. Dix, 1882, Houghton Library, Harvard University; T. R. Peale to B. J. Lossing, May 21, 1881, Harry Peale Haldt collection, quoted in Poesch,* Titian Ramsay Peale, *pp. 112–13.*

59 Memories of the Professional and Social Life of John E. Owens, by his Wife *(Baltimore, 1892) pp. 21–25; Wilbur H. Hunter,* The Story of America's Oldest Museum Building *(Baltimore, 1964).*

60 *Edward John Nygren, "Rubens Peale's Experiments with Mesmerism," APS,* Proceedings, *vol. 114 (1970), pp. 100–08; Barnum,* Struggles and Triumphs, *p. 158.*

61 *Rubens Peale, "Memorandums," pp. 21–22; "List of Articles comprising Peale's New York Museum and Gallery of the Fine Arts," Peale Papers, APS.*

62 New-York Mirror, *vol. 20 (1842), p. 71.*

63 *Rubens Peale to John T. Cairnes, Dec. 15, 1842, Peale Papers, APS; Neil Harris,* Humbug: The Art of P. T. Barnum *(Boston–Toronto, 1973), pp. 42–43.*

64 *Barnum to Moses Kimball, Feb. 5, 1843, Boston Athenaeum.*

65 *Boston Athenaeum.*

66 *Poesch,* Titian Ramsay Peale, *p. 95.*

Chapter 9

1 Alexander's Express Messenger, *Nov. 5, 1845;* North American, *Nov. 12, 16, 1845; Herman Cope to G. E. Sellers, June 22, 1841, on promissory note of June 1, 1836 ($32,000, reduced by subsequent payments), APS.*

2 Boston Transcript, *June 1, 1846.*

3 *Charles Durang,* History of the Philadelphia Stage between the Years 1749 and 1855 *(album of clippings from* The Sunday Dispatch, *HSP), vol. 2, pp. 296, 303–04; Michael B. Leavitt,* Fifty Years of Theatrical Management *(New York, 1912), p. 94.*

4 The Lover's Forget-me-not, and Songs of Beauty *(Philadelphia, 1847), p. 80; "Hose-houses" of the riotous firemen of the times.*

5 *Barnum to Kimball, April 9, May 10, 1847, New York Public Library; Philadelphia* Public Ledger, *beginning Jan. 15, 1848.*

6 *Durang,* History, *vol. 2, p. 306; Sheriff's Sale. Philadelphia Museum. Thomas & Sons, Auctioneers.* Catalogue of the Extensive and Valuable Collection

of National Portraits, Minerals, Birds, Shells, Fishes & Animals, and of the North American Indian Collection known as Peale's Philadelphia Museum . . . commencing on Thursday, June 8 . . . ; *Poster*, Sheriff's Sale . . . at the Masonic Hall . . . September 6, 1848 . . . , *Independence National Historical Park; George Escol Sellers to Charles Stetson, Oct. 18, 1848 (bank has taken all the pictures from Edmund Peale), Peale Papers, APS.*

7 *George Ord to Charles Waterton, Dec. 3, 1854 (admitting he does not know what had become of the mastodon), Peale Papers, APS; news of the presence of the skeleton at Darmstadt appeared in the Baltimore* Sun, *Nov. 22, 1954, and* The New Yorker, *Dec. 25, 1954.*

8 Public Ledger, *Mar. 24, 1849 (Peale's Museum);* Poulson's American Daily Advertiser, *Sept. 15, 1826 (Swaim's Panacea); Arthur Herman Wilson,* A History of the Philadelphia Theatre, 1835–1855 *(Philadelphia, 1935), pp. 34, 389–91, 395–400;* Memoirs and Auto-biography *of some of the Wealthy Citizens of Philadelphia (Philadelphia, 1846)), p. 60; J. Thomas Scharf and Thompson Westcott,* History of Philadelphia *(Philadelphia, 1884), vol. 1, p. 704n;* The Life of P. T. Barnum. Written by Himself *(New York, 1855), pp. 347–48.*

9 *P. T. Barnum Papers, Manuscripts and Archives Division, The New York Public Library (Astor, Lenox and Tilden Foundations).*

10 Ibid.

11 *George Garden, writing to his parents, Feb. 10, 1850, thought the Temperate and Intemperate Families "a Striking Contrast," but that the Last Supper figures "lookt as if a French barber had {been} imployed"; HSP.*

12 *Barnum,* Life, loc. cit.; *P. T. Barnum receipt book, May 21, 1849 to Aug. 7, 1851, Theatre Collection, Harvard College Library;* Public Ledger, *beginning June 2, 1850.*

13 Boston Transcript, *beginning Oct. 1, 1850; "Peter T. Barnum" on Temperance, ibid., Oct. 5, 1850.*

14 *P. T. Barnum,* Struggles and Triumphs; or, Forty Years' Recollections *(Buffalo, 1877), pp. 265, 280.*

15 *William Tappan Thompson (1812–1882),* Major Jones' Courtship; Cummings' Evening Bulletin, Daily Pennsylvanian, *and* Public Ledger, *Dec. 31, 1851.*

16 *A popular Victorian mounting, with birds on a bush growing from a vase, the whole set under a glass dome; shown in T. R. Peale's painting of the Museum interior.*

17 *Shown in T. R. Peale's painting of the Museum interior.*

18 *Leonard W. Labaree, ed.,* The Papers of Benjamin Franklin *(New Haven–London, 1959–), vol. 6, p. 7;* Philadelphia Record, *Oct. 18, 1944, "Cow Chace" acquired by A. S. W. Rosenbach.*

19 *Peabody Museum, Harvard University.*

20 *Obviously the Lewis and Clark robe, now at the Peabody Museum.*

21 *Record Book, 1807, p. 22; a painting by Miss Honeywell from the Museum was owned by Montroville W. Dickeson, 1869.*

22 *George E. Sellers to Coleman Sellers, June 7, 1892; to Albert Charles Peale, Mar. 29, 1898, stating that his meeting with Barnum took place soon after the fire, Peale Papers, APS; John Jay Smith,* Recollections *(Philadelphia, 1892), p. 213, states that*

many Peale's Museum pieces were lost in the burning "of Barnum's silly Philadelphia Theatrical Museum"; Barnum's American Museum Illustrated. A Pictorial Guide to that Far-famed Establishment *(New York, 1850),* p. *5; Samuel G. Goodrich,* The First Book of History. For Children and Youth. By the Author of Peter Parley's Tales *(Boston, 1833),* p. *58.*

23 City Museum, *broadside, APS;* Public Ledger, *Sept. 9, 1854; Nov. 26, 1868;* Peale's Museum Relics. Mason & Co.'s Fifth Philadelphia Sale. Catalogue of a Highly Interesting Collection of Aboriginal and other Relics, Illustrating American History, 262 of which are from the Celebrated Peale's Museum of Philadelphia, being a Portion of the Collection of Prof. Montroville Wilson Dickeson . . . to be Sold at Auction by Thomas Birch & Son . . . Philadelphia . . . October 13th & 14th, 1869.

24 Public Ledger, *Jan. 23, 24; Feb. 13, 14, 1850.*

25 Harmon A. Chambers, Catalogue of Rare and Valuable Coins, Meeds [sic], Minerals, Fossils, Corals, Shells, Manuscripts, Antiquities, &c. *(Carbondale, Pa., 1858).*

26 Catalogue of the Paintings, Portraits, Marble and Plaster Statuary, Engravings and Water Color Drawings in the Collection of the Boston Museum . . . together with . . . the Natural History Specimens, Curiosities, &c. *(Boston, 1847),* Rhyming Catalogue of the Rare, Curious and Valuable Collection of Curiosities and Works of Art in the Boston Museum *(Boston, n.d.);* Tom Pop's First Visit to the Boston Museum, with his Grandfather, giving an account of what he saw and what he thought. Dedicated to Pierpont Neal *(Boston, 1848).*

27 Boston Society of Natural History, Annual Report *(Boston, 1894),* p. *4; the elephant may have been "Columbus," recorded in Minutes, March 23–24, 1829.*

28 Walter Faxon, "Relics of Peale's Museum," Bulletin of the Museum of Comparative Zoology at Harvard College, *vol. 59 (1915),* p. *126, Charles J. Maynard to Witmer Stone, Feb. 18, 1900, Academy of Natural Sciences.*

29 Boston Society of Natural History, Proceedings, *vol. 29 (1899–1900), p. 354; J. D. Sornberger notes, Library of the Museum of Comparative Zoology; Elizabeth and Max Hall,* About the Exhibits *(Cambridge, Mass., 1964), pp. 42–44, and "George Washington's Pheasants,"* Harvard Magazine, *vol. 77 (1975), pp. 19–21.*

30 Record Book (e.g., Sept. 10, 1827); Franklin Peale, "Annotated Lists" and "Catalogue of Specimens received at Phila. Museum," Smithsonian Institution Archives.

31 Information courtesy of R. A. Langdon, Pacific Manuscripts Bureau, The Australian National University; T. R. Peale, "Collections of the United States South Seas Surveying and Exploring Expedition," Washington, D.C., 1846, Smithsonian Institution Archives; Tom Pop's First Visit, *pp. 22–23, illustrates part of Kimball's Pacific collection; T. R. Peale to Samuel G. Morton, July 14, 1846, Library Company of Philadelphia, reveals that both the Long expedition and Wilkes deposits had drifted away from the Museum.*

32 Rembrandt Peale, "Reminiscences," The Crayon, *vol. 3 (1856),* p. *101. The ribbon is a conspicuous feature of the Peale full-length portraits of Washington, 1776–80; it is first noticed as a Museum exhibit in Edward Thomas Coke,* A Subaltern's Furlough *(London, 1833),* p. *35.*

33 Charles Sellers to Coleman Sellers, Apr. 23, 1848; Ann Sellers to Ann Sellers,

April 1848, Peale Papers, APS; C. W. Peale, Curator, to Academy, Dec. 8, 1855, Academy of Natural Sciences.

34 *Unpublished autobiography of Alexander Bryan Johnson, courtesy of Professor Charles L. Todd; Joseph Henry, Address of Peale's Museum, c. 1876, Joseph Henry Papers, Smithsonian Institution.*

35 *G. E. Sellers to Charles Stetson, New York, Oct. 18, 1848; to Albert Charles Peale, Mar. 29, 1898, Peale Papers, APS.*

36 *G. E. Sellers to Horace Wells Sellers, Feb. 15, 1897, Peale Papers, APS;* Cincinnati Gazette, *Mar. 12, Sept. 26, 1851;* Catalogue of the National Portrait and Historical Gallery, Illustrative of American History. Formerly belonging to Peale's Museum, Philadelphia. Now exhibiting at Independence Hall, of Fourth Street, between Walnut and Vine, Cincinnati *(Cincinnati, 1852). The breast pin with Napoleon's hair and book of autographs are recorded in the Museum Record Book, HSP, as the gift of Mr. Rand, 1831.*

37 *T. J. Taylor for trustees of the bank to Morton McMichael, John Jordan, Jr., James L. Claghorn. Edward Armstrong, and Thomas S. Mitchell, July 6, 1854, HSP.*

38 Herbert and Marjorie Katz, Museums, U.S.A. *(Garden City, N.Y., 1965), p. 119.*

INDEX

A NOTE ABOUT THE AUTHOR

Charles Coleman Sellers was born in Overbrook, Pennsylvania, in 1903. He received his B.A. from Haverford College and his M.S. from Harvard University, where he studied American social history under Arthur M. Schlesinger, Sr.

Sellers is the author of the definitive biography of his ancestor Charles Willson Peale, as well as many other books on early American figures. In 1970 he received the Bancroft Prize in History for his biography of Peale.

In addition to his scholarly work in the field of American art history, Sellers has had a varied career. He has been an antiquarian bookseller (in New London, Connecticut), a playwright (with three staged plays to his credit), and, principally, a librarian. In the latter capacity, he served as Librarian of Dickinson College for many years; he is now the Librarian Emeritus. From 1956 to 1959 he was also the Librarian of the Waldron Phoenix Belknap Library of American Painting at the Winterthur Museum, where he edited American Colonial Painting.

Sellers has been awarded honorary doctorates from Temple University (in 1957) and from Dickinson College (in 1979). He lives and works in Carlisle, Pennsylvania.